Family Law in Practice

Authors

Maryam Akhavan-Tabib, Barrister, Coram Chambers

Simon Barry, Barrister, Lecturer, The City Law School

Susan Blake, Barrister, Reader, The City Law School

His Honour Judge Glenn Brasse

Emma Burgess, Barrister, former Senior Lecturer, The City Law School

Ros Carne, Barrister, Senior Lecturer, The City Law School

Virginia Dunn, Barrister, Senior Lecturer, The City Law School

Deirdre Fottrell, Barrister, Coram Chambers

Veronica Lachkovic, Barrister, Lecturer, The City Law School

Elpha Lecointe, Barrister, Coram Chambers

Lisa Parkinson, Mediator, Co-Founder of Family Mediators Association

Archna Thaman, Barrister

Editors

Virginia Dunn, Barrister, Senior Lecturer, The City Law School

Veronica Lachkovic, Barrister, Lecturer, The City Law School

Series Editor

Julie Browne, Barrister, Senior Lecturer, The City Law School

Family Law
in Practice

The City Law School, City University, London

OXFORD
UNIVERSITY PRESS

OXFORD

UNIVERSITY PRESS

Great Clarendon Street, Oxford OX2 6DP

Oxford University Press is a department of the University of Oxford.
It furthers the University's objective of excellence in research, scholarship,
and education by publishing worldwide in

Oxford New York

Auckland Cape Town Dar es Salaam Hong Kong Karachi
Kuala Lumpur Madrid Melbourne Mexico City Nairobi
New Delhi Shanghai Taipei Toronto

With offices in

Argentina Austria Brazil Chile Czech Republic France Greece
Guatemala Hungary Italy Japan Poland Portugal Singapore
South Korea Switzerland Thailand Turkey Ukraine Vietnam

Oxford is a registered trademark of Oxford University Press
in the UK and in certain other countries

Published in the United States
by Oxford University Press Inc., New York

British Library Cataloguing in Publication Data
Data available

Library of Congress Cataloging in Publication Data
Data available

Typeset by Laserwords Private Limited, Chennai, India
Printed in Great Britain on acid-free paper by
Ashford Colour Press Limited, Gosport, Hampshire

ISBN 978–0–19–957920–4

10 9 8 7 6 5 4 3 2 1

FOREWORD

I am delighted to write this foreword to the manuals which are written by practitioners and staff of the Inns of Court School of Law (ICSL [now The City Law School]). The manuals are designed primarily to support the training on the Bar Vocational Course (BVC). They now cover a wide range, embracing both the compulsory and the optional subjects of the BVC. They provide an outstanding resource for all those concerned to teach and acquire legal skills wherever the BVC is taught.

The manuals for the compulsory subjects are updated and revised annually. The manuals for the optional subjects are revised every two years. To complement the Series, the publishers will maintain a website for the manuals which will be used to keep them up-to-date throughout the academic year.

The manuals, continually updated, exemplify the practical and professional approach that is central to the BVC. I congratulate staff of The City Law School who have produced them to an excellent standard, and Oxford University Press for its commitment in securing their publication. As my predecessor the Hon. Mr Justice Gross so aptly said in a previous foreword, the manuals are an important ingredient in the constant drive to raise standards in the public interest.

Lord Justice Etherton
Chairman of the Advisory Board of the Institute of Law
City University, London

FOREWORD

OUTLINE CONTENTS

DETAILED CONTENTS

LIST OF ABBREVIATIONS

ADR	Alternative dispute resolution
AE	Additional element
BE	Basic element
CA 1989	Children Act 1989
CAFCASS	Children and Family Court Advisory and Support Service
CALM	Comprehensive Accredited Lawyer Mediators
CAO	Child assessment order
CCR	County Court Rules
CGT	Capital gains tax
CPR	Civil Procedure Rules
CSA	Child Support Agency
DPMCA 1978	Domestic Proceedings and Magistrates' Courts Act 1978
DVMPA 1976	Domestic Violence and Matrimonial Proceedings Act 1976
EPO	Emergency protection order
FA 1988	Finance Act 1988
FAO	Family assistance order
FLA 1996	Family Law Act 1996
FMA	Family Mediators Association
FMS	Family Mediation Scotland
FPC(MP)R 1991	Family Proceedings Courts (Matrimonial Proceedings etc) Rules 1991
FPCR 1991	Family Proceedings Courts (Children Act 1989) Rules 1991
FPR 1991	Family Proceedings Rules 1991
ICTA 1988	Income and Corporation Taxes Act 1988
ITA 1984	Inheritance Tax Act 1984
MCA 1973	Matrimonial Causes Act 1973
MHA 1983	Matrimonial Homes Act 1983
NFM	National Family Mediation
PET	Potentially exempt transfer
PSO	Prohibited steps order
SFLA	Solicitors Family Law Association
SIO	Specific issue order
TCGA	1992 Taxation of Chargeable Gains

TABLE OF CASES

Practice Directions and Notes

TABLE OF PRIMARY LEGISLATION

TABLE OF SECONDARY LEGISLATION

Introduction

Family law is a unique and largely self-contained area of practice at the Bar. Although it is civil law, it has its own rules of proceedings, the Family Proceedings Rules 1991 as amended, and to a large extent its own courts. At the magistrates' level, family cases are heard in the Family Proceedings Courts, where magistrates with specialist competence in family law sit and no other types of proceedings are heard. In the High Court, there is a Family Division with its own team of specialist family senior judges, headed by the President of the Family Division, Sir Mark Potter. In the county courts, you are most likely to find circuit judges and district judges who mix the hearing of family cases with other areas of civil practice, although some judges and courts specialise in family law matters. There is also the Principal Registry of the Family Division (PRFD), a unique court (in High Holborn, after a long time at Somerset House), which is staffed by a team of district judges of the High Court who specialise solely in family law and by circuit judges allocated to hear family proceedings, who all bring a high level of expertise and experience to their daily lists. Unlike the majority of court proceedings, family cases (other than committal proceedings) are heard in private but there is now a right of access by the media.

Despite its specialist qualities, most barristers who enter non-commercial practice will do some family work in their early years, so a working knowledge of how this area of law works and how to research within it is useful even to those who are not intending to pursue it as an area of specialisation. Almost all common law chambers and most sets who do some criminal or civil work will also have some family work passing through the clerks' room. There are specialist family sets, all of whose members are solely family practitioners. Some of those sets, and certainly many practitioners, specialise in one particular facet of family practice. The Family Law Bar Association (FLBA) is the specialist bar association for family barristers and has over 2,300 members. It produces *At A Glance*, an excellent and widely used ready reckoner for use in financial cases. It also produces an interesting newsletter, *Family Affairs*, which is well worth reading in order to pick up the working practitioner's perspective on issues in family practice.

As an area of practice, family law has a distinctive feel that can take a while to pick up and become familiar with. The issues involved are often highly emotive and even distressing and the parties involved can be extremely hostile to each other. Yet in terms of end results, this is one of the least adversarial areas of practice—most private law cases settle by consent. In most family cases, the processes are all about finding a solution, which for the parties and the advocates will involve building bridges, accepting compromise, letting matters go, seeing things from all sides, getting people to focus on the future instead of the past—all with a view to finding a way forward that the parties can live with and which will enable them to get on with their lives.

Most cases involve a sequence of hearings, usually for directions, that lead towards a final contested hearing. Every hearing is an opportunity to negotiate and, through a combination of such negotiations, solicitor correspondence and indications and guidance from judges, most cases wend their way towards an order made by consent without the need for a final contested hearing.

Although consensus is often the outcome in family cases, the process of getting there can involve some very tough bargaining and extremely adversarial positioning. Family practitioners are under the same duty as any other barrister to do the best for their client and the negotiating at court at the interim stages can be very tough indeed. Advocates at court will usually test the resolve and confidence of their opponents very directly, while retaining at the back of the mind a sense of ultimate compromise. At court, the advocate often feels that he or she is wearing two faces while involved in a kind of shuttle diplomacy: one explaining to the client why he or she needs to consider compromise and try to move on; the other telling the opponent why compromise is not possible and why your client's issues are still so relevant.

Another feature of family practice that gives it its distinct feel is the legislation itself. Family statutes tend to follow a pattern of governing situations by directing the court to have regard to all the circumstances and then providing a list of features or factors to which the court is to pay particular regard (see, eg, Family Law Act 1996, s 33(6), Children Act 1989, s 1(3), Matrimonial Causes Act 1973, s 25). The court will almost always have a discretion in how to exercise its powers. The approach is designed for the complex and personal situations that family law governs; every effort is made to avoid there being a sense of 'winners' and 'losers' and it would be inappropriate for outcomes to be achieved and the judge's hands tied by legal positioning, rather than by consideration of practical outcomes. So, usually the court must consider a set of factors or a checklist, which gives focus and consistency, but has a discretion in how to apply and balance those factors and to consider other circumstances, which gives flexibility and adaptability. Although intellectual ability is always an asset, it is probably true to say that family cases are often better argued by an approach that is fundamentally sensible rather than cerebral.

This Manual aims to lead into and complement the experience of a pupillage that includes family work and to prepare the newly qualified advocate for his or her first steps as a practitioner in the family courts. The three biggest areas of practice within family law are orders under s 8 of the Children Act 1989, ancillary relief and care proceedings. These areas are dealt with in detail, as is the law relating to domestic violence and occupation of the family home. The divorce process and other elements of financial provision are covered in less detail. There is a comprehensive checklist for committal proceedings, these being the ultimate sanction of the family courts for non-compliance. Other less common areas of family practice, which are not covered in this Manual, include adoption, child abduction, probate, issues under the Human Fertilisation and Embryology Act 1990 and issues relating to foreign divorce. There is a chapter on mediation, an increasingly important tool in the resolution of some family matters and also a continuing opportunity for practitioners to diversify their skills and their practices.

The first types of work in which new practitioners are likely to be instructed are applications for non-molestation orders and occupation orders and also directions hearings in other practitioners' cases. The former are a good way of taking responsibility for a simple, but entire, application and of impressing on instructing solicitors your ability to handle lay clients and achieve the desired result with a minimum of fuss.

Conducting other practitioners' directions hearings is a good way of getting exposed to more complicated briefs with minimal risk. Even if the directions are simple and the hearing a formality, you are well advised to take the opportunity to read and master the brief as if you were taking it through its course and to discuss the issues at court as much as you can with the other practitioners you meet. In this way, when you do have conduct of a more significant brief for the first time, in possibly more adversarial circumstances, you are less likely to be overwhelmed by a feeling of being there for the first time. This continues to be true for many years; even as you establish yourself with full conduct of simpler matters, you will always want to be getting exposure to more complex cases. Depending on the type of work that the chambers or firm does, the new practitioner can typically expect to have conduct of straightforward s 8 matters, simple claims for ancillary relief and perhaps early/interim applications by a local authority. Care cases, weightier claims for financial provision and contact or residence cases involving complex issues are not usually taken on by inexperienced advocates.

This Manual takes a practical approach and includes within the text relevant case law, legislation, rules of procedure and practice directions. Examples of commonly drafted documents are included. The relevant procedures are described along with observations and guidance on commonly occurring situations, interpretation and practical issues. Family practice involves the use of the full range of legal skills; negotiation and the ability to draft consent orders freehand at court are particularly prominent.

Social skills and understanding are also very important. It is not just a case of getting on well with a client—parties to cases are usually in circumstances of breakdown and change, involving personal issues, strong feelings, the need to confront uncertainty and allegations of personal shortcomings, and the loss of fundamental elements of their lives which may have been taken for granted for many years. Dealing with such clients requires sensitivity and maturity. Younger advocates who have been straight through university may be dealing with situations of which they have no direct life experience—this will not be a problem as long as they have the humility and self-confidence to listen to and learn from their clients and take the advice of their colleagues. In financial cases, numerical skills are at a premium. You will need to be able to prepare and present detailed breakdowns and summaries of incomes, assets and outgoings and to have a working knowledge of the more common financial products, mortgages, pensions and benefits. It is common at a financial dispute hearing for figures to be argued over and for the advocates and the judge to be tapping away together at calculators comparing results and looking for an agreed basis on which to proceed.

Current issues in family practice include:

- In public law, the debate, both in the profession and in the public at large, about the effectiveness of the care process to protect the most vulnerable children, following the *Baby P* case; the consequences for practitioners and the courts of the increased volume of care cases initiated since then.

- The advent of access of the media to family proceedings.

- In financial provision, the continuing development of the principles of *White v White* [2000] 2 FLR 981 and *Miller v Miller; MacFarlane v MacFarlane* and their outworking since *Charman* and, in particular, reasons for departing from equality. The recent developments by the Privy Council and the Court of Appeal in relation to the issue of pre-nuptial and post-nuptial agreements and the debate about whether pre-nuptial agreements should be recognised.

- The yet further new system for child support with the establishment of the Child Maintenance and Enforcement Commission.

- The continuing growth of mediation and alternative dispute resolution (ADR), both as a means of resolving disputes and as an area of practice and diversification for family lawyers.

- The increasingly urgent debate about the adequacy of fees for publicly funded work and the significant concern that those most vulnerable will be unrepresented in family proceedings.

- In Children Act matters, the importance of fact-finding hearings where there are allegations of domestic violence and the effect on contact disputes of the implementation of the Children and Adoption Act 2006.

Given the continuously developing nature of the law, it is incumbent on advocates to keep themselves abreast of developments and to use sources that are up to date. The monthly journal, *Family Law*, is an excellent source of comment and analysis, up-to-the minute case law and practical information. It has a website at <www.familylaw.co.uk>. The Family Law Reports are the dedicated law reports in universal use. So far as practitioner texts are concerned, it is generally better to use the readily updated loose-leaf binder publications; for financial matters, *Duckworth* is widely used; and for children's matters, *Hershman and MacFarlane* is the best-known text. The FLBA publication, *At A Glance*, is very useful and is published every year. Resolution (formerly the Solicitors' Family Law Association) produces a useful booklet of precedents, *Precedents for Consent Orders*, and other interesting publications, with details contained on its website at <www.resolution.org.uk.>

The law and procedure is stated as at 31 August 2009.

Domestic violence and occupation of the family home

2.1 Introduction

Modern living brings with it benefits, but at the price of increasing insecurity for many people—especially during times of economic instability. Sadly, this has an impact on family life and one manifestation is the inexorable rise in domestic violence, which accounts for nearly 25 per cent of recorded crime, despite the fact that only about one-third of such incidents are ever brought to the attention of the police. On average, two women die at the hands of an abusive partner each week. Although procedurally, the law in this area is coherent and rational, if not entirely straightforward, nevertheless it remains an aspect of family practice requiring great care and skill. Whether domestic violence is a cause or a by-product of family breakdown, it remains a traumatic occurrence.

Domestic violence is perhaps easier to identify than define precisely. The 1993 Home Affairs Select Committee (HASC) Report on Domestic Violence described it as 'any form of physical, sexual or emotional abuse which takes place within the context of a close relationship. In most cases, the relationship will be between partners (married, cohabiting, or otherwise) or ex-partners'. Although, typically, abusers are male and the abused, female; men in heterosexual relationships can be victims, as can same-sex partners. Children are also often affected—directly, or indirectly by witnessing the abuse of a parent.

After nearly a decade of relative legislative inactivity, significant changes were introduced relatively recently by two statutes designed to widen access to the court's protective powers and to improve the law's ability to deal with what seems an intractable problem. The civil law's basic legislative framework is by now tried and tested. It is found in Part IV of the Family Law Act 1996 (FLA 1996) which provides injunctive remedies in family proceedings to victims of domestic violence. Unlike the criminal law, which punishes past behaviour, remedies under the FLA 1996 are directed towards the future by regulating the conduct of perpetrators of domestic violence. This legislation was long overdue when it was passed, and replaced what had been a piecemeal approach to this area of practice with a comprehensive body of statute law. In many respects the FLA 1996 gave effect to the Law Commission's recommendations which preceded it ('Family Law: Domestic Violence and Occupation of the Family Home': Law Commission Report No 207, May 1992). It thus sought to give protection to a wide range of relationships in which domestic violence can take place, and attempted to give the courts very real powers to protect victims.

There was, however, an in-built bias towards heterosexual couples, which has now been removed by the combined effects of the Domestic Violence, Crime and Victims

Act 2004 (DVCVA 2004) and the Civil Partnership Act 2004 (CPA 2004). The latter gives same-sex couples who enter 'civil partnerships' equality of treatment with married couples and broadens the definition of 'cohabitant' to include same-sex couples. The former widens access to protection under the FLA 1996 and enlists the help of the criminal law for enforcement purposes. Unless otherwise indicated, all provisions referred to below have been brought into force.

This chapter will largely be devoted to explaining the somewhat intricate workings of the FLA 1996, as amended. Bear in mind, however, that domestic violence is not usually an isolated issue and may well have relevance to other aspects of family practice, especially contact between separated parents and their children (see **Chapter 8**) and, increasingly, financial provision after divorce (see **Chapters 4** and **5**). It is not at all uncommon that what begins as a domestic violence case evolves into a divorce and 'contest' over the children, and you need to keep alive to the implications for these other matters.

Remember, too, that understanding the law and procedure is only half the battle in this area of practice; it is important also to appreciate (but not identify too closely with) the personal anxieties involved. Legal redress, while contributing what it can to the cause of eradicating the disease of domestic violence, cannot by itself remove the distress suffered by its victims. When you are advising and representing lay clients, always try to remember that, more often than not, they will be in a highly volatile and emotional state. Decisions on how to proceed in a way which best protects the interests of your client usually means giving careful consideration not only to that person's individual needs, but the overall family situation as well.

2.2 The remedies

The FLA 1996 creates a single set of remedies, available from all courts having civil jurisdiction in family matters, to give personal protection from domestic violence and to regulate the occupation of the family home. A person seeking a remedy under the Act is called the 'applicant'; the person against whom the order is sought is called the 'respondent'.

There are two kinds of remedy, a **non-molestation order** and an **occupation order**, each with its own criteria, but capable of combination with one another and other family remedies. Both types of order may be made in relation to 'associated persons' (see **2.3**) and 'relevant child(ren)' (see **2.4**). An occupation order relates to persons living together under one roof and so has additional criteria making it available to a limited subclass of associated persons.

2.3 Associated persons

This is the entrée into the legislation and the initial prerequisite for those seeking protection under it. If the applicant and respondent are *not* 'associated', there is no scope for protection under this piece of legislation.

The FLA 1996 thus applies to 'associated persons', which from the outset was defined widely so as to encompass those living in almost any family or domestic living arrangement. The intention was to include many categories of people who had previously been excluded and so increase the availability of protection against domestic violence, especially non-molestation orders. The DVCVA 2004 and CPA 2004 have further widened access to protection by giving same-sex couples who have formed a civil partnership ('civil partners') equal status to spouses and by widening the class of associated persons generally.

Associated persons, is defined by s 62(3), as amended by the CPA 2004, to include: spouses or former spouses; cohabitants or former cohabitants (now defined by s 62(1)(a) as 'two persons who are neither married to each other nor civil partners of each other but are living together as husband and wife or as if they were civil partners'); couples who have agreed to marry or enter into a civil partnership, so long as the agreement was not terminated more than three years previously; parties to the same family proceedings (other than under the Act); and a variety of relatives (an interesting omission, perhaps, is in-laws or former in-laws). It also includes people who live or have lived *in the same household* other than as a mere employee, tenant, lodger or boarder (ie, a domestic rather than business relationship). In *Re H (A Minor) (Occupation Order: Power of Arrest)* [2001] FCR 370, for example, a father obtained a non-molestation and occupation order against this 17-year-old son.

The DVCVA 2004 added another category of 'associated person', namely persons 'who have or have had an intimate personal relationship with each other which is or was of significant duration'. The purpose behind this extension, which was brought into force in July 2007, is to give protection from abuse to those who meet the test of intimacy, but who are or were not living together (stereotypically, perhaps, a man and a mistress set up in separate accommodation). As originally drafted, the FLA 1996 was very focused on households, so that a cohabiting gay couple would have been associated, but a girlfriend and boyfriend who never lived (and had no children) together, would not. This new category of associated person would now cover some such couples, although the point at which dating becomes an intimate relationship of 'significant duration' awaits judicial interpretation.

Also 'associated' are the parents of the same child; individuals (not, eg, a local authority) who have or have had parental responsibility for the same child; and persons connected by virtue of the adoption process: s 62(5).

2.4 Relevant child

Children are a common feature of family life. Predictably, they also frequently figure in matters of family strife. The 'relevant child' is therefore a recurring concept in the legislation, and one which is very widely drawn, in effect including any child who needs protection from domestic violence.

By s 62(2), a 'relevant child' in relation to any proceedings under the FLA 1996 includes:

(a) any child living, or who might reasonably be expected to live with, either party to the proceedings;

(b) a child involved in existing children proceedings; and

(c) any other child whose interest the court considers relevant.

2.5 The non-molestation order

A non-molestation order is a form of injunction containing either or both of the following:

(a) a provision prohibiting the respondent from molesting another person who is associated with the respondent;

(b) a provision prohibiting the respondent from molesting a relevant child: s 42(1).

A great deal of thought was given to whether there should be a statutory definition of 'molestation'—a curiously archaic term used in previous legislation and which seemed incapable of simple, yet accurate modernisation. In the absence of any evidence of problems caused in the past by lack of a definition, and given the possibility that any delineation might become over-restrictive, it was decided to leave the term undefined in the FLA 1996. Thus the courts continue to be guided by the old case law which established that 'violence is a form of molestation but molestation may take place without the threat or use of violence and still be serious and inimical to mental or physical health' (*per* Viscount Dilhorne in *Davis v Johnson* [1979] AC 264). Lack of a statutory definition keeps the remedy flexible and able to adapt to novel circumstances.

In *Horner v Horner* [1982] 2 All ER 495 sending threatening letters and intercepting the applicant on the streets were regarded as molestation. In *Johnson v Walton* [1990] 1 FLR 350 it was suggested that sending partially nude photographs of the applicant to the press so as to cause her distress would amount to molestation. Thus, any serious form of pestering, intimidation or harassment is included in the concept.

There are, however, limits and the need for direct contact between perpetrator and victim was stressed in *C v C* [1998] 1 FLR 554. In that case, a husband and wife were in the process of divorcing. Newspaper articles, critical of the husband's marital conduct, were published with the assistance of information provided by his wife. The husband claimed the articles were harmful to him and sought an order restraining his wife from speaking to the press so as to procure further such articles. The issue on appeal was whether the wife's behaviour amounted to molestation. Sir Stephen Brown, then President of the Family Division, confirmed that molestation 'implies some quite deliberate conduct which is aimed at a high degree of harassment of the other party, so as to justify the intervention of the court'. But he held that the wife's revelations of her marital past 'come nowhere near molestation as envisaged by s 42'. He found the lack of direct communication between the parties relevant and concluded that the (by then ex-) husband was concerned with damage to his reputation rather than molestation as such. This case seems to confirm that molestation needs to be of a direct and personally troublesome nature, which excludes invasions of privacy which may be said to damage one's reputation. The remedy for the latter lies in defamation.

The court may make a non-molestation order either:

- *on application* by a person who is 'associated with the respondent' whether or not other family proceedings have been initiated (thus it can be, and usually is, a 'stand-alone' application, often in conjunction with an application for an occupation order, see **2.6**): s 42(2)(a); or

- *on its own initiative*, in any family proceedings to which the respondent is a party if it considers that the order should be made for the benefit of any other party to the proceedings or any relevant child: s 42(2)(b). More specifically, whenever the court is considering making an occupation order (see **2.6**), it must also consider whether to make, on its own initiative, a non-molestation order (see **2.5**): s 42 (4A) and (4B), inserted by DVCVA 2004, Sch 10, para 36. This is intended to give the court all options to deal with abuse in its many contexts.

In deciding whether to grant the non-molestation order, the court by virtue of s 42(5) shall have regard to *all of the circumstances* of the case, *including* the 'need to secure the health, safety and well-being' of the applicant (or, where applicable, the person for whose benefit the order is made) and any relevant child. Note the emphasis on the protection of the victim.

General molestation will be restrained by 'forbidding' the respondent from 'using violence against, threatening, harassing, intimidating or pestering' the victim (notice that the word 'molestation' does not appear in the actual order). In addition, specific kinds of behaviour may also be restrained by more precise wording—usually set out after the general prohibition.

Non-molestation orders may last for a specified period or until further order: s 42(7). This gives the court total flexibility. In general, non-molestation orders are intended as a temporary ameliorating measure to last only until a long-term solution is found (eg, reconciliation or separation), but every case is different and there will be occasions when a long-term or indefinite order is justified: see *Re B-J (A Child)*, *sub nom Re B-J (Power of Arrest)* [2001] 2 WLR 1660 where an indefinite non-molestation order, granted for the benefit of a child, was upheld by the Court of Appeal.

Note that a non-molestation order made in the course of other family proceedings will cease if those proceedings are dismissed or withdrawn: s 42(8).

One of the vexed problems with domestic violence is that it straddles the civil and criminal law, but victims (and perpetrators) too easily fall between these two very separate stools. In an attempt to engage in 'joined-up' solutions and signal the seriousness with which the law views domestic violence, a major change wrought by the DVCVA 2004 was to make breach of a non-molestation order a criminal offence: FLA 1996, s 42A. This is discussed in more detail below (see **2.14**).

2.6 Occupation orders: the general scheme

Known colloquially as 'ouster orders', these regulate the occupation of the family home to protect those remaining in it. Typically, they exclude a perpetrator of violence from the family home altogether or from some defined part of it. They may even preclude an abuser coming within a specified distance of the property. An abuser who has left the home can be prevented from returning.

Occupation orders are, in their nature, more limited in their scope than non-molestation orders. They come in various, if essentially standard, permutations and their availability depends on the rights and/or relationship of *both* parties to the application. *The greatest protection is given to those with property rights and people who have formalised their relationship (ie, married persons or civil partners).*

The FLA 1996 distinguishes, in the first instance, between applicants who are legally entitled to occupy the family home ('entitled applicants') and those who are not. Occupation orders, which effectively force people to leave their own homes, are draconian in their nature, and are therefore easiest to justify in the case of an applicant who is independently entitled to occupy the property. Conversely, they are most difficult to justify where the applicant has no such right but the respondent does. Therefore, an applicant who is, first, 'associated' with the respondent (see **2.3**) and second, 'entitled' to occupy the family home can get access to the fullest protection that is available under the Act, *irrespective* of the specific nature of her relationship to the respondent (although often it is this relationship which is the source of entitlement—see **2.8.1**).

Non-entitled applicants, on the other hand, may *only get orders against a former spouse, former civil partner, cohabitant or former cohabitant* (now redefined to include same-sex couples who are not civil partners) and are, to a degree, discriminated against in terms of the possible duration of such orders. In addition, a further distinction is made between those who have formalised their relationship and those who have not. Cohabitants are still specifically deprived of the potential benefits of the so-called 'balance of harm' test (see **2.8.4**), which in certain circumstances compels the court, when dealing with spouses/civil partners or former spouses/civil partners, to make an order in favour of the applicant.

These various permutations are reflected in the five separate, but subtly unequal sections, as amended, under which applications under the FLA 1996 are made. These are explained in detail below. In a nutshell the amendments effected by the CPA 2004 mean that civil partners are treated in the same way as married couples. Given that the parties must in any event be 'associated persons', which section is appropriate then depends on the status of the parties as follows:

- if the applicant is *'entitled'*—apply under s 33 (whatever the respondent's status) (see **2.8**);

- if the applicant is *not entitled*, but the respondent *is*: apply under s 35 if the parties are *former* spouses/civil partners (see **2.9.1**), or apply under s 36 if the parties are existing or former cohabitants (see **2.9.2**);

- if *neither* applicant nor respondent is entitled: apply under s 37 if the parties are spouses/civil partners or former spouses/civil partners (see **2.10.1**); or apply under s 38 if the parties are existing or former cohabitants (see **2.10.2**).

In all cases, when deciding whether to make an occupation order, the court should also consider its powers to make a non-molestation order (see **25**): s 42(4A), as added by DVCVA 2004.

2.7 Two types of occupation order

There are two types of occupation order: declaratory and regulatory. The latter, as the name suggests, regulates the occupation of the family house. The former declares, extends or creates rights and are a necessary prerequisite to a regulatory order where the respondent is already entitled, but the applicant is not.

Declaratory orders are possible in respect of any dwelling that is, has been or was intended to be a family home. They are not, however, applicable where neither party is 'entitled' (see **2.10**).

2.8 Entitled applicant: s 33

Under s 33(1)(a) (i) and (ii), an applicant is an 'entitled applicant' if he or she is entitled to occupy the dwelling-home by virtue of:

- a beneficial estate or interest (eg, resulting trust);
- a contract (eg, tenancy agreement);
- any enactment giving the right to remain in occupation; or
- 'home rights' in relation to the dwelling-house (see **2.8.1**).

2.8.1 Home rights

Both spouses and civil partners can acquire 'home rights'. Where one spouse has legal or other rights of occupation in the matrimonial home, and the other spouse does not, the latter is given equal occupation rights, or what the FLA 1996 originally called 'matrimonial home rights'. These have now been extended to civil partners in just the same way, and therefore renamed 'home rights': FLA 1996, s 30(1) as amended by CPA 2004, Sch 9. Home rights in effect give both parties to a marriage or civil partnership equal rights to occupy the family home.

Home rights are defined in s 30(2) as being—

(a) *if in occupation*: a right not to be evicted or excluded from the dwelling-house or any part of it by the other spouse or civil partner except with the leave of the court given by an order under s 33;

(b) *if not in occupation*: a right with the leave of the court to enter into and occupy the dwelling-house.

Home rights (like the Court's power to regulate the exercise of those rights) apply to any dwelling-house which is, has been or *was intended* to be the family residence: s 30(7)—not, eg, a property bought for investment purposes. In the normal course, such rights expire on divorce, termination of the civil partnership or the death of either spouse/partner, but can be extended by the court: s 33(5).

In practice, most applications under the FLA 1996 fall within s 33.

2.8.2 Possible s 33 orders

On application under s 33, the court may make any one or combination of the following 'regulatory' orders (s 33(3)):

(a) enforcing the applicant's entitlement to remain in occupation as against the respondent;

(b) requiring the respondent to permit the applicant to enter and remain in the dwelling-house or part of the dwelling-house;

(c) regulating the occupation of the dwelling-house by either or both parties;

(d) prohibiting, suspending or restricting the exercise by the respondent of his right to occupy the dwelling-house;

(e) restricting or terminating the respondent's home rights;

(f) requiring the respondent to leave the dwelling-house or part of the dwelling-house; or

(g) excluding the respondent from a defined area in which the dwelling-house is included.

This menu of possibilities is designed to deal with all eventualities. Thus, for example, there could be an order preventing the locks being changed by one party who is trying to stop the other from entering the premises; or an order requiring either party to vacate the premises at specific times; or an order preventing a respondent from entering a named part of the premises, eg, the main bedroom.

There is usually no need for a declaratory order under s 33, because the applicant, by definition, already has full entitlement to occupy the matrimonial home.

2.8.3   The criteria for s 33 orders

The test for regulatory orders is contained in s 33(6) and (7). In deciding whether, and in what terms, to make a regulatory order, the court must have regard to *all the circumstances* of the case and, *in particular* the:

- housing needs and resources of the parties and children;
- financial resources of the parties;
- likely effect of an order (or lack of one) on the health, safety and well-being of the parties or any relevant child; and
- conduct of the parties in relation to each other and otherwise.

These factors, which are essentially a matter of common sense, might usefully be described as the '*core criteria*' to be considered by the court. **They are common to *all* applications for occupation orders under the Act.**

2.8.4   The 'balance of harm' test

In addition, the court must apply the so-called 'balance of harm' test. This says the court *must* make a regulatory order *if* it appears that the applicant (or any relevant child) is likely to suffer *significant harm* (attributable to the respondent) if an order is not made *unless* it appears that the respondent (or relevant child) is likely to suffer equal or greater harm if the order is made (whether attributable to the applicant or not): see s 33(7).

Harm is defined in s 63. In relation to a child it means ill-treatment (specifically including sexual abuse) or the impairment of health or development. In relation to an adult it means ill-treatment (but, curiously, no mention of sexual abuse) or the impairment of health (but not development—apparently adults do not develop any further after a certain age!). Note that although the significant harm to the applicant referred to in s 33(7) must be 'attributable' to the respondent, it need not be intentional.

Although the core criteria are obviously relevant when weighing the balance of harm, subsections (6) and (7) are distinct stages of the decision-making process. In particular, the mandatory nature of subsection (7) only comes into play if the applicant or relevant child is likely to suffer 'significant harm'. The dictionary definition of 'significant' (ie, 'considerable, noteworthy or important')—accepted by Booth J in *Humberside County Council v Second Defendants* [1993] 1 FLR 257 (a Children Act case)—is taken as applying equally in this context (see s 63). In *Chalmers v Johns* [1999] 1 FLR 392, the Court of

Appeal allowed a husband's appeal against the making of an occupation order because the judge had wrongly applied the balance-of-harm test in a case where the harm which the applicant and child might suffer if the order were not made was, given the history, too slight to be considered 'significant'. Confirming both the draconian nature of ouster orders generally and the fact that subsection (7) is 'designed to cater for (the) more extreme situations', Thorpe LJ went on to say at p 396:

> The court has first to consider whether the evidence establishes that the applicant or any relevant child is likely to suffer significant harm attributable to the conduct of the respondent if the order is not made. If the court answers that question in the affirmative, then it must make the order unless balancing one harm against the other, the harm to the respondent or the child is likely to be as great. If, however, the court answers the question in the negative, then it enters the discretionary regime provided by sub-section (6).

One might have said 'returns' to rather than 'enters' the discretionary regime of subsection (6), since aspects of the core criteria set out there are obviously relevant to the question of risk of significant harm. The point is that where the court finds there is *not* a risk to the applicant of significant harm, it is *not bound* by the mandatory requirements of subsection (7) so that it has the *power* to make an order, taking into account the core criteria (ie, housing needs, conduct, etc), but is under *no obligation* to do so. See, eg, *G v G (Occupation Order: Conduct)* [2000] 2 FLR 36.

In the sad case of *Banks v Banks* [1999] 1 FLR 726, a husband, aged 75, applied for non-molestation and occupation orders against his wife, aged 79, who suffered from senile dementia. The wife could be both verbally and physically aggressive, but had never physically injured the husband. After a spell in hospital, her doctors thought it was in her best interests to be at home in familiar surroundings. Her husband, however, felt too frail, physically and emotionally, to cope and sought an occupation order under the FLA 1996—in effect to force her return to hospital. Although sympathetic to the husband, the court dismissed his application on the basis that there was no risk to him of significant injury if the order were not made, and so no compulsion to make an order arose. The judge also seemed to say that even had there been a risk of significant harm to the husband, the balance of harm in any event would have favoured the wife. (It is worth noting that a non-molestation order was also refused, principally because the wife would have been mentally incapable of understanding, much less abiding by it.)

In the all too prevalent cases, however, where the court does find that there is a likelihood of significant harm, the discretion becomes a duty and the court *must* make an order if, after weighing the harm likely to be suffered by both parties and by any relevant children, the 'balance of harm' favours the applicant (or relevant child). If the applicant is unable to show the risk of greater harm, then the court still has the *power,* but again is under *no duty,* to make an order. See, for example, *B v B (Occupation Order)* [1999] 1 FLR 715. In that case, after suffering substantial violence at the hands of her husband, a wife moved out of the family home with the couple's 2-year-old daughter. They were temporarily housed in bed and breakfast accommodation by the local authority while the husband remained in the family house with his 6-year-old son by a previous relationship. Both children were 'relevant' children. The wife obtained an occupation order against the husband. The husband appealed.

The Court of Appeal allowed the appeal against the order because the judge had wrongly applied subsection (7), in part due to his mistaken belief that the local authority would be obliged, were the husband excluded from his home, to provide him and his son with permanent housing. In fact, a husband removed from the family home on account of his own violence is considered intentionally homeless, requiring the local authority only to give advice and temporary shelter. By contrast, if the mother and daughter were made homeless on account of the husband's violence, the local authority was obliged to provide them with suitable permanent accommodation. The Court of Appeal thus held that:

- the judge had been perfectly correct to decide that the wife and daughter would suffer significant harm were an order not made; but

- he had erred in balancing the risks of harm. In weighing the risk as regards the two children, the balance came down not in the favour of the applicant and daughter, as the judge had supposed, but in favour of the husband's child, who would be very precariously housed were an occupation order made. Therefore, the judge had not been *required* by subsection (7) to make the order and in the circumstances, had he realised he had a choice, it was unlikely that he would have exercised his discretion to do so.

This case also confirms the fact that where there are significant risks to children, their interests are likely to become paramount in weighing up the balance of harm. Indeed, the Court of Appeal was at pains to ensure that the outcome of this case, which turned on a very particular set of facts, should not be viewed as condoning what had been very serious domestic violence.

2.8.5 Duration

Section 33(10) provides that orders under s 33 may be for a specified period, until the occurrence of a specified event, or until further order. In other words, these orders can be of unlimited duration.

The rest of the legislation follows the above pattern, with adaptations as appropriate to the circumstances, and to produce the result that the further away one gets from property rights or a formalised marital or civil partnership, the more dilute is the protection given under the FLA 1996.

2.9 Unentitled applicant and entitled respondent

2.9.1 Former spouses/civil partners: s 35

2.9.1.1 Possible orders

Possible regulatory orders under s 35(5) are an adaptation of those available under s 33. Because the applicant is (as yet) 'unentitled', those regulatory orders included in the s 33(3) list (see **2.8.2**), but excluded from the s 35(5) list, are orders (a), (b) and (e), which in this context need to be dealt with by way of declaratory order. The court cannot make a regulatory order under s 35 without first making the relevant declaratory order, in effect giving the applicant the same rights of occupation as the respondent before any regulation of those rights is then imposed. The declaratory order is, in essence, an equalising exercise.

Thus, where the court makes a regulatory order under s 35, it *must* also include a declaratory order giving the applicant relevant occupation rights, ie:

- *if the applicant is already in occupation of the property:* there must be a provision giving the applicant the right not to be evicted or excluded from the dwelling-house or any part of it by the respondent for the period specified in the order, plus a provision prohibiting the respondent from evicting the applicant during this period (s 35(3));

- *if the applicant is not in occupation:* there must be a provision giving the applicant the right to enter into and occupy the dwelling-house for the period specified, plus a provision requiring the respondent to permit the exercise of that right (s 35(4)).

It is possible (but uncommon) for a court to make a declaratory order without going on to make further regulatory orders.

2.9.1.2 Criteria for s 35 orders

In deciding whether, and in what terms, to make an s 35 declaratory order the court is to have regard to the *core criteria* (see **2.8.3**), plus certain additional matters relating to the circumstances; namely the length of time that has elapsed since the parties ceased living together, the length of time since the marriage or civil partnership was terminated and the existence of any relevant pending family proceedings (regarding property or children). These last might be viewed as relevant to the issue of how justified a declaratory order would be, given the applicant's lack of property rights vis-à-vis the respondent.

As to whether to go on to make further regulatory orders (which the court may, usually will, but need not necessarily do), the court shall have regard to the *core criteria*, plus the length of time which has elapsed since the parties ceased living together. In addition, the court *must* make a regulatory order under s 35(5) if the balance-of-harm test is satisfied (see **2.8.4**).

2.9.1.3 Duration

The duration of any order granted under FLA 1996, s 35 must, on the first occasion, not exceed six months, but may be extended on subsequent occasions for no more than six months at any one time: s 35(10).

2.9.2 Cohabitants and former cohabitants: s 36

2.9.2.1 Possible orders

The same menu of order possibilities applies for s 36 as for FLA 1996, s 35 (see **2.9.1**). Thus, if the court is to make a regulatory order under s 36, it must first make the relevant declaratory order: s 36(3) and (4). Declaratory orders can stand alone, but almost inevitably will be followed by a further regulatory order (s 36(5)).

The differences, and remaining discrimination against cohabitants (albeit that this term has been extended), arise in the following aspects of the legislation and are indicated in bold italics.

2.9.2.2 Criteria for s 36 orders

In deciding whether, and in what terms, to make an s 36 declaratory order the court is to have regard to the *core criteria* (see **2.8.3**), plus certain additional matters, again relating to the circumstances and the issue of whether such an order is justified; namely the length of time that the parties lived together, whether there are or were any children, the length of time which has elapsed since the parties ceased living together and the existence of any relevant pending family proceedings (regarding property or children). ***In addition the court must have regard to the nature of the party's relationship, and in particular the level of commitment involved in it*** (s 36(6)(e) as amended by DVCVA 2004). This latter requirement replaces a more judgemental (and rarely invoked) provision in the original legislation (inserted at the behest of the 'family values' lobby in the dying days of the last Tory government), by which the court was to have regard to the fact that the parties had 'not given each other the commitment of marriage'. This of course is legally impossible for gay couples and in any event accentuated the negative rather than the positive. Time, and the legislation, have moved on (although not as far as some would like).

2.9.2.3   Balance of harm: no duty

As to whether to go on to make further regulatory orders (which the court may, usually will, but again need not necessarily do), the court shall, in addition to the *core criteria*, have regard to:

- whether the applicant or any relevant child is likely to suffer significant harm attributable to the conduct of the respondent if a regulatory order is not included in the order; and
- whether the harm likely to be suffered by the respondent or child if the provision is included is as great or greater than the harm (attributable to the conduct of the respondent) which the applicant or child is likely to suffer if the provision is not made.

Note that in the s 36 context, these are merely additional factors to be taken into account and impose no duty. *There is thus no obligation on the court to make an s 36 order, even where it is the case that the applicant will suffer significant and the greater harm if an order is not made* (although in such circumstances the court would usually exercise its discretion to do so).

2.9.2.4   Duration

Like s 35, orders under FLA, s 36 are limited in the first instance to a specified period, not exceeding six months. *However, s 36 orders may only be extended on one occasion.*

2.10   Both applicant and respondent unentitled

In most cases, at least one of the parties will be entitled to occupy the property in question, so applications under this head will be relatively rare. Situations where both parties are unentitled include squatters and bare licensees (eg, a couple living with one of the party's parents).

2.10.1   Existing/former spouses/civil partners: s 37

2.10.1.1   Possible orders

Only regulatory orders are possible, ie from the list set out in FLA 1996, s 33(3) (see **2.8.2**), but excluding those, namely (a), (d) and (e), which enforce or restrict what, in this context, are non-existent rights. As *neither* party has any rights of occupation, equality between the parties already exists in this regard—there is thus no scope for an equalising declaratory order. In addition, s 37 orders cannot apply to *intended* family homes.

2.10.1.2   Criteria for s 37 orders

In deciding whether and in what terms to make a regulatory order under s 37, the court shall have regard to the *core criteria* (see **2.8.3**). In addition, the court *must* make a regulatory order if the balance-of-harm test (see **2.8.4**) is satisfied: s 37(4).

2.10.1.3   Duration

As under FLA 1996, s 35—see **2.9.1.3**.

2.10.2   Cohabitants/former cohabitants: s 38

2.10.2.1   Possible orders

The possibilities are the same here as under s 37 (see **2.10.1**).

2.10.2.2   Criteria for s 38 orders

In deciding whether and in what terms to make an order under s 38, the court shall have regard to the *core criteria* (see **2.8.3**). In addition, the court shall have regard to the risk of significant harm as set out above at **2.9.2.3**. As with s 36, the court has a discretion, but *no duty* to make an order were the balance of harm to favour the applicant or any relevant children.

2.10.2.3   Duration

As under s 36—see **2.9.2.4**.

2.11   Ancillary orders

When an occupation order has been made under any of FLA 1996, ss 33, 35 or 36 (ie, where at least one of the parties is entitled to occupy), the court has power to make appropriate orders related to the property. These may impose obligations relating to repair and maintenance, discharge of rent, mortgage repayments or other outgoings, and the use of furniture and other household equipment. Such ancillary orders, as they are called, may be particularly useful where the occupation order is to last for any length of time or where an order for financial provision following divorce is awaited.

2.12   Without notice applications

These are applications heard without notifying the respondent and therefore in his absence (and so without hearing, from him, his version of events). They used to be known as '*ex parte*' applications, and you may find this expression still being used sometimes. It is, as a matter of principle, very serious to seek and gain redress without giving the other side a chance to have his say, and so such applications are only appropriate in *emergencies*.

Therefore, where the situation is not urgent, applications must be made giving all parties notice of the date, place and time of the hearing. Formerly known as '*inter partes*' applications, these are now called on-notice applications.

Unfortunately, emergencies are all too common in domestic violence cases. The FLA 1996 therefore empowers the court to grant both occupation and non-molestation orders on an application without notice. However, in this context the approach to these two orders is very different. Orders to vacate the family home interfere with the respondent's legal rights and so such orders are rarely granted until both sides have been given an opportunity to tell their stories, unless the case is clearly made out or the risks extremely serious. The courts are less anxious about granting non-molestation orders without notice, since it is not such an infringement of a person's rights that he be prevented from doing something he should not be doing in the first place (although it would undoubtedly be an affront were the order unjustified).

Section 45(1) says that the court should only exercise its discretion to make a without notice order where it is 'just and convenient to do so'. In determining whether to grant the order or not the court must have regard to *all the circumstances* (s 45(2)), including:

(a) any risk of significant harm to the applicant or a relevant child, attributable to conduct of the respondent if the order is not made immediately;

(b) whether it is likely that the applicant will be deterred or prevented from pursuing the application if an order is not made immediately; and

(c) whether there is reason to believe that the respondent is aware of the proceedings, but is deliberately evading service and that the applicant or a relevant child will be seriously prejudiced by the delay involved in effecting service of the proceedings (where the court is a magistrates' court) or (in any other case) in effecting substituted service (now known in the mainstream civil courts as service by an alternative method, or alternative service).

These provisions encompass both the notion of urgency and the need for secrecy. Section 45(2)(b) represents an especially welcome recognition of the fact that some applicants may be so terrified of the respondent that the secrecy afforded a without notice application is needed to gain meaningful protection under the Act.

It is imperative that the application and supporting evidence explains *why* an application is being made without giving the respondent notice, since it should be the *exception*, not the rule to grant injunctive relief in such circumstances.

Section 45(3) provides that where the court does make an order on a without notice application it must give the respondent an opportunity to make representations as soon as 'just and convenient' at a full hearing, of which notice has been given to all the parties in accordance with rules of court. This suggests, and is taken by many district judges to mean, that an order made in these circumstances must specifically state a (prompt) return date (ie, the date when both parties return to put their cases). Equally, where a without notice application is refused, the court will usually ensure that a hearing where both parties are present takes place quickly, again often within a week.

2.13 Undertakings and power of arrest

2.13.1 Applications on notice

An **undertaking** is not an admission of guilt, but a *promise* made to the court to do, or not do, certain things, which is given to *avoid* a hearing and the making of a court order. A **power of arrest** is used as an aid to *enforcing* orders made at the end of FLA

1996 hearings. It allows the police to arrest, without a warrant, and bring before the relevant civil court a person whom they have reasonable cause to suspect of being in breach. There is an obvious tension between these two very different approaches to abuse cases, which has sometimes proved difficult to reconcile.

Traditionally, the acceptance by the court of undertakings, has been a useful, and often used, device in domestic violence cases. In appropriate cases, they can defuse fraught situations in that they avoid a traumatic court hearing, thereby saving time, saving tempers—and saving face (by allowing a party to avoid the stigma of the imposition of a court order). They can have real calming properties and are thus given statutory recognition in FLA 1996, s 46(1) which enables the court to accept an undertaking from any party where it has the power to make an occupation or a non-molestation order.

However, the legislation also wants to protect victims of domestic violence and to that end requires that where it 'appears' to the court that the respondent has *used or threatened violence* against the applicant or a relevant child, then it *must* ensure that any order it makes can be enforced by arrest without warrant unless it is satisfied that in the circumstances the applicant or the child in question will be adequately protected without this: FLA 1996, s 47 and 46(3A). In the case of occupation orders, this is achieved by attaching a power of arrest to the order. The same was true until very recently of non-molestation orders, but DVCVA 2004 went one crucial step further and made breach of a non-molestation order itself a criminal offence. It inserted a new s 42A into FLA 1996, which provides that 'a person who without reasonable excuse does anything that he is prohibited from doing by a non-molestation order is guilty of an offence'. This significant change (which came into force in July 2007) effectively renders the power of arrest redundant as far as non-molestation orders are concerned, and so they are abolished for such purposes (DVCVA 2004, Sch 10, para 38).

Arrest without warrant is *not* possible, however, where a respondent is in breach of an undertaking. This is because a power of arrest *cannot* be attached to an undertaking: FLA 1996, s 46(2). Furthermore, the court is expressly forbidden from accepting an undertaking in those cases where it would be required to ensure that any order it makes is enforceable by arrest without warrant. The combined effect of these provisions restricts the court's ability to accept undertakings and has been the object of some criticism for tying judges' hands. Having said that, it appears that a reasonable number manage to circumvent the legislation's constraints (eg, by not making relevant findings of fact about violence) because the proportion of cases settled by undertaking remains relatively high. In 2004, some 40 per cent of non-molestation applications were apparently concluded in this way (Judicial Statistics 2004 (2005) Table 5.9). The 2005 figures are similar, although until later statistics are released it will be difficult to know whether this pattern persists.

Be that as it may, before FLA 1996, it was exceptional for the court to attach a power of arrest to orders it made in domestic violence cases; over time it became the norm. It is now only relevant to occupation orders, breach of a non-molestation order having now become an arrestable offence itself. It is important to note, however, that where relevant, a power of arrest should *only* be attached to that part of the order to which it relates, ie, the terms protecting the applicant from the respondent's violence.

2.13.2 Applications without notice

A power of arrest (which has been abolished for non-molestation orders) may be attached to an occupation order made without notice where it is shown that the respondent has used or threatened violence against the applicant (or relevant child) *and* that there is a risk of significant harm to the applicant (or the child) from the respondent if the power of arrest is not attached immediately: s 47(3). This reflects the fact that attaching a power of arrest to an order when the respondent has not had the opportunity to be heard should be treated with some caution. However, where there has been some actual or threatened violence and there is additionally a risk of significant harm to the applicant or child, a power of arrest will be attached to an emergency occupation order.

The acceptance of undertakings in lieu of a court order is not, of course, applicable to applications where the respondent is not present, since he is not there to offer any.

2.14 Enforcement

The new offence of breach of a non-molestation order is an arrestable offence, triable either way. Arrested persons will be processed through the usual *criminal*, not civil channels. Upon conviction on indictment, the sentence is imprisonment for a term not exceeding five years, or a fine, or both; on summary conviction, the maximum sentence is 12 months' imprisonment, or a fine (not exceeding the statutory maximum), or both. Previously only non-molestation orders to which a power of arrest was attached were brought to the attention of the police. Now copies of any non-molestation order should be sent to the local police station once it has been served on the respondent, who may be arrested if there are reasonable grounds to believe he is in breach. Where a non-molestation order has been obtained without notice, a person can only be guilty of an offence under s 42A in respect of an order of which he has been made aware: s 42A(2).

As regards occupation orders, where (and to the extent that) a power of arrest has been attached, a police officer may arrest without warrant where he or she has reasonable cause for suspecting the respondent of being in breach of the relevant provisions of the order. The order and power of arrest form must be delivered to the local police station and state clearly to which parts of the order the power relates and when it expires. The benefit to the applicant is that no separate application to court need be made for a warrant of arrest to be issued. All she needs do is alert the police. If arrested, the respondent must be brought before the relevant civil court which made the order within 24 hours of the arrest.

Where there is no power of arrest attached to any (or some) part of an occupation order, and the respondent (having been properly served, and so on) is in breach of the order, or undertaking, the applicant can apply for a warrant for the respondent's arrest: FLA 1996, s 47. This is obviously a more drawn-out process, but is still an option in respect of both non-molestation and occupation orders, although as regards the former it is hard to imagine using this procedure when breach of the order is an arrestable offence anyway. The application is without notice and must be supported by evidence *on oath* to satisfy the court that there are reasonable grounds for believing that the respondent has failed to comply with the order/undertaking. If granted, the warrant for arrest is sent to the officer in charge at the relevant police station for it to be executed.

In any case, all orders and undertaking forms include what is known as a 'penal notice', ie, a warning to the respondent that a breach of the order amounts (at the very least, in the case of a non-molestation order) to a contempt of court which may be punishable by imprisonment. Committal proceedings (to determine if the respondent should be 'committed' to prison) are the oldest form of enforcement and so, not surprisingly, the most cumbersome. If the respondent fails to obey the order or undertaking, the applicant can apply to the same court that made the order to commit the respondent to prison for contempt ('committal hearing'). Such hearings are heard in public and so (somewhat unusually for family practitioners) require the wearing of robes. At the committal hearing, the respondent must 'show cause', ie, explain why he should not be sent to prison. It is relatively unusual for a respondent not to be given at least one more chance to comply before the most serious punishment is handed down. As regards non-molestation orders, it is not possible for a person both to be *convicted* of the new offence under s 42A and be punished for contempt (but contempt proceedings remain an alternative if criminal proceedings are not brought, or, presumably, where they are but the defendant is *not* convicted, although given that the standard of proof is the same for contempt and criminal proceedings, it would be a rare case where an acquittal could be followed by successful contempt proceedings).

See **Chapter 13** for a detailed guide to these various enforcement procedures.

2.15 Variation of occupation and non-molestation orders

Either the applicant or respondent can apply to vary or discharge any order made under FLA 1996. If the court has made an order of its own motion, then it can vary or discharge it: s 49.

2.16 Applications by children under the age of 16 years

A child under the age of 16 years (who will need to act through a litigation friend) may make an application for a non-molestation order or an occupation order but only with the permission of the court: s 43(1). Such applications should be made in the High Court. The test that the court applies in deciding whether to give permission is whether the court is 'satisfied that the child has sufficient understanding to make the proposed application': s 43(2). In the case of *Gillick v West Norfolk & Wisbech Area Health Authority* [1986] AC 112, Lord Scarman suggested that sufficiency of understanding came with 'the attainment by a child of an age of sufficient discretion to enable him or her to exercise a wise choice in his or her own interests'. Like the *Gillick* case itself, s 43 opens up wide-ranging possibilities, but has yet to generate much controversy. It seems more common for parents to be obtaining such orders against their teenage children, rather than the other way round. See, eg, *JH v RH* [2001] 1 FLR 641.

2.17 Jurisdiction

Section 57 of the FLA 1996 provides for a unified civil jurisdiction between the High Court, County courts and the magistrates' (ie, Family Proceedings) courts. In certain circumstances procedure varies slightly and/or proceedings must be commenced in a particular court. As a general proposition, however, the ethos and effect of the FLA 1996 is to create a single civil jurisdiction between all of the family courts, enabling choice as well as equality of access and speed for all parties seeking a remedy under the Act.

As the Court of Appeal observed, however, there remains a somewhat 'unsatisfactory ... interface between the criminal and family courts ... It is expensive, wasteful of resources and time-consuming. It is stressful for the victim to move from court to court in order to obtain redress and protection from the perpetrator': *Lomas v Parle* [2005] 1 WLR 1643, para 51. Local initiatives are presently taking place promoting and testing an integrated civil *and* criminal jurisdiction in the magistrates/Family Proceedings courts, but these are still very much at an experimental stage.

2.18   Rules of procedure

Applications for a non-molestation or occupation order are to be made in Form FL 401 whether the application is freestanding or in other proceedings. In the High Court and County courts, the application should be supported by evidence in the form of a sworn statement. In the Family Proceedings Court only a declaration of truth is required. Whatever form the supporting evidence takes, it should convey, as economically as possible, a clear and complete picture of why and on what grounds the order is sought. (See example at **2.23**.) The application will be heard in private ('in chambers') unless the court otherwise directs (but see **2.21** regarding media access).

The procedural rules governing applications under the FLA 1996 are to be found in:

- *In the High and County court*: the Family Proceedings Rules 1991 (SI 1991/1247), as amended.

- *In the Family Proceedings Court*: The Family Proceedings Courts (Matrimonial Proceedings etc.) Rules 1991 (SI 1991/1991), as amended.

- Allocation and Transfer of Proceedings Order 2008 (SI 2008/2836), supplemented by *Practice Direction: Allocation and Transfer of Proceedings*, 25 November 2008.

- The Family Proceedings Fees Order 2008 (SI 2008/1054).

- The Family Proceedings (Allocation to Judiciary) Directions 2009.

2.19   Amendments to the Children Act 1989

2.19.1   Temporary Exclusion order

Section 52 and Sch 6 of the FLA 1996 amended the Children Act 1989 (CA 1989), creating ss 38A, 38B, 39(3B), 44A, 44B, 45(8A) and 45(8B) and enabling the court to make an ouster order for the protection of children when making an interim care order (CA 1989, s 38) or an emergency protection order (CA 1989, s 44), but not an interim supervision order—see **Chapter 9**). These changes produced welcome improvements in the *emergency* protection of children by permitting the removal, albeit as a temporary short-term measure, of a suspected abuser from the family home rather than the removal of the child from the source of the suspected abuse. This power is intended to supplement the emergency protection order or interim care order, rather than provide a long-term alternative to a care order. To reinforce this supplemental aspect, the expression 'exclusion requirement' is used instead of 'ouster' or 'occupation order'.

2.19.2   The conditions

The conditions for attaching an exclusion requirement, as set out in the CA 1989, ss 38A(2) and 44(A) are:

(a) that there is reasonable cause to believe that, if a person ('the relevant person') is excluded from a dwelling-house in which the child lives, the child will cease to suffer, or cease to be likely to suffer significant harm; *and*

(b) that another person living in the dwelling-house (whether a parent of the child or some other person):

   (i)   is able and willing to give to the child the care which it would be reasonable to expect a parent to give him; *and*

   (ii) consents to the inclusion of the exclusion requirement.

These provisions do not seem to be utilised very much—presumably because of the difficulty of obtaining the necessary cooperation and consent from the child's other parent or carer. It is an unhappy feature of domestic child abuse that very often the relationship of that person with the suspected abuser is such that the former assumes the role, if not of co-abuser, then of colluder. Even if the collusion is the result of incompetence, rather than malice, it can still be difficult to be assured of the required level of responsibility from the remaining adult to give the child the necessary protection.

2.19.3   The nature of the exclusion requirement

The exclusion requirement provisions are set out in the CA 1989, s 38A(3)–(10). The requirement can be to leave a dwelling-house in which the child lives, not to enter a dwelling-house in which the child lives, or to be excluded from a defined area in which the dwelling-house where the child lives is situated. As to the evidential requirements, see *Re W* (*Exclusion: Statement of Evidence*) [2000] 2 FLR 666.

The court can attach a power of arrest to an exclusion requirement to last for the period of the main order or a shorter period. Enforcement procedure is the same as for any order with a power of arrest (see **2.13–14**).

An exclusion requirement ceases to have effect at the same time as the interim care order or emergency protection order comes to an end. The 'package' is thus intended as a temporary solution.

The court may accept an undertaking from a relevant person in lieu of attaching an exclusion requirement: CA 1989, ss 38B and 44B.

A person excluded can apply to vary or discharge the exclusion requirement whether or not he or she is entitled to make any application in relation to the main order itself: CA 1989, s 39(3A). If a power of arrest is attached, an application can be made for it to be discharged.

2.20   Protection from Harassment Act 1997

The range of people who can apply under the FLA 1996 for protection from domestic violence is now very wide, but there will still be those who fall outside the class of 'associated person' who will need to look elsewhere for assistance. The criminal law is one source of help, although it is not without its drawbacks, including the different standard of proof, a relatively slow process more orientated to football hooligans than domestic abuse, and the reluctance on the part of many (including victims) to criminalise their partners. In the past the common law had been willing to stretch the concepts of assault and bodily harm as necessary (eg, *R v Ireland; R v Burstow* [1998] 1 FLR 105), but it is the DVCVA 2004 which has attempted to give the criminal law greater capability to do its part to tackle domestic violence. Common assault is made an arrestable offence and there is a new offence of causing or allowing the death of a child or vulnerable adult. And of course, as discussed above, in an attempt to bring together the forces of the civil and criminal law to both protect and punish, breach of a non-molestation order is now a crime in itself.

This 'marriage' of the criminal and civil law in common cause is new, but not unique. The model is the Protection from Harassment Act 1997 (PHA 1997), passed shortly after the FLA 1996. The latter was implemented after a long public debate; the former seemed to slip onto the statute books almost unnoticed. Hastily drafted to provide protection against 'stalkers', it was found to have greater potential (and more pitfalls) than the legislators' anticipated and came to be used for a range of antisocial behaviour. Its innovative hallmark was the hybrid nature of the legislation in that in certain circumstances breach of a civil injunction against harassment became a crime, and criminal courts were given the ability to grant injunctive relief ('restraining orders') by way of sentence. This mixing and matching of the civil and criminal law is not without its difficulties and detractors, but it has been perpetuated in the DVCVA 2004, which made some significant amendments to the PHA 1997. Two of the more radical came into force in September 2009, when ss 12 and 13 of the DVCVA 2004 were implemented: it is now possible for the judge to impose a restraining order following the conviction of *any* offence, not simply behaviour associated with harassment. Even more controversially, the court now has the power to grant restraining orders against defendants who have been *acquitted* of an offence where it is thought 'necessary to do so to protect a person from harassment'.

There are obvious overlaps between the FLA 1996 and the PHA 1997, both of which deal with, and are capable of criminalising harassment, but the focus of the two pieces of legislation is still rather different. For example: applications under the former are family proceedings, whereas applications under the latter are mainstream civil proceedings; only 'associated persons' can apply under the FLA 1996 whereas anyone can apply under the PHA 1997; occupations orders are not a remedy available under the PHA 1997; damages, which can be awarded under the PHA 1997, are not available under the FLA 1996; emergency orders are specifically catered for in the FLA 1996 but not in the PHA 1997. Practitioners need to be well aware of both statutes, but if there is a choice, it would still seem that the FLA 1996 will be invoked to protect victims of abuse arising in the many domestic situations catered for in the legislation, as now enhanced by recent amendments.

2.21 The Human Rights Act 1998

The effect of the Human Rights Act 1998 (HRA 1998), which came into force on 2 October 2000, is to make rights under the European Convention for the Protection of Human Rights and Freedoms 'directly enforceable' against 'public authorities' (which is defined to include the courts), thus obviating the need for individuals to apply to the European Court of Human Rights. Under s 3, the courts must minimise interference with the Convention and interpret legislation so as to be compatible with it. In addition, domestic law must now be enacted, amended and interpreted so as to be compatible with the Convention. The higher courts can make declarations that legislation is 'incompatible' with a Convention right, although they cannot directly strike down primary legislation.

Because an occupation order usually has the effect of precluding an individual's exercising the right to occupy his or her home, it necessarily interferes with the right to 'private and family life' (European Convention, Art 8). But the right is qualified and the state is entitled to infringe it in certain circumstances, including in order to 'protect health or morals' or to 'protect the rights and freedom of others'. The FLA 1996 was drafted so as to comply with the Convention, and it seems that the balance which the latter strikes between the rights of the individual and the rights of others has been adequately reflected in the legislation.

The ability to obtain non-molestation and/or occupation orders on applications which have been made without giving the other side notice raises a possible conflict with Art 6 (the right to a fair trial). However, it seems that Art 6 is complied with so long as the need to apply without notice is made out (eg, urgency) and such orders last only for so long as it takes to hear the respondent's representations at a with notice hearing.

The requirement for a public hearing under Art 6 accepts the need for privacy in several circumstances, including the protection of the private life of the parties and the interests of children. It has long been assumed here that holding hearings in private was the best way to protect families dealing with the legal and personal fallout from domestic trauma. Increasingly, however, this came to be seen as a rather blanket approach, which, among other things, conflicts with the importance and benefits of ensuring that justice is not only done, but seen to be done. The widespread perception, for example, that non-resident parents (often fathers) are not treated fairly by the courts is in part perpetuated by lack of openness. There have, for many years, been strict restrictions on the *reporting* of certain information from family proceedings involving the welfare of children, although the courts do have power in some circumstances to lift these to an extent. The latest experiment in openness has a different focus. On 27 April 2009, the Family Proceedings (Amendment) (No 2) Rules 2009 came into force, which introduced provision for *attendance* of accredited journalists and similar parties at private hearings, subject to a contrary court direction. The idea is that the media (as representatives of the public) can see, and thus report on, how the system works (i.e. justice being seen to be done), and thereby hold the courts to account; but restrictions remain as to what documents journalists can see and the details on which they can report. Even so, there may be scope for tactical advantages being made from the risk or fear of public disclosure. These new rules are still in their infancy, but whether they will advance the cause of open justice remains to be seen. So far, celebrities have been a greater attraction than justice.

2.22 The Forced Marriage (Civil Protection) Act 2007

There is an obvious overlap between forced (as opposed to arranged) marriage and domestic violence. The hallmark of a forced marriage is the absence of valid consent on the part of both parties, and the presence of abuse or duress, whether physical, financial, emotion or otherwise. In *NS v MI* [2007] 1 FLR 66, Munby J said that 'the court must not hesitate to use every weapon in its protective arsenal if faced with what is, or appears to be, a case of forced marriage'. Until the Forced Marriage (Civil Protection) Act 2007 (FM(CP)A 2007), those weapons included care proceedings (if children were involved) or the (domestic) criminal law (assuming a victim would be willing to give evidence, which might well expose them and their families to more violence), the FLA 1996 as it then stood or the inherent jurisdiction of the High Court (eg, to grant injunctions). There were, however, limits to what the court could do. For example, one of the great challenges of forced marriage is its extra-jurisdictional nature; young people are often taken abroad for such purposes, and it is difficult for the arm of the law to reach that far.

The FM(CP)A 2007, which came into force on 25 November 2008, attempts to widen the ambit of the FLA 1996 to accommodate the complexities of forced marriage. It adds a new Part 4A to the FLA 1996, providing protection from having been or being 'forced into a marriage or from any attempt to be forced into a marriage'. The terms of the Forced Marriage Protection Order (FMPO) made under the new Part 4A may relate to conduct within *or outside* the jurisdiction of England and Wales and can be directed at a wide range of persons, whose identity may or may not be known to the court, who may be involved, however peripherally, with forcing an individual into marriage. An FMPO may not only contain the usual prohibitions (such as non-molestation orders, etc), but also 'restrictions, requirements or other terms', including, for example, an order that a respondent surrender the victim's passport (so as to prevent the latter being taken abroad against her will). An application may be made by the person to be protected or by a third party. The court is required to take into account the 'ascertainable' wishes and feelings of the victim when considering whether to make the order.

FMPOs can be made in the County or High Court, on notice or without notice, and a power of arrest can be attached in much the same way as occupation orders. The hope is that with proper training and understanding, and sufficient support from frontline services (eg, socials services, schools, doctors) this latest addition to the war on domestic violence will become more than 'a symbolic outlawing' of forced marriage and make a real contribution to its eradication. Time will tell.

OCCUPATION ORDERS

[of home which is, was, or was intended to be a common home]
Family Law Act 1996, as amended

Assuming R is 'associated' (now includes almost every domestic/enduringly intimate relationship) with A:

ASK:

Is A 'entitled to occupy'?

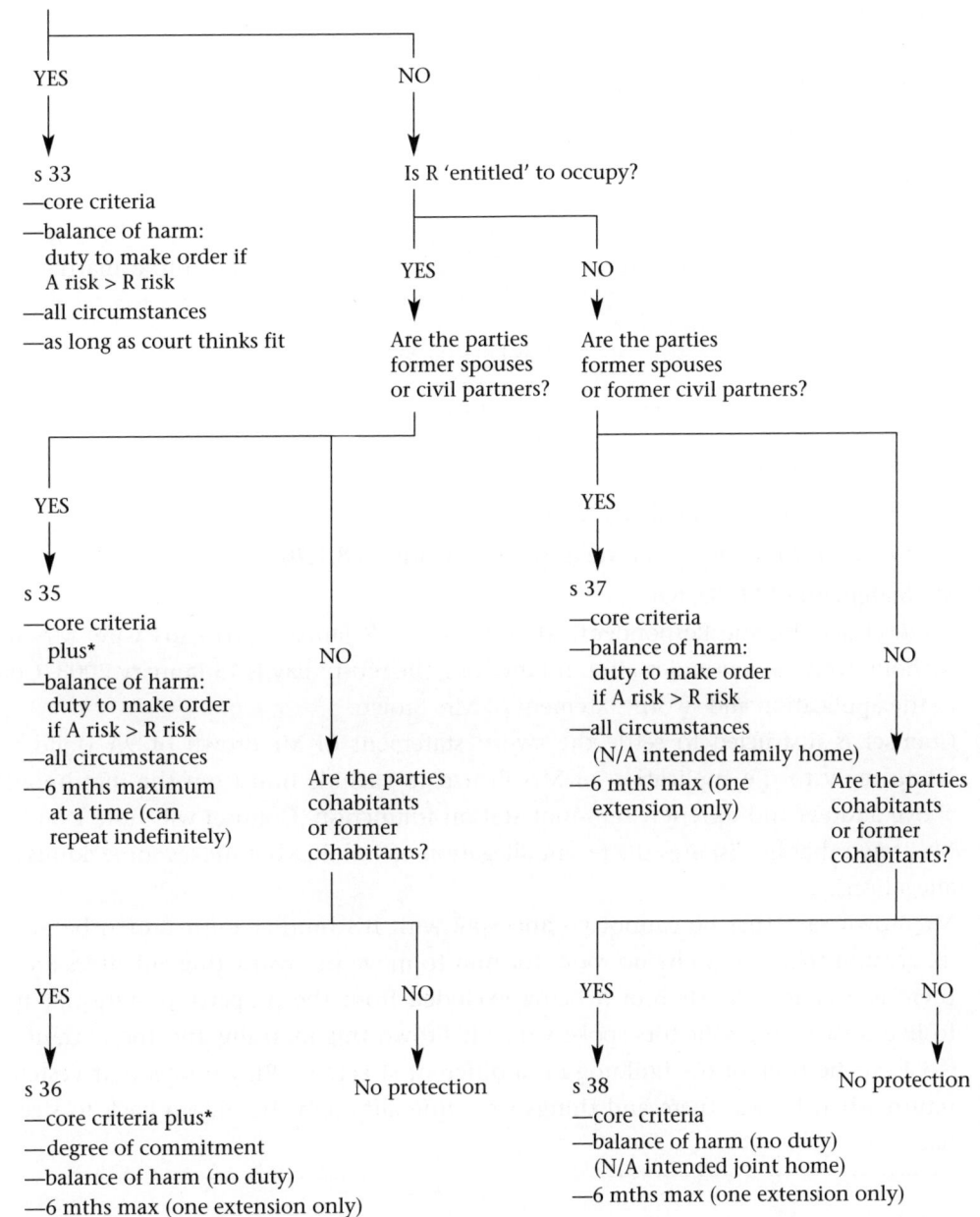

YES

s 33
—core criteria
—balance of harm:
  duty to make order if
  A risk > R risk
—all circumstances
—as long as court thinks fit

NO

Is R 'entitled' to occupy?

YES

Are the parties
former spouses
or civil partners?

NO

Are the parties
former spouses
or former civil partners?

YES

s 35
—core criteria
  plus*
—balance of harm:
  duty to make order
  if A risk > R risk
—all circumstances
—6 mths maximum
  at a time (can
  repeat indefinitely)

NO

Are the parties
cohabitants
or former
cohabitants?

YES

s 37
—core criteria
—balance of harm:
  duty to make order
  if A risk > R risk
—all circumstances
  (N/A intended family home)
—6 mths max (one
  extension only)

NO

Are the parties
cohabitants
or former
cohabitants?

YES

s 36
—core criteria plus*
—degree of commitment
—balance of harm (no duty)
—6 mths max (one extension only)

NO

No protection

YES

s 38
—core criteria
—balance of harm (no duty)
  (N/A intended joint home)
—6 mths max (one extension only)

NO

No protection

* ie, additional factors relevant to status, eg, how long together, etc

2.23   An example of domestic violence proceedings in the County court

This case study uses the most up-to-date forms available and/or adapts the old forms as necessary.

Instructions to counsel

IN THE CLERKENWELL COUNTY COURT   Case No 10/162

IN THE MATTER OF THE FAMILY LAW ACT 1996
BETWEEN

MS EMMA JANE BROWN   Applicant

and

MR DAVID MITCHELL BROWN   Respondent

INSTRUCTIONS TO COUNSEL

Counsel has herewith:

1.   Copy application dated 8.1.2010

2.   Copy sworn statement of the Applicant sworn on 8.1.2010

3.   Statement of Mr Brown

Counsel acts for the Respondent, Mr Brown. On 8 January 2010 his wife, Mrs Brown, obtained without notice a non-molestation injunction. The return day is 15 January 2008. Counsel is referred to the application and sworn statement of Mrs Brown.

Counsel is instructed to settle the sworn statement of Mr Brown of 9A Haliday Road, London N1 in reply to the application of Mrs Brown to exclude him from the matrimonial home at the above address and to renew non-molestation injunction. Counsel will note from the statement of Mr Brown that he disputes the recent allegation of violence but makes some admissions to the older allegations.

Mr Brown says that he cannot go and stay with his brother John Brown because he now has a lodger and there would be no room for him to move in. Instructing Solicitors are of the view that there is a chance of Mr Brown being excluded from the property despite not having anywhere to live. Instructing solicitors spoke with Mr Brown this morning and the entrance to the couple's flat is at the back of the building on a different street. Mr Brown says that yesterday his wife did return when he was there and things were fine although she did go back to sleep at her friend's flat.

Application for:
a non-molestation order
an occupation order

Family Law Act 1996 (Part IV)

The court CLERKENWELL COUNTY COURT

To be completed by the court

Date issued   8TH JANUARY 2010

Case number

10/162

Please read the accompanying notes as you complete this form.

1   About you (the applicant)

State your title (Mr, Mrs etc), full name, address, telephone number and date of birth (if under 18):

```
Mrs. Emma Jane Brown
9A Haliday Road
London N1 4CL

0795 234 1799
```

State your solicitor's name, address, reference, telephone, FAX and DX numbers:

```
Messrs Ling & Ton      tel:  020 7 226 4175
2 Upper Street         fax:  020 7 226 4299
London N1 2LT
```

2   About the respondent

State the respondent's name, address and date of birth (if known):

```
David Mitchell Brown
9A Haliday Road
London N1 4CL

dob 16 05 1984
```

3   The Order(s) for which you are applying

This application is for:

[x]   a non-molestation order

[x]   an occupation order

[x]   Tick this box if you wish the court to hear your application without notice being given to the respondent. The reasons relied on for an application being heard without notice must be stated in the statement in support.

1

4   Your relationship to the respondent (the person to be served with this application)

Your relationship to the respondent is:

(Please tick only one of the following)

1   [x] Married

2   ☐ Civil Partners

3   ☐ Were married

4   ☐ Former civil partners

5   ☐ Cohabiting

6   ☐ Were cohabiting

7   ☐ Both of you live or have lived in the same household

8   ☐ Relative
     State how related:

9   ☐ Agreed to marry.
     Give the date the agreement was made.
     If the agreement has ended, state when.

10   ☐ Agreed to form a civil partnership.
     Give the date the agreement was made.
     If the agreement has ended, state when.

11   ☐ Both of you are parents of, or have parental responsibility for, a child

12   ☐ One of you is a parent of a child and the other has parental responsibility for that child

13 ☐ One of you is the natural parent or grandparent of a child adopted, placed or freed for adoption, and the other is:

    (i)   the adoptive parent

    or (ii) a person who has applied for an adoption order for the child

    or (iii) a person with whom the child has been placed for adoption

    or (iv) the child who has been adopted, placed or freed for adoption.

State whether (i), (ii), (iii) or (iv):

14 ☐ Both of you are the parties to the same family proceedings (see also Section 11 below).

5 Application for a non-molestation order

If you wish to apply for a non-molestation order, state briefly in this section the order you want.

Give full details in support of your application in your supporting evidence.

```
The Respondent to be forbidden to use or threaten violence against
intimidate, harass or pester the Applicant or instruct, encourage or
suggest that any other person do so.
```

6 Application for an occupation order

If you do not wish to apply for an occupation order, please go to section 9 of this form.

(A) State the address of the dwelling-house to which your application relates:

```
9 Haliday Road
London N1 4CL
```

(B) State whether it is occupied by you or the respondent now or in the past, or whether it was intended to be occupied by you or the respondent:

```
Both Applicant and Respondent
```

(C) State whether you are entitled to occupy the dwelling-house: ☒ Yes   ☐ No

If yes, explain why:

```
Provided by Applicant's employer
```

(D) State whether the respondent is entitled to occupy
the dwelling-house: ☒ Yes ☐ No

If yes, explain why:

Home Rights

**On the basis of your answers to (C) and (D) above,
tick one of the boxes 1 to 6 below to show the category
into which you fit**

1 ☒ a spouse or civil partner who has home rights
in the dwelling-house, or a person who is
entitled to occupy it by virtue of a beneficial
estate or interest or contract or by virtue of
any enactment giving him or her the right to
remain in occupation.

If you tick box 1, state whether there is a
dispute or pending proceedings between you
and the respondent about your right to occupy
the dwelling-house.

2 ☐ a former spouse or former civil partner with no
existing right to occupy, where the respondent
spouse or civil partner is so entitled.

3 ☐ a cohabitant or former cohabitant with no
existing right to occupy, where the respondent
cohabitant or former cohabitant is so entitled.

4 ☐ a spouse or former spouse who is not entitled
to occupy, where the respondent spouse or
former spouse is also not entitled.

5 ☐ a civil partner or former civil partner who is not
entitled to occupy, where the respondent civil
partner or former civil partner is also not entitled.

6 ☐ a cohabitant or former cohabitant who is
not entitled to occupy, where the respondent
cohabitant or former cohabitant is also not
entitled.

Home Rights

If you do have home rights please:

State whether the title to the land is registered or unregistered (if known):

`unknown`

If registered, state the Land Registry title number (if known):

`unknown`

If you wish to apply for an occupation order, state briefly here the order you want. Give full details in support of your application in your supporting evidence:

`An order excluding the Respondent from the property known as 9A Haliday Road,`
`London N1 4CL`

7 Application for additional order(s) about the dwelling-house

If you want to apply for any of the orders listed in the notes to this section, state what order you would like the court to make:

8 Mortgage and rent

Is the dwelling-house subject to a mortgage?

☐ Yes   ☐ No

If yes, please provide the name and address of the mortgagee:

`Don't know`

Is the dwelling-house rented?

☒ Yes   ☐ No

If yes, please provide the name and address of the landlord:

`No details (I rent from my employers)`

9   At the court

Will you need an interpreter at court?

☐ Yes   ☒ No

If yes, specify the language:

If you require an interpreter, you must notify the court immediately so that one can be arranged.

If you have a disability for which you require special assistance or special facilities, please state what your needs are. The court staff will get in touch with you about your requirements.

10   Other information

State the name and date of birth of any child living with or staying with, or likely to live with or stay with, you or the respondent:

N/A

State the name of any other person living in the same household as you and the respondent, and say why they live there:

N/A

11   Other Proceedings and Orders

If there are any other current family proceedings or orders in force involving you and the respondent, state the type of proceedings or orders, the court and the case number. This includes any application for an occupation order or non-molestation order against you by the respondent.

None

This application is to be served upon the respondent

Signed: *Mssrs Ling & Ton*   Date: 08.01.10

Filed on behalf of Applicant
Deponent: E J Brown
Date of Swearing: 8.1.10
Date of Filing: 8.1.10
Case No 10/162

IN THE CLERKENWELL COUNTY COURT

IN THE MATTER OF THE FAMILY LAW ACT 1996

BETWEEN

MS EMMA JANE BROWN   Applicant

and

MR DAVID MITCHELL BROWN   Respondent

I, EMMA JANE BROWN, of 9A Haliday Road, London N1, canteen assistant, the above-named Applicant, MAKE OATH and say as follows:

Status

1. I make this sworn statement in support of my application herein for an injunction, forbidding the Respondent from using violence against me or from threatening, intimidating, harassing or pestering me. I also seek an order requiring the Respondent to vacate the matrimonial home at 9A Haliday Road aforesaid forthwith supported by a power of arrest.

2. I met the Respondent in February 2009 and we got married on 14 April 2009. He moved into my flat above the canteen where I work. It is a one bedroom flat.

Conduct

3. I did not know of the Respondent's serious drink problem until after we were married. Very shortly after our honeymoon he began to drink to excess on a regular basis. When he gets drunk he becomes abusive and violent but particularly his drunkenness manifests itself in an uncontrollable paranoia that I am engaging in affairs with different men.

4. The Respondent began visiting the canteen where I work, usually without warning, and sometimes many times in the day, to see if I had any men hidden behind the serving area or in the store cupboard. He was also rude to the male customers telling them to 'keep their hands off his missus' and not to 'eye me up'. This was extremely distressing for me and embarrassing for both me and my customers.

5. One day last July the Respondent and I were walking down the street when we met a married couple who are friends of mine. After we chatted for a few minutes the Respondent shouted at the man to 'stop imagining that you are having sex with my wife'. I did not know what to do or say so I just kept quiet.

6. On 8 August 2009 the Respondent and I went to a party where we met one of his friends. The friend complimented me in front of the Respondent who immediately lost his temper. He punched his friend in the face, broke his nose and there was blood everywhere. I was very embarrassed and frightened and did not dare say anything to the Respondent about this outburst.

7. The next day the Respondent noticed that I was wearing some silver earrings. I bought these before we were married and have worn them many times. However, he was convinced that they were a present from one of my customers. He grabbed me by the wrists, pulled the earrings out of my ears and tore my lobes as he did so.

8. Since then, the Respondent has assaulted me on more occasions than I can remember. He began going to the pub more and more and would often come home and beat me or kick me or bend back

my fingers. I felt too ashamed to go to the doctor for help. I wore trousers and long sleeved tops so that nobody noticed the bruises.

Significant harm

9.   Two nights ago the Respondent and I decided to hold a party with a Mexican theme for about twenty of the Respondent's friends and a couple of my girlfriends. I spent the whole day preparing the food whilst the Respondent provided the alcohol. Unfortunately he drank a glass of tequila with each guest as they arrived and got very drunk. He then got jealous of everyone complimenting me on the food, how pretty I looked in the Spanish dress that I was wearing and the attention that I was receiving. He got hold of a bowl of dip and threw it at me causing the dip to run down my dress. He shouted at me to 'stop behaving like a tart' and said 'now you will want to strip off your dress you slapper'. He then grabbed me by the wrists and dragged me to the bedroom trying to rip off my dress. He slapped me around the face and told me to change clothes. I felt humiliated because everyone was watching so I stayed in the bedroom and waited for everyone to go.

10.   About an hour later the Respondent staggered into the bedroom and hurled an empty bottle at me narrowly missing me and hitting the wall behind. He jumped on top of me on the bed and twisted back my arms. I received a large bruise on my left upper arm. Then he pulled my hair right back, slapped my face and then started to hit my head against the headboard. He only stopped when I poked his eyes with my fingers. He then rolled over and fell off the bed. I quickly ran to the bathroom and locked the door and stayed there all night.

11.   Last night I slept on the sofa of Janice Ham, a work colleague who lives close to the Angel. She has a small flat and I cannot stay there for more than a few days. I have nowhere else to stay. My flat is provided by my employers, at a very reasonable rent. I only earn £80 per week net and I cannot afford to rent any other accommodation. The Respondent can go and stay with his brother in Finchley where he lived prior to the marriage. His brother has a two bedroom house and it is not far for him to commute to work in his car. He is a garage mechanic working at Highbury Corner.

Emergency application

12.   I am too frightened to return to my flat. The Respondent behaves irrationally and I believe that he will continue to assault me if he is allowed to remain in the flat. I am frightened by how the Respondent will react to my applying for this injunction and I therefore seek an order without notice in the terms set out in paragraph 1 of this sworn statement.

Sworn this 8th day of January 2010
at 10 Highbury Crescent
London N1

Emma Jane Brown

Before me
Commissioner of Oaths

In the Clerkenwell County court

Brown v Brown   Case Number 10/162

Record of the Hearing on   8 January 2010

Applicant EMMA JANE BROWN
Ref:
Respondent DAVID MITCHELL BROWN
Ref:

On notice	Ex parte YES	

1. Attendances

Name	Present	Represented by
Applicant		Amanda Rice Ling & Ton (SD)

2. Evidence
    To be completed only when the court makes a finding of fact

The Court read the report(s)/statement(s) of	Dated
Applicant	8/1/10
The Court heard oral evidence [on oath] of	

FL405 Record of the Hearing

In the Clerkenwell County court

Brown v Brown	Case Number 10/162

[Order]   [Direction]
                                  Family Law Act 1996

Important Notice to the Respondent   DAVID MITCHELL BROWN

This order gives you instructions which you must follow. You should read it all carefully. If you do not understand anything in this order you should go to a solicitor, Legal Advice Centre or Citizens Advice Bureau. You have a right to ask the court to change or cancel the order but you must obey it unless the court does change or cancel it.

You must obey the instructions contained in this order. If you do not, you will be guilty of contempt of court and a criminal offence and you may be sent to prison.

It is ordered that:

1. The respondent, DAVID MITCHELL BROWN, is forbidden to use or threaten violence against the applicant, EMMA JANE BROWN, and must not instruct, encourage or in any way suggest that any other person should do so **AND/OR**

2. The respondent, DAVID MITCHELL BROWN, is forbidden to intimidate, harass or pester the applicant, EMMA JANE BROWN, and must not instruct, encourage or in any way suggest that any other person should do so.

3. This order shall last until 15 January 2010 or further order.

4. The respondent may apply to have this order varied or discharged.

5. Matter to be listed again for hearing on 15 January 2010.

6. Costs reserved

Ordered by   [Mr][Mrs] Justice
              [His][Her] Honour Judge
              [Deputy] District Judge [of the Family Division]   Swanson
              Justice[s] of the Peace
              [Assistant] Recorder

        on   8 January 2010

              FL404 Order or Directions

STATEMENT OF MR BROWN

I can't believe what she is saying. Whilst it is true that I used to go and visit her at work a lot, that was only because we had just got married and I missed her when we came back from our honeymoon. It was out of affection and not out of jealousy. I did accuse Emma of receiving the earrings from a customer but it is very difficult because she gets lots of builders and the like coming into her canteen and they are always being sweet on her. I asked her to take them off because it upset me seeing her wearing them and she refused. She just smiled and said nothing. She refused to answer my questions so I did take them off her. Maybe I was a bit heavy handed but they are very tricky things to remove. Anyway, she never complained about it at the time.

I admit that I did accuse Dave Canker of imagining that he was having sex with my wife when we met them in the street but that is because he has a reputation of having affairs and started chatting up Emma in front of Amy, his wife and she was getting all upset and crying and Emma was laughing at her and I wanted to help Amy because Dave is so thoughtless and would not stop.

I admit that I got drunk on the 8 of August last year and punched Frank Lee, but he asked for it. He has always been going on at me about how pretty Emma is and how he fancied her and so when he met her for the first time at that party and started coming on strong I was furious. I don't trust him an inch. He is a slippery fish and if he could get his hands on Emma he would.

Emma is very aware of the effect she has on men. She can switch on the charm and sex appeal when she wants to and she does it to tease me. It is true that I have hit her a couple of times in the past but that is only because she was trying to get my attention by chatting up other men. She knows that I get jealous and she does it on purpose. I have never kicked her. I have bent back her fingers but that is to stop her poking out my eyes. It is true that I go to the pub most evenings and some lunchtimes but that is because most of my mates go down there. As I have said, I do not get drunk and beat up Emma; rather, she teases me to get me jealous.

How Emma has described the Mexican party is a pack of lies. I did not drink a glass of tequila with every guest on their arrival. How would she know because she was not standing by the door greeting guests as they came in. Rather she was doing provocative dances with some of my mates from work. That is why I threw the food at her. It was the only way I could stop her dancing those close up Latin American dances. She was trying to attract my attention and to get me jealous. She stormed into the bedroom. When I came in later to see if she was alright she attacked me. She was screaming and kicking and when I tried to defend myself she tried to poke my eyes out.

I cannot stay with my brother in Finchley. He has rented out his spare room to a lodger and my car is not reliable enough to travel the distance to work. I cannot afford to be late for work because I already have a warning at work over my time-keeping. There is nobody else who has the room to put me up and I can't afford to rent because I am trying to pay off my credit card. I owe about £4,300 and I make payments of £200 a month. This comes out of my take home pay of £255 a week.

2.24 *Brown v Brown*: drafting the sworn statement in a support

The sworn statement is the party's evidence before the court and is an absolutely crucial document. It takes a high degree of skill—and lots of practice—to draft such statements effectively. Barristers are not often called upon to do this, but solicitors and other advocates will be.

When drafting a sworn (or other witness) statement you want to put forward the relevant facts as convincingly as possible. In effect your job is to present the evidence so that it has the best chance of achieving its purpose. Remember that judges often have to sit and read such statements all day long. If yours can be that much more compelling, clear and to the point than the rest, you will be doing yourself and your client a valuable service.

You should refer to Chapter 20 of the **Drafting Manual** for the rules of presentation of witness statements.

2.24.1   Content

It is imperative that the story you tell is the *client's* story—not your story or a story you think you would rather be telling. Obviously, you should never invent evidence.

In the sworn statement, your client should set out the relief or outcome sought and the eligibility for such relief, eg, the category of associated person and rights of occupation in the property. If the application is without notice, then the statement *must* include an explanation of why the application is being made without notice.

The statement should contain the relevant facts available to show why the party needs the court's protection or on what basis he or she resists the injunction(s) sought. It should focus on the main incidents said to justify the making (or not) of the order(s). The statement does not recite the law, but it needs to be drafted with the law clearly in mind. What it must do is set out the facts material to the criteria which the court will apply under the relevant section of the FLA 1996. If it is a sworn statement in reply, it should show why the criteria are not satisfied and/or why the court's discretion should be exercised in favour of the respondent and not the applicant.

2.24.2   Structure

It is important to tell your client's story well. The facts should be presented logically, setting out clearly the incidents of violence (or replying to each allegation of violence). A chronological telling is often easiest to follow. It may also help (but is not strictly necessary) to use sub-headings relating to the relevant legal provisions.

Try to develop a 'theory of the case' and draft accordingly. Describing a steady escalation of violence will require a different presentation from the portrayal of an out-of-the-blue series of attacks. Always set the scene carefully and think in terms of a 'strong finish'. Tailor the structure to meet the needs of your case; never use 'off-the-peg' statements.

Be as specific as you can. In Mrs Brown's statement she asserts that she has been assaulted on more occasions than she can remember. Unless she really has been attacked so many times it has affected her short-term memory, she will be challenged on this telling lack of detail.

A sworn statement in reply would normally adopt the order of the applicant's statement and should always respond to *every* allegation.

2.24.3   Language

The sworn statement is the witness's evidence and it is important to set out the facts so that his or her 'voice' comes through. Having said this, it is also important to recast sentences in the proof so that they are grammatically correct and readily comprehensible. The aim is not to make the statement unnecessarily formal but to make it clear and compelling. If it is appropriate to include the actual words spoken by a person, this should be done in the normal way using quotation marks.

2.24.4 Persuasiveness

The aim of the sworn statement is to persuade the court to make the order applied for or to resist the making of the order. Your 'theory of the case' must be an effective one; you must set out the facts in such a way that the inference you wish the judge to draw is credible and one which will achieve your goal. For example, Mrs Brown's theme might be that her husband is of a jealous disposition which especially manifests itself when he is drunk. He misinterprets situations, is increasingly violent towards her and will continue to do this unless she obtains protection from the court. She gives examples of his behaviour: he pesters her at work; he accuses her of having affairs; he tore out her earrings; he has developed a habit of getting drunk and using violence towards her. When there is a history of violence, an applicant is more likely to get the additional protection of an occupation order if he or she can show that it has escalated.

Mr Brown's theme might be that he does not misinterpret situations, but rather that his wife deliberately behaves in an alluring manner towards other men so as to make him jealous. While he does admit to occasions when he has lost his temper in response to such behaviour, eg, throwing the dip, he asserts that the allegations greatly exaggerate the situation and that his wife, who has voluntarily returned to the flat since her application, is herself capable of violence.

2.25 *Brown v Brown*: at the without notice hearing

This hearing, of which Mr Brown is not given notice, is brought in the County court and heard in chambers (ie, in private, but see **2.21**)—usually by a District Judge or a circuit judge. Mrs Brown's counsel will introduce himself or herself, explain that the application is for a non-molestation order and an order excluding Mr Brown from the matrimonial home situated at 9A Haliday Road, London, the latter to be supported by a power of arrest. Counsel will then briefly give some background facts—the very short courtship; the date of the marriage; the immediacy of Mr Brown's unfounded suspicions and pestering which escalated into violence first towards others and then to his wife.

The judge should then be given an opportunity to read the sworn statement if he or she has not done so already (always be prepared to read it out in full to the court but you will very rarely be called upon to do this).

Counsel will then get into the heart of the application. The essence of the case is that Mr Brown is of a jealous disposition which manifests itself when he is drunk and he uses violence towards his wife. Counsel will refer to the paragraphs in Mrs Brown's sworn statement to support this theory and the fact that Mr Brown's conduct towards his wife has got worse, eg, at the Mexican party he threw a bowl at her; grabbed her by the wrists; returned later and threw a bottle at his wife; jumped on top of her and twisted her arms back; pulled her hair back; slapped her face and started to hit her against the headboard. Highlight relevant facts and repeat useful detail, but do not merely recite whole paragraphs which the court has already read.

Counsel will then seek to persuade the judge that Mrs Brown needs proper protection and, importantly, draw attention to her reasons for applying without notice. Much will be made of the fact that Mrs Brown sought refuge in the bathroom and sanctuary at her friend's and that she cannot stay for long at Janice Ham's on the sofa but her husband could stay with his brother in Finchley and drive to work. In the absence of Mr Brown,

Mrs Brown's counsel must be mindful of the need for full and frank disclosure (which is sometimes difficult to achieve given the emotions involved in such family crises). In any case, you should always be aware of and be prepared to deal with weakness in the case (eg, a lack of medical evidence).

The outcome will likely be based on Mrs Brown's sworn statement and one would not expect her to be called unless, for example, the judge wishes to hear evidence of her injuries because there is no medical evidence to support her case (if possible, you should always get such evidence). Also, if there have been other incidents since the swearing of the statement then Mrs Brown can be called to give evidence of these.

The judge is unlikely to make an occupation order excluding Mr Brown because these are not exceptional circumstances (see **2.12**). He or she would, however, be likely to grant an injunction prohibiting Mr Brown from using violence or threatening violence and prohibiting Mr Brown from intimidating, harassing or pestering Mrs Brown. This no longer needs to be supported by a power of arrest, since its breach now amounts to a criminal offence.

The judge would then fix a return day for the with notice hearing which is usually about seven days later. Both parties will have the opportunity to put their case at this time. The without notice order will last until this later hearing.

Costs are usually reserved. If Mrs Brown is publicly funded (which would be indicated on the front page of the brief to her counsel), the judge might order an assessment of her costs. If not, counsel at the with notice hearing must remember to ask for it to be granted retrospectively. Counsel will then ask for a certificate for counsel.

The without notice hearing is likely to last only five to ten minutes. It is vital to present a focused and succinct application. Not only is this apt to be more persuasive, but the courts are very busy and will have a number of matters listed for the day.

Mrs Brown should have been advised before the hearing that she was unlikely to get the occupation order at this stage, and so should not be unduly surprised if she has not. She may, however, still have concerns so, after the hearing, counsel should explain the outcome, and especially the effect and added protection of the fact that it is a criminal offence to break a non-molestation order.

The order will only take effect once it has been drawn up and served upon Mr Brown personally—if appropriate, by an enquiry agent. Mrs Brown should be advised when the order has been served and what, in practical terms, to do if her husband is in breach of the terms.

2.26 *Brown v Brown*: at the with notice hearing

Again, the hearing is in private (but see **2.21**). This time, however, *both* parties are able to put their case, Mr Brown having by now sworn and served his statement in reply to Mrs Brown's.

Counsel for Mrs Brown will introduce the case (and both parties' advocates) and remind the court that a non-molestation injunction was ordered at the earlier hearing on 8 January 2010 and that this is the return day for the applications.

Counsel will refer the judge to the two sworn statements in the matter and then call Mrs Brown as a witness. Having taken the oath, she will be asked to identify herself and then to confirm that she did swear her statement on 8 January 2010 and that its contents contain her account of events to the date of its being sworn. If there are no other matters which need to come out, then generally Mrs Brown should not be asked questions-in-chief, but be tendered for cross-examination. As with the without notice hearing, if you want to get a power of arrest attached to the occupation order, you need the court to make a finding that there has been the use of or threat of violence. You may feel better able to show this if Mrs Brown tells her side of the story by relating the serious incidences of violence prior to cross-examination, but do not simply rehash what is in her statement (which otherwise stands as her evidence-in-chief). Some judges like to hear some oral evidence-in-chief in order to assess credibility. But others will stop you. You need to be flexible and learn to know your tribunal. If in conference before the hearing, Mrs Brown tells counsel of new matters since the statement was sworn, eg, new details of violence, accommodation and financial matters, then she can be asked questions-in-chief to elicit this information. Counsel for Mr Brown will then cross-examine Mrs Brown. He or she will question her on all the disputes of fact, putting Mr Brown's case to her. Counsel will seek to advance Mr Brown's theory of the case and to discredit hers. For example, counsel will seek to obtain from Mrs Brown admissions that she has behaved in an alluring manner to other men knowing that her husband would be provoked by this. Counsel might point out omissions in her sworn statement. For example, she cannot recall details of the other incidents which might indicate that they are invented, or the fact that in her sworn statement she says her husband bent her fingers back but omits to say that this was to avoid her poking out his eyes. There may be a suggestive lack of medical evidence.

Counsel for Mrs Brown will re-examine if necessary. Assuming there are no other witnesses, that concludes the case for the applicant. Remember to avoid surprise witnesses; if there are other people who can speak to relevant matters, ensure that their statements are available.

Counsel for the respondent then calls Mr Brown. The same points concerning examination-in-chief apply here and if Mr Brown is willing to give an undertaking not to use violence, threaten, intimidate, harass or pester his wife, make this clear to the court and make the appropriate forms available. Then, counsel for Mrs Brown will cross-examine him with any necessary re-examination to follow.

Finally, the closing speeches. The respondent goes first, giving the applicant the last word. The most effective submissions will take the judge through the s 33 'core criteria' and balance-of-harm test (see **2.8.3** and **2.8.4**), applying them to the facts. You are more likely to be successful if you relate each part of the test to the relevant facts and articulate your arguments fully while at the same time being concise and focused on matters likely to influence the decision.

The judge is well familiar with the legislation, so concentrate on persuading him or her that, *on the facts of the case*, your client is entitled to the remedy/outcome he or she seeks. As regards the occupation order, be aware of how s 33(6) and (7) relate to one another (see **2.8.4**). Apply the s 33(6) criteria to each party, relying on your own version of the events (as adapted through any concessions made in cross-examination), and compare and contrast with the version of events put forward by the other side.

When dealing with the balance-of-harm test contained in s 33(7), think both in terms of whether the test applies (ie, whether there is a risk of 'significant harm') and whether the balance favours your client. Set out the facts that support your submission on these points and contrast with any argument your opponent can make or has made. Deal with the mandatory/discretionary parts of s 33 in such a way that it advances your own case.

If he is present, the respondent will know the terms of any order made, but it should also be drawn up and served personally on him. Copies of any non-molestation order (and any occupation order to which a power of arrest is attached) should be given to the local police. In addition, if an occupation order is made under ss 33, 35 or 36, the applicant must serve a copy of the order on the mortgagee or landlord (as the case may be) of the property in question. Remember that breach of a non-molestation order is now a criminal offence and so arguments on accepting undertakings in lieu of such an order will focus on the applicant's need (or lack of it) for the protection that the order thus brings by way of enforcement. Costs will be apt to follow the event, although if both parties are publicly funded, the court will make no order as to costs. Counsel should ask for a certificate for counsel.

Again, after the hearing, counsel should spend a moment explaining the outcome of the case and its practical implications to the lay client and deal with any questions or concerns which he or she might still have.

2.27 Further reading

Bird, Roger, *Domestic Violence: Law and Practice* (Jordans, 2006).

'Compensation for Domestic Abuse after *Singh v Bhakar*' [2008] *Family Law Week*, 25 September; <www.familylawweek.co.uk>.

Domestic Violence: Guide to Civil Remedies and Criminal Sanctions, with useful glossary and further references, see the Family Justice Council website: <www.family-justice-council.org.uk/600.htm> (has been updated to 2007 only).

Hill, Robert N, 'Protection from Harassment' [2005] *Family Law*, May, p 364.

Petel, Hanisha, Rachel Landale, QC and Anne-Marie Hutchinson, OBE *Forced Marriage: the Concept and Law* [2009] *Family Law*, August.

Re Child X (Residence and Contact: Rights of Media Access: FPR Rule 10.28(4)[2009] EWHC 1728 (Fam), case notes [2009] *Family Law*, October.

Spon-Smith, Robin, *Civil Partnership Act 2004, Family Law*, vol 35, p 369.

Ward, Richard and Roger Bird, *Domestic Violence Crime and Victims Act 2004: A Practitioner's Guide* (Jordans, 2005).

The divorce process

This chapter provides a basic, practical outline of grounds upon which a divorce may be obtained, the procedure for getting a divorce and examples of relevant drafting. Irretrievable breakdown is the sole basis upon which a divorce may be sought, but this must be shown by alleging and proving one of five facts, three of which are entirely fault based. The current procedure has been subject to significant criticism for a variety of reasons:

- fault-based divorce encourages recrimination rather than resolution;
- using the model of petitioner and respondent encourages litigation rather than mediation and settlement;
- current procedure permits a divorce to be granted relatively quickly, with important matters relating to children and money remaining unresolved for some considerable time; and
- current procedure places little emphasis on seeking to retrieve a marriage that may be going through a difficult period.

A comprehensive attempt to address these problems was made in the Family Law Act 1996 (FLA 1996), which proposed the introduction of a wholly new procedure which was not based on fault, sought to support marriages that could be saved, encouraged mediation rather than litigation, and provided for the resolution of matters relating to children and money before a divorce was finalised. Because the changes being made were quite fundamental, various pilot projects were carried out before the legislation was brought into effect. Unfortunately, these projects highlighted difficulties with some of the proposed changes and, in January 2001, the government announced that it no longer intended to put the legislation into effect. While this decision is understandable, it is regrettable that the defects of the current system will therefore continue until alternative reform proposals are devised.

3.1 Getting married

It is a prerequisite of divorce that the couple be validly married. The law on the validity of marriage is not within the scope of this Manual, save where the marriage is void or voidable, see **3.7**. The rules governing capacity to marry can be found in the Matrimonial Causes Act 1973 (MCA 1973), s 11. In effect, they allow persons who are not closely related, who are of the opposite sex to one another, not already married and who are aged over 18, or over 16 with parental consent, to marry. Special rules allow those who are not domiciled in England or Wales to marry polygamously outside of England or Wales.

Even where the parties have the capacity to marry, the validity of the marriage may be questioned if the formalities have not been complied with (MCA 1973, s 11), or if the marriage has not been consummated or one of the parties either did not consent to it or had not the capacity to consent to it, or married a person who was pregnant by another or suffering from venereal disease at the time of the marriage (MCA 1973, s 12). Note that MCA 1973, s 13 provides defences to some of these grounds. See also **2.21** on forced marriage.

When s 12 applies, a decree annulling the marriage must be obtained; whereas when s 11 applies, a declaration from the court should be obtained.

Formalities for the marriage service are governed primarily by the Marriage Act 1949. The Act allows a marriage to take place in any approved building. Over 1,000 places have been approved, including several football stadia, London Zoo and a James Bond theme pub! See also the Marriage Ceremony (Prescribed Words) Act 1996.

Since 5 December 2005 it has been possible for two people of the same sex to enter a civil partnership under the Civil Partnership Act 2004 (CPA 2004). The ceremony must be performed in an approved building and registered. Civil partners have many of the same rights as a married couple in terms of maintenance, benefits, inheritance, etc.

3.2 The ground for divorce

If a person decides that his or her marriage is over, a divorce is available under the MCA 1973, s 1, only on the ground that the marriage has broken down irretrievably. This irretrievable breakdown may be shown in one of five ways:

(a) That the respondent has committed adultery and the petitioner finds it intolerable to live with the respondent.

(b) That the respondent has behaved in such a way that the petitioner cannot reasonably be expected to live with the respondent.

(c) That the respondent has deserted the petitioner for a continuous period of at least two years immediately preceding the presentation of the petition.

(d) That the parties to the marriage have lived apart for a continuous period of at least two years immediately preceding the presentation of the petition and the respondent consents to the decree being granted.

(e) That the parties to the marriage have lived apart for a continuous period of at least five years immediately preceding the presentation of the petition.

Only the first two involve no interval of time and can be used immediately, and therefore tend to be the most popular. However, both are based on the fault of the other spouse and are therefore to some extent antagonistic. The fourth ground is the only one which is consensual and makes no allegation of fault, but this requires two years of separation before a divorce can be granted.

There may be important considerations in deciding which basis for divorce to allege if there is any choice on the information provided by the client. Of course, the basis must be legally sound and supported by available evidence, but if there is a choice it should be carefully made. Adultery and behaviour are most commonly used as they allow for immediate divorce, whereas the alternatives require a wait of at least two years. Two years' separation and consent has the advantage of a parting by agreement. If more than one basis for divorce may be alleged, the choice may be based on the strength of available evidence, or on tactics. To give an example, an allegation of behaviour may be useful if it lays a foundation for claims to be made in financial or children hearings, but may be unwise if it upsets a spouse with whom it is hoped a good financial settlement will be negotiated.

3.3   The procedure for obtaining a divorce

The court must have jurisdiction to hear the divorce. This depends on the residence and domicile of the parties, and if there is an international element to the case it can be a complex issue. The details are beyond the scope of this Manual but should be researched if necessary. A spouse may wish to apply for a divorce in a particular country where he/she feels that financial provision rules may be more advantageous.

The great majority of divorce petitions are not defended and, in the case of an undefended divorce, there is a special procedure allowing the divorce to be granted without a hearing. A divorce can be defended on the basis that the facts alleged are not true or do not justify the grant of a decree. In the case of five years' separation there is a statutory defence if it can be shown that a divorce would result in grave financial or other hardship for the respondent (MCA 1973, s 5). This is rarely used, and may be avoided if it is possible to find some way of making financial provision.

Divorce is a two-stage process, consisting of an interim decree ('decree nisi') and a final decree ('decree absolute'), and the parties are only free to remarry once the decree absolute has been obtained. Generally, it is the petitioner who will apply for the decree absolute six weeks after the decree nisi has been granted by the court, but the respondent can apply once a further three months have elapsed if the petitioner has not applied. The hearing of ancillary matters relating to money and children is normally adjourned to be heard in private.

There may be a delay in the issue of the decree absolute if the judge feels it is necessary to use the court's powers with relation to the children (MCA 1973, s 41). Arrangements need not be detailed and final, but the judge must feel confident that there are no major potential problems. Formerly, there was a special hearing to consider this, but now a decision is taken on the basis of a written 'statement of arrangements'. If the judge is satisfied with these, the divorce will proceed under the special procedure. If the judge is not, he or she can ask for further evidence and if necessary there can be a hearing relating to the arrangements. The divorce can be delayed under s 41 if there are exceptional circumstances and it is felt that delay would be in the interests of the child(ren).

Under the current law, there are a variety of tactical and practical considerations that may be relevant in bringing or defending a divorce. Although it is possible to allege more than one basis in a petition, it is common, for costs reasons if no other, to plead only one basis, and a decision should be taken not only on the strength of the evidence but also on the likely reaction of the other side. The precise legal interpretation of each possible basis for divorce should be checked. For example, the test for behaviour is partly objective, but is also subjective; in *Birch v Birch* [1992] *Family Law* 290, the court allowed a wife to divorce a dogmatic and chauvinistic husband.

3.4 Drafting a divorce petition

A divorce must be originated by petition (Family Proceedings Rules 1991, r 2.2—FPR 1991). In recent years, with simplifications in procedure, it has become rare for a barrister to be asked to draft a petition, but it is still important for the barrister to be aware of what should be in a petition and to check it if briefed to appear on applications in connection with the divorce. The proposals for reform would have replaced the petition with a simpler form.

3.4.1 Rules for a petition

Rules for the contents of a petition are laid down in the FPR 1991, r 2.3 and Appendix 2, and a standard form is commonly used.

The petition to commence the divorce proceedings is filed in the local divorce County court or in the Divorce Registry in London, as appropriate. With it are filed:

(a) A statement of arrangements for children (if there are 'any children under 16 or over 16 but under 18 who are at school or college or are training for a trade, profession or vocation' (form M4)).

(b) The marriage certificate.

(c) A solicitors' certificate that reconciliation has been attempted (form M3).

(d) An affidavit in support of the petition (in short formal form).

Under the FPR 1991, r 2.4, a petitioner who seeks to rely on a conviction under the Civil Evidence Act 1968, ss 11 or 12, must give appropriate details in the petition.

Under the FPR 1991, r 2.5, a petition should be signed by counsel if settled by counsel, or by the solicitor or petitioner as appropriate.

Under the FPR 1991, r 2.7, a person with whom it is alleged the respondent has committed adultery should be made a party to the proceedings unless that person is not named in the petition, or is dead or the court otherwise directs. If some other improper association is alleged with a named person, the court may direct that that person be made a party.

In practical terms, a petition does not have to follow any set wording exactly, so long as it has the specified contents, but it is vital that it be complete and absolutely accurate.

3.4.2 Drafting a petition

Generally, paras 1 to 8 are formal and simply recount practical matters, such as the date of the marriage, the facts giving jurisdiction to the court, details about each spouse and about any children. As regards addresses, the petitioner may get leave to withhold his or her address if there is a real threat of danger from the respondent.

Details of children must include all children of the family, and of any other child born to the wife, giving name and date of birth of each.

Details of any proceedings affecting the marriage or the parties to it must also be given, including domestic violence proceedings, existing maintenance orders, etc.

Paragraphs 9 and 10 set out the ground of divorce, with the facts relied on and any appropriate particulars (MCA 1973, ss 1 and 2). In many cases, the facts can be alleged briefly and concisely, as is often the case for adultery or desertion, but all appropriate details must be given, for example, any periods of resumed cohabitation after separation.

More details are likely to be required where behaviour is relied on, and a full statement, acquired if necessary during a conference with the client, is a vital basis for pleading. It is important to organise allegations to produce a clear and strong draft. In general terms, when raising behaviour:

(a) Use an overall structure, whether it be chronological or putting the worst allegations first and then lesser allegations (or vice versa).

(b) Put each allegation in a separate numbered paragraph.

(c) Draft each allegation concisely and clearly.

(d) If there are many allegations, choose the strongest.

(e) Allege facts, not evidence.

(f) Try to include specific actions, rather than generalisations and emotions.

(g) Choose appropriate vocabulary, to put the client's words into a suitable form for presentation to the court.

It is technically possible to draft a petition relying on more than one basis in the alternative, but this should be avoided if possible as it is likely only to increase costs, and may suggest the case is weak.

The prayer is one of the most vital parts of the petition, as it should list all forms of relief which the spouse seeks, including financial relief, residence order, costs, etc. Relief sought should be checked with the client, but it is generally thought wise to claim widely at this early stage, thus keeping all options open.

3.4.3 Example petition

IN THE OXFORD COUNTY COURT   No. of matter

The petition of SANDRA ANNE CUTFORTH shows that:

1   On 18 August 2000 the Petitioner was lawfully married to James Andrew Cutforth (the Respondent) at the Tottenham Register Office, High Street, Tottenham, London N1.
2   The Petitioner and the Respondent last lived together at 13 Jasmine Road, Oxford, Oxfordshire.
3   The Petitioner is domiciled in England and Wales. The Petitioner is a receptionist and resides at 13 Jasmine Road, Oxford. The Respondent is a computer engineer and resides at Flat 3 Alexandra Mansions, New Way, London NW22.
4   There are two children of the family, namely Damian John Cutforth born on 4 April 2002 and Gemma Jane Cutforth born on 30 August 2003.
5   No other child now living has been born to the Petitioner during the marriage.
6   There are or have been no other proceedings in the court in England and Wales with reference to the marriage or the children of the family or between the Petitioner and the Respondent with reference to any property of either or both of them, save in that on 25 May 2009 the Oxford

County court made an order under the Family Law Act 1996 requiring the Respondent to leave the matrimonial home, and an order that the Respondent should not use or threaten to use violence against the person of the applicant.

7   The marriage has broken down irretrievably.

8   The Respondent has behaved in such a way that the Petitioner cannot reasonably be expected to live with the Respondent.

PARTICULARS

(i)   From about January 2006 the Respondent has become increasingly cold and neglectful towards the Petitioner, and unjustifiably critical of her abilities as a housewife.

(ii)   From March 2006 the Respondent began working late, often not returning home until the late evening. When the Petitioner asked about the reason for this the Respondent merely said that he liked work, and the Petitioner would not understand anything about his work.

(iii)   In May 2006 the Respondent refused to take the Petitioner to an important social function connected with his employment, saying that the function was only for those who supported their spouses in their work, and falsely claiming that she gave him no support at all.

(iv)   On several occasions over the summer of 2006 the Petitioner suggested that the Respondent should take her out for the evening, but he always refused, saying that he was too tired, and that in any event he found the Petitioner's company boring, and she should be spending more time keeping the house clean and learning to cook.

(v)   In December 2006 the Respondent invited several business associates to the matrimonial home, giving the Petitioner little notice of their arrival. When they left, the Respondent flew into a temper, throwing crockery at the Petitioner, and breaking several items from a dinner service that had been a wedding present from the Petitioner's parents.

(vi)   From March to September 2007 the Respondent insisted on attending a course which took him away from home most weekends, although the Petitioner requested him to spend more time with herself and the children of the family. When the Respondent was at home, he spent most of his time in his study, becoming angry with the children whenever he heard them playing. On one occasion in August 2007 he falsely accused the Petitioner of being an incompetent mother who could not control her own children. On completion of the course, the Respondent continued to spend many weekends away from the home, despite the entreaties of the Petitioner.

(vii)   From July 2008, the Respondent has consumed alcohol in excessive quantities. The Petitioner has remonstrated with him on several occasions, but the Respondent refuses to accept that he drinks excessively, saying only that he needs a drink to help him to relax. The Petitioner has become most concerned for the welfare of the children of the family when the Respondent is drunk.

(viii)   In November 2008 the Petitioner returned home early one evening to find the Respondent in a drunken stupor, although he had undertaken to look after the children of the family for the day, thereby putting the welfare of the children at risk.

(xi)   In May 2009 the Petitioner remonstrated with the Respondent on finding several empty whisky bottles secreted about the matrimonial home. The Respondent became extremely angry and struck the Petitioner, causing her injury which required hospital treatment and the insertion of five stitches on the side of her head. It was as a result of this incident that the Petitioner was granted the order referred to in paragraph 6 above. The Respondent left the matrimonial home as a result of this order and has not returned since.

The Petitioner therefore prays:

1   That the marriage may be dissolved.

2   That the children Damian John and Gemma Jane be ordered to reside with her.

3 That the court may order such payments by way of maintenance pending suit and may make such orders for financial provision or adjustment of property for the benefit of the Petitioner and the children as may be just.

4 That the Respondent may be ordered to pay the costs of this suit.

Anne O'Nimous

The name and address of the person to be served with this petition is:

James Cutforth
Flat 3
Alexandra Mansions
New Way
London NW22

The Petitioner's address for service is:
c/o Brown and Brown Solicitors
121 High Street
Oxford

3.4.4 Alternative bases for divorce

These are examples of how the various alternatives and particulars for para 8 of the petition might be drafted.

Adultery

The respondent has committed adultery and the petitioner finds it intolerable to live with the respondent.

1 The Respondent committed adultery with Mary Mopp (the Co-respondent) on 16 October 2008 at the Grand Hotel, Station Road, London SW40.

2 The Respondent also committed adultery with another woman the Petitioner could identify if called upon to do so.

3 The Respondent has since 1 July 2009 lived, cohabited and committed adultery with the Co-Respondent at 26 Wild Street, Dorchester, Dorset.

4 The Respondent on 30 April 2008 committed adultery at 11 Queen Street, Slough, Berkshire, with a person known to the Petitioner only as 'Jonnie'.

5 The Petitioner resumed cohabitation with the Respondent at 11 Queen Street, Slough, Berkshire from 1 May 2009 to 20 June 2009 a period amounting to less than six months.

Desertion

The respondent has deserted the petitioner for a continuous period of at least two years immediately preceding the presentation of the petition.

PARTICULARS

The Respondent informed the Petitioner on 17 December 2007 while she was in hospital that he was leaving the matrimonial home, since which day the parties have lived separate and apart.

Two years' separation and consent

The parties have lived apart from a continuous period of at least two years immediately preceding the presentation of the petition and the Respondent consents to a decree being granted.

PARTICULARS

The parties separated by agreement on 25 December 2006 since which day they have lived apart save that cohabitation was resumed for the following periods, namely: From 1 April 2007 to 1 June 2007 at 6 High Street and from 28 June 2008 to 30 June 2008 at 6 High Street, which periods amount to less than six months in all.

Five years' separation

The parties have lived apart for a continuous period of at least five years immediately preceding the presentation of the petition.

PARTICULARS

On 28 February 2004 the Petitioner ejected the Respondent from the matrimonial home, since which day the parties have lived separate and apart.

3.5 Drafting an answer

3.5.1 The role of the answer

The petition is served on the respondent with a form for acknowledgement of service, and a notice of proceedings informing the respondent what courses he or she can take. If the respondent wishes to defend the case, he or she should give notice of intention to defend within eight days.

It is not essential that an answer be filed at all. An answer is only required, within 21 days of the date for filing the notice of intention to defend, under the FPR 1991, r 2.12, if a respondent or co-respondent:

- wishes to defend the petition, or dispute any facts alleged in it;
- wishes to cross-petition, that is, to seek a divorce on an alternative basis; or
- wishes to oppose the grant of divorce under the MCA 1973, s 5 (petition alleging five years' separation and there is a defence of grave financial or other hardship).

It is not necessary to file an answer simply to be heard on ancillary matters relating to finance or the children. The decision whether to file an answer may involve practical considerations, bearing in mind that the majority of divorces are undefended and that defending will normally have the effect of making the divorce procedure longer and more expensive. This may require some discussion with the client, whose emotions may not immediately suggest the wisest course. In practical terms, an answer will be required:

- if the respondent does not want a divorce at all, and has some basis for defending the allegation in the petition;

- if the respondent really cannot accept the basis on which a divorce is sought in the petition, and has good reason for alleging an alternative basis; or

- if the petition makes allegations that may prejudice the respondent in the financial hearings or those concerned with children.

3.5.2   Contents of an answer

An answer effectively fulfils the role of a defence, and should thus generally deal with those allegations in the petition which are disputed and add any further relevant points (FPR 1991, r 2.15). There is no set format for an answer: it must be drafted to suit the case. An answer remains an important document, although relatively few cases are defended (*Lawlor v Lawlor* [1995] 1 FLR 269).

The heading, as in the example given in **3.5.4**, should set out the names of the petitioner and the respondent as parties. If any allegation of adultery with a named person is made in the petition, that person will be added as co-respondent. If any allegation of adultery is made against a named person in the answer, that person should be added as a party, called the 'party cited'.

The answer should start by dealing with any matters arising from the formal paragraphs in the petition. Generally, there will be no dispute on the basic facts of the marriage, occupation of spouses, etc, and there will therefore be no need to deal with these paragraphs of the petition at all. The respondent should, however, say whether or not he or she agrees with what is alleged regarding the children of the family.

It is then necessary to state whether or not the marriage has broken down. It should of course be admitted that the marriage has broken down if the respondent wants a divorce, even if he or she wishes to rely on a different basis.

The respondent must then deal with the basis for divorce relied on in the petition, pleading both to the fact alleged, and to any details provided. A bare denial is permissible (*Haque v Haque* [1977] 1 WLR 888) but it is a better policy to respond in more detail, especially as regards allegations of behaviour (*Andrews v Andrews* [1974] 3 All ER 643). Indeed, there may be good reason for responding to behaviour allegations in some detail, especially to confess and avoid, i.e. to give further information to explain, or to put a different interpretation on facts alleged.

Note that there is the specific statutory defence of grave financial or other hardship where the petition alleges five years' separation, and this should be specifically included in the answer, if it has to be relied on (MCA 1973, s 5).

3.5.3   Cross-petition

A cross-petition may be added to an answer, just as a counter-claim can be added to a defence. A cross-petition seeks a divorce on a basis other than that alleged in the petition. No sub-heading is required. One simply continues the numbered paragraphs to raise the basis alleged as one would in a petition.

3.5.4 Example answer and cross-petition

IN THE OXFORD COUNTY COURT   01 D No. 288

BETWEEN

MRS SANDRA ANNE CUTFORTH   Petitioner

and

MR JAMES ANDREW CUTFORTH   Respondent

and

MR JUSTIN REDMOND   Party Cited

The Respondent in ANSWER to the petition filed in this suit says that:

1   No other child now living has been born to the Petitioner during the marriage, so far as is known to the Respondent.

2   It is admitted that the marriage has broken down irretrievably.

3   It is denied that the Respondent has behaved in such a way that the Petitioner cannot reasonably be expected to live with him, as alleged in the petition or at all.

4   Save as is expressly admitted, the Respondent denies each and every allegation contained in paragraph 8 of the petition.

5   The Respondent denies that he became cold or neglectful towards the Petitioner as alleged or at all. He worked long hours, especially once he set up his own business, of which the Petitioner was unsupportive. Meanwhile, the matrimonial home was rarely cleaned, the Petitioner (who did not work outside the home) failed to discipline the children properly, and rarely presented proper meals, normally resorting to pre-packed dishes.

6   The Respondent admits that he frequently worked late. This was necessary as the joint bank account held by the Petitioner and the Respondent was frequently overdrawn, largely due to the sums spent by the Petitioner. The Respondent did not try to discuss his work with the Petitioner, as she frequently said that she did not understand how computers worked. The function in May 2006 was only open to employees of the Respondent's employer.

7   The Petitioner herself asked the Respondent to invite some of his colleagues from work to the matrimonial home. Having stated that she would cook a meal, the Petitioner merely provided light snacks, thereby causing much embarrassment to the Respondent.

8   The Respondent admits that he attended a course between March and September 2007. He did so in expectation of promotion at work. The Petitioner failed to support him in this enterprise, and indeed started an affair with the Party Cited in Spring 2008, causing the Respondent distress.

9   The Respondent denies that he has ever consumed alcohol in excessive quantities as alleged or at all. As to the incident referred to in November 2008, the Respondent in fact had a bad cold and had simply taken a cold remedy.

10   The Respondent admits that he did strike the Petitioner in May 2009, but this was an isolated incident, the Respondent not being a violent man. The injury to the Petitioner was accidental in that she hit her head on a table as she fell.

11   The Petitioner has committed adultery and the Respondent finds it intolerable to live with the Petitioner.

PARTICULARS

(a) The Petitioner committed adultery with Justin Redmond (the Party Cited) on a day or days unknown to the Respondent in about July 2008, at a place or places unknown to the Respondent.

(b) Since 8 April 2009 the Petitioner has committed adultery with Justin Redmond on a day or days unknown to the Respondent at a place or places unknown to the Respondent, but including 13 Jasmine Road, Oxford, Oxfordshire.

The Respondent therefore prays:

1. That the prayer of the petition may be rejected.
2. That the marriage may be dissolved.
3. That the children Damian John and Gemma Jane be ordered to reside with him.
4. That the Party Cited may be ordered to pay the costs of this suit.

Jonathan Brown

Name, addresses etc.

3.6 Reply

It is possible for the petitioner to respond with a reply to allegations made in the answer (FPR 1991, r 2.13). However, a reply is rare.

3.7 Void and voidable marriages

It should be kept in mind that divorce is not the only option if a client wishes to end a marriage. It is possible that the marriage may be void (MCA 1973, s 11) or voidable (MCA 1973, s 12). If either spouse is not domiciled in England and Wales, or was not so domiciled at the time of the marriage, then conflict of law points should be considered.

The grounds on which a marriage may be void are:

(a) That the parties are within a prohibited degree of relationship.

(b) That either party is under the age of 16.

(c) That vital formalities relating to the marriage were disregarded.

(d) That at the time of the marriage either party was already lawfully married.

(e) That the parties are not respectively male and female.

(f) That in the case of a polygamous marriage entered into outside England and Wales, either party was at the time of the marriage domiciled in England and Wales.

The grounds on which a marriage may be voidable are:

(a) That the marriage has not been consummated owing to the incapacity of either party.

(b) That the marriage has not been consummated owing to the wilful refusal of the respondent.

(c) That either party to the marriage did not validly consent to it, whether in consequence of duress, mistake, unsoundness of mind or otherwise.

(d) That at the time of the marriage either party was suffering from mental disorder of such a kind or to such an extent as to be unfitted for marriage.

(f) That at the time of the marriage the respondent was suffering from venereal disease in a communicable form, and the petitioner did not know this.

(g) That at the time of the marriage the respondent was pregnant by some person other than the petitioner, and the petitioner did not know this.

The last four of these may only be used within three years of the marriage. In the case of either a void or a voidable marriage, it is possible for the court to order financial provision and to make orders for the care of children.

3.8 Judicial separation

A final alternative is judicial separation (MCA 1973, s 17). This does not end the marriage, but is appropriate where the client does not want the marriage to end finally for emotional or religious reasons. A decree of judicial separation may be granted where one of the bases for a divorce is made out, and it is possible for the court to make orders for financial provision, and orders regarding the care of children when making an order that the parties live apart.

Financial provision—ancillary relief: law and practice

4.1 Introduction

Chapters 4 to **7** deal with the principles and practice involved in applications for financial provision. This chapter is intended to provide a broad framework on which to base the very practical work involved in applications for financial provision where couples are divorcing. This is known as ancillary relief (or more colloquially 'AR'), that is to say, applications for financial relief ancillary to divorce. Ancillary relief is by far the most common type of money-related procedure that occurs in family practice.

Also important in practice are financial applications relating to children. These mainly comprise applications under the Children Act 1989 (CA 1989), Sch 1 or applications to the Child Support Agency (CSA). Applications relating to children are dealt with in **Chapter 7**. It is important to note from the outset that the ancillary relief regime does not apply to separating unmarried couples or cohabitants. It is possible, though rare, for applications for financial provision to be made between partners to a marriage who are not divorcing—this uncommon situation is dealt with in **Chapter 6**.

In dealing with applications for ancillary relief, the importance of thorough and detailed fact management cannot be overemphasised. Obviously, it is essential to be fully conversant with the legal principles and factors that are applied to such applications and the procedure involved. As in other areas of family law, it can take the newcomer a while to get a feel for how practitioners and courts tend to interpret and use the checklist of factors that they are required by statute to take into account. However, unless you have a brief with an unusual feature, the biggest variables affecting the outcome of an application are the facts relating to the financial resources and needs of the parties. Most of the work in a typical ancillary relief brief revolves around acquiring, managing, updating and formulating arguments based on this factual information. The importance of numerical skills will become obvious.

There are several useful texts designed to assist the practitioner. The best known is *Matrimonial Property and Finance* by Peter Duckworth. Other well-known texts include the *Ancillary Relief Handbook* by Roger Bird, *Butterworths Family Law Service, Family Court Practice, Practical Matrimonial Precedents* and the FLBA's *At A Glance*.

4.1.1 The legal framework

Broad powers to order financial provision are provided by statute, primarily in the Matrimonial Causes Act 1973 (MCA 1973), as amended. Procedure is set out in the Family Proceedings Rules 1999 (FPR 1999) (SI 1991/1247), as amended. The powers of the court with regard to maintenance for children are limited by the Child Support Act 1991 (CSA 1991) (see **Chapter 7**). You must read and refer to the relevant law. The best place to start is always the more comprehensive practitioner texts, such as those set out above at **4.1**.

Because every case will involve different assets and different problems, the powers provided by statute are very wide to allow orders to be tailored to fit each individual case. For this reason, the statutory provisions themselves include only general guidance as to how the powers should be exercised. The MCA 1973, s 25 contains a list of matters to which the court must have regard when deciding how to exercise its powers. This list is widely referred to in practice as the s 25 factors and these factors govern all applications for ancillary relief. The words of the statute are plain and are designed to give judges latitude and discretion; practitioners will always seek to base their arguments, and judges their conclusions, on the words of the statute itself. Each case turns on its own facts and decided cases with apparently similar facts will rarely be persuasive or relevant. On occasion decided cases can assist with interpretation and general guidance on how the s 25 factors should be understood and applied in practice.

The court's powers under the statute and their application are dealt with in detail below at **4.2** to **4.4**.

4.1.1.1 The Civil Partnership Act 2004

The Civil Partnership Act 2004 (CPA 2004) came into force on 5 December 2005 and allowed same-sex couples to gain the rights and responsibilities of marriage, including the same sort of access to ancillary relief upon the dissolution of their partnership as married couples do upon divorce. The statutory provisions for civil partnership are virtually identical to those for marriage—the CPA 2004, Sch 5 mirrors the MCA 1973, Part II; the FPR 1991 apply.

Although the legal provisions are the same it remains to be seen whether civil partnerships bring new issues to the field of AR and in particular in respect to the application of the s 25 factors to same-sex relationships. Potential areas of new perspective include the absence of gender discrimination and the view of roles within the relationship and the significance of cohabitation prior to the partnership. At the time of writing there have been no significant reported cases.

4.1.2 Procedure

On 5 June 2000, a new set of procedural rules for dealing with applications for financial provision ancillary to divorce came into being (FPR 1991, rr 2.51A–2.70). These rules brought much greater efficiency into the decision-making process. The *powers* of the court to make financial orders are the same as before—it is the *procedure* which was changed.

The old procedure was based on sworn statements (affidavits) and was very adversarial. In practice, it was found to be inefficient in terms of defining issues and collecting information, and proved to be time-consuming and costly. This old procedure is now gone, but is mentioned, and you may see it referred to in older reported cases.

Modern procedure places greater emphasis on the completion and use of standard forms and involves tight timetables, a greater emphasis on defining issues and reaching agreements, and more court control. The procedure was extensively 'piloted' in various courts around the country and resulted in much cross-fertilisation with the reforms then being planned in civil practice generally. You will be familiar with the overriding objective from civil procedure, but the emphasis and objectives are slightly different in family law. A statement of the overriding objective is set out in the FPR 1991, r 2.51B. It provides that 'the ancillary relief rules are a procedural code with the overriding objective of enabling the court to deal with cases justly'. The rule goes on to expand on what dealing with cases justly means, including proportionality, an emphasis on saving expense, expedition, fairness and 'active case management'.

As you might expect, therefore, the main aims of the procedure are to:

- make expeditious progress towards resolution;
- give the court more control over the issues raised and the evidence used in each case;
- provide better ways of controlling costs;
- direct parties towards settlement where possible; and
- encourage full and frank disclosure, but discourage excessive and/or tactical requests for information.

The main elements of the procedure are:

(a) Once there has been an application for ancillary relief, there will be a first appointment (FA) within 12 to 16 weeks.

(b) Not less than 35 days before that appointment, there will be a simultaneous exchange of statements of the financial position of both spouses, containing specified information in a common format (Form E). Full supporting documentation will be attached.

(c) Not less than 14 days before that appointment, both parties will file a concise statement of the issues between the parties, a chronology and a questionnaire, seeking further information and specifying relevant documents to be produced.

(d) At the FA, the District Judge (DJ) will review the case with a view to limiting the issues and saving costs. The DJ will see if the FA can become a Financial Dispute Resolution hearing (FDR); if not, he will set a date for an FDR. Exceptionally, he may, if he considers an FDR inappropriate, set a date for a final hearing. He will give directions as to disclosure, documentation, valuations, evidence and any other case management directions necessary to prepare for the FDR.

(e) The FDR is to be treated as an opportunity for open discussion and negotiation. The DJ will facilitate and assist in this process. If appropriate, the DJ may adjourn and fix a date for a further FDR and give further directions or the DJ may fix a date for the final hearing, which must be before a different DJ. Before a final hearing, both parties must file a concise statement of the nature and amounts of the orders they will be inviting the court to make.

(f) Both sides must have an updated estimate of current costs available at each hearing (Form H).

Procedure, including issues relating to costs, is dealt with in detail in **Chapter 5**.

4.1.3 The practical approach

Statute provides general powers and a checklist of considerations. Case law, at best, merely provides examples of their application. So there is rarely a single, obvious answer as to the correct financial provision in any particular case. Although there is a defined set of factors, there is no set formula on how to apply them. Indeed, trying to apply the same formula to different circumstances would almost certainly be unjust. Instead, there are usually a variety of perspectives and approaches (from the facts, the instructions, the law, common sense and the advocate's own experience of practice) from which a case can be built, and an overall basis for provision proposed.

It is important to appreciate this. This is not an area where legal principles can simply be applied to calculate an outcome. Everything depends on a complete and thorough *factual* analysis of the individual case, and an intelligent development of arguments, in the light of the law. This makes a really practical approach vital—applying the s 25 factors to the unique facts and landscape of each situation and accompanying instructions. Although the powers of the courts are wide, advocates cannot make waffly arguments or general proposals. In each case, the facts must be carefully gathered and analysed, the detailed arithmetic done (and done properly, by you, so do get used to it), and specific and practical arguments and proposals formulated. Throughout, the client's objectives must be kept clearly in view.

This broad and non-linear approach can make it difficult for the newcomer to know where to start. Here are some tips for things to consider in order to get going with a brief:

(a) What sort of provision does the client want? In terms of capital? In terms of income?

(b) What assets do your client and the other side have?

(c) What income do your client and the other side have?

(d) What are the fundamental needs of your client and the other side? In particular: are there children? Who will be caring for them? Where will they live?

(e) What are the income needs of your client and the other side? Be realistic—what do they really need to live? How much will it really cost?

(f) How can these needs be met? Can the parties realistically be expected to work? Are there other sources of funds or support?

(g) What is the position in relation to pensions?

(h) What are the s 25 factors which seem most relevant to this case?

(i) What are the s 25 factors which strengthen/weaken your client's claims?

(j) Is a clean break possible?

(k) What then is the appropriate overall basis for provision? Are there any options?

(l) Work out full details for the proposal you are making. Do full arithmetic to show the position which each spouse will be left in if that provision is ordered, taking into account tax, etc. You should be aiming to devise a package that works for both parties.

(m) Check that the detailed proposals are practical, realistic and meet your client's objectives as far as possible.

(n) Check your proposal against the yardstick of equality. If your proposal does not amount to an equal division of resources, how can this be justified by reference to the s 25 factors?

(o) Remember that lawyers representing parties in a case have a duty to investigate figures fully and to advise their clients properly about their options.

(p) Use your common sense and maturity. They are indispensable tools.

4.2 Court powers to make orders

It is important to note from the very outset that the court does not exercise any of its powers in isolation from each other. After considering everything it is required to consider under the MCA 1973, s 25, the court will decide what result it wants to achieve and, choosing from among the powers available to it, will design a package of interrelating orders that best achieve its objectives. The most commonly used of these powers are found in the MCA Part II, especially ss 21–25C.

4.2.1 Overview and terminology

The court has the jurisdiction to make orders for ancillary relief on the grant of a decree of divorce, nullity or judicial separation. The FPR 1991, r 1.2 defines 'ancillary relief' as:

- an avoidance of disposition order;
- a financial provision order;
- an order for maintenance pending suit;
- a property adjustment order;
- a variation order;
- a pension-sharing order.

A variation order is defined as an order under the MCA 1973, s 31. Maintenance pending suit, which is an interim application for maintenance, is dealt with at **4.5**. There are other orders, not in the above list, that courts may consider making in proceedings for ancillary relief. The most significant of these are also dealt with in this section.

4.2.2 Financial provision orders: MCA 1973, s 23

4.2.2.1 Order for periodical payments to a party to the marriage or to/for a child of the family (s 23)

Periodical payments are an ongoing obligation to pay a sum at regular intervals, usually weekly or monthly. This type of order used to be called, and is still commonly referred to as, maintenance. Orders for periodical payments may be varied on further application, and may run for a set term or until the death of either of the parties or the remarriage of the person in whose favour the order is made. In considering an order for periodical payments, the court must weigh its obligation under the MCA 1973, s 25A to consider a clean break (see **4.4.3**).

4.2.2.2 Order for secured periodical payments to a party to the marriage or to/for a child of the family (s 23)

This is an order for periodical payments with an additional order that some kind of secure capital fund or asset be provided out of which the payments can be made or guaranteed. The main advantage of such an order is that the payments are protected against the death, insolvency or disappearance of the payer. Orders for secured periodical payments may be varied on further application, and may run for a set term or until the death or the remarriage of the person in whose favour the order is made. Again, the court must consider a clean break. Orders for secured periodical payments are comparatively rare.

4.2.2.3   Order that a lump sum be paid to a party to the marriage or to/for a child of the family
(s 23)

A lump sum order is intended to be a final order and, with limited exception, may
only be made once. A lump sum order is essentially a means of adjusting the balance
of capital resources between the parties. However, within the final package of orders
that a court makes they may serve a more specific purpose. Examples of such a purpose
include enabling a party to purchase property, or compensating a party for exiting a
jointly run business, or providing a fund to cover all purposes in big money cases, or
as a way of capitalising maintenance (known as a *Duxbury* fund). The statute refers
to 'lump sum or sums'. This still means that only one order may be made, but it
may provide for the payment of more than one lump sum, or for instalments, or for
payment to be deferred along with the payment of interest.

4.2.3   Property adjustment orders: MCA 1973, ss 24–24A

4.2.3.1   Transfer of property order, ie, an order that one party to the marriage transfer property
to the other party or to/for the benefit of a child of the family (s 24)

This can be any kind of property but is usually concerned with houses and land.
Usually, the housing needs of the parties and children are a high priority and in many
cases the former matrimonial home will be the sole or principal asset. The court may
not make more than one order but it may provide for the transfer of more than one
item of property in the same order. The property may be transferred outright, or it
may be transferred subject to a charge in favour of the transferor. This charge could be
realisable on a fixed date or on the occurring of a certain trigger event (eg, the youngest
child reaching 18).

4.2.3.2   Settlement of property order (s 24)

When used, these orders perform much the same function as transfer of property
orders, described above. Generally, courts use transfer of property orders and other
orders available under the statute to achieve the desired outcome and, as a result,
settlement orders are less frequently used nowadays.

4.2.3.3   An order varying the effect of any ante- or post-nuptial settlement (s 24)

Traditional marriage settlements are less common than they were; however, the use of
ante-nuptial settlements seems to be increasing. The powers to vary a settlement are
wide and include the power to give the capital or income in a settlement to either
party or the children, to extinguish the interest of a party under the settlement and to
terminate the settlement itself: see, by analogy, *MacLeod v Macleod* [2009] 1 FLR 641
and **4.4.8.2**.

4.2.3.4   Order for sale (s 24A)

This is not strictly speaking a property adjustment order but it is conveniently dealt
with here. The court may only make an order for sale when it has made a secured
periodical payments order or a lump sum order or a property adjustment order. The
purpose of the order for sale is to facilitate the capital order that it is ancillary to.

4.2.4   Pension-sharing orders: MCA 1973, ss 21A, 24B

Pension-sharing orders are available in respect of petitions for divorce or nullity (not
judicial separation) filed after 1 December 2000. The order provides that one party's

shareable pension rights (or state scheme rights) are subject to pension sharing for the benefit of another party. The order specifies the percentage value of the shareable pension rights to be transferred to the benefiting party. The pension arrangement as a whole is valued and the actual amount to be transferred is the percentage of that value. The actual amount the person in whose favour the order is made receives is known as the pension credit. After the order is made, the 'person responsible' for the pension arrangement (ie, trustees or managers) must within four months transfer the pension credit to a suitable pension scheme or an arrangement of the transferee's choice. For possible problems with pension-sharing orders, especially in relation to valuation, see the articles referred to at the end of **4.3.3.11**.

4.2.4.1   Other orders relating to pensions

The court has a range of orders available to it to deal with the complicated issues of pensions. Pension-sharing orders are the preferred way of dealing with most situations, but other orders are used in some circumstances. The orders made in a given case will depend on what the court is trying to achieve in relation to the issue of pension provision and on the other factors and considerations in the case (see **4.3.3.11**).

Offsetting
Offsetting is a way of compensating a wife for the loss of pension benefits by providing her with some additional capital, usually in the form of a lump sum or an enlargement of a lump sum already being considered. It is a useful tool, but requires there to be sufficient funds available from which the lump sum, or increased lump sum, can be paid.

Attachment orders
Attachment orders (formerly known as 'earmarking') are orders that oblige the persons responsible for a pension arrangement to pay to someone who is not a member of the pension fund, sums that would normally have gone to the member. All attachment orders are liable to applications for variation (which means that they may be varied before they are ever realised). They are also at risk from a change in the circumstances of the pension holder, such as bankruptcy. See *Re Nunn* (*Bankruptcy: Divorce: Pension Rights*) [2004] 1 FLR 1123, where an order that a husband pay his wife one-half of his pension lump sum was not enforceable after the bankruptcy of the husband, the whole pension fund going into the husband's estate in bankruptcy.

Attachment for income purposes (s 25B) This order will provide periodical payments to the person in whose favour the order is made, paid out of the pension fund. It is, in effect, an attachment of earnings order against the pension fund. It would cease to have effect on the death of either party.

Attachment for a capital sum (s 25B) This would be appropriate where the wife was to receive a deferred lump sum from the husband's pension entitlement, usually because there was insufficient capital to provide her with the appropriate amount at the time of the making of the order. A weakness of this order is that the court has no power to order the pension holder to take his pension at any particular time.

Attachment of death-in-service benefits (s 25C) This order would be appropriate where the wife continues to be dependent on the husband. If he died before retirement, any lump sum, or part of it, would be payable to the wife. The court has the power to force the husband to nominate his wife to be the person to receive some or all of the benefits (most pension schemes require the pension holder to nominate the person who will receive death-in-service benefits and the persons responsible for the scheme must follow this nomination).

4.2.5 Avoidance of disposition orders: MCA 1973, s 37 and other injunctions

The MCA 1973, s 37 gives the court the power, in ancillary relief proceedings, to prevent or set aside a disposition of property by one of the parties to the proceedings. This type of order is applied for and made when there is a suspicion that one of the parties is about to dispose, transfer or otherwise deal with property with a view to defeating or avoiding all or part of a claim for financial relief. That is, they are going to transform or dissipate an asset so as to put it beyond the reach of the court dealing with the ancillary relief proceedings. Alternatively, an order under s 37 can be made when the court is satisfied that such a disposal with such an intention has already been made.

So there are essentially two powers under this section. The first, dealing with the former situation described above, is pre-emptive and is an order to one of the parties not to deal with certain assets in certain ways. Copies of this order can be served on banks and any relevant institutions and the order usually has the effect of freezing or barring transactions concerning the asset. The second, dealing with the latter situation, is the power to set aside any disposition that has already been made. Such an order will require the person to whom the assets were transferred to transfer them back so that they will form part of the funds being considered in the proceedings for ancillary relief.

The burden is on the applicant (for the s 37 order) to prove that the disposition will be or has been made 'with the intention of defeating the claim for financial relief'. It is for the judge, however, to decide whether or not he is 'satisfied' that the condition is met and it has been held that further qualification of the standard of proof is not helpful (*K v K* (*Avoidance of Reviewable Disposition*) [1983] FLR 31). Although the intention can be inferred from conduct, the court must be careful in situations where there could be more than one reason for the disposition, most typically in situations where a party's livelihood or business activity depends on the movement of such assets as are under consideration. The court must be satisfied that the intention to defeat the claim exists—there is no general power to freeze assets as a holding or precautionary measure pending the outcome of a claim.

There are two further significant considerations relating to the power to set aside a disposition that has already been made. First, it must be a 'reviewable disposition' as defined in s 37(4). This essentially protects the bona fide purchaser for value without notice (in this case, without notice of the respondent's intention to defeat the applicant's claim). Unless the respondent can satisfy the court that the conditions in s 37(4) are met, it is presumed that the disposition is reviewable. Second, s 37(5) provides that in some situations there is a presumption of intention to defeat the claim. Essentially, the presumption applies where the disposition was made within three years before the date of the application and where the court is satisfied that the disposition has, or would have, the consequence of defeating the applicant's claim for ancillary relief.

Applications for s 37 injunctions should, if practicable, be heard at the same time as any related application for ancillary relief (FPR 1991, r 2.62(2)). Where there is urgency, the application can be made without notice and the court, if it grants the application, will fix an on notice return hearing at the earliest date.

Practitioners need to keep in mind the court's powers under s 37 and be prepared to exercise their judgement as to whether the circumstances warrant such an application. If so, then the application should be made without delay.

Three further types of injunctive relief are on occasion used by the family courts. They are used far less frequently than the s 37 order discussed above and so are dealt with in overview here.

In situations where the conditions of s 37 have not been made out but doing justice in the case requires the use of injunctive powers, the court can invoke its inherent jurisdiction. This means it can make such order as it sees fit in order to preserve the status quo (or achieve whatever end is required) (see *Shipman v Shipman* [1991] 1 FLR 250 and *Poon v Poon* [1994] 2 FLR 857). It is very doubtful that the County court has such an inherent jurisdiction; the practice in the Principal Registry is to transfer an application to invoke the inherent jurisdiction to the High Court. The Court of Appeal in *Wicks v Wicks* [1998] 1 FLR 470, has considered the limits of the inherent jurisdiction.

Freezing injunctions (formerly *Mareva* injunctions) are available to the civil courts generally. Essentially, a freezing order forbids the respondent from removing funds or assets from the jurisdiction of the court until trial. Such an injunction can be worldwide. The County court can grant an injunction in a family matter but under normal circumstances should transfer such applications to the High Court. The statutory basis is the Senior Courts Act 1981, s 37 and the procedural basis is dealt with in the Civil Procedure Rules (CPR), Part 25.

Search orders (formerly *Anton Piller* orders) may be made where it appears that the respondent has in his possession documents or materials which should have been disclosed and that he may destroy them imminently or if he is given notice of the intention to search for them. Thus, it is a without notice order. It empowers the applicant to enter the respondent's premises and seize and remove materials of the class(es) specified. Such orders are rarely made and if their execution does not turn up materials of the class sought, the applicant may be severely penalised in costs. Its statutory basis is the Civil Procedure Act 1997, s 7 and the procedure is also dealt with in CPR, Part 25.

4.2.6   Limitations on and duration of orders

Most of the significant features of the orders available to the court have been set out above. There are three further points to note:

(a) An application for ancillary relief, if it is made by the petitioner, should be included in the petition for divorce. (Note that the respondent to the divorce petition may also apply for ancillary relief.) If the petitioner does not include a prayer for ancillary relief in the petition then he or she must apply for leave to amend the petition. The court has no power to make orders until decree nisi has been granted (usually a formality done at the outset of proceedings). The orders of the court will not take effect until decree absolute has been granted; that is, they will take effect at the same time as the marriage is officially and finally dissolved.

(b) The MCA 1973, s 28 makes provisions relating to continuing financial provision orders. Periodical payments orders (secured or otherwise) may not be expressed to begin before the date of the application (ie, the court can 'backdate' an order to that point, but no earlier).

(c) The MCA 1973, s 29 makes provisions relating to continuing financial provision orders made in relation to children. Save in appropriate circumstances (eg, education beyond 16 or 18 or special need), no financial provision may be made in respect of a child who has reached 18 years of age. Further, orders for periodical payments to or for a child (which may begin from the date of application) shall not extend, in the first instance, beyond school-leaving age and in any event not beyond the date of the child's eighteenth birthday. Periodical payments orders to or for a child shall cease upon the death of the payer (save for any arrears).

4.2.7 Powers of the court relating to overseas divorce

This subject is not dealt with in detail in this Manual. Most of the relevant legislation is found in the Matrimonial and Family Proceedings Act 1984 (MFPA 1984) and in the Recognition of Divorces and Legal Separations Act 1971 (DLSA 1971). For the court to have jurisdiction, the separation must be recognised as valid under the DLSA 1971, ss 2–6 and the applicant must show a connection with England and Wales in accordance with the MFPA 1984, s 15. The applicant must then apply for leave. If granted, the court will hear the application—the powers and considerations of the court are very similar to those applicable to a domestic divorce and are contained in the MFPA 1984, ss 14 and 17–26.

4.3 The s 25 factors

4.3.1 The factors

On an application to court for financial provision, there is, as has been said, no standard formula for calculating appropriate provision. If it were that simple, there would be little role for the courts in considering the case. Although there may be similarities between cases, and there may be broad categories into which some cases will fall, the details of each are unique in terms of available assets and the needs of both parties. The system for determining provision has to be sufficiently flexible to allow for this, and therefore, rather than a single rule, the statute provides a list of relevant factors, to be taken into account by the court when deciding how to exercise its powers.

The factors are listed in the MCA 1973, s 25(1) (2) and are widely referred to as 'the s 25 factors'. The court must also take into account the provisions of s 25A, which direct the court to try to achieve a 'clean break' between the parties, if this is practicable (see **4.4.3**). It is worth emphasising from the outset the central role that the s 25 factors play in determining applications for ancillary relief. All the analysis and evaluation of the facts of the situation must be carried out by reference to the s 25 factors. All arguments and proposals made in the case must be framed in terms of the factors. All the orders that the court could make must be considered and justified in the light of s 25.

Section 25 provides:

(1) It shall be the duty of the court in deciding whether to exercise its powers under sections 23 or 24 or 24A or 24B above and, if so, in what manner, to have regard to all the circumstances of the case, first consideration being given to the welfare while a minor of any child of the family who has not attained the age of eighteen.

(2) As regards the exercise of the powers of the court under section 23(1)(a) (b) or (c), 24, 24A or 24B in relation to a party to the marriage, the court shall in particular have regard to the following matters—

(a) the income, earning capacity, property and other financial resources which each of the parties to the marriage has or is likely to have in the foreseeable future, including in the case of earning capacity any increase in that capacity which it would in the opinion of the court be reasonable to expect a party to the marriage to take steps to acquire;

(b) the financial needs, obligations and responsibilities which each of the parties to the marriage has or is likely to have in the foreseeable future;

(c) the standard of living enjoyed by the family before the breakdown of the marriage;

(d) the age of each party to the marriage and the duration of the marriage;

(e) any physical or mental disability of either of the parties to the marriage;

(f) the contributions which each of the parties has made or is likely in the foreseeable future to make to the welfare of the family, including any contribution by looking after the home or caring for the family;

(g) the conduct of each of the parties, if that conduct is such that it would in the opinion of the court be inequitable to disregard it,

(h) in the case of proceedings for divorce or nullity of marriage, the value to each of the parties to the marriage of any benefit which, by reason of the dissolution or annulment of the marriage, that party will lose the chance of acquiring.

(3) As regards the exercise of the powers of the court under sections 23(1)(d) (e) or (f) (2) or (4), 24 or 24A above in relation to a child of the family, the court shall in particular have regard to the following matters—

(a) the financial needs of the child;

(b) the income, earning capacity (if any), property and other financial resources of the child;

(c) any physical or mental disability of the child;

(d) the manner in which he was being and in which the parties to the marriage expected him to be educated or trained;

(e) the considerations mentioned in relation to the parties to the marriage in paragraphs (a) (b) (c) and (e) of subsection (2) above.

(4) As regards the exercise of the powers of the court under section 23(1)(d) (e) or (f) (2) or (4), 24 or 24A above against a party to a marriage in favour of a child of the family who is not the child of that party, the court shall also have regard—

(a) to whether that party assumed any responsibility for the child's maintenance, and, if so, to the extent to which, and the basis upon which, that party assumed such responsibility and to the length of time for which that party discharged such responsibility;

(b) to whether in assuming and discharging such responsibility that party did so knowing that the child was not his or her own;

(c) to the liability of any other person to maintain the child.

4.3.2 Using the factors

The factors listed by statute are effectively the building blocks from which the barrister constructs an argument in an individual case. No one factor is intrinsically more important than any of the others. However, in dealing with any given case, some factors will almost certainly be more central, and occupy more of the court's time, than others. Which factors are more important than others in any given case depends entirely on the circumstances of that case. Dealing with the relevant factors in a practical and professional way can only come with practice, but as a suggested starting point in a case:

(a) Identify which factors from the general list are relevant to the particular case.

(b) Weigh up each relevant factor, deciding by reference to the facts, which are central to the case and those which are less important.

(c) Remember that the factors can interrelate to each other. For example, *disability* is a factor in its own right but the fact of a disability will quite possibly relate to *earning capacity* and perhaps also to *needs*. *Age* is a factor and the older a person is, the lower their *earning capacity* is likely to be if they have been out of the labour market. Some facts may fit under more than one factor, for example, music lessons could be considered a *financial obligation* and/or an issue relating to the *welfare of a child of the family*.

(d) Clearly identify the relevant factors that favour your client, which will therefore be central to your case.

(e) Clearly identify the relevant factors that undermine your client's case or favour the other side, and which you will therefore have to try to counter.

If one factor overshadows all others in the case, it may suggest an overall basis for provision (see **4.4**). If no factor is substantially more important than others, all relevant factors will go into the balance.

4.3.3 What the factors mean

The meaning of the factors should be understood primarily from the words of the statute itself. Decided cases from appellate courts can provide guidance on interpretation and establishing the broad approach of the courts to certain issues. Other than this, decided cases are usually of little relevance in deciding how a court should exercise its discretion in a particular case. In *White v White* [1998] 2 FLR 310, CA, Butler-Sloss LJ said: 'There is a danger that practitioners in the field of family law attempt to apply too rigidly the decisions of this court and of the Family Division, without sufficiently recognising that each case involving a family has to be decided upon broad principles adapted to the facts of the individual case. It is the statutory wording and judicial reasoning in cases, not their outcome as such, which act as a guide to the meaning of the s 25 factors.

4.3.3.1 All the circumstances . . . (s 25(1))

The statute states: 'It shall be the duty of the court...to have regard to all the circumstances of the case...'. This means that the court must not confine itself to the listed factors but must consider any circumstance that is relevant. In practice, relevant circumstances almost always fall under one of the listed factors. However, this provision can be useful when formulating arguments and proposals, especially in a case that involves an unusual feature, so it is important to keep it in mind.

4.3.3.2 Welfare of the children of the family under 18 (s 25(1))

This consideration is limited to children of the family, which is defined as any child who has been treated by both of the parties to the marriage as a child of their family (MCA 1973, s 52(1)). This includes stepchildren. What it does not include is children conceived by one of the parties outside of the marriage, who were not part of the marital home. Such children can be considered under other factors, such as obligations, but not here. The statute says that the welfare of children of the family will be the 'first consideration'. This does not mean that it is a consideration that should take precedence over the other factors (although in the weighing of the circumstances of a case, the court usually comes to the view that it is)—it means that it is the first matter to which the court should direct its attention.

Maintenance for any children of the family used to be the province of the Child Support Agency (CSA), which was effectively reincarnated as the Child Maintenance and Enforcement Commission (C-MEC) in 2008. C-MEC's declared purpose is to maximise the number of effective child maintenance arrangements in place—whether private or statutory—for children who live apart from one or both parents. The emphasis on encouraging parents to reach private agreements for their children's maintenance is a welcome development (see generally **Chapter 7**).

The main issue in ancillary relief proceedings is usually housing the children. The court will want to ensure that the children are adequately housed in a location that takes into account their needs in terms of schooling, family relationships and social networks and activities (the latter varying according to age). The main carer will, of course, be housed with the children but this will primarily be a matter of the children's welfare—it is not a right or a benefit conferred on that carer. Either parent may or may not have a financial interest in some or all of the children's home—that will depend entirely on how the court decides to divide the assets. It is quite common for the resident carer to be required to sell the home and move to a smaller property once the children have left and no longer need it.

The needs of the child should not, however, unduly prejudice the need of the non-resident spouse for a home (*M v B (Ancillary Proceedings: Lump Sum)* [1998] 1 FLR 53). The court will, if possible, try to stretch the resources so that the latter has housing suitable for regular contact, including staying contact, with the children.

Generally, the younger a child is, the longer its needs will last, the more multifarious those needs are likely to be, and the further the court will go to try to balance available resources in order to ensure that they are adequately catered for. The closer a child is to 18, the less important its needs are likely to be in the overall balance.

4.3.3.3   Income, earning capacity, property and other financial resources . . . (s 25(2)(a))

The importance of getting full details and figures for capital and income cannot be overemphasised. Getting a complete and open picture of all the resources of the parties is one of the central features of ancillary relief procedure. Only when the court has determined what is available can it go on to determine how those assets should be allocated. The parties are under an ongoing obligation to make full and frank disclosure. There should be no partial disclosure nor should a party wait for the other side to ask for relevant information before disclosing it. The judge is required to consider penalising in costs a party who fails to disclose completely and voluntarily within the appropriate timescale.

A party's resources can be highly relevant not only to the amount, but also to the type of provision ordered. Lump sum payments, for example, require sufficient capital and/or income to raise the funds. Equally, if there is not sufficient income available to the person wanting to remain in the matrimonial home to pay the mortgage and outgoings, there may be no realistic alternative to selling it.

Note that 'any' financial resources are relevant, and this is widely interpreted to include benefits, for example, free or cheap accommodation available with a job. There are, however, some limits; for example, proceeds of crime that are liable to be confiscated might not be taken into account, depending on the circumstances. Neither an application for a confiscation order under the Drug Trafficking Act 1994, s 2, nor a claim for ancillary relief have priority over each other. The High Court must determine the outcome according to the public interest and applicable Convention rights. For the practice in this situation, see *Re MCA; HM Customs and Excise Commissioners and Long v A and A; A v A (Long Intervening)* [2003] 1 FLR 164 and, for the procedural effect of the Proceeds of Crime Act 2002 (POCA 2002), *Webber v Webber* [2007] 2 FLR 116 (and see *Stodgell v Stodgell* [2009] 2 FLR 218, discussed at **4.3.3.10**).

As regards earnings, it is important to appreciate that the court will also look to a party's *earning capacity*, ie, it will take into account not only what he or she is earning, but what he or she may be reasonably expected to earn if exploiting all opportunities fully, both in the short term and the long term. Parties who choose not to work or not to maximise their resources when they could do so are likely to have adverse inferences drawn against them. The subsection specifically requires the court to consider any increase in earning capacity that it would be reasonable to expect a party to take steps to acquire. The court will be realistic about what it is reasonable to expect people to do in the circumstances. For example, it is not likely to expect carers of very young children to go out to work full-time. If it takes the view that an applicant may need some time to retrain and/or otherwise adjust to future financial independence, the court may allow for this by making a fixed-term periodical payments order (as an alternative to a normal open-ended order which puts the onus on the paying party to apply for a variation).

'Property' is widely defined. It includes all real property, all personal property, any financial stock or other business assets or interests, any beneficial interest under a trust; this list is not exhaustive.

'Other financial resources' can include expectations, ie, property or income that a party is likely to have in the foreseeable future. Note that this does not include pensions, which are considered separately see **4.3.3.11**). Caution must be exercised in relation to an expectation—there must be evidence upon which the court can be satisfied as to the likelihood and extent of the expectation. An example of a common expectation is the prospect of being a beneficiary under a will (or an intestacy). The problems with this expectation are that it can be difficult to gauge life expectancy and to estimate the size of the potential benefit. A testator cannot be compelled to disclose his or her intentions. The court does have the power to adjourn the lump sum element of an application for financial provision, where there is an expectation of a significant inheritance and where the court considers it necessary to take this course in order to achieve fairness in a particular set of circumstances (*Re G (Financial Provision: Liberty to Restore Application for Lump Sum)* [2004] 1 FLR 997). Note that this is an exceptional course of action.

Regular financial support from a third party could, again with caution, be viewed as a resource. The court would need to be satisfied on evidence that it was reasonable to expect this support to continue in the foreseeable future. A recoverable debt owed by a third party would normally be seen as a resource.

Resources available from a cohabitee may also be relevant, but the position of a cohabitee cannot be fully equated with that of a spouse, and the income of a party's cohabitee will not simply be added to that of the party. It will be assumed, however, that the party and the cohabitee are mutually supportive of each other and this may have the effect of reducing that party's needs and obligations.

A court may draw inferences as to resources that are available provided there is sufficient reason to do so (*Thomas v Thomas* [1995] 2 FLR 668), especially if there is serious non-disclosure (*Baker v Baker* [1995] 2 FLR 829). A resource which is considered too remote (eg, a possible future inheritance) will be disregarded.

Although all assets and resources must be identified, not all will necessarily be available for redistribution. For example, a family business will have a net worth but it is also likely to provide essential income and so it may not be desirable to realise it as a capital asset. The situation may be different, however, if the business depended on the partnership of the divorcing couple for its efficacy, in which case it may be appropriate to order sale of the business and its assets. Specialist advice is often needed in cases involving businesses or other ventures a little out of the ordinary, such as farms or an Internet business, and case law often provides guidance, for example, see: *P v P (Financial Relief: Illiquid Assets)* [2005] 1 FLR 548, *D v D&B Ltd* [2007]2 FLR 548. A pragmatic approach needs to be adopted, however, in deciding whether an expert should be instructed to value a business: such an exercise is not an exact science and a detailed investigation is not only expensive but may not assist the court, see: *H v H* [2008] 2 FLR 2092. (See also **4.4.8.1**.)

Other assets that may or may not form part of the matrimonial pot are assets acquired prior to the marriage and assets acquired under an inheritance or under a family trust. It is a question of fact and judgement whether such assets become part of the matrimonial assets during the marriage, depending on how they are acquired, held and used. Since the House of Lords' decision *in Miller v Miller; McFarlane v McFarlane* [2006] 1 FLR 1186 the courts have much more routinely applied themselves to the question of determining what is and is not "matrimonial property". Although this issue receives a lot of coverage it is usually an issue in bigger-money cases, where there is more money than is required to meet the needs of all the parties. In that decision Lord Nicholls and Baroness Hale differed in their views as to the distinction between matrimonial and non-matrimonial property. *Per* Lord Nicholls, non-matrimonial property is viewed as all property which the parties bring with them into the marriage or acquire by inheritance or gift during the marriage (plus perhaps the income or fruits of that property), while matrimonial property is viewed as all other property. Baroness Hale's approach is that non-matrimonial property includes not merely: (a) property which the parties bring with them with into the marriage or acquire by inheritance or gift during the marriage (plus perhaps its income or fruits); but also (b) business or investment assets generated solely or mainly by the efforts of one party during the marriage. For recent cases, see: *Rossi v Rossi* [2007] 1 FLR 790, *S v S* (*Non-Matrimonial Property; Conduct*) [2007] 1 FLR 1496. In *Charman v Charman* [2007] EWCA Civ 503 Potter P stated that the newly elevated 'sharing principle' (see **4.4.4**) applied to all property, but, to the extent that property is non-matrimonial, there is likely to be better reason for a departure from equality. He also preferred the more generous (to the payee) view of matrimonial property, despite its minority status in the House of Lords' judgment.

So far as pensions in particular are concerned, as a resource they are relevant no matter how far in the future the benefit might be realised. See s 25B MCA 1973, as added by the Pensions Act 1995. For more on pensions generally, see **4.3.3.11**.

4.3.3.4   Financial needs, obligations and responsibilities . . . (s 25(2)(b))

As regards needs, it is necessary to get accurate details of all the household expenses, such as the mortgage, gas and electricity bills, etc. The term 'needs' can be interpreted widely to include any reasonable expense of living, and this should be fully investigated—get the client to think of everything that has to be paid for. Remember that for your client you would try to include all arguable needs, whereas in relation to the other side's needs, you might be more apt to claim that they should be pruned and kept within more reasonable bounds. In low-to-average income cases, the subsistence level indicated by current state benefit levels plus housing costs is often used in practice as a yardstick for minimum needs.

The term 'obligations' can include any legal or moral obligation to meet an expense, including obligations to third parties, such as relatives, cohabitees or children who are being supported. In some cases, this may mean that the resources of one person have to be divided between their former spouse and their new spouse or cohabitee, and any children. This can be very contentious, especially when resources are overstretched. While the court will try to give precedence to the first family, it has to be realistic—for example, it is often easier for the former wife on her own to claim benefits than the new cohabitee living with a person of average income.

Where there is a purported debt that is being claimed by a third party, then the court cannot anticipate the outcome of other proceedings. The court will decide if the debt is significant and if so will either adjourn to await the outcome, or have the cases heard in tandem by the same judge (*George v George* [2004] 1 FLR 421).

It used to be that different considerations applied to 'big-money' cases and the concept of 'reasonable requirements' was used in place of needs. However, since the House of Lords' decision in *White v White* [2000] 2 FLR 981, this approach has been disapproved and it is established that, in the context of s 25(2)(b), consideration of needs is what the statute requires in all cases.

4.3.3.5 The standard of living of the family before the breakdown (s 25(2)(c))

In most cases, it will not be possible to maintain the standard of living that the parties enjoyed during the marriage. Except in big-money cases, if the money that has financed a single household has to be split to finance two, there will almost certainly have to be some drop in the standard of living.

The concern of the court will be to see that the standard of living does not slip more than is necessary and to ensure that one party does not suffer a significantly greater drop in living standards than the other.

It is worth noting that the subsection refers to the standard of living of the family, not the parties. This means that the standard of living of the children must also be considered.

4.3.3.6 The age of each party (s 25(2)(d))

The main relevance of age is in relation to earning capacity and to the importance of providing for retirement. A young wife will normally be seen as having an earning potential, whereas an older person, who has not worked for years, will have less ability to enter the labour market and less time to accrue savings or investments for the future. For an older person, it will also be more expensive to pay a mortgage as the 25-year term will not be available.

In the case of a younger person, a clean break or deferred clean break is more likely to be possible. With an older person, there is more likely to be a dependency and it will be important to investigate the pension situation.

4.3.3.7 The duration of the marriage (s 25(2)(d))

For marriages of average or greater length, the duration is not normally relevant, as the usual guidelines will apply. Duration is usually most relevant if the marriage is short. In the case of an extremely short marriage, the court may order no financial provision at all, for example where a marriage effectively lasted only two weeks (*Krystman v Krystman* [1973] 1 WLR 927). It is particularly likely that no provision will be ordered where neither spouse has suffered financially as a result of the marriage. For a marriage that has lasted more than a few weeks, it is quite possible that some provision will be ordered, even if it is at a low level, such as the award of a small lump sum or a limited term of periodical payments to allow the claimant to readjust.

In a short marriage, other s 25 factors may be less significant—there will probably have been far less by way of contribution and earning potential is likely to be higher. On the other hand the existence of children of the marriage will be very significant. Even after a short marriage, the needs and welfare of any children must be properly catered for (see *B v B (Mesher Order)* [2003] 2 FLR 285, and see further at **4.4.7**).

In *Miller; McFarlane* [2006] 1 FLR 1186 Lord Nicholls expressed clearly the view that a short marriage was no less a partnership of equals than a long marriage and disapproved the approach that a party's entitlement increased over time. The short duration of a marriage might affect the amount of matrimonial property at stake between the parties—but the entitlement of the parties would be still subject to the yardstick of equality before considering whether there was a good reason for departure.

Baroness Hale differed slightly in recognising that duration was a factor that the courts are required to consider. In her view non-matrimonial assets were more likely to be excludable from the common pot in a shorter marriage, whereas in the normal course of events such distinctions would be likely to fade and such assets become part of the common enterprise—in this sense a short marriage might justify a departure from equality.

What is clear is that, post-*Miller*, the line of authorities for short-marriage cases pre-*White*, which focused on the needs of the wife, cannot now be relied upon, and the post-*White* authority of *Foster v Foster* [2003] 2 FLR 299 is approved. The principle of sharing and the yardstick of equality apply—the significance of short duration is that it may justify departure or it may diminish what is at stake.

When considering the length of the marriage, the court has traditionally taken it as lasting from the time of marriage to the time of breakdown. Cohabitation before (or after) the marriage was not normally relevant to duration (*Foley v Foley* [1980] Fam 160), unless the circumstances were exceptional; eg, a 25-year cohabitation as a family where the husband could not marry for legal reasons (*Kokosinski v Kokosinski* [1980] Fam 72).

Recently, however, the courts have shown greater willingness to treat a period of cohabitation as being part of the effective duration of the marriage. In *GW v RW (Financial Provision: Departure from Equality)* [2003] 2 FLR 108, Nicholas Mostyn, QC included 18 months' cohabitation as part of the duration of the marriage, concluding that, 'where a marriage moves seamlessly from cohabitation to marriage without any major alteration in the way the couple live, it is unreal and artificial to treat the periods differently'. He commented that, since the decision in *Foley*, public opinion had moved on and was more willing to recognise fully committed relationships outside of marriage. He also thought it relevant to consider how the parties themselves define their period of cohabitation. In *CO v CO (Ancillary Relief: Pre-marriage Cohabitation)* [2004] 1 FLR 1095, Coleridge J gave full weight to eight years' cohabitation preceding a four-year marriage. He held that, contingent on the parties having eventually married, committed and settled relationships outside marriage should be treated with the same validity as relationships which had publicly recorded that same degree of commitment by marrying.

This development has been criticised in some quarters; for some strong counter-arguments see the article in [2004] *Family Law* 205. One of many is that cohabiting couples should not be deprived of the ability consciously to distinguish their state from that of married couples by an erosion of the distinction between the two.

Recent cases set no precedent but it is clear that the latitude of the courts' discretion is now open to the argument, based on the intention and conduct of cohabiting parties, that a relationship period longer than the marriage itself may be the appropriate measure. See **4.4.7**.

4.3.3.8   Any physical or mental disability of either of the parties (s 25(2)(e))

This point is fairly straightforward. If either spouse has a physical or mental disability which makes it difficult or impossible to be self-supporting, then that will be a factor in its own right as well as being relevant to earning capacity and possibly to needs.

However, the fact of the disability must be put in context. If the spouse who has a disability can claim social security benefits, while the spouse against whom a claim is made has a limited income, it is possible that no order will be made (see *Ashley v Blackman* [1988] Fam 85).

4.3.3.9 Contributions to the welfare of the family . . . (s 25(2)(f))

Contributions to the welfare of the family can take many forms. One form is financial, but this provision also puts value on non-monetary contributions by making particular reference to looking after the household. So far as it can gauge them, the court will take into account contributions in the future as well as in the past.

Financial contributions include the earnings of the spouses over the course of the marriage and any capital sums or property that they bring or acquire during the marriage. As to inheritances, windfalls, family trusts and assets acquired before the marriage, see **4.3.3.3**.

Non-monetary contributions are usually those of the spouse who does not work in order to bring up children and look after the household. From the 1970s, there has been steadily increasing recognition of the value and status of such contributions. Now, since the House of Lords' decision in *White v White* [2000] 2 FLR 981, we have arrived at a position of direct equality between financial and non-financial contributions, at least as a starting point. In that case it was held to be a principle 'of universal application' that there should be no discrimination between husband and wife in their respective roles. A marriage involves a division of labour and, however this labour is divided, there should be no bias in favour of the breadwinner at the expense of the homemaker and child-carer. (For further consideration of *White*, see **4.4.4**.) Other types of non-monetary contributions, such as caring for an elderly or sick family member, or playing a support role to the career of the main earner, should not be overlooked where they are relevant.

Consideration of future contributions includes both financial and non-financial contributions. Where one party will be caring for children, this will be a relevant factor and the longer the dependency, the greater its significance. The likelihood of making financial contributions in the form of child support over a significant period of time will also be a relevant consideration.

4.3.3.10 Conduct . . . (s 25(2)(g))

You will almost certainly have to explain to your client at some point that this factor is not concerned with the 'normal' types of misbehaviour often associated with the breakup of a marriage. This is not an easy issue on divorce. One spouse may be very upset at the way that the other has behaved—indeed that conduct may to them personally be the most important issue in the case. However, the court is loath to go into a detailed examination of the causes and effects of marital breakdown, as this can be very expensive in terms of time and money, and is rarely relevant to deciding the best way forward for the future. In *McCartney v Mills* [2008] 1 FLR 1508, Bennett J declined to hear evidence or argument about conduct on the basis that it would make little or no difference to the final result. As a result, the court will only take the most serious misconduct into account.

The statute provides that conduct will only be taken into account if it is such that 'in the opinion of the court it would be inequitable to disregard it'. In fact, there have been relatively few reported cases where the court has held that conduct is sufficiently bad to have a substantial effect on the level of provision ordered.

A departure from this well-established approach was suggested by the Court of Appeal in *Miller v Miller* [2006] 1 FLR 151, where Thorpe LJ cited the fact that the husband was responsible (in no extreme way) for the breakdown of the marriage as a factor influencing the balancing exercise. This aspect of that judgment drew much adverse comment and when *Miller* went to the House of Lords this point was expressly overruled. Conduct can only be taken into account if it is such that it would be inequitable to disregard it.

It is clear that adultery will not be sufficiently serious to be taken into account unless there is some aggravating factor, for example, if the adultery is with a father-in-law (*Bailey v Tolliday* (1982) 4 FLR 542). Where a person's right to apply for ancillary relief has been based on deceitful or criminal behaviour, such as bigamy, then it has been held that they should not be entitled to benefit from their deceitful act (*Whiston v Whiston* [1995] 2 FLR 268). However, bigamy is not an automatic bar to entitlement; it will depend on the circumstances, including the other spouse's degree of knowledge and complicity (*Rampal v Rampal (No 2)* [2001] 2 FLR 1179) (though see [2003] *Family Law* 415 for a trenchant criticism of this decision). Serious violence has been held to be relevant conduct. In *H v H (Financial Provisions: Conduct)* [1994] 2 FLR 801, the husband had been imprisoned for violently assaulting and raping his wife; this was held to be relevant and the court further took into account that he had put himself in a position where he could not support the family. In *Evans v Evans* [1989] 1 FLR 351, it was held that a wife's right to maintenance should end after she was convicted of inciting the murder of her husband. In *K v K (Financial Provision: Conduct)* [1988] 1 FLR 469, a wife's conduct in assisting her husband's suicide attempts was held to be relevant to her level of entitlement. In *H v H (Financial Relief: Attempted Murder as Conduct)* [2006] 1 FLR 990, a husband convicted of the attempted murder of his wife received only a small portion of the matrimonial assets. Coleridge J stated that, 'The court should not be punitive or confiscatory for its own sake. The proper way to have regard to the conduct is as a potentially magnifying factor when considering the other subsections and criteria. It places the wife's needs as a much higher priority to those of the husband because the situation the wife finds herself in is, in a very real way, his fault.'

Serious financial misconduct may also be relevant. In cases where a party dissipates or fritters away family assets, or brings about financial ruin through obviously selfish and unreasonable behaviour, then the court may take the view that he or she is not entitled to claim a part of what remains on an equal footing with the other spouse. For examples, see *Beach v Beach* [1995] 2 FLR 160 and *Le Foe v Le Foe and Woolwich plc* [2001] 2 FLR 970. The case of *Stodgell v Stodgell* [2009] 2 FLR 218 is a dramatic example of the effects of serious financial misconduct. It deals with the conflict between a criminal confiscation order (made after the husband's conviction for tax evasion and fraud) and the wife's ancillary relief claim. Holman J held that neither the MCA 1973 nor the Criminal Justice Act 1988 took priority over the other and that the husband's fraudulent activities amounted to conduct it would be inequitable to disregard. However, the husband's total assessed tax liabilities were virtually identical to his whole assets (£900,000) and the confiscation order prevailed. Leave to appeal was refused [2009] 2 FLR 244, even though it was likely that the wife would then be forced to turn to the state for assistance.

Misconduct in the course of the proceedings, such as misrepresentation, making false statements or wilful non-disclosure, may well be relevant to the court's considerations. In *P v P (Financial Relief: Non-disclosure)* [1994] 2 FLR 381, Thorpe LJ held that, though the conduct was such that it would be inequitable to disregard it, this should be reflected in the order for costs rather than in the apportioning of the assets. However, in, *M v M (Ancillary Relief: Conduct: Disclosure)* [2006] 2 FLR 1253, the husband had gambled away a significant amount of assets and had repeatedly failed to disclose matters, leading to penal notices and eventually a subpoena. The judge took account of both elements of bad conduct in the balancing exercise, rather than just confining the litigation element to a costs penalty.

4.3.3.11   Value of any benefit the parties will lose the chance of acquiring (s 25B(1))

The Pensions Act 1995 deleted the reference to pensions that used be part of s 25(2)(h) and inserted s 25B, which is entirely concerned with pensions. Issues other than pensions that may fall for consideration under this factor might include early retirement or redundancy rights, or in some circumstances inheritance rights.

Section 25B(1) added considerations to the s 25(2) factors. It provides:

> *(1) The matters to which the court is to have regard under section 25(2) above include—*
>
> *(a) in the case of paragraph (a), any benefits under a pension arrangement which a party to the marriage has or is likely to have, and*
>
> *(b) in the case of paragraph (h), any benefits under a pension arrangement which, by reason of the dissolution or annulment of the marriage, a party to the marriage will lose the chance of acquiring, and, accordingly, in relation to benefits under a pension arrangement, section 25(2)(a) above shall have effect as if 'in the foreseeable future' were omitted.*

Thus, the court is now required in every case to consider, no matter how remote these events may be, the benefits that the parties might receive from a pension scheme and the effect of the commensurate loss on the paying party. In most cases, there are two types of loss. The first is the loss of the ability to share with the husband the benefits of the payments he will receive on retirement. The second is the loss of the protection, most commonly the widow's pension, which the scheme will confer on the death of the husband.

Although the court is obliged to consider pension benefits, such consideration is not a separate consideration outside of the s 25 approach. The court considers whether and how pension considerations, just as with any other factor, should affect the terms of the order it is considering making. Having considered pension issues, the court may give them as much or as little weight, including disregarding them altogether, as it thinks appropriate.

Considering pension rights is a process that can become very complex. It may involve, for example, detailed evaluation of intricate financial products, calculations of future worth and application of discounts for accelerated receipt and contingency. In complex cases, it may be appropriate to obtain expert actuarial advice. What is given here is an overview of the appropriate steps to take in considering pension rights; see also a useful introductory article 'A Beginner's Guide to Pensions within Family Proceedings' [2009] *Family Law* 341.

Valuation

Regulations, made under the MCA 1973, have been made for the value of any benefit under a pension scheme to be valued and verified for the purposes of making an order under the Act. These regulations are the Divorce etc (Pensions) Regulations 2000 (SI 2000/1123), and the Pensions on Divorce etc (Provision of Information) Regulations 2000 (SI 2000/1048), which themselves refer to the Pension Schemes Act 1993, ss 93–101. The value of the pension arrangement shall be taken as at a day to be specified by the court. The method of valuation is to calculate the cash equivalent transfer value (CETV). The process has been complicated by the introduction of new regulations from 1 October 2008 which apply to some pensions, but not others (the Occupational Pensions Schemes (Transfer Values) (Amendment) Regulations 2008 (SI 2008/1050)). Calculating the CETV is a specialist process—essentially it calculates a present (ie, the date specified by the court) cash value for the value of the member's payments on retirement and other pension benefits. The CETV does not include death–in–service benefits nor discretionary benefits. The managers of pension schemes must provide a CETV within three months of being ordered to do so by the court.

The CETV is the standard method of valuation but it is not the only one and the method has its critics (see the article referred to at the end of this section). Most criticisms argue that the CETV, for various reasons, tends to undervalue the actual value of the fund that will be accrued or the benefit that will be conferred. Although the court is required to use the CETV, it can also take other methods into account, provided that it is satisfied by expert evidence that it is appropriate to do so.

Weight

The next thing to consider is what weight to attach to the value of the benefits. The most significant facts here are the ages of the parties, the length of the marriage and the amount of time remaining until retirement. With younger couples, the prospect of retirement will be far away and courts will tend to regard any future lost benefits as being too remote to be justly considered. The duration of the marriage is likely to be shorter, so the shareable benefits will be smaller. Additionally, younger divorcees will have plenty of time to make provision for their futures—so there will be considerably less need under this factor and considerably less dependency, if any, on any existing pension arrangement. Conversely, the older a couple is, the closer in time will be the anticipated losses and the more important it will be for the court to make provision for them. The amount of time spent together accruing benefits is likely to be longer and therefore the value and significance of shareable benefits will be higher. Most importantly, the wife may only have a short time until retirement during which she will probably not be in a strong position in the labour market. She will therefore have little time and means by which to provide for her retirement and will be dependent, perhaps heavily or even solely, on the retirement arrangements of her husband.

Another basic consideration is to decide the time over which the pension benefit was accruing. In *H v H (Financial Provision: Capital Allowance)* [1993] 2 FLR 335, Thorpe J, as he was then, set out an approach that is commonly followed. He said that the value of what was earned during the period of cohabitation was more relevant than what may be earned during the period between separation and retirement. In that case, the pension had been earned over 13 years of service but there had only been seven years of cohabitation. The CETV was divided by the number of years of service and multiplied by the number of years of cohabitation.

District judges often follow this 'straight line' fractional approach. However there is criticism of this approach—see below.

As can be imagined, the courts are reluctant to prescribe any periods of time or specific conditions for the relevance or otherwise of pension arrangements. However, decided cases tend to follow some broad principles and considerations:

(a) Where the parties, especially the wife, are young, possibly up to early thirties, the value of the pension may have little or no relevance.

(b) Similarly, if the pension is realisable more than 20 years into the future, it may well be of little or no relevance.

(c) Taking into account the case as a whole, what are the wife's reasonable needs for income or capital after retirement? Where there is not a clean break, there is more likely to be a future dependency.

(d) It is important to consider the position the wife will be in if the husband dies.

(e) In most cases, the court will have given priority to considering the wife's and any children's housing needs and income needs—if substantial provision has been made here, this may, taking into account the overall balance, affect the weight given to the wife's retirement needs.

(f) The needs of the husband must not be forgotten, especially in limited assets cases where the balance has gone against him in terms of housing and/or income.

(g) It is most important to bear in mind that these are merely illustrative tendencies derived from decided cases—every case will turn on its own facts!

The final order

The final thing to consider is how to reflect the value and weight of pension benefits in the final order. Pension benefits constitute a consideration under the overall s 25 exercise. When considering what, if any, orders to make in relation to pensions, the overall balance of all the relevant factors and circumstances must be borne in mind. There is no need to interfere with pension entitlement unless it is justified by reference to relevant factors or to the overall yardstick of equality (see **4.4.4**).

In circumstances where there are sufficient funds to meet all the wife's income and capital needs for life, it may be appropriate to consider offsetting, ideally in the form of a *Duxbury* fund (see **4.2.2.3**). Offsetting may also be appropriate where there is a younger couple and the wife has no serious requirement justifying adjustment of the husband's pension entitlement—but it may be considered just to reflect some loss of provision in a lump sum.

In circumstances where it is foreseen that there is likely to be an ongoing dependency crossing over into retirement, an attachment order for periodical payments could meet this purpose. In some circumstances, for example where the dependency is strong, or where there are dependent children being provided for, or where the husband is significantly older than the wife, it may be appropriate to strengthen the wife's protection by providing for the possible death of the husband, which can be achieved by an order for attachment of death-in-service benefits.

If there were insufficient funds at the time of the proceedings to make such lump sum order as the court considered appropriate, an attachment order for a lump sum could be used. This is in effect a deferred lump sum order.

In cases where there is a clean break and it is desired to provide for the wife with a share of the husband's pension, a pension-sharing order will usually be appropriate. There does not have to be a clean break—a pension-sharing order can be combined with an order for periodical payments. It is not possible to combine pension sharing with an attachment order—so the less independent a wife is, the less appropriate a pension-sharing order is likely to be. An advantage of a pension-sharing order is that it gives the wife a sum that is not subject to variation, nor at risk from changes in the husband's circumstances, such as bankruptcy—once she has her pension credit it is hers for life.

For a description of these various types of orders, see **4.2.4**.

Criticism of current practice

In the post-*White* era of fairness there is a greater trend towards pension-sharing orders. However the straightforward approach adopted by many judges may not be doing justice to the complexity of pensions. Comparing CETV values between different pension schemes can be very misleading in that those values can be quite unrelated to the actual income streams that the given pensions will produce. For further discussion of this and related problems, see 'Pensions and Equality' [2007] *Family Law* 310.

For further articles expressing detailed concern at the CETV valuation method and the problems with pension-sharing orders, see 'The Reality of Pension Sharing—Part One' [2003] *Family Law* 517 and 'Part Two' [2003] *Family Law* 679.

4.3.4 Keeping an open mind

Examples have been given in this section of some of the most common issues that may arise in relation to the s 25 factors and of some of the most common approaches that may be adopted in relation to them.

However, it is repeated throughout this chapter, and we are constantly reminded in leading judgments, that every case is individual and must be approached with an open mind. With any brief, you must consider all the s 25 factors with a fresh perspective and be prepared to make a sensible argument supporting a sensible proposal based on them.

4.4 Bases for provision

4.4.1 Introduction

An identification and balancing of the relevant factors in the case must finally be brought into focus in deciding on an overall basis for provision using the orders available to the court. The fact that the statutory powers to make orders and to take factors into account are wide may seem to provide a bewildering array of possibilities, but for every case a coherent solution must be found. This requires the development of professional expertise.

In any case, the overall basis may suggest itself from one, or more than one, salient or dominant feature of the circumstances. Statute directs the court to consider whether a clean break is possible and also to consider the needs of any children of the family first; either of these considerations could, if appropriate, become a basis for shaping the overall package. In particular circumstances, one of the factors in the case may be so important that it overrides all others; or a combination of two or more factors may provide the basic objectives around which a package of measures can be constructed.

The following notes offer a broad summary of possibilities rather than a comprehensive study. A basic overall guide suggesting an approach for deciding on an appropriate basis can be found at **4.4.9**.

4.4.2 Consider the needs of children first

The welfare of any children is stated by statute to be a first consideration (MCA 1973, s 25(1)). However, this does not mean that the children are entitled to be given outright assets belonging to their parents, but rather that provision for the children should be taken into account in dividing the assets of the parents. The most common effect of this principle is that where there are young children, the matrimonial home will often be used to provide a home for them either by settling it (that is, by apportioning beneficial interest in the home between the parties) or transferring it to the custodial parent.

Although stability in the life of children is important, the existence of children will not always mean that the matrimonial home is preserved. In some cases, especially where the husband too has need of rehousing, or if the house is larger than is strictly required by the children of the family and the parent with care, it will have to be sold to provide capital and smaller properties purchased.

The welfare of children is also important in terms of income, and child support liability (see **Chapter 7**) means that in practice payments of maintenance for children will need to take priority. This will inevitably have an effect on overall settlements and may make it less likely that generous capital provision will be made.

4.4.3 The clean break

The idea of the clean break is that resources should be divided once and for all between the spouses, leaving no further financial obligations between them, and leaving each free to start a new life. This can usually only be achieved if there are sufficient available assets to satisfy the reasonable claims of the applicant, and if both spouses have such income or earning potential that maintenance payments will not be necessary.

4.4.3.1 Legislative framework

The objective of trying to achieve a clean break between spouses on divorce was made statutory in 1984, when s 25A was inserted into the MCA 1973. There are three subsections to s 25A.

Subsection (1) provides that whenever the court exercises its powers under ss 22A–24A, it is under a duty to consider whether it should do so in a way that terminates the financial obligations of the parties to each other as soon after decree absolute as the court considers just and reasonable. If the court does not conclude that termination is appropriate, then subsection (2) requires the court, when it makes an order for periodical payments (secured or otherwise), to consider whether it is appropriate to set a term for the payments that lasts only as long as necessary to allow the benefiting party to adjust without undue hardship to the termination of their financial dependency on the other party. Subsection (3) provides that if the court dismisses the application for periodical payments (secured or otherwise), then it may do so with an order barring further applications in relation to that marriage. The desirability of self-sufficiency may also be read in the 1984 amendment to s 25(2)(a) directing the court to consider any increase in earning capacity that it would be reasonable to expect a party to take steps to acquire (see **4.3.3.3**).

4.4.3.2 The approach of the courts

The court must make these considerations in every case. However, it should only do so after consideration of all the s 25 factors and not in isolation from them. Although the court is required to try to achieve a clean break, it is under no obligation to pursue one as a priority or at the expense of other considerations.

In most cases, the court will have two decisions to make: should there be an immediate clean break (*per* s 25A(1)); or should there be a clean break at some future time (a deferred clean break) (*per* s 25A(2))? When considering a deferred clean break, the court must further consider whether to make an order under s 28(1A), which prohibits the party in whose favour the order is made from making further applications for extension or variation under s 31.

In considering what is appropriate, there are three broad categories that cases might fall into: 'big money', 'no money' and 'normal money'. In 'big-money' cases, a clean break can often be achieved, because whatever the wife's short- or long-term entitlements, there is enough money to meet them for her lifetime by providing her with some form of capital fund, such as a *Duxbury* fund. All continuing claims can be dismissed because the capital fund provides real self-sufficiency. In such cases, however, the liquidity of any business assets can be a highly relevant factor—see *F v F* (*Clean Break: Balance of Fairness*) [2003] 1 FLR 847 for an example of a case where it was held to be inappropriate to order a clean break in order to preserve a significant and illiquid business that generated income for the parties. In *Miller; McFarlane* [2006] 1 FLR 1186 the House of Lords confirmed the principle that periodical payments can be ordered to provide a spouse with a fair share of the matrimonial assets where there was insufficient capital to do so. This is a departure from the previous view that periodical payments could only be used to meet ongoing needs. It is probably limited to big-money cases where the payer is unusually 'capital-poor' but 'income-rich'—even here critics wonder whether a lump sum order in instalments would not fit the purpose better.

In 'no-money' cases, a clean break may be ordered on the basis that there is no possibility nor prospect of the husband paying periodical payments. In such circumstances, the clean break at least avoids ongoing uncertainty, litigation and cost. It should be said that even with no clean break, where there is no money, there is less possibility of such complication.

It is the 'normal-money' cases that present the most difficulty in considering the clean break possibilities. Often the husband does not have enough money to make payments without hardship but the wife does not have an earning capacity that would enable her to be self-supporting. The most significant fact is whether or not there are children of the family—wherever there are children, a clean break becomes very hard to achieve and is unlikely to be attempted. This is for very practical reasons including the obvious fact that, with children, the caring parent will have greater needs and diminished earning capacity. With children present, the parties are going to have a serious and long-term ongoing joint responsibility so achieving a clean break is less important.

In balancing available money against needs, it is important to consider the latter side of the balance carefully, especially with childless couples. If the needs are not great, then a clean break may still be achieved even where there is not a great deal of money. Needs may be fewer where there has been a short marriage, or the parties are young, or where they both have careers.

Authoritative guidance on how to approach the question of a clean break was given by Ward LJ in *C v C* (*Financial Relief: Short Marriage*) [1997] 2 FLR 26. Although that case involved a short marriage, the guidance is of general application. To summarise:

(a) The first task is to consider whether an immediate clean break is appropriate. Section 25A(2) provides the test of the payee being able 'to adjust [to the termination of dependency] without undue hardship' in considering a deferred clean break. It is commonly inferred from decided cases that this same test applies to considering an immediate clean break (even though it is not written in the statute).

(b) If the court decides to order periodical payments of some sort, then it must also consider whether to set such payments for a finite term. It should only do this if satisfied that the payee will at the end of the term have adjusted to the termination of support without undue hardship. There must be evidence before the court to support such a conclusion.

(c) What is appropriate must depend on all the circumstances of the case, including the welfare of any minor child and the s 25 factors. The duration of the marriage may be of particular relevance but a short marriage does not always lead to a clean break.

(d) In considering whether and when the payee can cope with the termination of financial dependence, the question is *can* she adjust, not *should* she adjust. In answering that question, the court will pay attention not only to the duration of the marriage but to the effect of the marriage and its breakdown; the need to care for minor children and the effect of this on the earning capacity of the payee; and any difficulties she will have in entering the labour market, resuming a fractured career and making up any lost ground.

(e) If there is doubt about whether the payee will be able to adjust, then it is wrong to set a term with the onus on the payee to apply for an extension. The proper course is to set no term and leave the payer to apply for variation.

4.4.3.3   The Inheritance (Provision for Family and Dependants) Act 1975

The Inheritance (Provision for Family and Dependants) Act 1975, s 1(1)(b) (I(PFD)A 1975) allows former spouses to make a claim for financial relief against the estate of a deceased person. This would not be appropriate in a case where the court had effected a clean break. Section 15(1) of the I(PFD)A 1975 provides that, on a decree of divorce, separation or nullity the court can, if it considers it just to do so, make an order that the other party shall not be entitled to apply under the I(PFD)A 1975 against the estate of the deceased party. This is commonly done in clean break cases but it is a separate consideration and will not always be appropriate, for example, in the 'no-money' cases discussed above. The court will not make this order unless asked so you should take care not to overlook it.

4.4.3.4   Extension of terms

Where there is a direction under the MCA 1973, s 28(1A) barring applications for an extension/variation of the term, that is final and the court cannot reconsider it.

According to the guidance in *C v C*, there should not be a situation where a fixed-term order for periodical payments is made without an s 28(1A) order. However, it does happen and when it does the payee may apply for an extension/variation under s 31. He or she must do so before the term expires, as once the term has expired the right to apply for extensions is lost.

4.4.3.5   Advising the client

It is vital to appreciate, and to make it clear to the client, that a clean break will, except in exceptional circumstances, bring a permanent *end* to all the client's claims for provision (see *Hewitson v Hewitson* [1995] 1 All ER 472). Contrast this with a nominal maintenance order. This is an order for periodical payments of a low or token sum, which can be varied if circumstances change. Clean break orders are not susceptible to variation. Appeals or applications for further provision will only be possible in cases of fraud or the like. This will be an advantage for the person against whom provision is sought, but it must be considered seriously by the spouse seeking provision. Sometimes clients are very keen to get a clean break even when your advice is that they would be, or might in the future be, entitled to maintenance. In such circumstances, if a client insists on instructing you to obtain a clean break, you should get them to endorse your brief to confirm that they have listened to and understood your advice.

4.4.3.6   Summary of common orders

Open-ended order for maintenance
This is appropriate where the dependency of the payee will continue for a long time or for life or where there is uncertainty. This is often the case where there are young

children or where the payee is older and the court is uncertain that she will be able to become self-sufficient.

Maintenance order with a term and s 28 (1A) direction

This will most often be used where the court is satisfied that after a period of readjustment the payee will be able to achieve a state of self-sufficiency, for example, a younger wife with a large part of her working life ahead of her.

Maintenance order with a term without s 28(1A) direction

This is contrary to judicial guidance, which says that if there is uncertainty then an order without term should be made (see **4.4.3.2**). However, this may be appropriate, for example, where there are older dependent children and the wife does have the means to achieve self-sufficiency, but the future dependency of the children cannot be ascertained with certainty.

Immediate clean break on income

This will be appropriate in circumstances where the court considers that there should not be an ongoing dependency, for example, where there are no children, the marriage is short, the wife is able to become self-supporting immediately or is already self-sufficient. It may be that the wife could have been entitled to some kind of maintenance but she gave that up in return for a greater share elsewhere in the package, such as an increased share in property, which preserved the overall balance and may also have decreased her income needs.

Capitalised maintenance, no periodical payments

This is a lump sum out of which the payee can provide maintenance for herself. This kind of solution can be used where there is a dependency but there is sufficient money to provide for that dependency with a capital fund and thus make a clean break possible.

Nominal maintenance order

This is an order for periodical payments of a token sum such as five pence per year. This kind of order can be used where it is thought that a clean break is possible and/or desirable but the circumstances are such that the payee should not be left without the ability to reapply. For example, if the payee is cohabiting but not remarried, she may be supported by the cohabitant for the time being but she does not have the certainty nor the legal rights that come with remarriage. Another situation where nominal payments may be appropriate is where the husband simply cannot afford maintenance but there is a chance that his situation will improve, so it should be left open to the wife to reapply if he becomes able to afford to support her.

4.4.4 Finding a starting point—fairness, non-discrimination and equality

The s 25 factors govern the exercise of the court's discretion—but it is necessary to consider what the court, in the exercise of its discretion, is trying to achieve. Is there a fundamental basis, or starting point, for the court in deciding how to approach issues of financial relief? In decided cases, there is regular reference to the objectives of 'achieving fairness' and 'doing justice'. In *White v White* [1998] 2 FLR 310, Butler-Sloss LJ stated: 'Sections 25 and 25A provide the guidelines and require the court to have regard to all the circumstances of the individual case and to exercise the discretion of the court to do justice between the parties.' In *Cowan v Cowan* [2001] 2 FLR 192 at 213, Thorpe LJ stated that: 'the unexpressed objective of the [s 25] exercise is to arrive at a fair solution'. It is helpful to consider now what 'doing justice' and 'arriving at a fair solution' have been held to mean in more practical terms.

After the passing of the MCA 1973, the first major case to deal generally with how discretion should be exercised was *Wachtel v Wachtel* [1973] Fam 72. This case proposed the use of the 'one-third rule' as a starting point for evaluating how to apportion the assets of the marriage. Essentially, it meant that a fair division of assets in a standard situation could mean one-third going to the wife and two-thirds going to the husband. Within a few years this 'rule' became subject to regular criticism and numerous court decisions emphasised that the only proper approach was to consider the statutory factors. The 'one-third rule' is now totally extinct and is of historic interest only.

A principle that partly replaced the 'one-third rule', at least for cases where there was a significant level of income and capital, was that of seeking to meet the applicant's 'reasonable needs'. This term was developed by the courts as a way of interpreting the statutory factors and achieved widespread use, even outside of bigger-money cases. However, there are many situations where there is insufficient money to meet all 'reasonable needs', or where such a principle is inappropriate, as both spouses have built up and have good claims to income and capital.

The principle of 'reasonable needs' has now been replaced by the guidance of the House of Lords in *White v White* [2000] 2 FLR 981 and the subsequent line of authority, although not without some comment and difference of opinion. Although *White* was a case involving significant assets, which were more than sufficient to meet needs, Lord Nicholls set out some principles to be followed in future cases.

(a) It is a principle 'of universal application' that there should be no discrimination between husband and wife in their respective roles. Fairness dictates that, whatever the division of labour, this should not prejudice either party when considering the statutory factors.

(b) When considering how to give effect to the factors, the judge should check his or her provisional views against 'the yardstick of equality of division'. 'As a general guide, equality should be departed from only if, and to the extent that, there is good reason for doing so.'

(c) However, although equality is a 'yardstick' or a 'cross-check', it is not a 'starting point' nor a 'presumption'.

(d) The concept of 'reasonable needs' is a misconception. The wording of the statute is simply 'needs' and no general qualification of this is desirable.

There has been some debate about how much *White* applies outside of big-money cases. Lord Nicholls' speech makes it clear that the non-discrimination principle is 'of universal application'. The 'yardstick of equality' is a little less straightforward, being a 'yardstick' but not a 'starting point'.

In *Cowan v Cowan* (which was a big-money case), the Court of Appeal declined to take the opportunity to provide authoritative guidance on how *White* should be applied across all types of cases, but Thorpe LJ said in his judgment: 'The decision in *White* clearly does not introduce a rule of equality. The yardstick of equality is a cross check against discrimination. Fairness is the rule . . .'. In *Cordle v Cordle* [2002] 1 FLR 207 (which was not a big-money case), Thorpe LJ said: 'There is no rule in *White* that district judges must produce equality of outcome unless there are good reasons to justify departure.'

In *Miller v Miller; McFarlane v McFarlane* [2006] 1 FLR 1186 the House of Lords again considered the question of fairness: 'In arriving at a fair outcome, three elements must be considered: the needs of the parties and children; compensation for any economic disadvantage arising from the marriage; and sharing the fruits of the matrimonial partnership.' Baroness Hale added this important qualification: 'The ultimate objective is to give each party an equal start on the road to independent living.' In addition the remit of periodical payments was extended beyond maintenance to include compensation in appropriate cases (see **4.4.3.2** above).

In the High Court the new guidance was applied with a sense of restraint. In *RP v RP* [2006] EWHC 3409 (Fam) Coleridge J said care had to be taken in ensuring that the guidance in *Miller* was not elevated to some kind of quasi-statutory amendment—it was the commentary of the House of Lords on a well-trodden statute now in its fourth decade. He stated that it was questionable whether 'compensation', which did not appear in the statute, added anything to 'financial . . . obligations and responsibilities' under s 25(2)(b). In *H v H* [2007] EWHC 459 (Fam) Charles J said the fact that both parties to a marital relationship are free to bring it to an end, along with its cooperation and common goals, leads to the conclusion that by reference to the rationale of compensation or sharing, the lower-income earner is not, and should not be, entitled to long-term economic parity.

The Court of Appeal however has pulled in a slightly different direction. In *Charman v Charman* [2007] EWCA Civ 503 Potter P states that the 'sharing principle' (of the three strands identified by the House of Lords in *Miller; McFarlane*) is the dominant principle in big-money cases and that it should be the starting point of ancillary relief consideration—rather than come at the end of the exercise. He says that the sharing principle should come before needs, unless needs produces a bigger award. He also limits Baroness Hale's views on non-matrimonial property as applying only to short-marriage cases and as being less preferable to Lord Nicholls' more 'logical' view.

Some commentators said that this marked the end of the 'yardstick of equality' and that the principle of fairness should now be understood as having a starting point of sharing. This was a little premature—it has to be remembered that this is a big-money case and that in most cases courts are mainly concerned with stretching available resources to cover adequately the needs of the parties—as Lord Nicholls put it in *Miller; McFarlane*: 'In most cases the search for fairness begins and ends at that stage.'

The yardstick of equality, involving in any given case a calculation of what equal division would be, should still be a useful cross-check against discrimination—a tool rather than an objective. In most cases, resources are limited. Various factors, such as cost of living and children and the need to house everyone, will have such weight that, after they are carefully balanced in a non-discriminatory way, they may well produce an outcome that is unequal (in terms of the allocation of resources), but fair (in terms of all the circumstances and relevant factors).

In most 'normal' cases there will be little or nothing remaining over which to have a protracted debate about the value of various types of contribution. This is often true even in 'well-off' families with well-above-average incomes, as the perceived needs and entitlements tend to be of higher value—the houses cost more, the living standard to be met is higher, there are school fees and other private outgoings—so there is still nothing remaining that is perceived as a surplus to needs. It should be said that in normal-money cases, even though contribution may not be a leading factor, it is still relevant and the non-discrimination principle will apply. It may be more important in cases where there is a small enterprise to be divided or where there are no children; see *Foster v Foster* [2003] 2 FLR 299, CA for the principle applied to a small business in a short, childless marriage.

Two years post-*Charman*, it is still true that the only overall objective that is always relevant and can never be departed from is fairness—and the starting point for achieving this is always the s 25 factors. It is well described by Thorpe LJ in *Cordle*, at 214:

> The second difficulty that needs mention is the impact the decision of their Lordships in *White* has had upon what may be described as a routine district judge case...The first point, that cannot be overemphasised, is that there is no rule that district judges must produce equality of outcome...The cross-check of equality of outcome is intended to be a safeguard against discrimination...it is the first duty of the court to apply the s 25 criteria in search of the overarching objective of fairness...in the typical...case the district judge will always look first to the housing needs of the parties...the court's first concern will be to provide a home for the primary carer and the children...where there is sufficient to go beyond that, the court's concern will be to provide the means for the absent parent to rehouse...Another factor that should be considered is buttressing the ability of one or other of the parties to work...if there be cash beyond that the judge has to look to what in his estimation is the fair result.

These considerations will apply in many standard cases, but they are, of course, not exclusive. The only universal rule is to apply the s 25(2) criteria to all the circumstances of the case (giving first consideration to the welfare of the children) and to arrive at a fair result that avoids discrimination. This approach has recently been reiterated by the Court of Appeal in *B v B (Ancillary Relief)* [2008] 2 FLR 1627, where the court emphasised that there is no rule that equal division is the starting point in all cases, but that the financial position of the parties and s 25 factors are the starting point. The Court of Appeal emphasised that in all cases the objective was fairness and that the yardstick of equality is to be applied to every outcome and only to be departed from to the extent that there is a good reason for doing so: paras [24] and [25].

4.4.5   The rich couple

The application of reasonable needs has been done away with by *White*. So, too, in theory anyway, has the discrimination between wealth-creating work and 'homely management' of the house and children. In big-money cases, there has been great emphasis on the need to justify departure from the yardstick of equality. In doing this, there is often (although not exclusively) a focus on contribution. This is partly because wealth tends to render most of the other factors irrelevant; but it also shows that, while the courts are anxious to avoid discriminating with regard to the nature of the contribution made by the parties, they have still been willing to find differences in the level of contribution made and to reflect that in the division of the assets. In *Cowan*, departure from equality was justified by the fact that 'the husband's contribution...was truly exceptional'. In *Lambert v Lambert*, at first instance, departure was justified by 'the really special contribution of the husband'. However, on appeal (*Lambert v Lambert* [2003] 1 FLR 139), the Court of Appeal became much more wary of the issue of special contribution, making 'a cautious acknowledgement that special contribution remains a legitimate possibility but only in special circumstances'. Courts continued to limit the concept of special contribution and in *Miller; McFarlane* [2006] 1 FLR 1186 the House of Lords stated that 'the question of contributions should be approached in much the same way as conduct. Exceptional or special contributions should only be regarded as a factor pointing away from equality of division when it would be inequitable to proceed otherwise.'

It will generally be easier to achieve a clean break where there are substantial assets, but continuing maintenance may be ordered, for example, where it is not reasonable to expect the claimant spouse to go out to work or where the payer's huge salary may come to a predictable end. An alternative may sometimes be for a sufficiently large lump sum to be ordered to buy out the right to continuing maintenance (see **4.4.3.4**).

4.4.6   The poor couple

There are unfortunately many cases where the joint assets of the spouses are not sufficient to provide properly for both. Where the money that has managed to finance one household is split, there may simply not be enough to go around. This is, perhaps, the most obvious and frequently used reason for departing from 'the yardstick of equality'. There may not be an easy solution in such cases, and you will need a particularly practical understanding of the problems that such a couple may face, and a thorough understanding of the social security benefit system. This knowledge will need to be both detailed and up to date.

One spouse cannot normally expect the state to take over the expense of caring for the other spouse, as that is a legal liability of the spouse. However, it is appropriate when assessing the potential income of a party to include non-means-related state benefits. Generally, parties are expected to apply for benefits designed to assist people in their position; a commonly occurring example is the working family tax credit. Clearly, it would be unreasonable and illogical to order a spouse to pay maintenance if that would put the payer below subsistence level, as the effect would simply be that the payer would be in need of state benefit him or herself (*Stockford v Stockford* [1981] 3 FLR 58) and in such a situation a maintenance order will not normally be made. This is not an invariable rule, particularly in cases where a paying party has taken on new liabilities irresponsibly and without proper regard for his or her obligations to his or her children and/or former spouse (*Campbell v Campbell* [1998] 1 FLR 828). Generally, though, in a case where joint resources are so low that it is inevitable that one spouse will have to rely on state benefits, it may be appropriate that a nominal order or no order be made for maintenance, and the claimant spouse be left to rely on state benefits.

Where resources are limited, the 'net-effect' approach can be used in considering maintenance payments. This was first enunciated in *Stockford* by Ormrod LJ and is still useful practice. The point is to calculate as accurately as possible how much the payer can afford to pay towards the maintenance of the other spouse in any case where the need for financial provision may outweigh the available resources. Attention is centred on the sum each party will have left to live on. The object is to ensure that the payer's net income (after deductions, including the maintenance payable to the spouse) is not reduced below subsistence level (that is, the income needs of the payer's new household as indicated by the appropriate income support level and the cost of his or her accommodation).

There is no set formula for what is basically a common-sense exercise. It involves ascertaining the net income from all sources for each of the parties, adding or subtracting to that according to the amount of the proposed order and allowing for any tax changes that may result. This gives the income of each party if the proposed order were made, which figures can be compared and related to their respective needs, and the hypothetical order adjusted accordingly.

Where there are children, note that a child support calculation will have to be made first. If the payer is not well off, this may well leave little or nothing for any additional maintenance for the caring spouse.

4.4.7 The short marriage

Since *Miller; McFarlane* [2006] 1 FLR 1186 (see **4.3.3.7** above) all pre-*White* authorities on the effect of a short marriage must be treated with caution.

Probably authorities relating to very short marriages—relationships that in effect never got off the ground—are still useful guidance. If a marriage is short, then this may be an overriding factor which in effect dictates the whole basis for provision. After a very short marriage (lasting weeks), there may be no provision at all (although a brief marriage can be debilitating; see *C v C* (*Financial Relief: Short Marriage*) [1997] 2 FLR 26). After a marriage lasting months, provision is likely to be on the basis of what the applicant has lost by the marriage. Another feature may be to provide the wife with maintenance for a limited term sufficient to enable her to rejoin the labour market, although note the *dicta* of Ward LJ in *C v C* to the effect that, just because the marriage is short, it does not automatically mean that there should be a term.

However, while these may be the effects of a short marriage on the overall package of provision, it is essential to note that, as always, all the circumstances and factors must be considered. The existence of a child of the marriage will almost certainly alter the picture completely. Foreign cultural factors may also alter the court's approach to a short marriage (see **4.4.8.4**).

For marriages long enough to be measured in years the best starting point is probably *Foster v Foster* [2003] 2 FLR 299, CA, which was cited with approval in *Miller; McFarlane*. In this case, a four-year marriage without children, Hale LJ restored a DJ's order that intended to give back to the parties what they had brought into the marriage (and spent after separation) while sharing equally between them, despite different levels of financial contribution, the assets they had accumulated during the marriage. For an example of a very short marriage of less than a year where there was a child, see *B v B* (*Mesher Order*) [2003] 2 FLR 285, Family Division. Munby J made large (relative to the assets) orders for indefinite periodical payments and a lump sum (for housing) that left the husband short of capital. The judge said that the existence of the child meant that effectively the wife would be making a contribution to this marriage for two decades, and that her earning capacity would be severely reduced, while the husband's large earning capacity meant that he would be able to rebuild his capital. These factors meant that it was fair and necessary to make significant and long-term provision in her favour.

In cases where there is a surplus after meeting the parties' needs, short duration is a factor that might justify departure from equality, particularly in respect of non-matrimonial property (see **4.3.3.3** for the leading views in *Miller; McFarlane*) Baroness Hale takes a slightly more expansive view of the possible effect of a short marriage, noting that it is a statutory requirement to consider it.

See also **4.3.3.7**.

4.4.8 Special circumstances and assets

The facts of an individual case may reveal some special circumstances in the position of either spouse, or with regard to the assets available for provision, which may inevitably have some practical bearing on the basis on which financial provision can be ordered.

4.4.8.1 A business forming part of the assets

One type of asset that may require special consideration is a business or an interest in a business. If either or both spouses are involved in the running of a business, there may be complex problems in deciding to what extent the business should be taken into account, how the business should be valued and how provision might be made from a business, as it may be difficult to extract money from a business without prejudicing its chances of success. Expert assistance may well be required in dealing with accounts, taxation, the marketability of shares and future projections for business success. For examples, see *Mubarak v Mubarak* [2001] 1 FLR 673 and *A v A* [2000] *Family Law* 470. For thorough consideration of how to value a business for ancillary relief purposes, see [2004] *Family Law* 187.

Historically, there has been a reluctance by the courts to 'kill the goose that lays the golden egg'. The income generated by a business is often more important than the cash that could be raised by selling it. However, if one of the parties is retiring from the business or if the business was run together by the separating parties, then it may be appropriate to realise the value of the business. After *White*, there was a trend, in big-money cases, in favour of selling business assets if necessary to reflect equality of contribution; see *Parra v Parra* [2003] 1 FLR 942 (and also discussion of *Lambert* and *Cowan* at **4.4.5**). However, there is now a greater tendency to try to find ways of preserving the business. See *F v F* (*Clean Break: Balance of Fairness*) [2003] 1 FLR 847, dealing with the fairly common situation of an illiquid business. Singer J preserved the business by ordering ongoing maintenance (rather than a lump sum that could only be raised by selling the business) to the wife in a situation where a clean break would otherwise have been quite appropriate. For a very creative solution to illiquidity, see *R v R* (*Lump Sum Repayments*) [2004] 1 FLR 928, where, without selling the family business, the husband would have been left with £448,000 and the wife with £30,000, which was obviously not an acceptable outcome. The High Court ordered the husband to make a lump sum payment by 240 monthly instalments; as a lump sum order these payments would continue if the wife remarried and also were subject to variation if there were unforeseen circumstances. In *R v R* (*Financial Relief: Company Valuation*) [2005] 2 FLR 365 the husband was given five years to pay a lump sum of £1,000,000 but was incentivised by early payment discounts of up to 20 per cent.

4.4.8.2   Agreements

At the time of writing, there has been an increased interest by the press (and perhaps the public) in the topic of pre-marital agreements (these are also called 'ante-marital' and 'pre-nuptial' agreements). This has been stimulated by two significant cases: *MacLeod v MacLeod* [2009] 1 FLR 641 (a Privy Council case on appeal from the Isle of Man) and *Radmacher v Granatino* [2009] 1 FLR 1566. These cases reflect the significant movement by the courts to give greater weight to agreements reached between the parties in relation to their finances. Care needs to be taken, however, when approaching the issue of agreements, to distinguish between three different types, since the court's approach to each is not wholly the same. They are: pre-marital agreements, post-marital (or 'post-nuptial') agreements and post-separation agreements. There is growing pressure, evident in the legal press, for the first of these categories to be made binding. *MacLeod* suggests that this should only happen through legislation. The Law Commission is considering the effect of pre-marital agreements and is due to report in 2012. Unless and until there is such a change in the law, what is not in doubt is that no type of agreement between the parties whose marriage ends in divorce can oust the jurisdiction of the courts (*Hyman v Hyman* [1929] AC 601). This was reiterated in relation to pre-marital agreements in *MacLeod* (at para 31). The existence of an agreement between the parties is a circumstance that the court is required to take into account. The more difficult question is how much weight to attach to it. A first consideration will be to assess whether the agreement was reached in good faith; the presence of fraud, misrepresentation, duress or mistake would almost certainly render the agreement worthless, in the same way that it would in any civil case.

In relation to pre-marital agreements, guidance was given in *K v K* [2003] 1 FLR 120, where the court set out a comprehensive checklist of factors to be considered. Recently, in *Crossley v Crossley* [2008] 1 FLR 1467, Thorpe LJ expressed the view that, on the facts of that case (short, childless marriage between two independent, wealthy individuals who had both been previously married and both consulted lawyers), the pre-nuptial agreement was a factor of 'magnetic' importance. In *Radmacher v Granatino*, the Court of Appeal went so far as to suggest that they should be treated like any other contract; certainly it was not prepared to give much weight to some of the factors in the *K v K* list: the need for independent legal advice, full and frank disclosure, provision for children in the event they are born and fairness in meeting the needs of the parties. Emphasis was placed firmly on the issue of the consent of the contracting parties. At para 78, Rix LJ put it this way:

> barring misrepresentation or fraud, or undue influence, or such other defect serious enough to remove the necessary basis of consent, the pre-nuptial agreement, whether viewed as a contract or a mere legally ineffective agreement, stands as a matter to which regard must be had for the purposes of section 25.

The rationale for this (at para 38) appears to be that fairness and justice require the exercise of the court's discretion, but also that weight should be given to the parties' autonomy in making such agreements. This somewhat controversial case is most helpfully considered in [2009] *Family Law* 816, where the point is made that since it could be argued that the Court of Appeal declined to be bound by *MacLeod*, an appeal to the Supreme Court may well follow. Interesting as these developments are, one should not lose sight of the fact that these issues will probably only be relevant in a very small number of cases (where there are substantial assets) and are unlikely to be those met in the early days of practice.

As far as post-marital agreements are concerned, this was the main issue in *MacLeod*. The Privy Council held that such agreements are valid and enforceable, subject to the issue of whether they have been reached in good faith. They are subject to the court's powers of variation under MCA 1973, s 35. The court will look at the circumstances when the agreement was made and consider whether there has been a significant change which could render the financial arrangements manifestly unjust. For an example of undue influence in a post-nuptial agreement, see *NA v MA* [2006] EWHC 2900 (Fam), where Baron J considered the subtle and particular pressures that parties can be subject to within a marriage relationship. Here the husband had effectively threatened to end the marriage if she did not sign and such legal advice that she received was poor. The judge gave no weight to the agreement.

Post-separation agreements are the third type of agreements which might be considered by the courts. These are governed by the line of authorities following *Edgar v Edgar* [1980] 3 All ER 887. Ormrod LJ said that regard must be had to the conduct of both parties leading up to the agreement and their subsequent conduct in consequence of it. He highlighted circumstances that would be relevant: undue pressure, exploitation of a dominant position, inadequate knowledge, (possibly) bad legal advice, an unforeseen change of circumstance. He also stated the principle that formal agreements, properly and fairly arrived at, should not be displaced unless there are good and substantial grounds for believing that an injustice will otherwise be done.

The issue of bad legal advice was considered by the Court of Appeal in *Harris v Manahan* [1997] 1 FLR 205. Although bad legal advice is a circumstance to be taken into account, where there was a consent order it was a matter of public policy that there had to be a finality in litigation and the order would not be interfered with save in the most exceptional case of the cruellest injustice.

Where the parties reach a separation agreement and subsequently apply for ancillary relief, the court will consider the *Edgar* principles. If the agreement was fairly reached, then the court will hold it to be one of the most important factors which is highly persuasive, but not binding. In *A v B (Financial Relief: Agreements)* [2005] 2 FLR 730, Black J held that an agreement of this kind should be taken into account under the heading of conduct, as one of the considerations to which the judge must give weight in applying the statutory criteria. See also *S v S (Ancillary Relief)* [2009] 1 FLR 254 where Eleanor King J held that a post-separation agreement reached after round-table meetings, which was then encapsulated in a draft order, was of such magnetic importance that it must necessarily dominate the discretionary process. It was appropriate for the case to proceed on the notice to show cause why the draft order should be perfected.

4.4.8.3   The millionaire's defence

This 'defence' is essentially a defence against disclosure in cases involving very substantial assets, where the respondent says that he will meet any order the court might make (*Thyssen-Bornemisza v Thyssen-Bornemisza (No 2)* [1985] FLR 1069). If the court considers that any difference between the, say, £400 million that the husband admits to having and the, say, £1,000 million that the wife is claiming he has will not make any significant difference to the award it is likely to make, then it can agree to dispense with lengthy and costly disclosure. Whether the 'defence' survives post-*White* is uncertain.

In *J v V (Disclosure: Offshore Corporations)* [2004] 1 FLR 1042, Coleridge J said that there may still be a role for such concessions in some circumstances, such as a marriage involving independently obtained wealth that was of short or medium duration, or where the parties wanted to avoid acrimonious proceedings and where there was to be a presumption of no order as to costs.

However, in *McFarlane v McFarlane* and *Parlour v Parlour* [2004] EWCA Civ 872, where the wealthy husbands had not bothered with proper financial disclosure, Thorpe LJ stated *obiter*, 'We were told by the Bar that a practice has grown up for substantial earners to decline any statement of their needs on the grounds that they can afford any order that the court is likely to make. These appeals must put an end to that practice.' That sounds like the final word. But in that case the court was annoyed by the husbands' cavalier attitude to disclosure. In addition the husbands were certainly not saying to the court, 'make any order you like and I'll pay it'. Probably they were not able to make that offer—wealthy though they were, they did not possess the sums involved in *Thyssen*.

Perhaps there is scope for the defence to survive—but only as the *billionaire's* defence!

4.4.8.4   Foreign cultural factors

If the foreign or cultural background of the parties imports significant features relating to marriage or divorce, then the court can take these into account. The court can consider how the matter would be dealt with in the foreign jurisdiction and treat this as a relevant factor, giving it whatever weight seems appropriate to achieve a fair outcome (*Otobo v Otobo* [2003] 1 FLR 192). In *A v T (Ancillary Relief: Cultural Factors)* [2004] 1 FLR 977, an Iranian couple had married under shariah law in Iran but the matrimonial home was in England. The marriage broke down after only seven weeks and the wife returned to Iran. The Iranian court ordered the husband to pay the marriage portion—a sum of £60,000—but took no further action. The wife applied for divorce in England. It was held that the husband should pay the wife a lump sum of £35,000 if he gave her a talaq divorce within a specified time, otherwise he must pay the full marriage portion of £60,000, as this was the sum she would have received from the Iranian court in the circumstances.

4.4.9   Deciding on the appropriate basis

After consideration of all the factors and circumstances, an appropriate overall basis must be settled upon for each case. There are no shortcuts; every case turns on its own facts. However, it is possible to make some general observations. They are not comprehensive, and they can overlap, or even conflict in a case, but as a very simple general guide:

    (a) If there are young children, their needs will be central to the overall package. Depending on the assets available and the husband's housing needs, this may require that the former matrimonial home be transferred or settled.

    (b) If there are no children, the primary objective will be to achieve a clean break, if this is possible with the assets available. A clean break cannot be achieved if the court is not satisfied on the evidence that an applicant spouse can become self-sufficient.

    (c) If any factor clearly dominates the case, such as the shortness of the marriage or very bad conduct (rare), this may determine the overall basis for provision.

    (d) Even where there are no children, one of the primary concerns of the court will be to ensure that the parties are adequately housed.

    (e) As regards level of provision, the balance of needs against ability to provide will be the basic approach. Pensions should be considered as part of this balance.

    (f) In any event, whatever broad starting point is appropriate, all the factors can go into the balance in deciding the overall package.

There will not always be a single appropriate basis for a case. There may be alternatives, for example, between a clean break and continuing provision. If there are, the options should be fully discussed with the client.

4.4.10   The home and the overall package

Once the relevant factors have been assessed and a suitable overall basis for provision has been identified, the details of the overall package must be considered, balancing capital provision, income provision, provision for children, housing needs, pension needs, etc. *The interrelation of all the elements of a package must be considered.* For example, if a spouse gets a capital asset, such as a house, will he or she have sufficient income to pay for it and maintain it? Alternatively, if a spouse has to borrow money to pay a lump sum, the effect of the repayments on his or her own income and the income available to pay maintenance must be considered.

    In many cases, where the couple own their own home, that will be central to the package, as it will be the main asset they own. In considering what should happen to the home, it is important to check whether the house is in a sole name or joint names, what its value is, what mortgage attaches to it, and who has made mortgage or other payments in respect of the house.

To outline the main possibilities for the home:

(a) The house may simply be sold, especially if there is to be a clean break. Consideration should be given to the share of the proceeds each spouse will get (noting that it is generally better to do this in terms of proportionate shares, expressed as a percentage of whatever equity is eventually realised, rather than set figures, in case the expected value is not achieved). Sale may not be a fair option if a spouse is old or ill, or may have trouble finding alternative accommodation. The costs of sale need to be taken into account: this usually includes solicitors' and estate agents' fees.

(b) The home may be left in or transferred outright into the name of one spouse only. Again this may form the basis for a clean break, and it should help to avoid continuing problems about paying for repairs, and possible future tax liability. However, if the home is the sole capital asset of the parties, it may simply be unfair for one spouse to get the full value, depriving the other spouse of all his or her capital. In such a case, some sort of settlement or charge may be fairer.

(c) The home may be transferred to the ownership of one spouse, subject to a charge in favour of the other, especially if it is needed as a home for the children. This may be an advantage for the custodial spouse, but ties up the interest of the other spouse. It is usually better to express the value of the charge as a percentage of the net equity realised on eventual sale. It is very important to be very clear and unambiguous about when and in what circumstances the charge will be realisable (often referred to as 'triggers').

(d) The home may be settled under a trust for sale, although this happens less often these days, the charge back being more commonly used. There are potential difficulties and uncertainty with a settlement, the effect of which leaves both parties in ownership of the former matrimonial home and, therefore, in a continuing financial relationship and both of them dependant on its future sale. Great care must be given to deciding the terms of the settlement, especially what interest each is to have in the house, and when it will be sold. Again, proportionate shares are better than cash figures. Two widely known examples of such trusts follow:

   (i) *Mesher v Mesher* [1980] 1 All ER 126. Home settled to be sold when the children were 18 or left full-time education. The wife to pay the rates and the spouses to pay half the mortgage each (note that this particular feature is very unusual these days—the resident spouse will usually be expected to pay). Each spouse to have a half share in the proceeds of sale.

   (ii) *Martin v Martin* [1978] Fam 12. No children, husband had alternative accommodation. Home settled, not to be sold while the wife was unmarried and lived in it. Each spouse to get half of the proceeds on sale.

(e) If the home is not owned but is rented, then, unless both spouses are to move out, consider what names are on the lease, and whether there may be a possibility, if appropriate, of transferring the lease into another name.

4.4.11 Being realistic

Every aspect of the proposed overall package must be checked to ensure that it 'works'. It must be realistic as regards resources available for payments, realistic as to needs and realistic in terms of what each spouse has left to live on. Check that it is adequate for the payee and affordable by the payer.

Just as you find out full details of the resources each has before the application is made, you should look at the precise position that both parties will be left in if the suggested provision is ordered. You should do the arithmetic and make it clear to your client what he or she will have in income and capital terms, so that future plans can be made. You should do the same exercise for the other side; you will need to be able to persuade them that your proposals are a practical solution, or, failing settlement, persuade the court of this.

Look ahead as far as possible. It is important to bear in mind what changes in your client's position are reasonably foreseeable, and to make sure that the provision made does provide for the future as far as is reasonably possible. For example, if a house is settled, consider what position the spouses might be left in when it is sold, looking at what their ages and resources are likely to be then.

4.4.12 Taxation and benefits

The potential relevance of state benefits must be taken into account and explained to your client. It has been made clear by the courts that it is also part of the barrister's duty in every case to calculate tax implications and explain them to the client.

The principles for the taxation of maintenance are outlined in **Chapter 12**. The income tax effects for the payer and the recipient of maintenance should be calculated and explained to them.

The possibilities of a charge to capital gains tax should never be ignored on divorce, especially if the couple are relatively wealthy (for an example, see *M v M* [1988] 1 FLR 389). The possibility of future liability to capital gains tax where a house is settled is also important, as the spouse who is not living in the home will have no exemption from tax when the house is sold.

4.5 Maintenance pending suit

Marital breakdown can cause immediate financial strains. Maintenance pending suit is simply an interim application for short-term maintenance intended to 'tide' a party over, where necessary, until a final determination of the application(s) for financial provision can be made and put into effect. Such orders, which take the form of requiring one spouse to make periodical payments to the other, are therefore very much a temporary measure.

4.5.1 Law

Once a petition has been filed, maintenance pending suit may be ordered to be paid by one spouse to the other. Of necessity, it will not be possible to have full information available at this stage of the case, so the court will only seek to determine what figure is reasonable for immediate needs and what the respondent's short-term ability to pay is, rather than seeking to make complex calculations or to apply all the factors outlined above. However, it is still important to present the figures you do have and the arguments for what is reasonable as clearly as possible. It may also be necessary to seek a separate maintenance order in favour of any children.

The MCA 1973, s 22 states as follows:

On a petition for divorce, nullity of marriage or judicial separation, the court may make an order for maintenance pending suit, that is to say, an order requiring either party to the marriage to make to the other such periodical payments for his or her maintenance and for such term, being a term beginning not earlier than the date of the presentation of the petition and ending with the date of the determination of the suit, as the court thinks reasonable.

Do not confuse maintenance pending suit (made before the court has power to make a final order for financial provision) with other interim financial provision orders. The latter are appropriate where the court has *power* to make a final order (ie, after decree absolute), but is not yet in a *position* to do so—perhaps because some relevant information is still outstanding. Interim orders for financial provision are also usually confined to periodical payments orders (*Wicks v Wicks* [1998] 3 FLR 470).

4.5.2   Procedure

The procedure for obtaining maintenance pending suit (and other interim orders) was modified by the Family Proceedings (Amendment No 2) Rules 1999 and is set out in the FPR 1991, r 2.69F. An application can be made at any stage in the proceedings by issuing a notice of application, the date fixed for hearing being at least 14 days later. If the application is made before Form E (which provides details of financial resources and needs) has been filed, the applicant must file and serve on the respondent a draft of the order sought, together with a short sworn statement that provides relevant information about means and explains why the order sought is necessary. Similarly, if the respondent has not yet filed a copy of Form E, he or she must file a short sworn statement of means at least seven days before the date fixed for hearing. Applications for maintenance pending suit are commonly made at the first appointment (see **5.3.8**).

4.5.3   Practice

When preparing for the hearing, you should bear in mind that at this stage the court will focus on what the applicant really needs to cover reasonable outgoings, together with what the respondent can reasonably afford to pay. To present information on this clearly and concisely, it is best to draw up a schedule which summarises the income of each party from all sources and the reasonable outgoings of each. If relevant, also include other liabilities and assets that may have a bearing on the appropriate order. Ensure that all figures are given on the same basis, ie, monthly or weekly, net or gross.

If you act for the applicant, your first objective will be to show the shortfall between your client's income and reasonable outgoings; your second is to show how the respondent can reasonably afford to cover this gap. If you act for the respondent, your main aims will be to show that the applicant could earn more, and/or is extravagant, and/or that in any event your client cannot afford to pay the order sought. To convince the judge of your case and your credibility, it is very important to use accurate and full figures.

At the interim stage, the DJ will be concerned to meet immediate needs, not to try to prejudge in any detail what will be ordered when financial provision is finally decided. Therefore, awards tend to be on the low side. It is not possible to obtain interim lump sum orders under s 22—a lacuna which has been much criticised, especially in light of the increasing number of orders that contain an element to cater for legal costs, which would be much more sensibly dealt with by a lump sum.

It is permissible for the court to include in any award an element of legal costs; see *A v A* (*Maintenance Pending Suit: Provision for Legal Fees*) [2001] 1 FLR 377 and *G v G* (*Maintenance Pending Suit: Payment of Costs*) [2003] *Family Law* 393. As sources of funding for ancillary relief applications diminish this method of funding litigation is gaining in importance (as are any other ideas for funding, including bank loans, see [2007] *Family Law*, April, 'Funding Ancillary Relief Cases: The New Costs Rules').

Uncertainty was caused by the (apparently inadvertent) introduction of an exceptional circumstance test by Thorpe LJ in *Moses–Taiga v Taiga* [2006] 1 FLR 1074. This was cleared up by the Court of Appeal in *Currey v Currey* [2007] 1 FLR 946, which is now the leading authority. The initial overarching enquiry is into whether the applicant for a costs allowance can demonstrate that she cannot reasonably procure legal advice and representation by any other means. For a case on the process, see *Re G* (*Maintenance Pending Suit*) [2007] 1 FLR 1674 and for an article outlining the problems caused by continuous cuts in legal aid and remuneration see [2007] *Family Law*, March, 'Maintenance Pending Suit and the Costs Allowance'. The position is not likely to improve, given the imminent implementation of further cuts.

4.6 The Proceeds of Crime Act 2002

The POCA 2002 came into force on 24 February 2003 and caused lawyers in all areas of practice to reconsider carefully how they go about advising and representing their clients. It seemed to impose a duty on all lawyers in their dealings with clients, to make a report to the National Criminal Intelligence Service (NCIS) (now the Serious Organised Crime Agency (SOCA)) any time they had a suspicion that criminal property might be involved. Criminal property is widely defined and includes any money on which tax might not have been paid, where it should have been. In ancillary relief, where there is such emphasis on a thorough investigation of the finances of the parties, it is not uncommon to come across an element of a party's property that might not have been disclosed to the Inland Revenue. Often the amounts involved are very small, but POCA 2002 covers every sum, no matter how trivial. Having been compelled to make a disclosure to NCIS, the lawyer then also had to cease acting for the client until getting consent to do so from NCIS and, further, was not allowed to tell the client about the disclosure. It is a criminal offence under POCA 2002 to be involved in an arrangement concerning property and not disclose it to NCIS, with a maximum penalty of five years' imprisonment. Tipping the client off about the disclosure is a further criminal offence.

Happily, recent developments have reined back the ambit of POCA 2002. However, the Act in its amended form still exists and there are many activities which lawyers may perform in the course of their profession that may be caught by it. It is important to know the legislation, know the history of its implementation and to know the guidance from the Bar Council and other bodies. The most recent guidance from the Bar Council in relation to POCA 2002 and the Money Laundering Regulations 2007 (MLR 2007) (which came into force on 15 December 2007) was given in January 2008. Most of all it is important to understand that it is the barrister's individual responsibility to be familiar and up to date with all the developments and guidance relating to POCA 2002.

The relevant sections of POCA 2002 are summarised here. Essentially, s 328 creates the offence of 'being involved in an arrangement with criminal property' and the ordinary conduct of litigation can be caught under this definition (when, in conducting litigation, the lawyer comes to know about property that he suspects may be tainted).

For wider consideration of POCA 2002, see the **Professional Conduct Manual**, **Chapter 8**.

4.6.1 The legislation

Section 340 defines 'money laundering', 'criminal conduct' and 'criminal property'. The definitions are wide and include any property that may not have been declared for taxation purposes.

Sections 327–329 create offences of, respectively, dealing with criminal property, being involved in an arrangement concerning criminal property and possessing criminal property. It is a defence under ss 327–329 to make an authorised disclosure to the authorities, usually SOCA.

Section 330 creates an offence of failing to disclose where the person who should make the disclosure is in the regulated sector. Barristers are considered to be within the regulated sector (under MLR 2007).

Section 333, which created an offence of 'tipping off', has been amended (now s 33 A–D) and now only applies within the regulated sector. After a disclosure has been made to the authorities, it is an offence to make any disclosure (eg, to your client) that may prejudice any investigation. There is also an offence under s 342 of prejudicing an investigation *before* any disclosure has been made (eg, destroying relevant evidence). Various defences are available, including legal professional privilege.

Section 338 deals with the making of an authorised disclosure, which provides a defence to s 328.

4.6.2 Relevance to practice

This legislation had a strong effect on the practice of several areas of law, ancillary relief being one of them. The whole ancillary relief regime relies on an ethos of full and frank disclosure. With such disclosure putting clients at risk of prosecution, and lawyers in a position where they have to disclose hitherto confidential information to the police, and proceedings at risk of having to be halted every time this happens to await consent to continue from NCIS (now SOCA)—it is not hard to imagine how obstructive this could be to the administration of justice. In effect, in situations governed by POCA 2002, the concept of legal professional privilege had been done away with.

The matter was radically changed by the Court of Appeal in *Bowman v Fels* [2005] EWCA Civ 226, which effectively overrules *P v P (Ancillary Relief; Proceeds of Crime)* [2003] EWHC Fam 2260. The former was a relatively minor civil case concerning interests in a house, where disclosure had been made to NCIS over some work done on the property. The Bar Council, Law Society and NCIS intervened in order that the POCA issues could be fully argued in front of a senior constitution of the court. After dealing with the inconvenient fact that the parties in the substantive matter had settled their dispute at the door of court and the consequent problem of jurisdiction to continue the hearing, Brooke LJ went on to give an exhaustive examination of the issues. His conclusion was that the ordinary conduct of litigation by lawyers was not covered by POCA 2002, s 328. This includes any step taken by lawyers in litigation from the issue of proceedings and the securing of injunctive relief or a freezing order up to its final disposal by judgment. He stated that, 'Parliament cannot have intended that . . . steps taken by lawyers in order to determine or secure legal rights and remedies for their clients should involve them in "becoming concerned in an arrangement which . . . facilitates the acquisition, retention, use or control of criminal property", even if they suspected that the outcome of such proceedings might have such an effect.' He went on to say that s 328 was not intended to override legal professional privilege nor does it affect the terms on which lawyers are to have access to documents disclosed in the litigation process.

It is important to stress that there are professional activities that may be covered by POCA 2002 and by the MLR 2007. The Regulations and POCA 2002, s 330 apply to activities in the 'regulated sector' and some situations remain where s 328 could still apply to lawyers.

Lawyers acting in the course of business who are deemed to be 'relevant persons' will be subject to additional requirements under the MLR 2007 and are also at risk of criminal liability. Members of the Chancery Bar are those who are most likely to fall within the ambit of the MLR 2007, if they are involved in non-contentious advisory work, particularly in relation to business, taxation or property transactions and the setting up of trusts and companies, see MLR 2007, regs 3(1) and 3(9). You are advised to refer to the Bar Council Guidance on the MLR 2007, issued in January 2008.

The additional requirements under the MLR 2007 include such matters as having procedures for the proper identification of clients, for record keeping, for internal reporting and for the training of staff (see regs 5–9 and 19–21).

The risk of criminal liability is under POCA 2002, s 330 which is an offence by someone in the regulated sector of failing to disclose. If such a person suspects, or has reasonable grounds to suspect, on the basis of information that comes to them in the conduct of business in the regulated sector, that another person is engaged in money laundering, then they must make a disclosure to SOCA. Failure to do so is an offence. However, it is a defence if the person is a professional legal adviser and the information came to him in privileged circumstances (s 330(6)(b)). Section 330(10) clarifies situations of legal professional privilege but s 330(11) provides that the defence of privilege will not apply where the information is communicated with the intention of furthering a criminal purpose. The standard is objective and not subjective. It is important, therefore, for any piece of work that you do, to consider whether you have an obligation to disclose under s 330 and, if so, whether the defence under s 330(6) applies.

Note that there are other criminal offences that can be committed under POCA 2002, notably the amended offences of tipping off (s 333A–D) (see **4.6.1**).

So, while most activities are not covered by s 328 and most activities covered by the MLR 2007 are protected by privilege, there are areas that are subject to the force of some or all of the legislation. In his decision Brooke LJ dealt with the situation when parties agreed to the issues between them by settlement rather than in the direct conduct of litigation. His view was that such consensual resolution in a litigious context must also be covered by privilege and exempt from s 328, as, 'The consensual resolution of issues is an integral part of the conduct of ordinary civil litigation.' What is less clear is whether consensual resolution before issue of proceedings is covered. It seems most likely that it is and that the phrase 'consensual resolution in a litigious context' would also cover such situations. To summarise:

- If the settlement is made in contemplation of legal proceedings then it is normally covered by the ordinary definition of legal professional privilege and there is no obvious reason why POCA 2002 should displace it.

- If parties settle matters during exchanges that take place under the guidance or spirit of a pre-action protocol, then they are doing exactly what the CPR intends and encourages them to do—to borrow his Lordship's words: such resolution is also an integral part of the conduct of ordinary civil litigation.

It is then hard to conclude that these situations should be treated any differently in relation to POCA 2002. What his Lordship does make clear is that where litigation is known or suspected to be no more than a pretext for the acquisition, retention, use or control of criminal property, then there would be no protection and s 328 would apply.

It must be stressed again that it is essential that the individual takes responsibility for keeping abreast of the law and the guidance from professional bodies and Bar associations and for assessing whether any work carried out is affected by some or all of the legislation.

Guidance can be found on the Bar Council website at <www.barcouncil.org.uk>. At the time of writing—look under the guidance link, at the alphabetical list, go to 'P' for POCA 2002. There you will find 'Proceeds of Crime Act 2002 and Money Laundering Regulations—Guidance for the Bar'.

5

Financial provision—ancillary relief: preparation and process

5.1 Pre-application protocol

A pre-application protocol for ancillary relief procedure was created by *Practice Direction* (*Ancillary Relief Procedure*) [2000] 1 FLR 997 to coincide with the nationwide implementation of what was then a new procedure. This is essentially of concern to solicitors.

The ancillary relief pre-action protocol is an adaptation of the Civil Procedure Rules (CPR) pre-action protocols and in one sense its aims are broadly similar—to achieve a fair and consensual settlement without recourse to litigation where this is possible. Therefore if the parties can and will make full and frank disclosure, sensibly instruct experts jointly and negotiate in a meaningful way without having to apply to the court, then they should do so.

However, in practice not all (some would say not many) disputed ancillary relief cases will be suited to attempts to resolve the matter pre-action and the protocol explicitly caters for this. Indeed para 2.4 of the notes of guidance states that 'making an application to the court should not be regarded as a hostile step or a last resort, rather as a way of starting the court timetable'. So where, for example, disclosure is at issue or the parties are at odds (as they often are), it may be more appropriate, both in terms of saving time and costs, to proceed directly to the court managed process (para 2.2).

The Financial Dispute Resolution hearing (FDR) is the central feature of the ensuing process and is the point at which parties are expected to be prepared to make every possible effort to settle their own affairs without the need for a full contest.

Note that by virtue of the Civil Partnership Act 2004 (CPA 2004), same-sex couples who have registered their union will have the same sort of access to ancillary relief upon the dissolution of their partnership as married couples do upon divorce. Thus references here to 'spouse' and 'divorce', etc should be read to encompass civil partnerships.

5.2 Getting started: information about your client's position

Getting detailed information about the (lay) client's financial position is very important. This will involve careful investigation, clarity of thought, and realism as to what information may be available. It is often not sufficient simply to ask the client general questions—many will not realise what is relevant. Counsel must be aware of all the details that may be required. The most successful ancillary relief application will be that which is based on the soundest preparation.

The first source of information for the barrister will usually be the brief, which is likely to include some form of statement of the client's means. The amount of detail available initially will vary considerably, depending on the stage at which the counsel is instructed and the amount of preparatory work which the solicitor has done. It is, however, unlikely that the statement provided in the brief will be complete, as the client may well not have supplied full information to the solicitor, and the solicitor may well leave it to counsel to suggest what further information should be sought.

Whatever information is supplied in the initial brief must be carefully analysed. What is there must be sorted out, and any gaps or implications that need to be clarified must be identified. A list of further information that will be required from the solicitor, from the client and from any other sources should be drawn up.

Depending on the complexity of the case, the next stage may be either a telephone call to the solicitor seeking further information, the arranging of a conference with the client or the writing of an opinion on the case. In any event the following general points will apply.

Get your standpoint clear: is your client seeking provision or trying to resist an application for provision? What are the client's objectives, and which of these is most important? Do not automatically assume that your client will wish to get as much, or pay as little as possible. Many divorcing parents are prepared to make reasonable provision, especially for children. Is one specific asset of particular importance to the client? Does your client want to stay in the matrimonial home or move? In considering objectives, be aware of the effects of emotion. One party may want an asset as a matter of status or spite rather than objective need. While the barrister should seek to fulfil the client's objectives, it may sometimes be necessary to talk to him or her about what is reasonable.

This is just the beginning of a process of gathering and assimilating a large amount of financial and other factual detail. An important aspect of your job is to marshal this information as it comes to you, and not to be overwhelmed by it. You need to understand clearly the context in which it is required and received—and learn how to keep it readily accessible and up to date. Various techniques are used to achieve this, to which you will be introduced in the following paragraphs.

Start, first of all, by getting a clear view, with actual or possible values, of the assets that your client has. As a basic checklist, consider the following.

Income

Employment (including wages, commission, etc)	£
Value of fringe benefits	£
Any other work or business	£
State benefits	£
Pensions	£
Unearned income (ed. dividends, interest)	£
Income regularly provided from another source (eg, from a cohabitee)	£
From any other source	£

Total £

Outgoings

Mortgage repayments or rent	£
Other costs of the home (eg, water rates, repairs)	£
Cost of services: electricity, gas, telephone	£
Council tax	£
Food	£
Clothes	£
Regular hire-purchase and credit sale payments	£
Costs and expenses of work or business	£
Cost of holidays	£
Other regular obligations (eg, supporting a third party)	£
Any other expenses	£
	Total £

Ensure that all income and expenditure figures relate to the same period, for example, to the same calendar or financial year, and that all figures are annual, monthly or weekly. You need to be able to compare like with like.

Capital assets

Value of home (or share of home)	£
Savings	£
Shares	£
Other investments	£
Household goods, furniture, etc	£
Car	£
Other capital assets (eg, jewellery)	£
	Total £

Debts (liabilities not covered by expenditure)

Balance due on credit card	£
Bank loan	£
	Total £

Make sure that a client gives a current rather than a historical value. In considering the matrimonial home, be clear who owns it and what mortgage may be attached to it, and perhaps whether a non-owner spouse may already have an equitable claim to a share in it. If either or both spouses have interests in a business, assessing its value may present particular problems, especially if it is a small business. Other issues, such as the transferability of the shares in an unquoted company, or the value of goodwill due to the involvement of the spouse may need to be considered.

To get a clear picture you need to look at the position as regards both income and capital, so that you can see clearly if the client can afford his or her current lifestyle, or has any money to spare.

Do not just ask for figures, but advise getting written verification where possible. Not only may this be required as proof when the matter comes up for hearing, but some clients do make mistakes or overlook points in the replies they give. Think about payslips, bank statements, mortgage statements, receipts, bills, accounts, building society statements, etc. Be realistic about what records the client may or may not have, but anticipate the documents which will have to be disclosed. In some cases, copies may be available where originals have been lost, for example, bank statements. Also be realistic about the amount of paperwork collected, bearing costs in mind.

Do not just get figures for each item, but also consider the practical aspects. Could an asset be sold easily or not? Are there any important points regarding the history of the asset? Could an asset be used as security for a loan or not? Does an asset have particular sentimental value to one spouse?

In taking this wide and realistic view, a knowledge of accounts, company law, partnership law, insolvency, revenue law, etc will be valuable where appropriate.

When pursuing a claim, the procedural timetable is essentially divided into three stages: (a) application to first appointment (FA); (b) FA to FDR; (c) FDR to final hearing.

5.3 Stage one: application to first appointment

5.3.1 Making the application

This is the initial stage, which is dominated by the mutual exchange of relevant information and getting a 'handle' on the case. A petitioner should ask for the whole range of financial relief in the divorce petition, to keep all options open. The application is then 'activated' by filing Form A. Respondents to the petition should seek relief in their answer, if there is one. Otherwise, they should initiate their application using Form A.

When Form A is filed the court will list an FA to take place between 12 and 16 weeks from the date of filing. Notice of the FA (in Form C) is served by the court on the respondent, along with a copy of the application. Once the date of the first appointment has been fixed, it can be changed only with the permission of the court.

Consider the following case study, *Cutforth v Cutforth*.

Mr and Mrs Cutforth were married in 2000 when they were in their mid to late twenties. They have two children, now aged 6 and 8. Before the marriage, Mrs C, who has degrees in modern languages and speaks Russian and German, had a well-paid job as an interpreter, working largely at international business conferences. She met Mr C during this time. She gave up work when their children were born. She now works part-time in a local toyshop. The matrimonial home has four bedrooms and three reception rooms. Its value is somewhere between £425,000 and £500,000. The couple separated following an allegation and finding of domestic violence resulting in a court order that Mr C vacate the property. He lives in modest rented accommodation and pays all the outgoings on the former matrimonial home. Even so, Mrs C finds it difficult maintaining her standard of living. She does not wish to move and wants a new car. The elder child will go to boarding school soon. Mr C is employed as a computer engineer and set up his own company in 2003, the value of which is unclear. He can make ends meet, but feels Mrs C was unsupportive of him and his company venture. He is unhappy at the role of Justin Redwood, Mrs C's boyfriend, and cited by Mr Cutforth in the divorce. His affair with his wife, he says, hastened the breakup of the marriage and caused the row leading to the ouster order. Mr Redwood has been joined to the proceedings as a 'Party Cited'.

5.3.2 Preparing for the first appointment

Before the FA, the following should happen (r 2.61B):

(a) A simultaneous exchange of financial information on Form E must occur not less than 35 days before the first appointment. This is a 25-page, standard-form document and replaces the narrative affidavit of the past, which sometimes shed more heat than light on a case. The purpose of Form E is to eliminate the emotion as well as the lottery involved in finding the lawyers with the best (or better) drafting skills. The overriding objective seeks to ensure that the parties are kept, so far as possible, on an equal footing—and standard forms are one way of achieving this. In any case, Form E contains several boxes inviting comment on standard of living, conduct, contributions (of both a financial and non-financial kind) and the like, so all is not lost for drafters.

Designated documents must attached to the form. All must be filed and served on the other side. Exchange between the parties is to occur at the same time, which is sometimes easier said than done. Form E is the only vehicle for disclosure leading up to the FA, once the application has been made.

Counsel will not often be asked to assist with completing this financial statement. If you are, or even when you analyse the forms, useful advice can be found in *Ancillary Relief: A Guide to the New Rules*, Nicholas Mostyn, QC and John Nicholson (Butterworths, 2000), though be aware that in some other respects, this handbook is out of date. See also *W v W (Financial Provision: Form E)* [2004] 1 FLR 494.

(b) No later than 14 days before the FA, each party must file and serve on the other(s) the following documents:

   (i)   A concise statement of issues (see **5.3.4**).

   (ii) A chronology (see **5.3.3**).

   (iii) Either a questionnaire, indicating what further disclosure is needed and why, or a statement confirming that no further information is required (see **5.3.6**).

(c) No later than 14 days before the FA, both sides should file and serve a notice in Form G stating whether they are in a position to use some or all of the first appointment as an FDR hearing (see **5.4.4**).

(d) No later than 14 days before the FA, the applicant must file and serve on the respondent confirmation that relevant notice provisions have been complied with (eg, notice to mortgagors, pension funds, etc).

(e) Each side must come to the FA with an estimate of costs (on Form H) up to that point (as they must do at every appointment or hearing).

5.3.3 Chronologies

A chronology is an obvious and effective way of getting to grips with a case. It helps you to assimilate the detail and present the history in a meaningful and accessible way.

As a matter of common sense, it is one of the first things you will do with a set of papers.

Judges like chronologies too because they help them to keep the background of a case at their fingertips—this is why parties are required to file one before the FA. Note that in this context there may be scope for inserting a bit of 'colour', for these purposes. The chronology is likely to be the judge's initial exposure to the parties, and it may be useful to introduce information to give the court a rounded view of the case.

For example, Mr Cutforth may want to try to 'neutralise' the effect of the occupation order made against him in the following way.

Cutforth v Cutforth—Chronology (Respondent husband)	
DATE	EVENT
14.11.69	Respondent born (40)
7.2.76	Petitioner born (34)
12.12.98	Parties meet
3.6.99	Purchase of matrimonial home for £275,000 (4 bedrooms in Mankshott, Oxfordshire)
18.8.2000	Parties marry
4.4.02	Damian born (8)
5.6.03	Respondent invests £10,000 in own software business, Jactrad Ltd.
30.8.03	Gemma born (6)
Spring 08	Petitioner starts affair with Justin Redmond
Winter 08/09	Petitioner promises to end affair
25.5.09	Respondent leaves MR after row about Petitioner's extramarital relationship and court order
4.6.09	Respondent moves into one-bedroom flat
12.7.09	Petitioner issues divorce petition
18.9.09	Decree nisi
18.12.09	Petitioner files Form A

Whether and to what extent you want to put such information into the chronology is a matter of tactics—and good sense. You would not want to antagonise the other side if he or she is negotiating constructively, or appear to be giving an inaccurate picture to the court. But sometimes it feels right to try to present a 'balanced' picture here, unless the information already appears elsewhere (eg, the petition or Form E).

5.3.4 Statement of issues

This is an important document. It should set out clearly and succinctly what the areas of dispute are. The aim is to help to identify and narrow the real (not petty) issues, which is the purpose of the FA. In the *Cutforth* case, for example, the dispute over the matrimonial home and the wife's earning capacity might be described as set out below.

ISSUE	WIFE'S CASE	HUSBAND'S CASE
Housing	The wife should remain in the family home. She needs four bedrooms and the children need continuity. She cannot buy other suitable accommodation near the children's school for less than the value of the family home.	The family home should be sold. A three-bedroom house, of the type illustrated in the particulars annexed to the husband's Form E, could be purchased by the wife with some of the proceeds; thus releasing about £50,000 for his housing needs.
The wife's earning capacity	The wife is only able to work part-time and locally until the children are much older. Her language skills are no longer of commercial use; she has been out of the market too long.	The wife has skills she can exploit in the labour market. She can work part-time as a translator from home.

Note that one tends, for the sake of clarity, to refer to the parties as 'husband' and 'wife' (or by name), rather than simply the 'petitioner' and 'respondent', except when drafting formal documents. It is not always the case that the wife is the petitioner, or that the petitioner and the person seeking ancillary relief are the same!

5.3.5 Getting information about the other side

Your client's claim for financial provision, or resistance to such a claim, can only be fully considered in the overall context of the income and capital available to both sides. Ideally, you need to know as much about the assets of the other side as you do about your own client's assets. Realistically, it may not always be easy to get such information if the other side is being obstructive.

Initially, you will ask your own client what he or she knows about his or her ex-spouse's assets. Even if your client has little detailed knowledge, he or she may have a general idea what the other party earns and owns, or at least be able to suggest points to be pursued. This source of information may be inaccurate, may have an emotional rather than an objective basis, and may well include conjecture and hearsay. But it may at least suggest some starting points; and eventually, a useful basis of comparison.

The next source of information is of course the financial statement provided by the other side. As already suggested, you should go through this with your client, checking it for inaccuracies and omissions. Where the information is vague or incomplete, appropriate steps should be taken, either by way of asking for Form E to be completed or seeking additional information by way of questionnaire (see **5.3.6**). Only ask for information you really need from the other side; questionnaires are not the place for scoring tactical points.

5.3.6 Questionnaires

As with the mainstream civil courts, one of the aims of the new rules was to put an end to cases getting bogged down in endless, expensive and often overwhelming requests for disclosure. This has been achieved in two ways. First, several of the sorts of documents routinely requested by parties in the past are required to accompany their Form E financial statements. These are set out in the Schedule of Documents at the end of Form E and include:

(a) Any recent valuations of the matrimonial home.

(b) The last 12 months' bank statements for all accounts listed.

(c) Surrender value quotations of all life insurance policies.

(d) The last two years' accounts of any business in which the other party has an interest.

(e) The last three payslips, and most recent P60.

(f) The last two years' accounts for any self-employment, or any relevant partnership.

(g) A valuation of pension rights if these are available.

A curious omission is credit card statements, so this will remain a typical request in the questionnaire, as will the disclosure of any of the above documents which were not annexed with Form E when it was served and filed.

Second, only documents listed in the checklist may be attached to a party's Form E and requests for further disclosure will not be granted if it would not further the overriding objective. Questionnaires should be *thorough* and ask for what is needed, but every request *must be related to an issue in the case and, crucially, be proportionate*. This is especially important when seeking orders against third parties. The intention is that the District Judge (DJ) deals with *all* disclosure issues based on requests made at the FA, so it is important to get the formal request right. Only with the court's permission will a party be able to require further disclosure after the FA.

Like any other form of drafting, it is necessary to be precise to be effective. Keep the requests as tightly worded as possible. Don't ask: 'Does the Respondent have a credit card.' Be specific.

By way of example, some of Mrs Cutforth's requests might be drafted as set out below.

***Cutforth v Cutforth*—Petitioner's Questionnaire and Request for Documents**

1. The Respondent states in his Form E that Jactrad Ltd 'has few assets and negligible income' but he failed to annex the last two years' accounts as required. Please provide a copy of these accounts, plus any documentary evidence relating to the ownership of shares in and value of the company. Please provide any draft accounts in respect of the period since the last prepared accounts.

2. The Respondent refers in his Form E to monthly payments of £450 on the matrimonial home, which appears to exceed the amount due under the mortgage. Please explain, by reference to a recent mortgage statement, the basis for this figure.

3. The Respondent says he cannot afford the Petitioner's stated needs, but does not make clear on what he spends his income. Please provide a schedule of all credit, charge and store cards held by him during the last 12 months, whether in his sole name, joint names or upon which he has signing rights, together with copy statements for the said period.

In his questionnaire, Mr Cutforth might ask as set out below.

Cutforth v Cutforth—Respondent's Questionnaire and Request for Documents

1. What is the Petitioner's case as to her earning capacity? In particular:

   (a) Does the Applicant contend that, in order to exploit her language skills, she needs to take some form of refresher course or further education? If so, please give details of the course or courses, including cost and duration.

   (b) Is it disputed that, as a translator working from home, the Petitioner could earn approximately £20,000 gross?

2. Does the Petitioner have any and, if so, what intention to marry or cohabit with the Party Cited? Without prejudice to the generality of this question, please state with appropriate narrative the precise nature of the Petitioner's relationship with the Party Cited, giving full details of any direct or indirect financial support the Petitioner has received from the Party Cited since the beginning of their relationship or expects to receive in future.

Questionnaire requests will tend to focus on controversial matters. There should be an obvious link to the issues in dispute. **You must be clear about the purpose of each question and know what you want to achieve, and why, so you can justify the request to the court**. Nuisance questions, or those which are unnecessarily antagonistic, will be frowned upon—and can be counter-productive.

The court does have powers to make more draconian orders regarding disclosure, where that is deemed necessary and proportionate. These include search orders and freezing orders, the setting aside of transactions intended to defeat or reduce a proper claim for financial provision (MCA 1973, s 37; see **4.2.5**) or even imprisonment (*Lightfoot v Lightfoot* [1989] 1 FLR 414). None of these, of course, will be granted lightly.

If a spouse fails to provide information when an order is made, there are various implications:

(a) A party who fails to make proper disclosure can be ordered to pay costs occasioned by that failure (*P v P* (*Financial Relief: Non-disclosure*) [1994] 2 FLR 381). See also **5.6**.

(b) A party who fails to produce documents may be imprisoned for contempt if appropriate, but only as a last resort (see *Bluffield v Curtis* [1988] 1 FLR 170).

(c) A party who is very obstructive in providing information may be penalised in the order made (see *Mason v Mason* [1986] 2 FLR 212).

5.3.7 Use of financial schedules

It is vital to put the financial information you receive into an accessible form. One look at the size and layout of Form E will tell you that however useful for neutrally conveying a large amount of information, it is not convenient for ease of assimilation or reference. This is where the financial schedules come in. They are a crucial part of both the preparation and presentation of a case. They encapsulate the relevant figures in a useful form, and help you, the client and the court focus on the implications of the orders sought. Ensure that they are up to date before use in court and that your opponent and the judge have copies.

There is no prescribed format for preparing a schedule—in practice, you will be able to see what other practitioners do and form a view as to what is most effective—but in general the schedule should try to do the following:

(a) Summarise the current position as to income, outgoings and the capital position (assets and liabilities) of both parties insofar as it is relevant to the application under consideration (eg, if you are applying for maintenance pending suit, you do not need a full summary of the capital position, though it might be relevant to bring in capital that is available to meet immediate needs).

(b) Summarise the proposed position as to income, expenditure and capital that both parties will be in if the order sought is made (which needs to show how this will put your client into a satisfactory position if you are applying for the order, and how this will put your client into an untenable position if you are resisting an application for an unrealistic order). The idea is to demonstrate that the order sought will 'work' for *both* parties—or not, depending on whether you are seeking or resisting the order!

(c) Be adaptable—it is useful to have a format that can be used flexibly, so that, for example, it is easy to work out what the effect would be if an order of £10 per week less than that sought were made, etc.

Styles vary, but the following sort of format might be used to support the case of Mrs Cutforth.

Schedule of Income and Assets

Wife: age 34
Husband: age 40

Damian: age 8 (resides with wife)
Gemma: age 6 (resides with wife)

Wife: Income and Outgoings

Current position

Income

Employment	£	500.00 per month (net)
Payments from respondent (for children)	£	433.00 per month
Child benefit	£	143.86 per month
Building Society interest	£	1.30 per month

Total £ 1,078.16

Outgoings

Listed on separate sheet (does not include housing costs)	£	1,040.00 per month

Balance

This shows a small surplus of	£	38.16 per month

Proposed position

Income

Employment	£	500.00 per month (net)
Child benefit	£	143.86 per month
Building society interest	£	1.30 per month
Increased payment by respondent	£	450.00 per month for wife
	£	433.00 per month for children

Total £ 1,528.16

Outgoings

(As before, plus outgoings on matrimonial home as detailed by the respondent)	£ 1,470.00 per month

Balance

This shows a small surplus of   £   58.16 per month

Husband: Income and Outgoings

Current position

Monthly income	Total	£	2,000.00 (net)
Monthly expenditure	Total	£	1,520.00 (including outgoings on MH)

Surplus per month	£	480.00

Proposed position

Income

Monthly income	Total	£	2,000 (net)

Outgoings

Estimated monthly expenditure (Wife to assume outgoings on MH; includes estimated housing costs and relevant outgoings on H's Form E)	£	1,350.00
Proposed payments to petitioner	£	450.00
(Total	£	1,800.00)

Surplus per month	£	200.00

Whether one wants to include a 'proposed position' section (and on the same sheet) will depend on the circumstances and the use being made of the Schedule, which in any event should go on to list capital assets and liabilities (joint as well as individual). Nowadays, pension details would be apt to be listed under a separate heading.

5.3.8 The first appointment

Counsel is often instructed to attend the FA (which you might also now find being referred to as the first directions appointment, or FDA—not to be confused with the FDR: see **5.4**). Both parties must do so, unless they are excused by the court. The appointment is usually listed for 30 minutes and it should not be adjourned or vacated unless there is a good reason. Non-service or late service of the other side's Form E could constitute a good reason for an adjournment. You or your instructing solicitors will have prepared and served the documents set out above. Confirmation that the trustees or managers of a pension scheme have been served, if seeking a pension-sharing or attachment order, and confirmation that the mortgagees have been served, should also be filed. The person responsible for the pension arrangement is entitled to be represented at this appointment.

The DJ conducts the first appointment and determines the extent to which any questionnaire filed should be answered and what documents or further information should be produced, making such directions as are necessary (which, if appropriate, can include an order that a non-party (eg, co-habitee or business partner) attend and produce specified documents at what has come to be known as an 'inspection hearing'). He or she will also give directions as to the valuation of assets (including pensions), obtaining and exchanging experts' evidence and any evidence to be adduced by each party, and as to any chronologies or schedules to be filed by each party. It is helpful, when answering questionnaires, to reproduce the original request.

An application may be made for maintenance pending suit. If you are applying for maintenance pending suit, then notify the court beforehand to request a longer hearing.

The court may be reluctant to order extensive expert evidence at this stage. In any event, such evidence should be provided by a single joint expert where possible. In fact, family law has been the pioneer in this respect (where do you think the CPR got the idea?). Welfare reports in Children Act cases, for example, have long been provided by a single expert. See now *Best Practice Guide for Instructing a Single Joint Expert* [2003] 1 FLR 573, issued by the President of the Family Division's Ancillary Relief Advisory Group. See also *Martin-Dye v Martin-Dye* [2006] 2 FLR 901.

Rule 2.61D states that 'the first appointment must be conducted with the objective of defining the issues and saving costs', so protracted and indiscriminate disclosure is actively discouraged. A party is only 'entitled' to further disclosure if it has been ordered at the first appointment or with leave of the court (r 2.61D(3)). Remember that the judge will be thinking in terms of the need to identify the real issues and keep costs down. For these reasons, you will not necessarily obtain all that you request unless you have prepared cogent reasons for disclosure. Voluntary disclosure happens in practice and advanced disclosure is now part of the pre-action protocol.

Procedure varies slightly from court to court. Applicants usually open, giving reasons for the directions they seek, and the other side responds in kind. Remember that requests will need to be justified by reference to the overriding objective.

If it appears that agreement between the parties may be possible at this stage, the first appointment can be 'converted' into an FDR (see below), in which case any discussion about further disclosure or evidence would await the success or failure of the attempt to settle. In the overwhelming majority of cases, however, the judge will fix an FDR, although a further directions/inspection hearing might be ordered in exceptional circumstances (eg, where a party has failed to file a Form E). If an FDR, which is effectively court-monitored conciliation, seems a waste of time, a date for a final hearing can be fixed at this stage, with any further pertinent directions (including level of court), as can a date for the hearing of an application for an interim order. The case can also be adjourned for out-of-court mediation or private negotiation or, in exceptional cases, generally: reg 2.61D(2)(d), as amended.

On rare occasions there may be a good reason for departing from normal procedure to let the court adjudicate on a single issue which will effectively determine the outcome of the case. This might happen, for example, where there has been a pre-nuptial agreement dictating the parties' financial position post-divorce: *Crossley v Crossley* [2008] 1 FLR 1467.

The FA is heard in private. The new rules on media access to private hearings specifically excludes those, like the FDR, which amount to judicially assisted negotiation and conciliation; but not it seems the FA, unless it is treated as a FDA (or a party's Art 8 rights of privacy prevail). This distinction could well affect one or other party's approach to the FA, for better or worse.

5.4 Stage two: first appointment to FDR

5.4.1 Analysis of evidence

Whenever, and however, disclosure of financial evidence is made, it is imperative to analyse the information carefully and cross-check it with assertions made by the disclosing party.

When you look at payslips, for example, check that they support the figure presented in Form E. Compare them with the P60.

When going through bank statements, it is important to look out for regular payments which suggest a source of income which has not been disclosed. Alternatively, a statement might reveal a bank account, pension, savings account or life assurance policy which has not been disclosed. Check transfers to and from other bank accounts and regular direct debits or standing orders. You will need to look at such statements over time, but by way of example, see the sample here.

UK	Statement of Account	IM 1X 09
BANK	Sheet No. 6	
Account Number: 0432366	Sort Code: 30-20-10	
MRS S CUTFORTH	Telephone: 01473 111 222	
	Facsimile: 01473 111 333	
	Date issued: 1 September 2009	

Type of Account: Premier   When overdrawn marked OD

Date	Particulars		Payments out		Receipts		Balance	
2009	Opening Balance						1,553	51
1 AUG	STMARYSSTREETC/P 3		100	00			1,453	51
7 AUG		000073	152	37			1,301	14
		000075	500	00[1]			801	14
	STMARYSSTREETC/P 3							
	DATEOFWITHDRAWAL	05 AUG	100	00			701	14
	STMARYSSTREETC/P 3							
	DATEOFWITHDRAWAL	06 AUG	20	00			681	14
8 AUG	SOLIHULLC/P 3		60	00			621	14
11 AUG	CR 92600476 CHB				122	63	743	77
		000076	400	00			343	77
14 AUG		000077	10	94			332	83
15 AUG	MARKSTREETC/P 3		20	00			312	83
	SCOTTISHWIDOWSD/D[2]		44	10			268	73
21 AUG	CR TRANSFER[3]				200	00	468	73
22 AUG		000074	15	35			453	38
25 AUG		000078	120	50			332	88
	TRAVELFACILITIES[4]		300	00			32	88
	POUNDSTREETC/P 3							
	DATEOFWITHDRAWAL	23 AUG	40	00			7	12 OD
26 AUG	CR CAREBEARTOYS				500	00	492	88
	CREDIT S/O							
		000080	22	03			470	85
28 AUG		000081	17	63			453	22
		000082	250	00			203	22
		000079	16	27			186	95
29 AUG	CRNETINTEREST					18	187	13
29 AUG	CRCHQ	10048			433	00[5]	620	13

The items and balance shown should be verified. Any interest rates shown are the rates in force only on the date shown. Details of all other rates and calculations of any interest charged are available on request to your branch.

Notes:

1 Investigate large and/or regular withdrawals. Do they correspond to claimed expenditure?
2 Check direct debits/standing orders. Do they tally with Form E? Identify their purpose.
3 Transfers indicate another source of funds.
4 Look for the purpose of significant payments out.
5 Investigate large and/or regular deposits. Cross-refer to Form E.

Reading and cross-checking the bank statements and credit card statements can give clues as to the standard of living of that party, eg, look out for frequent holidays and restaurant bills when a party is pleading poverty.

When you look at business accounts, look at the balance sheet carefully. Look out for benefits a party receives through the business, eg, entertainment, motor expenses and director's loan accounts and drawings. Also, look at the tax returns and see if they are consistent with the accounts (and do not confuse personal and business tax liability).

5.4.2   Conferences

At an appropriate point, there should be a conference with the client. A conference may take place at a very early stage, perhaps even before the divorce proceedings are commenced, if there is a need to discuss what the client hopes to achieve, or if the facts of the case are complex, or if there are substantial assets. In any case, conferences may be needed at the various procedural staging posts, eg, before Form E is filed (if counsel is asked to draft this); before the FA; before any FDR appointments and; if no agreement is reached, before the final hearing. Earlier conferences will focus on aspirations and evidence; later ones on priorities, reality, tactics and possibilities of settlement.

It goes without saying, therefore, that good conference skills are important in this context. Getting full information from the client will take great care, and perhaps some diplomacy! You will also need to give clear and practical advice. Special skill will be needed to deal with the emotional reactions of clients, and the effect that such feelings may have on their perspective. Reality can be a bitter pill to swallow.

5.4.3   Writing opinions

General points

Counsel may be asked to provide an opinion at any stage, but the main possibilities are (a) that an opinion may be sought at an early stage when there is little detail of the financial position but the solicitor and client want general advice, and/or (b) that an opinion or a further opinion may be sought at a later stage when more detailed figures are available. Counsel may be asked to deal with overall entitlement or with particular issues.

The following general checklist for the contents of an opinion dealing with financial provision will of course need to be fully adapted for each individual case. The opinion should:

(a) Show clear appreciation of the standpoint and objectives of the client, and of any particular concerns that the client has.

(b) Identify clearly the factors in the case which favour the client.

(c) Identify clearly the factors in the case which weaken the client's case or favour the other side.

(d) Advise clearly on the likely basis or alternative possible bases for provision.

(e) Deal clearly and comprehensively with the resources and assets that are available.

(f) Use the available figures to practical effect. Be specific.

(g) Advise clearly on further information or figures that should be sought.

(h) Ensure that a summary of clear, practical advice is provided.

In essence, it is vital to be clear, practical and thorough. Do not generalise about statutory provisions and the options available, or deal superficially with figures.

Example opinion

CUTFORTH v CUTFORTH
OPINION

1. I am asked to advise the Petitioner, Sandra Cutforth, with regard to her application for financial provision on divorce. She has made the usual global application in the Petition. In particular she seeks ownership of the former matrimonial home, a lump sum payment sufficient to enable her to purchase a car and pay off her current credit card bill as well as sufficient income to maintain, for herself and her children, the standard of living enjoyed during the marriage. She has also applied for maintenance pending suit. The Respondent, Mr Cutforth, is seeking sale of the matrimonial home and a clean break.

Background

2. The parties married in 2000, a year after moving into the matrimonial home together. Mrs Cutforth is now 34 years old; Mr Cutforth is 40. They have two children, Damian (now aged 8) and Gemma (now aged 6). The parties separated in May 2009, Mr Cutforth having been ordered to vacate the matrimonial home. The children remain there with their mother. Decree nisi has been granted; perhaps instructing solicitors could confirm whether decree absolute has followed.

3. After some rather acrimonious pre-action discussion, Form A was issued by Mrs Cutforth on 18 December 2009. Both parties have filed Form E statements. The first appointment (FA) is listed for 22 March 2010, where the further information required from Mr Cutforth mentioned below should, if not forthcoming before that time, be sought.

Summary advice

4. Although several of the s 25 factors favour Mrs Cutforth, I take the view that she will not be able to 'have it all'. Although a clean break seems unlikely in view of the ages of the children, Mrs Cutforth may have to choose between, on the one hand, more financial independence in exchange for the larger share of the matrimonial home and, on the other, sharing the latter more equally in exchange for a reasonable level of maintenance.

5. This is, of necessity, a provisional view because there is still important information which needs to be gathered, especially as regards the value of the family assets. Until I have these details, I cannot advise more conclusively.

Needs of children

6. In exercising their powers, the court will treat the welfare of the children as the first consideration. There seems to be no dispute about the children living with their mother or having reasonable contact with their father. Mr Cutforth currently pays £100 per week to his wife—she says it is for the two children, but he describes it as 'maintenance for petitioner'. These, of course, are two entirely different things. Assuming the money is intended as child support (and assuming his income figures are accurate), it seems acceptable (possibly generous) by the standards of the new child support regime. If Mr Cutforth continues to pay for the children at this rate, I certainly would not advise an application to the Child Support Agency (CSA), but would expect his payments to be taken into account when considering spousal maintenance.

7. There is also no mention of who will be responsible for any school fees (it seems one of the children will soon attend boarding school). This can be catered for in a court order, but it is not

clear what the parties intend. If Mr Cutforth is to pay for this, it would add a significant amount to his outgoings.

8. The children are likely to remain with Mrs Cutforth for the foreseeable future and they will need a suitable home for the period of their continued dependency. Mrs Cutforth would like to remain in the former matrimonial home, which is a four-bedroom semi-detached property. The advantages for the children of her doing so are clear, ie, continuity and a sense of security. However, there is some question as to whether the property may be bigger than they need (as Mr Cutforth claims) and whether suitable alternative housing in the same neighbourhood is affordable (Mrs Cutforth says it is not). Perhaps Mrs Cutforth could collect particulars of (and see) some three- and four-bedroom properties in the area to help to resolve this point.

9. The parties also take very different views of the value of the former matrimonial home: Mrs Cutforth estimates it to be about £425,000, whereas Mr Cutforth puts it at £500,000. Clearly, this discrepancy needs to be resolved, so it is vital to get an agreed, up-to-date assessment. As a matter of priority, could those instructing please invite the respondent's solicitors to agree a valuer to carry out a valuation as soon as possible. It may be worth getting a view on how the house's value has fared and will fare if sold in the current economic climate.

10. Mr Cutforth discloses an outstanding mortgage on the matrimonial home of £50,000. He also says in his Form E that he pays £450 per month 'on the property'—a figure apparently exceeding the probable mortgage (even repayments at, say, 7 per cent would be closer to £370). Mrs Cutforth says Mr Cutforth also pays all the outgoings on the property, so the likelihood is that his figure of £450 per month includes other expenditure, but this needs clarifying. The figure seems rather high for the mortgage alone, especially in view of reduced interest rates. What sort of mortgage do the parties have? Variable rate mortgages became very inexpensive at one point, but of course they have a limited lifespan. Accurate information as to the costs of Mrs Cutforth's remaining in the house is critical to her application for a transfer of the property into her name. This includes the cost of any mortgage she would have to pay. It is unlikely in my view that the court would make an outright transfer to her if she were unable to afford to live there without significant maintenance from Mr Cutforth.

Mrs Cutforth's needs, resources etc

11. At present, Mrs Cutforth apparently has a monthly income (including Mr Cutforth's child support) of £1,078 to meet current monthly expenses in excess of about £1,040. Although Mr Cutforth pays all of the outgoings on the house, Mrs Cutforth still struggles to maintain the standard of living the family enjoyed during the marriage, and has found herself falling into debt. In effect she would like the money Mr Cutforth now pays towards the matrimonial home, paid to her by way of maintenance. She also says she needs a car and looks to Mr Cutforth to provide this.

Earning capacity

12. However, there remains the question of her earning capacity, cited by Mr Cutforth under Part 4 of his Form E. At present, she is working part-time as a receptionist at a small local toy factory but, as she herself says, the pay is inadequate to meet her needs. Mrs Cutforth has a good degree in languages and prior to her marriage had a well-paid job with good career prospects. Not surprisingly, Mr Cutforth is therefore claiming that she is not exploiting her full earning potential, and this is likely to be an important issue in the case. Could instructing solicitors get from Mrs Cutforth further information on this point. What are her qualifications? What jobs might be open to her as an interpreter? Has she made enquiries about this herself? If so, what did she find out? Could she work as a translator or teacher from home? How much do such jobs

pay? Could she take a course to update her skills or increase her job prospects? The other side is bound to ask about these matters at the FA.

13. The court, however, will only expect Mrs Cutforth to act reasonably. It may, for example, be the case that, while the children are young, she has to work locally and could not take on more lucrative work as an interpreter because this would involve long hours and a substantial amount of travel. Clearly, if Mrs Cutforth can only earn what she earns now, this will support her claim for maintenance for herself. On the other hand, if she could earn more, the court will take this into account in any decision it might make. If she can earn more, it might be more realistic to argue that she should get the house outright as she will then be in a position to meet the outgoings on it. What are Mrs Cutforth's views on this? At the moment, it would seem that to cover the existing mortgage as well as the other outgoings on the house would cost at least £450 per month, the figure given by Mr Cutforth.

Mr Redmond

14. There is also the added complication of Mr Redmond. Mr Cutforth claims that Mrs Cutforth's relationship with Mr Redmond should be taken into account in determining her ancillary relief application. It seems that while Mrs Cutforth has formed a relationship with Mr Redmond (which has endured for some time), it does not yet have the hallmarks of permanent cohabitation. Mrs Cutforth says that he stays the night from time to time and pays for occasional meals and family entertainment, but makes no direct contribution to the running of the household. She is non-committal about the future of the relationship. On this basis, it would seem that the relationship with Mr Redmond is not relevant to the outcome of Mrs Cutforth's application. If, on the other hand, the overnight stays were to become a regular event, they would become cogent evidence of cohabitation and it would be taken for granted that Mr Redwood contributes to the expenses of the household in which he lives. Mrs Cutforth should confirm that no such contributions are being made (or intended). It should reassure Mr Cutforth (who felt strongly enough to cite Mr Redmond as a party to the divorce) to know that any agreement between him and Mrs Cutforth could be upset were the situation to have been shown to be otherwise. Instructing solicitors will no doubt bear in mind and advise Mrs Cutforth of the effects of remarriage should this be relevant.

Mr Cutforth's needs, resources etc

15. Mr Cutforth says he has a monthly income of about £2,000 (net) to meet current expenses of about £1,520. Were he to pay for Damian's schooling, this would obviously increase his outgoings considerably. Buying a property for himself to live in would also increase his expenditure, although for these purposes he seems to have some 'slack'.

16. It would seem that, in addition to other fringe benefits from his employment, Mr Cutforth has earned various bonuses over the years. It seems likely that these might continue and details should be sought. As to the loan opportunities available to Mr Cutforth referred to by Mrs Cutforth, there is some doubt as to whether Mr Cutforth could qualify because he may leave this employment in the next couple of years.

17. I have very little detail on Mr Cutforth's housing needs. At present, he lives in modest rented accommodation, but the court will want if possible to leave him with sufficient resources to buy suitable accommodation. This would require him to have enough capital for a deposit and sufficient income for mortgage repayments. He will need a property suitable for having the children for overnight stays (ie, at least two bedrooms). Costs of such properties need to be investigated. If he could borrow money on favourable terms from his employer, then this would be relevant to his purchasing ability, as would his being relieved of mortgage payments on the former matrimonial home. Details of the loan scheme should be requested.

Capital assets

18. As to capital resources, although the former matrimonial home is registered in Mr Cutforth's sole name, Mrs Cutforth undoubtedly has as equitable interest in it. She apparently put £10,000 towards adding a conservatory (although Mr Cutforth describes this contribution somewhat less generously), but in any event may be taken to be up to 50 per cent entitled if, as seems likely, her contributions to the family over the years assisted Mr Cutforth in making the mortgage repayments. It was apparently agreed, after all, that she gave up a promising career to look after the children. Until I have the information on the value of the property, however, it is impossible to put an accurate value on the parties' existing share in what appears to be the major matrimonial asset.

19. In addition, Mrs Cutforth has £10,000 in savings and £15,000 worth of furniture which she inherited from her parents. As to the value of Jactrad Ltd, there is a dispute between the parties. According to Mr Cutforth, this is a company of few assets but this needs to be clarified. Mr Cutforth's Form E indicates that the accounts of the business will follow. If they do not, they should be sought at the FA. If the company turns out to be of value, then clearly this will improve Mrs Cutforth's prospects as regards her claims. There is, perhaps, a curious lack of disclosure by Mr Cutforth of any other capital assets—does this accord with Mrs Cutforth's memory?

Other factors

20. Although the marriage was not especially long, the court will undoubtedly recognise that Mrs Cutforth has made, and will continue to make, substantial contributions to the family in assuming the primary care of the children. There is also a clear disparity in income and earning capacity between the parties—Mrs Cutforth has been economically handicapped by her withdrawal from the labour market over 10 years ago to have and care for her children. Mr Cutforth suggests that his wife was less than energetic in helping to build up Jactrad Ltd, which he says was intended as a family enterprise. These allegations strike me as too vague to amount to conduct that would be relevant to Mrs Cutforth's application for financial provision, but it would be useful to have her reaction to them. The standard of living enjoyed during the marriage seems to have been a comfortable one—divorce usually requires both sides to make adjustments in this regard and the court will be alert to the need to ensure the financial burdens are shared as equally as possible. Given the parties' ages and the length of marriage, I doubt that the court would ascribe much value to loss of pension rights in this case, but a degree of offsetting may well take place.

Conclusion

21. It is early days yet and the outcome of this case depends very much on what we find out about the value of the family's capital assets, Mrs Cutforth's true earning potential and the costs of alternative housing. Up-to-date tax advice might also be useful. What I can say at this point is that the court would be very slow to deprive Mr Cutforth of all of his interest in the matrimonial home, unless he is able to raise or has access to other capital for housing purposes. Nor would it, on the other hand, grant a clean break where an applicant's ability to be self-sufficient has been, and continues to be, handicapped by the responsibilities of parenthood. The issue is whether Mrs Cutforth can adjust without undue hardship to the end of financial independence, not whether she ought to do so: *C v C (Financial Relief: Short Marriage)* [1997] 2 FLR 26, CA. It may seem unlikely that she would not use her specialist skills if she could.

22. Even were Mrs Cutforth to double her income from employment, there would still be a sizeable disparity between the parties' incomes, so it seems likely that a maintenance order would be made, possibly for a term if the court finds that Mrs Cutforth merely needs time to adjust to the change. She is still quite young and apparently well qualified. In return, Mr Cutforth would keep

an interest in the home, either as proceeds of sale or a chargeback. The actual division would depend on the further information sought. In effect, there is likely to be something of a trade-off between provision of income and transfer of property.

23. Even were the court to decide that Mrs Cutforth could become financially independent, I take the view that they would in that case transfer the matrimonial home to her with a nominal maintenance order which could be varied in certain events, eg, Mr Cutforth's business trading at a certain level. This would give her something of a safety net, but feel like (and have some of the psychological benefits of) a clean break for Mr Cutforth. If owning the home outright is a greater priority than remaining in it for the time being, this is perhaps an outcome worth investigating.

24. Whether and to what extent the lump sum payment will form part of the package will again depend on the figures. On the face of it, Mrs Cutforth's need to have a car and pay her credit card bill is reasonable, as both partly relate to the care of the children. Indeed, if having a car would facilitate her realising her earning potential, this would give a boost to her claim. However, unless there is a source of capital from which Mr Cutforth could make such a payment, the court may decide that Mrs Cutforth should look to her own capital to meet some, if not all, of these needs.

Next steps

25. Once the information I have identified is to hand, a clearer picture of the realistic possibilities will emerge. To recap, this includes:
    - an agreed valuation of the matrimonial home (para 9);
    - prices of three and four bedroom properties in the area (para 8);
    - more precise information on the nature and value of Jactrad Ltd, including the loan scheme (paras 18/19);
    - more precise information on Mr Cutforth's resources and expenditure (para 17 ff);
    - who will pay Damian's boarding-school fees? (para 7);
    - details of Mrs Cutforth's qualifications and employment prospects (para 12);
    - Mrs Cutforth's priorities in term of outcome (paras 22/23).

    In the meantime, if Mrs Cutforth is falling into debt, the claim for maintenance pending suit should be pursued. The courts will award a reasonable amount to tide her over for the time being, but will not prejudge the outcome of the main claim for financial provision. This should assist her to meet her immediate needs.

26. As soon as it is feasible, attempts should again be made to narrow the issues and agree an outcome with the other side. Neither party is publicly funded and, as always, it is important that costs should not be built up unnecessarily. To the extent that agreement has not been reached, the FA should help serve this purpose. At that time, a written estimate of costs should be provided to the court.

301 Gray's Inn Place Chambers   *Sue D. Nym*
10 February 2010

5.4.4 The FDR hearing

The FDR is the focal point of any case; its aim is to achieve settlement through 'discussion and negotiation' (r 2.61E(1)). It is important to arrive early and, again, unless the court orders otherwise, both parties must attend. Legal representatives are expected to have a full working knowledge of the case so that the opportunity for settlement is not wasted. Not later than seven days beforehand, the applicant should have filed details of all offers and proposals, with responses, although the FDR appointment is conducted on a privileged basis.

Hearings are in private—FDRs are specifically exempted from the new rules on media access to private hearings, since they are 'conducted for the purpose of judicially assisted conciliation or negotiation' (r 10.28(1)).

At the appointment, you should use your 'best endeavours' to reach an agreement, as indeed should all concerned. Be prepared to open the case to the judge. It is essential to have prepared a schedule of assets, liabilities, income and outgoings. You must be able to make brief submissions in support of the orders you seek. The FDR gives each side the opportunity to put their positions to the district judge, who will guide the case towards a settlement, if that is possible. In particular, the judge should point out to either party any argument or expectation which he or she considers unrealistic. If you reach an agreement, you should be ready to draw up a consent order for the judge to make at the hearing or submit after the hearing for his or her consideration (see **5.9**). If you are close to agreement, but need more time, the judge can give you more time, fix another date for a further FDR, or the FDR can be adjourned for out-of-court mediation. If there is no agreement, the proceedings are usually listed for a final hearing. You should then collect all documents containing offers, proposals and responses. The appointment is without prejudice and none of these documents should stay on the court file.

In *W v W* (*Ancillary Relief: Practice*) The Times, 15 March 2000, it was suggested that if, at the FDR, it is clear that the case is 'going to fight', the FDR judge may order 'narrative affidavits' to be filed if this would help 'illuminate' the conduct and contributions of each party.

In *Rose v Rose* [2002] 1 FLR 978, the Court of Appeal considered a number of aspects of the FDR. It was said that the judge might offer an early, but **considered** neutral view of the case, along with an objective risk assessment should the case go to a contested final hearing. This could well concentrate the minds of the parties on what is, and what is not, important, and so conduce to settlement. Having said that, there will still be cases where the issues cannot be properly determined without a full hearing.

Note that the judge who hears the FDR is not permitted to have any further dealings with the case, except to make trial directions, hold further FDR appointments or grant consent orders. It is unclear whether a judge who granted a consent order can hear the application to vary it: *Myerson v Myerson* [2008] EWCA Civ 1376.

The FDR appointment is a crucial feature of the process and it is important to explain to your client just what it is all about and what may or may not happen. In their book (see above), Nicholas Mostyn and John Nicholson set out some useful dos and don'ts as you and your clients approach the FDR, including being very clear about what your 'bottom line' is so that you do not lose sight of it in the heat of negotiation. It is also imperative to reduce any agreement into writing, ideally as a proper consent order or at the very least set out in sufficient detail to qualify as an 'unperfected order' (which can later be perfected by the court): see *Rose v Rose* (above), where the husband sought to resile from an agreement which had not been properly drawn up at the end of the FDR due to lack of time. The CA treated it as an 'unperfected order' and the husband was held to it.

5.4.5   Negotiations and offers to settle

The importance of trying to negotiate agreed terms for financial provision cannot be overstated. One way or another, the costs of any case will come out of the family coffers.

Leaving aside the impetus and requirements of the new rules, an agreed settlement offers many advantages for the parties:

(a) Terms can be fine-tuned to meet the needs of a particular case.

(b) An agreement can include terms which a judge might not have power to order.

(c) An agreement gives the client more control over the outcome than going to court (subject to the wide powers of the court).

(d) Spouses are more likely to abide by an order they have agreed to.

(e) An agreed solution can save costs.

For more comment on the process and skills of negotiating a settlement, see the **Negotiation Manual**.

A move to try to negotiate an agreement is most likely to be formally made when sufficiently detailed information is available (eg, after Form Es have been filed), although you should be prepared to consider a settlement at any stage (note the pre-action protocol). To negotiate sensibly, it is crucial to have a thorough knowledge of the facts and figures of the case since once the settlement is agreed, an appeal or an application for further provision may be impossible. In preparing for a negotiation, you must have a *clear view* of what the client wants, and the parameters of the *most* and the *least* that the client might reasonably get and/or be prepared to accept.

Until recently, the so-called '*Calderbank* offer' was very much part of the ancillary relief negotiation landscape. This worked like Part 36 offers in mainstream civil cases, and conduced to settlement by means of putting pressure on the other side so far as costs were concerned. However, it became increasingly apparent that there was potential, if not actual conflict between the open offer(s) which the court knows about and the *Calderbank* offer, which it does not (until the question of costs is determined). This posed problems, the solution to which has been found in the decision to depart, in ancillary relief cases, from the notion that 'costs follow the event'. This has effectively killed off the *Calderbank* letter (see **5.6**).

Because the negotiated settlement will usually end all the client's claims, it cannot be stressed too strongly that the terms must be clear and comprehensive—and clearly explained to and sanctioned by the client.

5.5 Stage three: FDR to final hearing

For cases which do not settle, the finale comes in the final hearing.

5.5.1 Preparation

Certain matters must be given particular attention when preparing for the final hearing:

(a) *Bundles*. A bundle of documents relevant to both parties' cases should be prepared for the hearing *by the applicant*, properly indexed and paginated. For a complete guide to what goes into the bundle, see: *Practice Direction (Family Proceedings: Court Bundles) (Universal Practice to be Applied in All Courts Other Than the Family Proceedings Court)* [2006] 2 FLR 199. What follows is an outline summary only. The trial bundles must now be divided into separate sections, namely:

(i)   preliminary and other case management documents;

(ii)   applications and orders;

(iii) statements and affidavits;

(iv)   experts and other reports;

(v)   care plan (where relevant); and

(vi)   other documents.

Bearing in mind that each case is different, the sorts of documents which might typically be relevant and so be included in the bundle would be:

- pay slips;
- relevant P60 forms;
- business accounts (if either party is self-employed or a director of a small company);
- bank and building society statements (going back over an informative but not excessive period);
- investment details;
- pension details;
- insurance policy details;
- credit card statements (going back over an informative but not excessive period);
- property valuations; and
- mortgage redemption figure.

At the beginning of the bundle should be:

(i)   a short (one-page if possible) up-to-date summary of the background to the case;

(ii)   statement of issues;

(iii) summary of orders/directions sought by each party;

(iv)   a chronology (if a final hearing or the summary of background is insufficient);

(v)   skeleton arguments as appropriate (see *Drafting Manual*, **Chapter 23**); and

(vi)   list of essential reading.

It is the applicant's responsibility to prepare and keep track of the bundle, which should if possible be agreed with the respondent. The bundle, which should include a time estimate for the hearing, must be lodged before the relevant hearing and in accordance with the rules. A paginated index to the bundle must be given to all parties not less than four working days before the hearing, regardless of whether the bundle has been agreed or not. Bundles are now lodged and relodged as a case progresses.

(b) The *issues in dispute*. Continue to review the evidence carefully so that you do not waste time on matters which are agreed, but are able to deal effectively with areas in dispute. Decide in advance how relevant facts will be proved. Consider what evidence may be needed to support relevant allegations, eg, regarding costs of alternative accommodation (estate agents), availability of (re)mortgage lender, availability of council housing (local authority). Plan any cross-examination so that it will be focused and efficient. You must also have a clear and accurate view of the range of possible outcomes. Before the hearing, a Statement of Issues and Open Offers (setting out the order(s) sought) must be filed with the court and served on your opponent: R 2.69E. *Calderbank* offers have effectively been consigned to history (although the new rules are not retrospective), but ancillary relief cases often settle at the door of the court and so, right up to the very last minute, you must be able to recognise and make acceptable offers of compromise.

(c) *Tax considerations.* It is important to calculate in advance (so far as this is possible) the likely tax implications for all parties of any order sought. In some courts, judges require such calculations to be agreed between the parties.

(d) *Benefit considerations.* Similarly, if any party is in receipt of any state benefits, it is important to consider in advance the effect that any order may have on entitlement or the amount of such benefit.

(e) *Child Support.* If there are children in respect of whom a statutory child support assessment will, may or could be made, an estimate of the level of the amount of such payment ought to be made and included in the bundle.

(f) *Schedules.* A schedule summarising your client's income/assets and outgoings/ liabilities as at the date of the hearing should be prepared—for your use as well as the courts (see **5.3.7**). Not only will it concentrate your own mind on the realistic possibilities, it will help the judge to have this information available 'at a glance'.

(g) *Chattels.* Do not overlook this aspect of the case. Ideally, this should be dealt with before the final hearing, with a clear schedule included in the bundle setting out who is getting what. But this is not always possible—couples who get this far are often willing to fight over the strangest things. In such cases, a Scott Schedule should be drawn up setting out who claims what, and why. See generally *K v K (Financial Relief: Management of Difficult Cases)* [2005] 2 FLR 1137.

(h) *Costs estimates.* Each party should prepare an estimate of costs, including an estimate of costs to date, an estimate of the anticipated costs of the hearing and any anticipated consequential costs such as costs of sale, purchase or remortgage of any property (see *Practice Direction (Family Division: Costs)* [1988] 2 All ER 63 and Family Proceedings Rues 1991 (FPR 1991), r 2.61F(1) (as amended)). This is now to be filed and served in Form H1, which is a far more detailed document than Form H (which has been used on all previous occasions). Its purpose is to enable the court to take account of the parties' costs liabilities when deciding the outcome of the case. This is particularly important in publicly funded cases, where the effect of the statutory charge must be borne in mind at all times (see **5.7**). It is an expensive exercise in itself to complete form H1 and there may be occasions when the court can be persuaded that using Form H would be more proportionate.

5.5.2 The hearing

The hearing usually takes place before a DJ (except in complex cases when it may be heard by a more senior judge). Even if the parties have agreed terms for provision, these should be referred to the judge for the court's approval, with sufficient information as to the resources of the parties. The hearing is in private, but (like the FA), there is now scope, it seems, for media access, and publication of what was heard or seen (subject to long-standing restrictions relating to the welfare of children).

It is usual for the parties to attend the hearing to give oral evidence, as the other side will wish to cross-examine them. Others may also be asked to attend to give evidence; for example, expert valuers, if a valuation is not agreed. The basic evidence of the parties' means will be contained in Form E, but the judge has a discretion over the evidence received.

Some judges set their own procedural agendas (eg, by inviting discussion on a provisional view he or she has taken on the papers), but many require proceedings to run as follows.

Counsel for the applicant (whether this is the petitioner or respondent to the divorce proceedings) will, as a general rule, go first. Where there are cross-applications, the convention is that the first in time opens, but if logic or convenience suggests otherwise, a different order may be adopted by agreement and with the leave of the court. The party opening has the advantage of the first and last word.

The applicant's opening

Ensure that the judge has all relevant documents, including the chronology, any schedules and, as appropriate, your skeleton argument.

In the opening, you should:

- introduce yourself and the other advocates, indicating who is appearing on behalf of whom;

- outline briefly the nature of the application, referring to any relevant dates and application forms;

- give a brief outline of the background to the case (ie, names and ages of parties, date of marriage, names and dates of birth of children, etc) referring to any chronology which has been filed. This puts the application into context, but should not be overlong. In particular, remember that marital conduct (or misconduct!) is usually not relevant to applications for financial provision and so should not be emphasised. Any attempt to make capital out of the behaviour of the other party (unless it is relevant) is likely to backfire;

- set out the parties' financial position, using your schedule. Refer as necessary to any relevant documents in the agreed bundle (eg, revaluation of the matrimonial home);

- summarise the evidence you intend to call, making reference to the more important paragraphs in the written evidence, reports, etc. Check, as you go along, that the judge has all of the documents to which reference will be made;

- indicate whether agreement has been reached on any issue and make clear what the outstanding issues in dispute are;

- tell the judge what order your client is seeking and why, indicating briefly the factors under the MCA 1973, s 25, on which you rely. For example, a case might be such that you would argue: 'the children reside with the applicant wife. They need to be housed and she is resisting sale of the former matrimonial home because the husband is already adequately housed. And while his share in the equity will be tied up by way of a charge, this is justified because of the contributions the wife made, and will continue to make, to the welfare of the family and her reduced earning capacity.' If appropriate, outline any points of law, making brief references to any skeleton argument and/or authorities to be cited; and

- lastly, give a costs estimate of each of the parties.

Pace yourself so that the judge can easily follow you and ensure that he or she has had or is given the opportunity to read the statements, reports, etc. Even if the judge has read the file before you open your case, you should still summarise the main issues and deal with the matters above. However, do so *briefly*—be as concise and to the point as possible. In particular, be receptive to any hints the judge gives you that he or she has understood the point being made (and would like you to move on to the next one).

At the end of the opening (and once the judge has read the file) indicate that, unless the court wishes to hear further on any preliminary matter, you propose to proceed to the evidence.

The applicant's evidence

As a general proposition, Form E and other disclosed documents will contain all the relevant information. It will not normally be necessary (or desirable) to read or repeat this wholesale to the court. Keep the oral evidence succinct and to the point.

The evidence of the applicant will usually be tendered first but other witnesses may be taken first, for convenience sake.

Where the witness has sworn a statement and is then called upon to give oral evidence, this must be given on oath or affirmation. Get the witness to state his or her name and address and confirm that the contents of the relevant statement were correct at the time of swearing. Examination-in-chief is now limited to:

- updating the witness's evidence, if there has been a change in circumstances;

- allowing the witness to expand on issues in dispute—for example, why the applicant can only work part-time when the other party says he or she can work full-time; or why the alternative properties suggested by the respondent are not suitable (a good tip, in this context, is to advise the client to go and look at the properties which have been put forward by the other side); and

- allowing the applicant to say what order is being sought from the court and how that order would meet his or her needs.

Cross-examination will then follow. Keep it polite and purposeful. Discursive or discourteous cross-examination is counter-productive and should be avoided. Common areas of cross-examination of a party include: questions on bank statements; questions on lifestyle and expenditure; questions on rehousing; questions on cohabitees and their contributions to the household. There should be a link between questions asked/put and the points you hope to make in your closing.

Any re-examination should be kept very brief. Remember only to use re-examination to clarify matters arising out of the cross-examination.

After cross-examination and (if appropriate) re-examination of the applicant, each succeeding witness will be called and dealt with in the same way. In the unlikely event that a witness is called to give oral evidence without first having sworn a statement, then all of that witness's evidence will have to be brought out in examination-in-chief and tested in cross-examination in accordance with general principles.

After all of the evidence for the applicant has been called, indicate to the court that the applicant's case is closed.

The respondent's case

As with any conventional civil case, the respondent is not entitled, as of right, to an opening speech. Otherwise, the respondent's case should be presented in the same way as the applicant's case.

Closing speeches

It is usual for the applicant who opened the hearing to make the final speech, preceded by the other party. However, the court has a wide discretion as to the order of speeches and the judge may determine, or the parties (with the court's permission) may agree, a different order.

Your closing speech should, in short, attempt to *persuade* the court to make the order your client seeks. This is done by reference to your 'theory of the case' (which should have informed your questioning of witnesses), backed up by the relevant facts as disclosed by the evidence, and in particular those factors under the MCA 1973, s 25, which support your case. Be practical and realistic. Demonstrate, by use of the relevant figures, how the order would work *in practice* (from both the applicant's and respondent's perspectives). It is rarely relevant what happened in some other case, but any pertinent law should be cited. Use common sense and keep your closing speech focused.

Counsel should not, of course, go over ground that was covered in an opening speech. Do not be tempted to regurgitate all of the evidence the judge has just heard—simply highlight the important points. Be persuasive not long-winded. If you have omitted, or not had the opportunity to give an up-to-date costs estimate, do so in your closing speech.

Costs

Once judgment has been given, there may follow argument on costs. If there is a reason to depart from the general rule, which in such cases now is that the court shall make no order as to costs (ie leaving each party to pay their own costs), then these should be put forward (see **5.6**). Remember to ask for a detailed assessment of costs and also, if necessary, for a declaration pursuant to the Community Legal Service (Financial) Regulations 2000, reg 52, which allows postponement of the legal aid charge against a property if applicable (see **5.7**). You will also need to ask for a certificate for counsel.

Court order

Having made his or her decision, it is possible that the judge will ask the parties to draw up the terms of the order to be referred back to the judge for approval. If appropriate, the court may refer the order for financial provision to conveyancing counsel if the order involves complexities in securing payments or in a property adjustment order (MCA 1973, s 30). This is very rare.

5.6 Costs

Keeping track of and controlling the costs of securing a financial provision order is a very important aspect of ancillary relief litigation. Parties are kept informed about the costs of the litigation as the case progresses, while the overriding objective and active case management means that costs are kept proportionate. After all, whoever pays the costs, the amount will effectively reduce the total available family resources.

Until 2006, costs in ancillary relief cases followed the philosophy of mainstream civil cases, ie costs followed the event. It was a context in which the *Calderbank* offer thrived (see **5.4.5**). However, over time, it became clear that there were more differences than similarities between family feuds over money and, say, your average negligence action. Three main criticisms were levelled at the *Calderbank* friendly costs regime. First, the costs order made in such cases, which might be for a significant sum, sometimes had a destabilising effect on the substantive order. Second, the *Calderbank* system had come to be used more and more as a tactical tool, rather than a genuine offer of settlement. It was likened to a form of spread betting where parties essentially gambled on the predictions of their lawyers; they had to decide on how much risk they were/were not prepared to take on for a *potentially* higher/lower payback. Third, the whole issue of costs gave rise to an increasing amount of expensive and time-consuming satellite litigation, which was often conducted with some venom. In such circumstances, the issues between the parties were not being disposed of at final hearing, as was the intention. Although the system had its proponents, most practitioners felt the time had come for a change.

This came in the form of the Family Proceedings (Amendment) Rules 2006 (SI 2006/352), which amended FPR 2.71, as explained in the accompanying *President's Direction* (*Ancillary Relief: Costs*) [2006] 1 FLR 865. As a result, for all claims for ancillary relief commenced on or after 3 April 2006, the **general** rule is that 'the court will not make an order requiring one party to pay the costs of the other party': r 2.71(4)(a). In other words the fundamental presumption is that each side should be responsible for his or her own costs (which is the position in Children Act cases). The (unstated) idea was that the costs which have been expended by each party (which is obvious to the court from the running total set out on Forms H and H1) should be treated as part of the financial needs of each, to be accounted/paid for when dividing up the family assets. This approach has been generally upheld as sound: see, eg, *Currey v Currey* [2007] 1 FLR 946.

Notwithstanding the general principle, the rules go on to say that a costs order can be made at any stage of the case where a party's **litigation** (not matrimonial) **conduct** (whether before or during the proceedings) justifies it: r 2.71(4)(b). A checklist has been set out in FPR 2.71(5) of the matters to which the court is to have regards, namely:

- any failure by a party to comply with the rules, or any relevant order or practice direction;

- any *open* offer to settle made by a party (my emphasis);

- whether or not it was reasonable for a party to raise, pursue or contest a particular allegation or issue;

- the manner in which a party has pursued or responded to the application or a particular allegation or issue;

- any other aspect of a party's conduct in relation to the proceedings which the court finds relevant;

- the financial effect on the parties of any costs order.

Note the explicit reference to *open* offers; the court is no longer able (after the FDR anyway) to look at *Calderbank* letters (ie, without-prejudice offers) in determining liability for costs. But it will look at litigation behaviour and this includes how a party responds to offers of settlement (whether in the form of a counter-offer or not), as Heather Mills found (quite literally) to her cost: *McCartney v Mills McCartney* [2008] 1 FLR 1508. The President's Direction makes clear that where a party is seeking an order for costs against the other, this should be made clear in open correspondence or in skeleton arguments before the date of the hearing. In addition, that party must serve a written notice of the costs concerned in Form N260. If the judge does decide to make an order for costs, all of the options open to the mainstream courts are available (modified as necessary) in family proceedings (see, eg CPR 44.3(6), which lays down various permutations which can be adopted and adapted to the circumstances of the case). For detailed guidance on the new rules, see David Burrows, *The New Ancillary Relief Costs Regime* (Jordans, 2006).

Remember that when negotiating a consent order, the payment of costs should form part of the agreement (see **5.9**).

Note, too, the possibility that a lawyer may be liable for wasted costs (*C v C* (*Wasted Costs Order*) [1994] 2 FLR 34 and *Ridehaugh v Horsefield* [1994] 2 FLR 194).

5.7 Public funding

One or both of the spouses may have the assistance of public funding. Although being publicly funded can be considered advantageous, potential problems regarding the statutory charge must be kept in mind, and explained to the client (see *Singer v Sharegin* [1984] FLR 114). This arises under the Access to Justice Act 1999, s 10(7), imposing a first charge in respect of the costs of the action on any property 'recovered or preserved' in the proceedings. The charge can attach to any property that is in issue in the proceedings, not just property which changes hands (*Hanlon v Law Society* [1981] AC 124). The charge can arise even if the claim for provision is settled (*Curling v Law Society* [1985] 1 WLR 470).

The problems of the charge arise whenever a *capital* lump sum is recovered, as the charge can then be realised immediately, even if the lump sum is awarded in lieu of continuing maintenance (*Stewart v Law Society* [1987] 1 FLR 223). The same could happen if the lump sum were awarded for the purchase of a house (*Simpson v Law Society* [1987] AC 861), but it is provided that if a lump sum is specifically ordered for this purpose, the charge (registered against the property) can be postponed until that house is sold. If a house is sold, costs can be enforced from the proceeds of sale (*Chaggar v Chaggar* [1996] 1 FLR 450).

Before 2005, as a special, if relatively small, concession in ancillary relief cases, the first £3,000 of property liable to the statutory charge was exempt. This exemption has now been abolished for applications made after April 2005: Community Legal Services (Financial) (Amendment) Regulations 2005 (SI 589/2005), reg 18. So too has any 'cost protection' for funded parties.

In many cases, the major asset is the matrimonial home, which may need to be preserved as a home for a spouse and for children. In appreciation of this, where the matrimonial home or an interest in it is transferred on divorce, the statutory charge can be postponed until the home is sold. It is also possible for the charge to be transferred from one house to another if the spouse moves. This is clearly an advantage but, where a charge is postponed, interest will now accrue on the charge. Consideration must always be given to paying off the charge if, and as soon as, possible.

There are various ways of keeping the potential effects of a charge to a minimum:

(a) All reasonable efforts (by the parties and the courts) should be made to keep costs down as the case progresses.

(b) Efforts should be made to reach a reasonable settlement rather than pursue the matter to trial and build up costs. The most obvious way to avoid the impact of the charge is to settle the case through mediation, not litigation (see **Chapter 11**).

(c) If your client is publicly funded and the other side is not, try to get agreement that the latter pay the costs (this can be part of the 'deal') or, where appropriate (see **5.6**), seek an order that they do so from the court.

(d) Orders for periodical payments to a spouse will not be caught by the charge, nor will any provision ordered for children. Courts may have regard to the implications of the type, as well as the amount of any order it makes.

(e) Try to keep the property that is in issue in a case to the minimum. If, eg, both sides agree that the applicant owns half the matrimonial home, it may be arguable that only the other half will be 'up for grabs'. This is a complex area and much will depend on the facts of the case.

(f) If there will inevitably be a charge, try to ensure that it attaches to a home and can therefore be postponed, though note that this option is not so attractive now that interest is payable on the charge.

Clearly, the effects of any charge must be taken into account in agreeing provision. The approach taken by the courts is not entirely clear. It has been said that a judge should take the effects of a charge into account when ordering provision (*Simmons v Simmons* [1984] Fam 17). However, it has more recently been suggested that a judge should not do so (*Collins v Collins* [1987] 1 FLR 226).

It is less clear the extent to which the principles and provisions relating to possible costs orders against funded parties and against the Community Legal Service Fund itself still apply to family law cases. See, eg, Roger Bird, *Ancillary Relief Handbook* (Jordans, 2009), paras 17.24–17.27.

5.8 Tactics

Tactics in the negative sense (eg, delaying tactics) have been largely eliminated by the new rules. But there are still lots of positive tactical decisions to be made, from how things are worded, to offers put and concessions made in negotiations.

Be aware of other factors that may be tied in with a financial provision application. For example, one spouse may be prepared to consent to a divorce under the MCA 1973, s 1(2)(d) (that is, two years' separation and consent) if the other is prepared to make some financial concession. As a different example, a dispute over the custody of children may be tied in with an application for financial provision where the spouse who gets custody is likely to have a better claim to stay in the matrimonial home.

An understanding of the relationship between the spouses can also help you in doing the best for the client. Emotional strain can cloud the judgment of some divorcing couples, but others will be able to behave reasonably to each other, and will wish to achieve a fair solution. Few couples want to see their children suffer unnecessarily. The relationship between the parties may be critical to getting information and in reaching a solution.

As so many cases result in agreed orders, effective negotiation skills are clearly important. Even if a consensual outcome is likely, there are still decisions to be made as to which side should make the first offer, what precisely they should offer, and when.

5.9 Orders and consent orders

5.9.1 Orders

Although the court will, officially, be the one to make or sanction the order for financial provision, it is vital to know how to draft these effectively and efficiently. Whether drawing up agreed terms or responding to suggestions from the other side (or indeed a request from the court to do the drafting!), you are likely to be actively involved in this aspect of the case. Ancillary relief orders need to be drafted with care and foresight—the devil is often in the detail. This is particularly critical when drafting consent orders.

The importance of reaching a consensual order has been mentioned and is strongly underlined in the procedure for seeking financial provision. The overriding objective in FPR 1991, r 2.51B provides that active case management should help the parties to settle the whole or part of the case and encourages the parties to use mediation where appropriate. As regards the FDR appointment, r 2.61E provides that details of all offers and responses should be filed, and that at the appointment parties should use their best endeavours to reach agreement on all matters in issue, with the express possibility of a consent order being made at the end of the hearing.

In fact, the impetus to settle permeates the rules from beginning to end. Early on, Form E requires both parties to provide detailed information and set out the orders they are seeking. Rule 2.69E requires that, shortly before the final hearing, updated offers and statement of orders sought be filed and exchanged. The new costs rules are designed the stop parties gambling on the outcome.

5.9.2   Powers to make consent orders

The judge hearing an application for financial provision on divorce has an inherent power to make an order in terms suggested by the parties, but can refuse if he or she thinks the terms are clearly inappropriate. The court should not interfere lightly, but equally it is not a mere 'rubber stamp': *Pounds v Pounds* [1994] 1 FLR 775.

The new procedure makes it possible for a consent order to be made at a first hearing in a straightforward case, and does all it can to encourage a consent order by the end of the FDR appointment through the clarification of issues and offers.

Note that a consent order can only be made after a decree nisi (*Pounds v Pounds*, above), and that orders relating to capital can only become effective after decree absolute. This may need to be taken into account if drafting at an early stage.

5.9.3   The role of the consent order

Although negotiations for financial relief are common, a settlement must never be seen as an easy way out. The settlement should be based on full information just as much as a contested court order would be.

It is vital that the lawyer and the client keep at the front of their minds that, save in exceptional circumstances, the consent order will form a final settlement of all claims. An application for variation may not be possible (see **5.11.3**). In *H v B* [1987] 1 WLR 113 it was held that once a spouse has agreed to a consent order, he or she cannot seek further provision. There is a duty to make full disclosure in carrying out negotiations for a consent order, or the order may be set aside (*Livesey v Jenkins* [1985] AC 424).

The terms of a consent order must be clearly explained to the client. Although an agreement may have advantages, there should be no undue pressure on a client to accept terms, particularly bearing in mind that the spouse may be very emotional at the time of a divorce (*Tommey v Tommey* [1983] Fam 15). As always, you must act within the client's instructions in negotiating. In the exceptional case of *Dutfield v Gilbert H Stephens & Sons* [1988] *Family Law* 473, a wife sought a quick divorce settlement but later sued her solicitors for not thoroughly investigating her husband's assets. The wife failed in her claim as her solicitors had acted within her instructions. Note, however, that it is no defence to a claim for negligence against a lawyer that a court has approved a consent order (*B v Miller & Co* [1996] 2 FLR 23).

5.9.4 Drafting an order

The draft order must be clear, comprehensive and accurate (*Dinch v Dinch* [1987] 1 WLR 252). Judges have frequently criticised poor drafting in this area, as in the case of *Dinch* itself, in which Lord Oliver of Aylmerton said:

The appeal is yet another example of the unhappy results flowing from the failure to which I ventured to draw attention in *Sandford v Sandford* [1986] 1 FLR 412 to take sufficient care in the drafting of consent orders in matrimonial proceedings to define with precision exactly what the parties were intending to do in relation to the disposal of the petitioner's claims for ancillary relief so as to avoid any future misunderstanding as to whether those claims, or any of them, were or were not to be kept alive. The hardship and injustice that such failure inevitably causes, particularly in cases where one or both parties are legally aided and the only substantial asset consists of the family home, are so glaring in the instant case that I feel impelled once again to stress in the most emphatic terms that it is in all cases the imperative professional duty of those invested with the task of advising the parties to these unfortunate disputes to consider with due care the impact which any terms that they agree on behalf of the clients have and are intended to have upon any outstanding application for ancillary relief and to ensure that such appropriate provision is inserted in any consent order made as will leave no room for any future doubt or misunderstanding or saddle the parties with the wasteful burden of wholly unnecessary costs. It is, of course, also the duty of any court called upon to make such a consent order to consider for itself, before the order is drawn up and entered, the jurisdiction which it is being called upon to exercise and to make clear what claims for ancillary relief are being finally disposed of. I would, however, like to emphasise that the primary duty in this regard must lie upon those concerned with the negotiation and drafting of the terms of the order and that any failure to fulfil such duty occurring hereafter cannot be excused simply by reference to some inadvertent lack of vigilance on the part of the court or its officers in passing the order in a form which the parties have approved.

The vital importance of absolute accuracy in drafting is illustrated by *Richardson v Richardson* [1994] 1 FLR 286. It was recorded in the consent order that maintenance for a wife should continue at the rate of £8,000 for three years. Shortly before the end of the three-year period (which the husband thought was about to bring to an end his liability to pay maintenance) the wife applied to increase the amount payable and to extend the period of the order. It was held that this could be done as nothing in the wording of the consent order prevented this. Precise wording may be vital for many purposes, eg, possible tax relief (*Billingham v John* [1998] *Family Law* 175). See also *B v B (Consent Order: Variation)* [1995] 1 FLR 9, *L v L (Lump Sum: Interest)* [1994] 2 FLR 324 and *Richardson v Richardson (No 2)* [1997] *Family Law* 14.

Once terms are agreed, the draft order may be prepared by lawyers for both sides acting together, or may be prepared by the lawyer for one side and then sent to the other for amendment and approval. See r 2.61 FLR 1991 which deals with the procedure for seeking consent orders, Form M for setting out the prescribed information required for the court, and r 2.70(11) for notification required where the order includes provision for pension attachment.

The draft must follow the formal structure of a court order, illustrated in the examples below (see **5.9.7**).

It is important to note that, in addition to including orders, the order can include undertakings. It is important to decide which of the agreed terms can and should be orders (see **5.9.5**) and which could usefully be added as undertakings (see **5.9.6**). Each item agreed should be set out in a separate paragraph. The possible problems of failing to draft in sufficient detail were illustrated in *Rooker v Rooker* [1988] 1 FLR 219, where there was a consent order that the home be sold, but the husband failed to sell for two years. It was held that the wife could get no compensation for this delay. It would have been far better if the original order had been drafted to protect her.

Adequate flexibility is also important. In *Masefield v Alexander* [1995] 1 FLR 100 it was only on appeal that a husband escaped difficulties brought about by a strict time limit in the order, and in *N v N (Valuation: Charge-Back Order)* [1996] 1 FLR 361 the husband found that he could not avoid problems arising from a specific valuation clause.

Everything that is agreed by the parties should normally be included as an order or undertaking. Although it might be argued that an agreed term could be enforced even if it is not in the order, any omission may lead to real difficulties.(see *Edgar v Edgar* [1980] 3 All ER 887 and *Brown v Brown* [1980] 1 FLR 322).

5.9.5 Orders

The court can make orders it is empowered to make (eg, MCA 1973, ss 23 and 24). These will be contained in the body of the document.

As a basic checklist for what might be ordered:

(a) Maintenance for a spouse. How much? At what intervals (weekly, monthly)? When should payments start? Should payments be for a set period? Should any provision for review be built in? Even if there is no substantial order for maintenance, should a nominal order be included? On potential problems here, see *Richardson v Richardson* (above) and *Flavell v Flavell* [1997] *Family Law* 211.

(b) Maintenance for children. Is an order necessary, or is this dealt with by the statutory authority? How much? How often? When should it start? Should it be paid to the child or the custodial parent? Any overlap with future statutory payments?

(c) Lump sum. If a lump sum is to be paid, how much? When? Linked to any other part of the order? Payable by instalments? Any penalty if it is not paid on time? Interest?

(d) Sale of the home. If the home is to be sold, do you need a time limit linked with a penalty for delay? How should the proceeds be divided? Who should conduct the sale? What about price? What if it doesn't sell?

(e) Settlement of the home. Be very clear about the terms of settlement. When should the home be sold? Should there be any options for time of sale? How should the proceeds be divided? Who should occupy the home? Are other orders or undertakings needed to deal with the mortgage or other obligations?

(f) Transfer of property. Precisely what is to be transferred? When? Any penalty for failure to comply? Does it need to be linked to, eg, a lump sum payment?

(g) Pensions. This is a complex area. If either a pension-sharing or pension attachment order is included, relevant information must be annexed (in form P1 or P2). For further guidance consult specialist texts.

(h) Dismissing claims. Should the court be asked to dismiss any further possible claims by a spouse? It is especially important to consider this where there is to be a clean break. For example, the possibility of claims for maintenance in the future, and the possibility of claims for provision from the estate of the spouse on death may be dismissed.

(i) Costs. If, and to the extent, that one party is to pay the other's costs, this must be recorded. If a party is publicly funded, additional provisions (eg, relating to the statutory charge) may be necessary.

(j) Liberty to apply. This can be given to allow the parties to return to court if there are any difficulties in enforcing the order, but not to deal with substantive issues.

If orders are required in respect of the children, the practice is that they should be separately recorded on the appropriate form. Care is needed if a decision on any application is adjourned (*D v D* (*Lump Sum Order: Adjournment of Application*) [2001] *Family Law* 254).

5.9.6 Preamble and undertakings

The lead-in to the substantive order is sometimes referred to as the preamble. If appropriate, this records the basis of the order or any relevant historical detail. In particular, it also includes any relevant undertakings.

Undertakings are not an essential element of a consent order. In a relatively straight-forward case, no undertakings may be required. However, the undertaking is an extremely useful and flexible way of adding extra details to an order. The point is that the court can only actually order those things which it has the *power* to order by statute, which includes the items outlined in **5.9.5**. If the parties wish to agree to further details, such as one party allowing something to be done, or one party making specific payments to third parties, this cannot be directly ordered by the court, but may be the subject of an undertaking. For example, in *Milne v Milne* [1981] 2 FLR 286 it was held that a party could not be ordered to take out a mortgage or an insurance policy, but these matters could be the subject of undertakings.

The status of an undertaking must be appreciated. As it is not an order, it cannot be directly enforced as if it were. It is rather a promise given to the court, and therefore any breach would be a contempt, and could be treated as such, for example, by the imposition of a fine or a term of imprisonment. Because of possible enforcement problems, if something can be ordered, it is better that it be the subject of an order rather than an undertaking. On enforcing undertakings, see *Symmons v Symmons* [1993] *Family Law* 135.

5.9.7 Sample consent orders

The following samples are intended to cover some of the most common types of financial provision, and to illustrate possible variations in drafting style. All the samples are loosely based on the *Cutforth* case study used in this chapter, but they make use of a range of scenarios so that it is possible to illustrate a variety of possible orders. Note that if child maintenance is being left entirely to a CSA assessment, it does not need to be referred to at all in the order.

For further examples, see *Practical Matrimonial Precedents*, a loose-leaf publication (Sweet & Maxwell), and in particular, the supplement 'At Court—Ancillary Relief and Precedents'. See also examples in R. Bird, *Ancillary Relief Handbook* (Jordans, 2009).

5.9.7.1 Consent order providing for a clean break based on a transfer of property order, and ordering child maintenance by consent. Neither party in receipt of public funding

This is a fairly simple and straightforward order, appropriate where property is to be divided and there will be a complete clean break, save as regards children, for whom provision is agreed in the form of maintenance and school fees.

IN THE OXFORD COUNTY COURT   Matter No D

BETWEEN

MRS SANDRA ANNE CUTFORTH   <u>Petitioner</u>

and

MR JAMES ANDREW CUTFORTH   <u>Respondent</u>

and

MR JUSTIN REDMOND   <u>Party Cited</u>

CONSENT ORDER

BEFORE District Judge   on the   day of   2010

UPON hearing Counsel for both parties and upon reading Form E evidence of each party;

AND UPON the Petitioner undertaking to make application for decree absolute in this matter forthwith;

AND UPON the Petitioner undertaking

(a) to pay from the date of the transfer to her sole name of the property at 13 Jasmine Close, Oxford, Oxfordshire (registered at HM Land Registry title no) ('the property') all instalments in respect of the mortgage in favour of the Bland Building Society (Roll No 123456) ('the mortgage') secured upon the property as they fall due;

(b) to use her best endeavours to secure the release of the Respondent from his covenants and liabilities in respect of the mortgage, and in any event to indemnify him against any claims and liabilities in respect thereof;

AND UPON the Respondent undertaking to pay or cause to be paid all payments due under the mortgage and collateral endowment premiums relating to the property up to the date of transfer of his legal and beneficial interest in the property to the Petitioner;

AND UPON it being deemed that the Petitioner and the Respondent have made all forms of application for ancillary relief under sections 21A, 23, 24 and 25 of the Matrimonial Causes Act 1973;

BY CONSENT IT IS ORDERED THAT:

(1) The Respondent within 28 days of the date of the order shall transfer all his legal and beneficial interest in the property to the Petitioner, subject to the existing mortgage in favour of the Bland Building Society but otherwise free of encumbrance.

(2) Simultaneously with the transfer referred to in paragraph (1), the Petitioner shall execute a charge upon the property in favour of the Respondent as to 25 per cent of the net equity therein (as defined in paragraph 3 below). The said charge shall be realisable upon the earliest of the following events:

— the remarriage of the Petitioner

— the Petitioner cohabiting with another man for a continuous period of six months or more

— the death of the Petitioner

— the youngest surviving child of the family attaining the age of 18, or finishing full-time education if later, save that in any event the charge shall become realisable upon that child attaining the age of 21 years

Upon the occurrence of the earliest of these events, the property shall be placed upon the market for sale and sold at the best price reasonably obtainable, save that the Petitioner shall have the option of buying out the Respondent's charge for a sum calculated in accordance with paragraph (3) below.

(3) The term 'net equity' as referred to above is defined as the selling price of the property less the mortgage thereon at the time of the realisation of the charge, and less reasonable legal and estate agent costs of sale. In the event that the Petitioner shall exercise her right to buy out the charge, the net equity will be calculated with reference to value of the property at that time rather than the selling price. In the event of any dispute as to the value or selling price of the property, the valuation of a jointly agreed and paid surveyor (being a member of the Royal Institute of Chartered Surveyors) shall be final.

(4) The Respondent shall pay periodical payments to the Petitioner for the benefit of the children of the family, Damian John Cutforth and Gemma Jane Cutforth, at the rate of £50 per week in respect of each child, the first payments to be made on 1 June 2010 and the payments to last until each child respectively attains the age of 17 years or ceases full-time education (whichever is the later) or until further order.

(5) Upon the transfer and charge referred to in paragraphs (1) and (2) above, the claims of both parties for periodical payments, secured periodical payments, lump sum or sums, property adjustment orders and pension-sharing orders (all such claims being deemed to have been made) shall stand dismissed, and it is directed that neither party shall be entitled to make any further application in relation to the marriage for an order under s 23(1)(a) or (b) of the Matrimonial Causes Act 1973 or the Married Women's Property Act 1882 as amended.

(6) Further, upon the transfer and payment referred to in paragraphs (1) and (2) above, the court considering it just to do so, neither party shall on the death of the other be entitled to apply for an order under s 2 of the Inheritance (Provision for Family and Dependants) Act 1975.

(7) There be liberty to apply as regards the timing and implementation of the terms of this order.

(8) No order as to costs.

Note the following:

(a) There is an undertaking to apply for the decree to be made absolute as the property orders can only come into effect after decree absolute.

(b) It is important to describe the property fully, including the Land Registry title number at one point in the order. Note the link between the transfer of the property to the Petitioner and her taking over the mortgage payments.

(c) Undertakings as regards the mortgage can be useful where the property has been in joint names and will be put into one name. The Building Society that has granted a mortgage cannot be directly ordered to change any responsibilities under the mortgage so all that can be achieved here is through undertakings. An undertaking may not be necessary if there is no doubt that the party getting sole ownership will pay the mortgage (which it will be in his or her interests to do).

Note the use of the expression 'best endeavours'. This is used where the consent or cooperation of a third party is necessary to achieve the desired result.

(d) If one party is to get sole ownership of the home, it will often be fair for the other party to get some of the capital value. This may be achieved by an immediate lump sum payment if possible, or by a deferred charge back (as here) if there is no free capital to pay an immediate lump sum.

(e) When dealing with shares in or charges on capital, it is important to be clear about how figures will be calculated, eg, by defining net equity.

(f) Child support is now often a matter for the statutory authority so that no order may be required although parents are to be encouraged to agree maintenance (see **Chapter 7**).

(g) A clean break is achieved by the court ordering that no further applications can be made. Here there can be no other applications by either spouse. However, it is possible to order a clean break as regards only one spouse, leaving open the possibility for the other to make applications.

(h) 'Liberty to apply' only relates to the detailed enforcement of the order and cannot be used to go back to court on a substantive issue.

(i) You should be explicit that there is to be no order as to costs, if that is what is agreed.

5.9.7.2 **Consent order providing for a clean break based on the sale of the matrimonial home, a lump sum payment by instalments, and additional child maintenance to cover school fees. Neither party is publicly funded**

This is again a fairly simple and straightforward order, appropriate where the home has to be sold and the proceeds divided as the basis for a clean break. Note that here the clean break is delayed by maintenance payments for the wife for a limited period (appropriate where she is likely to be able to support herself after retraining or when the children are old enough for her to work). Here it is assumed that a CSA assessment will provide for child maintenance, although there is an order to cover school fees.

IN THE OXFORD COUNTY COURT   Matter No D

BETWEEN

MRS SANDRA ANNE CUTFORTH   Petitioner

and

MR JAMES ANDREW CUTFORTH   Respondent

and

MR JUSTIN REDMOND   Party Cited

CONSENT ORDER

BEFORE District Judge   on the   day of 2010
UPON hearing Counsel for both parties and upon reading the sworn Form E evidence of each party filed herein;

AND UPON the parties agreeing that the contents of the former matrimonial home are the absolute property of the Petitioner;

AND UPON the parties further agreeing that the Respondent shall pay the amounts ordered in (4) below directly to the Bursar of the said school, and that receipt by that payee shall be a sufficient discharge;

AND UPON it being deemed that the Petitioner and the Respondent have made all forms of application for ancillary relief under sections 21A, 23, 24 and 25 of the Matrimonial Causes Act 1973;

BY CONSENT IT IS ORDERED THAT:

(1) The property at 13 Jasmine Road, Oxford, Oxfordshire (registered at HM Land Registry title no ('the property') shall be placed on the market for sale forthwith, and upon sale the net proceeds of sale shall be divided between the Petitioner and the Respondent as to two-thirds to the Petitioner and one-third to the Respondent. The term net proceeds of sale shall mean the gross sale price less the amount outstanding in respect of the mortgage in favour of the Bland Building Society and the legal costs and estate agent charges in respect of sale.

(2) The Respondent shall pay to the Petitioner a lump sum of £30,000 payable as follows:

— £5,000 within 28 days of the date of this order

— £5,000 within three months of the date of this order

— £20,000 within six months of the date of this order

(3) The Respondent shall pay or cause to be paid to the Petitioner periodical payments at the rate of £400 per calendar month, payable in advance, for a period of three years commencing on 1 April 2010 (and it is directed that the Petitioner shall not be entitled to apply for any extension of the period of three years).

(4) As from the date of this order, the Respondent shall pay or cause to be paid to the Petitioner for the benefit of Gemma Jane Cutforth, until such time as she shall cease full-time secondary education or until further order, periodical payments of an amount equal to the fees payable at the Royal Grammar School, Oxford (including reasonable extras), such sums being payable on the first day of each school term.

(5) Upon the sale and payment referred to in paragraphs (1) and (2) above, the Petitioner's and Respondent's claims for lump sum, property adjustment orders and pension-sharing orders (all such claims being deemed to have been made) shall stand dismissed, and neither party shall be entitled to make any further application in relation to the marriage for orders of a capital nature pursuant to the Matrimonial Causes Act 1973 or the Married Women's Property Act 1882 as amended.

(6) Further, upon the same events referred to in paragraph (5) above, the Respondent's claims against the Petitioner for periodical payments or secured periodical payments shall stand dismissed and it is directed that he shall not be entitled to make any further application in relation to the marriage for an order under section 23(1)(a) or (b) of the Matrimonial Causes Act 1973.

(7) The Respondent shall not be entitled on the death of the Petitioner to apply for an order under section 2 of the Inheritance (Provision for Family and Dependants) Act 1975, the Court considering it just to so order.

(8) There be liberty to apply as regards the timing and implementation of the terms of this order.

(9) The Respondent shall pay the Petitioner's costs on the standard basis, to be assessed if not agreed, including the costs of negotiations, up to a maximum of £7,500.

Note the following:

(a) There does not need to be an undertaking to apply for decree absolute if that decree has already been granted, as is assumed for this draft.

(b) An agreement about personal property may usefully be recorded in the undertakings section for the avoidance of doubt.

(c) A payment of school fees involves third parties who are not involved in the divorce, and this must be carefully dealt with in deciding on appropriate orders/undertakings.

(d) If a property is to be sold, the court can make detailed orders as regards the carrying out of the sale. The sample order here is very short and simple.

(e) The court can make detailed orders about the payment of lump sums, including instalments, interest, etc (compare the lump sum order in the next example). An order needs to reflect the reality of what can reasonably be raised and when payments can be made.

(f) Ideally, if a home is to be sold, all capital provision would be dealt with in the division of the proceeds of sale without a separate lump sum. This is not done here purely to provide a wide range of sample orders.

(g) Maintenance payments for the former wife are here limited to three years. Such a limitation would depend entirely on the practicalities of the individual situation. Note that, as a result, the clean break orders in paras 5 and 6 leave open applications as regards maintenance by the wife for the time being.

(h) Here the agreement is that the husband will pay the wife's costs (within certain limits, which detail is recorded).

5.9.7.3   Consent order providing for a continuing financial relationship between the parties, with periodical payments and a settlement of the house. Petitioner is publicly funded

If there will be ongoing provision, the order may need to be more complex than that for a clean break as the ongoing terms will need to be clear and there will be more possible eventualities to be provided for. The following is a fairly simple example.

IN THE OXFORD COUNTY COURT   Matter No D

BETWEEN

MRS SANDRA ANNE CUTFORTH   Petitioner

and

MR JAMES ANDREW CUTFORTH   Respondent

and

MR JUSTIN REDMOND   <u>Party Cited</u>

CONSENT ORDER

BEFORE District Judge   on the   day of   2010

UPON hearing Counsel for both parties and upon reading Form E evidence of each party;

AND UPON the Petitioner undertaking to make application for decree absolute in this matter forthwith;

AND UPON the Petitioner undertaking to pay or cause to be paid as from the date of this order all monies which shall become payable in respect of the former matrimonial home at 13 Jasmine Road, Oxford, Oxfordshire (registered at HM Land Registry title no) ('the property') and the building insurance premium, the water rates and the council tax on the property;

AND UPON the parties agreeing that all property and possessions shall remain the property of the party in whose possession they currently lie save as otherwise provided in the order below;

BY CONSENT IT IS ORDERED THAT:

(1) The Respondent shall pay or cause to be paid to the Petitioner from 1 June 2010 periodical payments for herself during their joint lives or until the Petitioner shall remarry or until further order at the rate of £800 per month, payable monthly in advance.

(2) The Respondent shall forthwith transfer the property into the joint names of himself and the Petitioner, to be held by the Petitioner and the Respondent upon trust for themselves as beneficial tenants in common in equal shares, on condition that the property shall not be sold until the earliest of the following events:

— the death of the Petitioner

— the remarriage or cohabitation for a period in excess of six months of the Petitioner

— the children of the family both attain the age of 18 years or cease full-time education (whichever is the later)

(3) The Respondent within 28 days of the date of this order shall pay or cause to be paid to the Petitioner a lump sum of £10,000, the sum to carry interest at the rate of 10 per cent per annum if not paid by the due date.

(4) The Petitioner shall forthwith transfer to the Respondent all legal and beneficial interest in the Peugeot 306, car registration number CUT 13.

(5) It is hereby certified for the purposes of the Community Legal Service (Financial) Regulations 2000, regulation 52 that the property at 13 Jasmine Road, Oxford, Oxfordshire has been preserved/recovered by the Petitioner for use as a home by herself and her dependants.

(6) There shall be no order as to costs save Public Funding Detailed assessment of the Petitioner's cost.

Note the following:

(a) If a home is to be settled rather than sold or transferred to the ownership of one spouse, the details of who pays all the household bills will need to be agreed. The court cannot make orders as regards specific liabilities, but this can be covered by undertakings.

(b) A settlement of a house may be quite complicated and the sample order here is a relatively simple one. It is vital to reflect accurately whether the house is or is not already jointly owned, and to include any appropriate details of the settlement of the house.

(c) It is possible for the court to order the transfer of ownership of any specific asset if required.

(d) The final paragraphs may be relevant where the applicant is publicly funded.

5.10 Enforcement of orders

5.10.1 The importance of enforcement

The detailed possibilities for enforcing orders should be researched if necessary. It is typically a solicitor's area of expertise. These notes merely give a general guide.

The most important point is that many possible enforcement problems can and should be avoided. In a financial provision case, problems with enforcement are often foreseeable, due to the assets involved, the attitude of one or both spouses, or the circumstances of the case. Going back to the court for enforcement will itself cost money and cause stress, so any need to return to court should be avoided if at all possible. As suggestions for avoiding or alleviating enforcement problems:

(a) If the spouses can agree the details of provision they are more likely to abide by them, so a negotiated settlement should be reached where possible.

(b) The precise effects of an order should be explained to the client to avoid any misunderstanding.

(c) The details of every order must be carefully drafted to avoid ambiguities and omissions that may cause problems.

(d) Some provision for enforcement may be included in an order, for example, by providing a penalty if something is not done by a set date, or only dismissing a spouse's claims once the other spouse has fulfilled a term (but avoid doing this if it would simply make the order more complex, or be irritating rather than productive).

(e) If there are any alternatives in making provision, consider whether one may be easier to enforce than another.

As an obvious practical point, once an order is made, the solicitor should if appropriate check with the client that the steps ordered are being taken, and should take action quickly if there is any delay or difficulty. Delay in enforcement may of itself cause problems, if, for example, the capital value of property alters, or arrears of maintenance accumulate to such an extent that they have to be remitted.

Enforcement is primarily a matter of returning to court once there has been some default on an existing obligation, but because of the delays and difficulties this can cause, the powers of the High Court and of the county court when making a maintenance order have been extended by the Maintenance Enforcement Act 1991 (MEA 1991), s 1. These courts may now order that payments be made by standing order or some similar method, and may order the payer to open a bank account for this purpose. It is now also possible to make an attachment of earnings order when making the maintenance order rather than waiting for a default in payment.

5.10.2   Modes of enforcement

An appropriate mode of enforcement must be chosen, depending on the type of order breached, and the form of the breach. Procedural points relating to enforcement must be kept in mind. For example, even though an order is not made in the Family Proceedings court (ie magistrates' court), it can be enforced there if it is first registered there (Maintenance Orders Act 1958).

5.10.2.1   Attachment of earnings

An order can be sought to get maintenance paid directly from an individual's salary to the recipient under the Attachment of Earnings Act 1971. This Act has been amended by the MEA 1991, primarily to allow attachment orders to be made at the same time as the maintenance order is made. This can be useful, but only if the payer is in steady employment. It can also be used to deduct payments from a pension.

5.10.2.2   General civil remedies

Many forms of enforcement for civil claims are appropriate in a family case, for example, a charging order, execution against goods, third-party debt orders (formerly known as garnishee proceedings), or a judgment summons (see the *Civil Litigation Manual* and, for example, *Gandolfo v Gandolfo* [1981] QB 359). The appropriateness of such proceedings must be properly considered (see, for example, *Clark v Clark* [1989] 1 FLR 174 where lawyers were criticised for seeking sequestration where the resulting funds did not cover costs, let alone the sum due).

5.10.2.3   Imprisonment

This is a last resort, which will not generally be available or used for a simple failure to pay. However, it may be a possibility where a spouse has flouted court orders and is therefore in contempt of court, as in *Lightfoot v Lightfoot* [1989] 1 FLR 414.

5.10.2.4   The international element and reciprocal enforcement procedures

If an ex-spouse lives or moves abroad, it may be possible to register and enforce an order in the country in question. Similarly, orders made abroad can sometimes be enforced here. This is a complex area, and you will need to refer to relevant reciprocal enforcement orders and conventions.

5.11   Returning to court: appeal and variation

5.11.1   Context

A party may appeal against an order or, if appropriate, seek a variation or further provision. However, there are limits and difficulties in returning to court which must not be overlooked in considering the original order.

The different possibilities for returning to court should be clearly distinguished and the correct option chosen for each case:

(a) Returning to the court which made the order. This may be done without commencing new proceedings, but generally only to clarify the terms of the order made, not to make any radical alteration or addition. To allow the parties to return to the court if necessary, 'liberty to apply' may be added to an order.

(b) Appeal. On normal principles, an appeal will lie to challenge an order made if there is cause. Attempts to set aside a consent order, which is effectively an agreement between the parties, pose special problems (see **5.11.2**).

(c) Variation. If there is a later change of circumstances, a party may be able to apply to court to vary the original order (see **5.11.3**).

(d) Additional orders. A further order may be sought in some circumstances. For example, the powers of the court on divorce under the MCA 1973, ss 23 and 24 may be exercised on divorce or at any time thereafter. Note, however, that a court will be slow to add to an existing order without good reason, especially if the existing order was made by consent and was intended to end all claims.

It may be possible to vary or add to an order without actually returning to court. This may be done either if the terms of the original order allow for variation without return to court, or if the parties agree to a variation by consent.

Problems arise particularly in the case of a consent order, where the court will be very slow to interfere where the parties have expressly agreed provision; and in the case of a clean break, where the court will be reluctant to undermine the order by making further provision.

There is in practice a variety of procedural options for the route by which a case can be returned to court for appeal or variation, and a variety of overlapping factors relevant to whether an appeal or variation may be granted. There have been calls for a more unified procedural approach, but reform has proved problematic.

5.11.2   Appeals and setting aside

Where an order is made by a District Judge following a contested hearing, either party may appeal, if dissatisfied with the outcome, to a judge in chambers. A notice of appeal is necessary, which must set out the grounds (but permission is not required). Until 2001, such appeals were heard by way of re-hearing, but the combined effect the Court of Appeal decision in *Cordle v Cordle* [2002] 1 FLR 207 and subsequent amendments to the wording of FPR r 8.1 now means that:

(a) the decision of the DJ should only be interfered with if it was clearly wrong;

(b) the appeal is limited to a review of the DJ's decision unless the court considers that in all the circumstances it would be in the interests of justice to hold a rehearing;

(c) the court may hear oral or other evidence not before the DJ if it considers that in the circumstances it would be in the interests of justice to do so.

In the case of a consent order, the possibilities for setting aside are very limited. A party who has agreed to an order will rarely be allowed simply to change his or her mind, or the finality of consent orders would be in doubt. For example:

(a) *Barber v Barber* [1987] *Family Law* 125. As a wife knew of her husband's pension rights when she agreed to provision, she could not later seek to set aside the agreement to get further provision in respect of those pension rights.

(b) *Cook v Cook* [1988] 1 FLR 521. As it was agreed that the wife should get the home in any event, the fact that she was cohabiting with another man did not undermine this agreement. Equally, if a wife agrees to leave on cohabitation, that is enforceable (*Omeilan v Omeilan* [1996] 2 FLR 306).

(c) *Cornick v Cornick* [1995] 2 FLR 490, *Harris v Manahan* [1997] 1 FLR 205. A dramatic change in the value of property, if at all foreseeable, cannot be a basis for setting aside. However, an appeal will be allowed if one party has knowingly misled the other (*Middleton v Middleton* [1998] 2 FLR 821).

Only where the order has been undermined by a procedural irregularity or by serious misconduct, such as fraud, material non-disclosure or mistake, will it be set aside. For example:

(a) *Munks v Munks* [1985] FLR 576. Consent order set aside because the fact that it was made before decree nisi was a procedural irregularity.

(b) *Redmond v Redmond* [1986] 2 FLR 173. A wife's application to set aside was allowed when she agreed to provision on the basis that her husband would not apply for redundancy, which he later did.

(v) *Vicary v Vicary* [1992] 2 FLR 271, CA. A consent order was made on the basis that the husband's assets, including his shares in a private company, were £430,000. He did not disclose the fact that negotiations were taking place for the sale of the company, which included the sale of his shares for £2.8 million. The order was set aside (but compare this with the case discussed in the next paragraph).

(d) *I v I* (*Ancillary Relief: Disclosure*) [2008] EWCA 1167 (Fam), where a consent order had been made after a FDR at which the husband failed to disclose that he was negotiating a new employment contract. The wife applied to set aside the order on grounds of material non-disclosure. It was held that, even had the situation been disclosed, it would have made very little difference to the final order and so the appeal was dismissed.

5.11.3 Variation

After a divorce, a former spouse may wish to vary the provision agreed and/or ordered for many reasons. There may be a significant change in the financial circumstances of one former spouse, such as a significant inheritance of capital or a redundancy. Alternatively, one of the former spouses may change his or her views as to how or where he or she wishes to live, for example, taking early retirement. The details of variation of orders are beyond the scope of this Manual, but it is important to be aware broadly of when variation may or may not be possible in negotiating and drawing up the original order.

The court has little power to make more than one lump sum or property transfer order, and it cannot vary a transfer or settlement of property. It is therefore best to work on the basis that variation of such capital orders will be unlikely or impossible and that the widest view of potential events should be taken when drawing up the original order.

However, variation may be possible in a case where there is *ongoing* provision for maintenance. Not only may the amount and term of maintenance be ordered, but a lump sum may be ordered to replace maintenance (thereby potentially achieving a clean break some time after the divorce). The powers for variation are contained in the MCA 1973, s 31, as amended by the Family Law Act 1996, Sch 8. It should be noted that these powers can be used even where an order has been made by consent, and that an order can relate to pension provision (*Burrow v Burrow* [1999] 1 FLR 508).

In deciding whether a variation should be ordered, the court will consider any material change respecting either party since the order was made. This will often primarily consist of reviewing changes in financial resources and/or needs, and therefore such should be fully investigated as they would be before an initial application. The court will also take into account any change in other factors that are relevant to provision. The court might consider, for example, whether one of the spouses is now cohabiting and therefore has extra resources or liabilities.

If there has been a material change then the court will reassess financial provision to decide what is now appropriate, taking into account all the factors it would take into account on an original application. Having said that, the court will try not to deviate from the *spirit* of the original order: see, eg, *VB v JP* [2008] 1 FLR 742.

As with an appeal, it may be difficult for a party to seek a variation of an order to which he or she has consented. It is possible to apply (*Jessel v Jessel* [1979] 1 WLR 1148) but the court will be slow to order the variation without good reason. In *T v T* [1988] 1 FLR 480 there was a consent order for provision for a wife to last until she married or her ex-husband retired. When the latter did retire, it was held that she could not have these terms varied to provide extra provision. If claims for financial provision have been dismissed, it will not be possible to seek a variation to get provision (*De Lasala v De Lasala* [1980] AC 546). On a variation linked to a clean break, see *Jones v Jones* [2000] *Family Law* 607.

Variation may be possible if the welfare of a child is at stake (*N v N (Consent order: Variation)* [1993] 2 FLR 868).

Some limited relief may be available in exceptional circumstances. In *Thwaite v Thwaite* [1982] Fam 1 it was held that, although the consent order could not be varied, the court would refuse to enforce it in favour of a party who had not complied with its terms.

5.11.4 Professional negligence

If other routes fail, the client may feel driven to blame the lawyers for an unsatisfactory divorce settlement. This is an unhappy situation for all concerned and should be avoided. Bear in mind that the legal advisor should always ensure that a client is fully advised of the terms and implications of any settlement, including any possible drawbacks, and that the client is aware of options and takes informed personal decisions.

In *Kelley v Corston* [1998] 1 FLR 986 a barrister advised a client to accept a 'door of the court' settlement, but she then complained that the settlement left her unable to fund the mortgage on her home. It was held that the barrister was immune from proceedings, either because actions at the door of the court were immune in the same way as actions in court, or because the settlement had been approved by the judge. But this was further considered in other cases that were consolidated for hearing in the House of Lords in a decision reported as *Hall and Co v Simons* [2000] 2 FLR 545. In summary, it is clear from these cases that advice given before a hearing will not necessarily be immune from legal action. This makes it more important than ever that clear and accurate advice is given as regards what financial relief may be awarded on divorce, and what might be offered or accepted by way of settlement.

See also 'Professional Negligence Claims arising out of Consent Orders in Family Proceedings' [1999] *Family Law* 773.

Financial provision within marriage

This chapter outlines briefly the power of the courts to deal with financial matters when no divorce is pending. Although there are circumstances in which it may be necessary or desirable to seek, vary or enforce orders for financial provision even though no divorce proceedings are pending or contemplated these provisions are infrequently used. Spouses may separate experimentally, or temporarily or there may be personal or practical reasons why they wish to separate without divorcing, and it is in this area that most of those provisions continue to have some application. Financial problems can arise very quickly if there are housing and food bills to be met and previous financial arrangements have broken down. When the long-debated divorce reforms were enacted in the Family Law Act 1996, Parts I–III (FLA 1996) it was thought that the main provisions in this area would again be used much more widely. One of the orders provided for under FLA 1996 was a 'separation order' and amendments to the Matrimonial Causes Act 1973, s 27 (MCA 1973) and the Domestic Proceedings and Magistrates' Courts Act 1978 (DPMCA 1978) were contained in FLA 1996 to adapt them to the new divorce/separation regime. However, FLA 1996, Parts I–III were never brought into force and have since been abandoned by the government. More practical detail on how to prepare and present a case is provided in **Chapter 5**. Financial provision for children is dealt with in more detail in **Chapter 7**.

6.1 The High Court and County courts

The High Court and the County courts have the following powers to make orders relating to financial provision and property rights when no divorce is sought. Applications must be supported by appropriate evidence.

6.1.1 Financial provision in case of neglect to maintain

Either party to a marriage can seek a maintenance order that the other should provide maintenance on the basis of:

- failure to provide reasonable maintenance for the applicant; or
- failure to provide or make a proper contribution towards reasonable maintenance for any child of the family.

The relevant statutory provision is MCA 1973, s 27. The orders that can be made and the factors that are relevant to the level of provision made are similar to those on divorce. In fact, s 27 directs the court to have regard to the factors mentioned in s 25(2) (see **4.3**).

Applications for failure to maintain are uncommon and, where they are made, are more likely to use the fuller provisions under DPMCA 1978 (see **6.2**).

6.1.2   Maintenance agreements

It is possible for spouses to make enforceable agreements for the payment of maintenance by contract or deed without going to court. There are powers relating to the validity and variation of maintenance agreements in MCA 1973, ss 34–36, although these are not widely used.

6.1.3   Ownership of property

Orders as to the ownership of property can be made under the Married Women's Property Act 1882, s 17. Note that this section does not provide any discretion, but simply a power to declare existing rights. One spouse may have an interest in property owned by the other under an implied, constructive or resulting trust, due to contributions made to the purchase price, etc.

6.2   Family proceedings courts

Although they have no jurisdiction in respect of divorce, family proceedings courts have powers to order financial provision for spouses and children. The powers of the magistrates and the factors that they can take into account in making orders are closely aligned to the powers of the higher courts, but their jurisdiction is much more limited. The powers of the court are set out in the Domestic Proceedings and Magistrates' Courts Act 1978 (DPMCA 1978). Orders made under this Act are often referred to, inaccurately, as 'separation orders'.

The possible advantages of going to a family proceedings court are that it may be cheaper, and possibly also quicker, as the procedure is relatively straightforward. There are limits on the orders that can be made and the purpose behind the Act is really one of maintenance rather than significant consideration of capital.

6.2.1   Powers to award maintenance and lump sums

The powers of the family proceedings courts (see DPMCA 1978, ss 1 and 2) are broadly similar to those of the High Court and the County courts already outlined, but the powers are wider in that, in addition to being able to make an order where there is a failure to provide reasonable maintenance for a spouse or child, an order can be made where the respondent has deserted the applicant, or has behaved in such a way that the applicant cannot reasonably be expected to live with the respondent. An order may provide for periodical payments or a lump sum, but cannot include secured periodical payments, or a lump sum in excess of £500. The factors relevant to making an order are similar to those on divorce.

The duration of any order should be specified and is essentially at the discretion of the court. An order cannot be backdated before the making of the application for provision, although the order can cover liabilities and expenses already reasonably incurred. It is quite common for periodical payments to be payable for a set period of years, or 'until further order'. The courts can make interim orders (s 19) and can vary or revoke orders (s 20).

Payments to or for the benefit of a child will not normally be made under DPMCA 1978 since the enactment of the Children Act 1989, Sch 1 (CA 1989) and Child Support Act 1991, s 8(3) (see **Chapter 7**). In fact DPMCA, s 8 mandates that the court shall not dismiss or make a final order under the Act until it has decided whether to exercise any of its powers under the CA 1989 with respect to the child. Where such orders are made they will normally stop when the child reaches school-leaving age, and should in any event cease when a child is 18 unless the child is still undergoing education or training or there are other special circumstances justifying ongoing provision (DPMCA 1978, ss 4 and 5).

6.2.2 Agreed provision

Magistrates have powers under the DPMCA 1978, ss 6 to 7, to make an order where provision has been agreed. An order can be made where the court is satisfied that there is an agreement that provision be made and it would not be contrary to the interests of justice to make an order in those terms (s 6). Alternatively, an order can be made where the parties have been living apart for at least three months and maintenance has in fact been paid, to ensure that such maintenance continues and becomes enforceable (s 7). Orders under these sections can include maintenance for a spouse or child. An order by agreement under s 6 can also include a lump sum.

6.2.3 Procedure

The proceedings for an order under the DPMCA 1978, ss 2 or 6, are commenced by written application. Following this, a summons will be issued to the spouse from whom provision is sought. Affidavits do not have to be filed, but it is necessary for a statement of means to be completed, for which there is a standard form. The documents are lodged with the court for service on the respondent.

The applicant will make his or her claim and the other side will reply. Evidence will be partly oral, with skills in examination-in-chief and cross-examination required in getting out the facts of the case. There is advance disclosure of argument and evidence, including a schedule of figures relating to the current and proposed financial position of the client. As you might expect, the practical arithmetic of the situation is at the heart of the case.

7

Financial provision for children

7.1 Introduction

These materials seek to provide no more than an introduction to the principles in this area and a general guide to child support calculations. A final section deals with applications for financial provision for children under the Children Act 1989, Sch 1 (CA 1989).

This is a complex area as there have been a number of changes to the child support system since its introduction in 1991 with the enactment of the Child Support Act 1991 (CSA 1991). The principal changes implemented by the Child Support, Pensions and Social Security Act 2000 (CSPSSA 2000) were outlined in the previous edition of this Manual. Since then, new legislation, the Child Maintenance and Other Payments Act 2008 (CMOPA 2008), has been introduced. This act further amends the CSA 1991. At the time of writing, applications for child support are still calculated under both the 1991 and 2000 regimes. However, by the end of 2010 there could be three systems of child support running concurrently, depending on the date on which the parent with care (PWC) made an application to the Child Support Agency (CSA).

At the time of writing (August 2009), the major practitioner's works have not been fully updated to take into account the changes brought about by the CMOPA 2008. The exception is *Child Maintenance: The New Law*, by Roger Bird and David Burrows (Jordan Publishing, 2009) which is likely to become a standard text on the legislation. The earlier *Child Support: The New Law*, also by Roger Bird (Jordan Publishing, 2002, 5th edn) is a thorough guide to the system in force under the CSPSSA 2000. The annual publication *At a Glance* (Family Law Bar Association) includes an introduction to the new legislation in its 2008–9 edition and promises fuller coverage in later editions. There are useful calculation tables covering the 1991 and the 2000 child support regimes. The CSA's website can be found at <www.csa.gov.uk>.

Although calculation of child maintenance is still primarily the responsibility of the CSA, it is vital that all lawyers working in the field of family law should be familiar with the system (for the role of the new Child Maintenance and Enforcement Commission, see **7.1.3** and **7.5**). At the very least, approximate calculations of child support will need to be made in all ancillary relief cases involving children, in order to ensure that orders sought by a client are both just and practicable. Thus, lawyers also need to be familiar with the terminology employed under the relevant statutes and regulations. This is becoming an increasingly complex area. Professor Nick Wikeley of Southampton University, sums up the problem memorably in 'Child Support: the Brave New World'

[2008] *Family Law Journal*, October. Speaking of the effect of the new legislation, he writes:

As a result, the 1991 Act is even more of a patchwork quilt than before—or rather separate patchwork quilts, as there will be different versions of the Act for cases which entered the system at different times.

7.1.1 The Child Support Agency and the courts

The theory behind the CSA 1991 (which came into force on 5 April 1993) was that parents should take proper financial responsibility for their children. Child support payments should be set at a realistic and reasonably uniform level by the use of a standard formula for calculation. The CSA was set up to gather relevant information, make assessments using the set formula and assist in the enforcement of payments due.

The establishment of the CSA took control and responsibility for child maintenance out of the hands of the court system. In essence, where the CSA has power to make a maintenance calculation, the court may not make an order for child maintenance (CSA 1991, s 8(3)). 'Maintenance' generally means the making of orders for periodical payments. However there are residual areas of jurisdiction for the court and the interrelationship between the powers of the court and the CSA is not simple (see **7.3**). Where the court does have the power to order maintenance for children, one of three statutes will apply:

- the Matrimonial Causes Act 1973—financial provision on divorce;
- the Domestic Proceedings and Magistrates Courts Act 1978—married parents; or
- the Children Act 1989—unmarried parents or the child itself.

7.1.2 Inflexibility—the old system

The CSA 1991 in its original form was unfair in a number of ways. The formula for calculating child maintenance was both too complicated and too inflexible. In particular, the original legislation made no allowance for pre-existing settlements. For example, an absent parent might have transferred his share of the matrimonial property to his former wife on divorce. In return, it might have been agreed that he would not pay any form of child maintenance or periodical payments to his former wife (a form of settlement known as a 'clean break'—see **4.4.3**). However, with the introduction of the CSA 1991, the same former husband would be liable for child support notwithstanding that he had made the transfer on the understanding that he would be excused any such payments (see *Crozier v Crozier* [1994] 1 FLR 126). This inflexibility was in part addressed by a system of 'departures' introduced by the Child Support Act 1995. Under this system, where a maintenance agreement or capital settlement was made before April 1993, or where specific costs had not been taken into account by the formula for assessment, a parent could apply for a 'departure' from the strict terms of the formula.

7.1.3 Child Support, Pensions and Social Security Act 2000

The 'departures' system has now been superseded in new cases by a system of 'variations', introduced by the CSPSSA 2000. Most of the significant provisions enacted by this statute came into force on 3 March 2003. At the time of writing, the majority of clients using the CSA are likely to be in receipt of, or waiting to receive, child support under these provisions. For this reason the amendments which have taken effect under the 2000 statute will be considered in some detail. The changes brought about, and due to be brought about, under CMOPA 2008 are set out as they arise and more fully in section **7.5** of this chapter.

The CSPSSA 2000 made a number of important amendments to the CSA 1991. These amendments are set out in the CSPSSA 2000, Sch 3, and result in a complete change to the way child support is calculated. The CSPSSA 2000 also introduced tougher penalties for non-payment, including, not entirely logically, disqualification from driving (CSA 1991, s 39A(2)). It should be noted that CMOPA 2008 has toughened enforcement procedures still further to include a possible order for the surrender of passports and even a curfew.

Any application for an assessment with an effective date earlier than 3 March 2003 is under the 1991 regime. The main relevance of the 1991 regime for practitioners is for appeals against assessments made under it—in 2006 there were about 800,000 cases under the old regime.

For cases with an effective date on or after 3 March 2003 the 2000 regime applies. In 2006 there were about 600,000 cases under the 2000 regime. The failure of the CSA to implement fully and effectively the child support regime has been the subject of considerable criticism. In December 2006, following publication of a report by Sir David Henshaw, the government published its White Paper 'A New System of Child Maintenance', the consultation period for which ended on 13 March 2007. This resulted in the enactment of CMOPA 2008. The act makes a number of fundamental reforms to the system and alters the percentage basis for child support calculations. The CMOPA 2008 has led to the establishment of the Child Maintenance and Enforcement Commission (CMEC). The CMEC at present has a largely advisory and support role but it is anticipated that it will take over the functions of the CSA at some point in the future. As indicated above, new applications under the CMOPA 2008 are expected to be accepted some time in 2010. For a summary of the 2008 provisions see **7.5**.

If the patchwork is beginning to seem horribly confused, it may at least be some consolation that the terminology introduced by the CSPSSA 2000 is unchanged by the CMOPA 2008. The 'absent' parent remains the non-resident parent (NRP); the child maintenance assessment remains the 'calculation'. The claimant, almost always the parent with care (PWC) has always been, and still is, described as 'she' in all three statutes. This chapter adopts the same approach for the sake of simplicity, though of course a PWC could be either mother or father. It should also be noted that in spite of the establishment of the CMEC, the CSA remains, at the time of writing, the body responsible for calculating and distributing child support. The plan is that the existing functions of the CSA should be transferred to the CMEC (see <www.csa.gov.uk/en/about/changes-at-the-csa>) but no date has yet been set for this transition.

7.2 The Child Support Agency

7.2.1 Jurisdiction of the Child Support Agency

Essentially, the CSA has jurisdiction where there is a parent with care (PWC), a non-resident parent (NRP) and a 'qualifying' child within the United Kingdom. It should be noted that a qualifying child must be the natural or adoptive child of the parent

(CSA 1991, s 3(1)). The definition is different from that employed in the Matrimonial Causes Act 1973 (MCA 1973) where 'child of the family' may include a stepchild. Any claim for child maintenance from a step-parent must be pursued through the courts. The court will also have jurisdiction to make an order where two parents are living in the same house, even if they are living separate lives. So if a couple in the process of divorce are still living together, it would be possible to seek an interim maintenance order for the benefit of a child at the first appointment (FA) or the financial dispute resolution (FDR) hearing.

7.2.2 The Child Support Agency and parents receiving benefit

Under the new legislation, the much criticised system, whereby parents with care could have their benefits suspended if they failed to make an application for child support, has been abolished (CMOPA 2008, s 15 repeals CSA 1991, s 6). From 14 July 2008 any PWC who makes a claim for income support will have the same choice as any other PWC. She may agree a private maintenance with her ex-partner or she can apply to the CSA for a statutory assessment. She may not wish to make any arrangement at all for child maintenance.

7.2.3 Procedure for child support application

A PWC who chooses to make an application for child support may do so either orally, on-line or in writing, using a prescribed form

7.2.4 The formula for calculating what is payable under CSPSSA 2000

The original formula introduced by the CSA 1991 was a complex system depending on the net income of both parents, housing costs, council tax, travelling costs and a number of other variables. In order to simplify the formula, the starting point under the 2000 regime system is the net income of the paying parent and the number of children in each household. Note that this will change under the 2008 regime when the starting point will be the gross income of the NRP. This will result in a change in the percentage basis of the calculation (see **7.5**). The income of the parent in receipt is ignored for the purposes of the calculation. The CSA 1991, Sch 1 lays down four rates:

- the basic rate;
- the reduced rate;
- the flat rate; and
- the nil rate.

7.2.4.1 The basic rate

One qualifying child	15% of net weekly income
Two qualifying children	20% of net weekly income
Three or more qualifying children	25% of net weekly income

Where the NRP has 'relevant other children' the amount payable is reduced. Relevant other children are defined in the CSA 1991, Sch 1, para 10C(2) as 'children other than qualifying children in respect of whom the non resident parent or his partner receives child benefit', in other words, children living with the NRP, either his own or his partner's.

7.2.4.2 The reduced rate

A reduced rate is payable where the NRP's net income is between £100 and £200 per week. For example, the reduced rate for one child will range from a minimum of £5 to a maximum of £27.50 per week.

7.2.4.3 The flat rate

A flat rate of £5 is payable where:

- the NRP has a net income of less than £100 per week;
- he or his partner are on income support or income-based jobseeker's allowance; or
- he is in receipt of a state pension, incapacity benefit, invalid care allowance or certain other benefits set out in the Child Support (Maintenance Calculations and Special Cases) Regulations 2000, reg 4.

If points 1 or 2 apply and the NRP looks after a qualifying child for at least 52 nights a year, he is eligible for the nil rate.4

7.2.4.4 The nil rate

Nothing is payable where the NRP is:

- a student;
- a pensioner;
- a geriatric patient;
- a prisoner;
- a child;
- a person whose net weekly income is less than £5;
- a person in receipt of an allowance in respect of work-based training for young people.

7.2.5 Apportionment

Where an NRP has qualifying children living with different parents, a simple apportionment system is applied (CSA 1991, Sch 1, para 6.1). For example, an NRP earns £400 per week and has three qualifying children aged 2, 5 and 14. The two younger children live with A and the eldest lives with B. The NRP's maintenance liability would be £100 (25 per cent of £400). A would receive two-thirds of this sum (£66.66) and B would receive one-third (£33.33). The ages of the children are immaterial.

7.2.6 Shared care

Under the 1991 legislation, 'absent' parents who had a qualifying child staying with them for more than a certain number of nights each year were given relief in the amount payable by way of child support. These provisions have been extended by the 2000 legislation (CSA 1991, Sch 1, paras 7–9). A sliding scale of reduction in payment applies depending on the number of nights the child stays with the NRP. The scale starts at one-seventh of the amount payable where the NRP has a qualifying child stay between 52 nights a year rising to one-half at 175 nights each year. If a child stays with the NRP for more than half the year, the NRP can apply to claim child benefit and thus become the PWC. See *At a Glance* for the full table.

7.2.7 Cap

Under the 2000 regime, net weekly income over £2,000 is ignored for the purpose of child support. The court retains the power to top up under the CSA 1991, s 8(6).

7.2.8 Variations

The system has always endeavoured to make allowance for situations where the strict application of the rules would lead to unfairness. 'Special cases' and 'departures' in the old regime are replaced in the new regime by the rules on 'variation' (CSA 1991, ss 28A–28G). The system of variations is complex and is described here in outline only.

Either parent may make an application for a variation. The application may be made by telephone initially, but the agency may then ask for an application in writing. The word 'variation' suggests a degree of discretion on the part of the CSA but, in fact, the grounds for variation are currently limited to the following (CSA 1991, Sch 4B, Part 1):

(a) Special expenses in connection with any of the following:
  (i)   costs incurred in keeping in contact with a qualifying child;
  (ii) costs attributable to the long-term illness or disability of a relevant other child;
  (iii) debts incurred when the parents were living together for the benefit of themselves or their children. This can include loans on mortgages;
  (iv) boarding school fees of the qualifying child;
  (v)   payments on the mortgage of the home of the qualifying child where the NRP has no continuing interest in the property.

(b) Pre-April 1993 property transactions.

(c) Too much capital, for example, where the NRP has an interest or assets exceeding £65,000 in value. This does not include assets used in the course of a business, compensation for personal injury, property which is home, or any other asset which the CSA considers to be 'reasonable in all the circumstances'.

(d) Unreasonable manipulation of income.

(e) Lifestyle inconsistent with declared income.

7.2.9 The variation jurisdiction

The Secretary of State may only allow a variation if it would be 'just and equitable'. In coming to this decision, the CSA is to have regard to the welfare of the child affected and other factors laid out in the CSA 1991, Sch 4B and the Child Support (Variations) Modification of Statutory Provisions Regulations 2000. These are:

• whether a variation would be likely to result in the NRP falling out of work;

• whether the NRP already has a liability to any child maintenance under a court order or agreement;

• whether the NRP who claims to have special expenses could in fact rearrange his financial affairs so as to afford those expenses.

The Regulations also set out factors that must not be taken into account. These include matters such as the conduct of the parents and whether or not the child in question was planned. The Regulations also allow for 'thresholds' for special expenses. For example, if an expense claimed as special is less than £10 a week and the relevant weekly income is £200, the expense will not be taken into account.

7.2.10 Default maintenance decisions

Under the new regime, the punitive system of interim assessments is abolished. Instead, where the CSA is required to make a maintenance calculation and does not have sufficient material to enable it to do so, it may impose a 'default' maintenance decision. This requires the NRP to pay a fixed rate set by the Child Support (Maintenance Calculation Procedure) Regulations 2000. These rates are currently £30 for one qualifying child, £40 for two qualifying children and £50 where there are three or more qualifying children.

7.2.11 Appeals

Where a parent is aggrieved by a decision of the Secretary of State, the first step is an application for 'revision'. If this fails and where the right of appeal exists, the parent may apply to the Child Support Appeal Tribunal. The next stage, if the right of appeal exists, is to the Child Support Commissioner. There may be an appeal from the Child Support Commissioner, but only on a point of law, to the Court of Appeal. Judicial review of the Secretary of State's decision may be possible in some cases. A number of cases have made it clear that the CSA, as an independent agency, is outside the court system and there can be no appeal to a court on the substance of the agency's decision (*Farley v SSW&P* [2006]1WLR HL; *Secretary of State for Social Security v Shotton* [1996] 2 FLR 241).

7.3 The powers of the court

7.3.1 Areas where the court retains jurisdiction

The court retains the power to order financial provision for children in cases that stand outside the jurisdiction of the CSA. The main circumstances where the CSA has no jurisdiction and the court can therefore make an order are:

(a) Where the parents are still living together.

(b) Where one of the parents is not habitually resident in the UK. Note that there is a special provision introduced by the CSA 1991, s 44(2A) that exempts certain individuals from this category. Thus, a civil servant working overseas, a member of the Armed Forces stationed abroad or employees of certain companies that employ people to work overseas but make calculation and payment arrangements in the UK would be liable for CSA calculations.

(c) If the child is not a qualifying child but is, for example, a stepchild.

(d) If the child is aged 17–19 but not in full-time education.

(e) If the parent earns more than £2,000 net per week and a top-up is appropriate. Under the 2008 regime the figure would be £3,000 gross. But as the CSA is not yet accepting applications under this regime, parents who earn more than £2,000 net but less than £3,000 gross could still be the subject of an application through the courts.

(f) If the order is for school fees.

(g) If the child is disabled and has special needs in addition to normal maintenance.

(h) If the order is for a lump sum or property adjustment rather than maintenance. Note, however, that in *Phillips v Pearce* [1996] 2 FLR 230, Johnson J made it clear that the court must not award a lump sum as a form of capitalised maintenance when the matter is within the jurisdiction of the CSA.

7.3.2 Written agreements

There is also a limited provision for the court to make orders based on written agreements (CSA 1991, s 9). These will usually be consent orders. Under the old regime parents could 'contract out' of the CSA system by means of a written agreement. Under the new regime any court order made before 3 March 2003 having that effect will continue to do so. However, any such court order made after that date will only be 'protected' from the CSA for a period of 12 months, after which either parent may make an application for an interim assessment followed by a full child support calculation (CSA 1991, s 4(10)). The CMOPA 2008 does not mention consent orders. This provision is therefore unchanged.

7.3.3 Other areas of overlap between the courts and the CSA

If maintenance for a child is set by agreement, or if an application is made to vary a court order, the figure the CSA might award is relevant for the court to consider, although not decisive (*E v C* [1996] 1 FLR 472).

7.3.4 Wording an order for financial provision

Where a practitioner is seeking to draft a consent order for financial provision in divorce proceedings or for the benefit of a child of unmarried parents, it is important where possible to put the order in context as regards the CSA.
Note the following:

(a) If a consent order for financial provision, known as 'periodical payments', is made on divorce, it may still be useful to record that a CSA calculation will be made to meet the needs of the children.

(b) It is possible, and often advisable, to word an order to allow for the replacement of court-ordered maintenance by child support. Such an order is commonly known as a 'Segal' order, named after the District Judge who initiated the practice in the Principal Registry of the Family Division. Note that such an order may only serve as a holding operation until the CSA takes on responsibility for child maintenance and there must be a 'substantial' element of spousal support (see *Dorney-Kingdom v Dorney-Kingdom* [2000] 3 FCR 20).

(c) If the court is making an order that it has power to make in any event, eg, for school fees, the order can be worded in a conventional way but it may help to clarify the situation to state whether the order is in addition to a CSA calculation.

7.4   Child support: summary of 2000 regime

The 2000 regime makes rough calculations much easier than they were under the 1991 arrangements. Practitioners cannot be expected to remember every detail of the system, so you will want to refer to loose-leaf books and Internet-based resources. However, as a bare minimum, it is important to remember the following points:

(a) A PWC who lives in the UK and is not living with her child's father *may* at any time make an application for a child support calculation in relation to her biological or adopted child or children provided (with some exceptions) the father lives in the UK (CSA 1991, s 4).

(b) Similarly, a PWC who is receiving certain state benefits and is not living with her child's father may make an application for a child support calculation in relation to her biological or adopted child or children. CSA 1991 s 6 has been repealed and there is no longer any obligation to make such an application.

(c) The CSPSSA 2000, amends the CSA 1991 and allows for a system of 'variations', currently confined to certain special cases (CSA 1991, ss 28A–28G).

(d) Where the CSA has jurisdiction, the court may not make an order for child support unless such an order is by way of confirmation of a written agreement (CSA 1991, s 8(5)). Such an order, if made after 5 April 2002, cannot oust the jurisdiction of the CSA permanently. One year after the making of such an order, either party may apply to the CSA for a calculation.

(e) Under the CSPSSA 2000, the income of the PWC is irrelevant.

7.5   The Child Maintenance and Other Payments Act 2008 and the future of child support

The Child Maintenance and Enforcement Commission, established by virtue of CMOPA 2008, s1, is a non-departmental public body whose main objective is:

to maximise the number of those children, who live apart from one or both of their parents, for whom effective maintenance arrangements are in place. (CMOPA 2008, s 2)

The CMEC currently has an advisory and support role while the CSA continues to effect the calculation and recovery of child support. It is anticipated that the CMEC will take over the functions of the CSA but it is unclear how or when this will come about. Transfer of 1991 and 2000 cases to the new regime is expected to begin in 2010 and to be completed in 2013.

Key features of the 2008 system include:

• use of gross rather than net income for assessment basis

• a change to the percentage rates to be used for calculation. For gross incomes of £200 or more per week up to £800 pw basic rates will be 12%, 16% or 19% for 1, 2 or 3 children respectively. In excess of £800 the percentages are 9%, 12% and 15% respectively. Gross weekly income in excess of £3,000 will be disregarded;

- a reduced rate for gross incomes between £100 and £200 per week;

- flat rate of £7 per week for gross income under £100 per week;

- nil rate on similar terms as 2000 regime;

- more emphasis on encouraging agreed arrangements between parents;

- abolition of the rule requiring parents receiving benefits to make a child support application (dealt with at **7.2.2** above);

- awards fixed for yearly terms with restriction on applications for variation; and

- more effective enforcement procedures including curfews and passport confiscation.

There was extensive criticism of the proposed new regime prior to the enactment of CMOPA 2008. As will be apparent from the previous paragraphs, one major problem is the impracticality of running three systems during the transitional period. At the time of writing it is not clear when the first 2008 regime applications will be processed. Another concern is the continuing limitation on the powers of the court to deal with child maintenance disputes.

For further observations on the effect of the CMOPA 2008, readers are referred to the following articles: 'Child Support: the Brave New World' [2008] *Family Law*, October; 'Child Support: Carrots and Sticks' [2008] *Family Law*, November; 'Child Support Appeals: Disclosure of Papers' [2009] *Family Law*, January; 'Arrears of Child Support: The Magistrates' Court Function' [2009] *Family Law*, April.

7.6 Applications under the Children Act 1989, Sch 1

Where a PWC seeks provision for a child or children from the other parent to whom he or she is not married, the appropriate statutory provision is the CA 1989, s 15 and Sch 1. A person over the age of 18 whose parents are living separately may also in certain circumstances make an application for an order on his or her own behalf (CA 1989, Sch 1, para 2(a) and (b)).

Orders under the CA 1989, Sch 1 continue in force until the child's seventeenth birthday unless the court thinks it right to specify a date not beyond the child's eighteenth birthday. Orders may be extended beyond the eighteenth birthday if the child is a student or there are special circumstances. These special circumstances are not set out in the statute but might include, for example, disablement.

The language of the Schedule echoes that of the MCA 1973, s 23 and the orders that can be made are as follows:

- periodical payments;

- secured periodical payments;

- lump sum orders;

- settlements;

- transfer of property orders;

- interim periodical payment orders; and

- orders altering a maintenance agreement.

Such orders may be sought in the County court or the Family Proceedings Court (FPC), although the FPC is restricted to making orders for periodical payments, interim periodical payments and lump sum orders to the level of £1,000.

Orders under the CA 1989, Sch 1 may direct payment to the child itself or to the applicant 'for the benefit of the child'. Thus, it is possible for the court to order the transfer of a tenancy into the sole name of a parent for the benefit of a child (see *K v K (Minors: Property Transfer)* [1992] 2 FLR 220).

Where, as in most cases, the court has no jurisdiction to make periodical payments for the benefit of the child as a result of the CSA 1991, s 8(3), lump sum orders may still be awarded and this is the main use of Schedule 1 in practice. For an article on the development of Schedule 1 proceedings since 2003, see 'Schedule 1 to the Children Act 1989: Consider the Mother's Future' [2007] *Family Law*, March.

7.6.1 Definitions

In contrast to the CSA 1991, under CA 1989, Sch 1, a 'parent' includes any party to a marriage in relation to whom the child concerned is a child of the family. Unmarried fathers are included whether or not they have parental responsibility for the child concerned. However, for the purposes of the CA 1989, Sch 1, an unmarried cohabitee who is not the father or mother of the child is not a parent however long he or she has lived with the child. If the parties marry, the parent will become a step-parent and thus a 'parent' for the purpose of Sch 1.

7.6.2 Procedure

The procedure for making an application under the CA 1989, Sch 1 is almost identical to that required in making any other application under the CA 1989 (see the Family Proceedings Rules 1991 (SI 1991/1247), r 4 and the Family Proceedings Courts (Children Act) Rules 1991/1395, r 4). In addition, the applicant is required to fill out a form setting out the financial details he or she believes to be relevant to the application (Form C10A).

An application under the CA 1989 may be free-standing or may be attached to an application for any other order under the Act. It is also possible for the court to make a Sch 1 order of its own motion whenever it makes or discharges a residence order (CA 1989, Sch 1, para 1(6)). This is, however, somewhat unusual.

7.6.3 Statutory criteria

Once again, the language of the CA 1989, Sch 1 echoes that of the MCA 1973. The relevant paragraph is set out below:

4 Matters to which court is to have regard in making orders for financial relief

(1) In deciding whether to exercise its powers under paragraph 1 or 2, and if so in what manner, the court shall have regard to all the circumstances including—

(a) the income, earning capacity, property and other financial resources which each person mentioned in sub-paragraph (4) has or is likely to have in the foreseeable future;

(b) the financial needs, obligations and responsibilities which each person mentioned in sub-paragraph (4) has or is likely to have in the foreseeable future;

(c) the financial needs of the child;

(d) the income, earning capacity (if any), property and other financial resources of the child;

(e) any physical or mental disability of the child;

(f) the manner in which the child was being or was expected to be educated or trained.

(2) In deciding whether to exercise its powers under paragraph 1 against a person who is not the mother or father of the child, and if so in what manner, the court shall in addition have regard to—

(a) whether that person has assumed responsibility for the maintenance of the child and, if so, the extent to which and basis on which he assumed that responsibility and the length of the period during which he met that responsibility;

(b) whether he did so knowing that the child was not his child;

(c) the liability of any other person to maintain the child.

(3) Where the court makes an order under paragraph 1 against a person who is not the father of the child, it shall record in the order that the order is made on the basis that the person against whom the order is made is not the child's father.

(4) The persons mentioned in sub-paragraph (1) are—

(a) in relation to a decision whether to exercise its powers under paragraph 1, any parent of the child;

(b) in relation to a decision whether to exercise its powers under paragraph 2, the mother and father of the child;

(c) the applicant for the order;

(d) any other person in whose favour the court proposes to make the order.

The child's welfare, while relevant, is not required to be the court's paramount concern as the court is not determining a question with respect to the 'upbringing' of the child (CA 1989, s 1). Nor does the 'no order' principle (CA 1989 s 1(5)) apply in such an application (*K v H (Child Maintenance)* [1993] 2 FLR 61).

8

Children—private law

8.1 Introduction

The law relating to children in both private law and public law situations (see **Chapters 9** and **10**) can mainly be found in the Children Act 1989 (CA 1989), as amended by the Adoption and Children Act 2002 (ACA 2002) and the Children and Adoption Act 2006 (CAA 2006). The main rules governing jurisdiction and procedure are:

- in the magistrates' court, the Family Proceedings Courts (Children Act 1989) Rules 1991 (SI 1991/1395) (FPCR 1991);

- in the County court and High Court, the Family Proceedings Rules 1991 (SI 1991/1247) (FPR 1991); and

- in the domestic court, the Family Proceedings Courts (Matrimonial Proceedings etc) Rules 1991 (SI 1991/1991) (FPC(MP)R 1991).

But note that these rules must now be read subject to the procedural guidance introduced from July 2005 in the Private Law Programme. The aim is to speed up proceedings, achieve greater resolution by consent and give courts greater case management responsibility: see **8.6.1**. Forms must be used in all applications. Where no form is provided, then a written request should be made to the court.

Much of the philosophy underpinning the legislation is of non-intervention—a belief that, in the main, parents know best what is good for their children and will act in their children's best interests. It also provides for a unified structure of both law and jurisdiction, with concurrent jurisdiction and cases capable of being transferred from one court to another.

The Handbook of Best Practice in Children Act Cases (HMSO, June 1997) contains detailed guidance from the Children Act Advisory Committee.

The Human Rights Act 1998 (HRA 1998) also has an impact in child cases as it incorporates the European Convention on Human Rights directly into UK law. There are a number of areas where the HRA 1998 is relevant in child cases, in particular Art 6 which provides the right to a fair trial and Art 8 which provides the right to respect for family life. The HRA 1998 imposes obligations on the state, both negative and positive, and applies to public authorities. The individual is, therefore, able either to bring proceedings directly against public authorities under the HRA 1998 or rely on Convention rights in any legal proceedings. The most obvious areas in which the HRA 1998 applies in child cases relate to unmarried fathers, same-sex couples, care plans, the enforcement of contact orders, abduction and the disclosure of information (see *TP and KM v United Kingdom*, Application No 28945/95 [2001] 2 FLR 549). Where a local authority fails to act to protect children from abuse, then Art 3 (inhuman and degrading treatment) can be used (see *Z and Others v United Kingdom*, Application

No 29392/95 [2001] 2 FLR 612, where pecuniary damages were awarded for this breach under Art 13). A breach of Art 8 has been found where following the granting of a care order, the local authority abandoned the care plan without informing the mother (*Re C* (*Breach of Human Rights; Damages*) [2007] 1 FLR 1957).

8.1.1 'Old terminology'

Old terminology used prior to the HRA 1998 such as 'custody' may still be used (particularly by litigants-in-person), it is important to have some familiarity with the former law if you practise in this area.

On divorce or separation, a parent could apply for an order for 'custody' of a child, which if awarded would give the person with custody the right to take most major decisions 'with regard' to the child. Custody was normally awarded to one parent alone and might therefore be strongly contested, though a joint order could be made if it was thought there would be cooperation.

A separate order for 'care and control' could be made for the day-to-day care of the child as distinct from the power to take decisions about the child. There might therefore be an order for joint custody of a child with care and control to one parent.

An order could also be made for 'access', which was roughly equivalent to the current contact order.

8.2 Parental responsibility (PR)

This concept makes clear that being a parent creates responsibilities rather than rights, and hence that these responsibilities exist whatever the state of the parents' relationship with each other. It emphasises the view that each will retain a (shared) continuing responsibility for the children. Where more than one person has PR for a child, each of them is given power to act alone (CA 1989, s 2(7)) unless each person with PR is by law required to give his or her consent, for example, to adoption. PR can be shared by a range of people and with a local authority where the child is in care, and an order can be made even though the child was neither born nor is resident in the UK.

8.2.1 What does parental responsibility mean?

The concept of PR replaced that of custody while incorporating into it much of the common law meaning of custody. The CA 1989, s 3(1), states that PR encompasses 'all the rights, duties, powers, responsibilities and authority which by law a parent of a child has in relation to the child and his property'. At common law the meaning of custody has never been absolutely clear with most writers relying on the definition of it by Sachs LJ in *Hewer v Bryant* [1970] 1 QB 357, at p 373:

'custody'...embraces...a 'bundle of powers'...These include power to control education, the choice of religion, and the administration of the infant's property. They include entitlement to veto the issue of a passport and to withhold consent to marriage. They include, also, both the personal power physically to control the infant until the years of discretion and the right...to apply to the courts to exercise the powers of the Crown as *parens patriae*.

In practice parental responsibility impacts on such matters as deciding the child's name, religion, consenting to medical treatment, using corporal punishment and giving consent to marriage. The 'bundle of powers' has often been described as a dwindling one because the more mature the child is, the more difficult it is for a parent to justify exercising total power over him or her. A particular example of this can be seen in the discussion surrounding the power to control the medical treatment of a child (see *Gillick v West Norfolk & Wisbech Area Health Authority* [1986] AC 112).

The main addition is to make clear that there are responsibilities which automatically follow parenthood. The Children (Scotland) Act 1995 defines PR and includes matters such items as safeguarding and promoting the child's health, development and welfare, giving direction and guidance, the maintenance of personal relations and direct personal contact, and the right to live with the child (see s 1(1)).

8.2.2 Who has parental responsibility?

(a) **Mother**: always has **PR**—s 2 CA 1989 (ACA 2002)

(b) **Father**: if married to the mother at the time of the child's birth, he will automatically acquire **PR** s 2(1) CA 1989.

Previously fathers not married to the mother at the time of the child's birth did not have **PR** unless the following positive steps were taken:

(i) Entering into a PR agreement with the mother. An agreement must comply with the Parental Responsibility Regulations 1991 (SI 1991/1478), reg 2 (as amended by SI 1994/3157). Agreements must be signed, there must be proof of identity of the parents and the child; the agreement must then be registered in the Principal Registry of the Family Division. It should be noted that an agreement can be terminated by order of the court either on application by a person with parental responsibility or, with leave, by a child with sufficient understanding (CA 1989, s 4(3) and (4) (see *Re A* [1994] 2 FCR 709, CA).

(ii) Court order

If the mother does not consent to the father obtaining PR, it is open to the father to apply to Court.

The European Convention on Human Rights has been used by unmarried fathers to gain rights. In *X, Y and Z v UK* [1995] 2 FLR 892 and *Keegan v Ireland* (1994) 18 EHRR 342 the court was asked to consider the meaning of family life (Art 8) in relation to unmarried fathers and concluded that a number of factors would be relevant as to whether Art 8 was engaged, including whether the couple had lived together, length of the relationship and whether they had demonstrated their commitment to each other by having children.

The court considers the child's welfare as the paramount consideration (*Re G (A Minor) (Parental Responsibility Order)* [1994] 1 FLR 504, and the making of the order must be better for the child than making no order at all. Factors that will be taken into account include the degree of commitment shown to the child, the degree of attachment that exists and the reasons for applying (see *Re H (No 3)* [1991] Fam 151).

(iii) Obtaining a residence order

Section 12(1) CA 1989 directs the court to make a PR order under s 4 if the father obtains an RO and does not have PR.

(iv) Marrying the child's mother

(v) Being appointed a guardian

(Appointment in this manner can relate to another person other than the father too.)

(vi) Adopting the child

The unmarried father never automatically acquired **PR**.

Section 4 CA 1989 was amended by ACA 2002, s 111 in December 2003, which altered the unsatisfactory position in relation to unmarried father's and PR.

The position now is that an unmarried father can obtain PR from 1 December 2003 when his name is included on the child's birth certificate CA 1989, s 4(1)(a).

In relation to a birth registration which does not mention the father's name the birth can be reregistered—see Births and Deaths Registration Act 1953, s 10A.

If reregistering the birth is not an option, the unmarried father can attempt to obtain **PR** by any of the routes detailed in (i)–(vi).

(c) Step-parent

They will be able to use the procedure open to a father by applying for a court order or entering into an agreement with the mother to share responsibility (**ACA**, s 112 amending **CA 1989**, s 4).

If an **RO** is made in favour of step-parent then he will have **PR** for the duration of the **RO**. There are number of restrictions to the exercise of step-parent's **PR**—see **CA** 1989, s 12(2)–(4).

There are other parties who may apply for an **RO** (see **8.3.4**)—if they are successful in such an application they will acquire **PR**, subject to the same restrictions as step-parent.

(d) Local authority

The local authority obtain **PR** when an interim care order, a full care order or an Emergency Protection order is made (see **9.5.3.1**).

(e) Adoption

When a child is placed for adoption, PR vests in the adoption agency and the prospective adopters (**ACA** 2002, s 25(2) and 25(3)). (When the child is placed for adoption, the adoption agency may restrict the PR of any parent or guardian (**ACA** 2002, s 25(4)). When the adoption order is made, the PR of all others save for the adopter or the adopters is extinguished (**ACA** 2002, s 46(2)).

8.2.3 Transferring PR

A person who has **PR** may not transfer responsibility to another. However, he or she can arrange for the responsibility to be met by some other person acting on his or her behalf (including someone who has **PR** for that child) while remaining responsible for the failure by that delegate to act (CA 1989, s 2(9)–(11)).

8.3 Section 8 orders

8.3.1 Types of s 8 order

Section 8 of the Children Act 1989 empowers the court to make, vary or discharge the following orders:

(a) *Contact order* (*CO*). This is an order which imposes on the person with whom the child lives a legal obligation to allow the child to have direct contact with the person named in the CO. this may include for example, a visit, stays, including overnight, long or short visits and holidays, telephone calls and contact at contact centres. Contact can however be restricted to indirect contact, for example, letters, birthday or Christmas cards, as in *Re P (Contact: Indirect Contact)* [1999] 2 FLR 893 where a father who had just served a long prison sentence was limited to sending cards to the child.

Supervised contact is used where a child has suffered or is at risk of suffering harm during contact where a third party provides one-to-one supervision to ensure that nothing untoward occurs, it is only justified if the person presents a risk to the child. A local authority cannot be directed to supervise contact and finding funding for supervised contact can prove problematic. Supported contact where contact takes places in a confined area alongside other children having contact with people monitoring the contact is less intrusive and is preferred by the courts to supervision.

Orders can be made for 'no contact' and this will mean that contact is prohibited. Contact orders are directed against the person with whom the child is living, and so, when the court is seeking to prevent that person allowing contact with someone unsuitable, a no contact order will be appropriate. However, it may be more effective to seek an order prohibiting contact (see **8.3.1**(c)) when this is directed to the person who is not to have contact as it can then be enforced against that person.

There is a presumption of contact between parents and their children (see **8.4**). The same presumption does not apply as between children and their step-parents or grandparents. A contact order made in favour of a parent no longer living with his or her spouse and children will cease to have effect if the parents resume cohabitation for a continuous period exceeding six months (CA 1989, s 11(6)). Orders can be made without notice or by consent, on written evidence or after an oral hearing and in favour of any person, including grandparents and siblings.

A contact order may contain directions about how it is to be carried out or may impose certain conditions to be complied with by any person to whom the conditions are expressed to apply, for example, that the child should not be exposed to a particular religious group, that contact be supervised by another person, that contact must be at a particular location, etc. Further conditions may be imposed concerning the duration of the order or concerning the duration of express provisions of the order. The court may also make any incidental, supplemental or consequential directions as it sees fit (CA 1989, s 11(7)) or it may order that a particular activity is undertaken alongside a contact order (CA 1989, s 11A as amended by CAA 2006, s 1).

Where matters have to be investigated, eg, allegations of violence and/or inquiry by the Courts and Family Court Advisory and Support Service (CAF-CASS—see **8.4.1**), the outcome of which may effect whether a contact order should be made or the type of contact that should be ordered, an interim contact order may be appropriate pending a final hearing. This is always a short-term position. In cases where allegations of domestic violence are made regard must be had to the case of *Re L (Contact; Domestic Violence)* [2000] 2 FLR 334. In particular it is important to have regard to the impact of domestic violence on children and how this in turn may require the imposition of safeguards or conditions around contact. Where allegations of violence are made a fact finding hearing should be listed at the earliest possible date to deal with this issue. The best practice in such cases was detailed in *Re A (Contact; Risk of Violence)* [2005] EWHC 851. This has now been supplemented by a practice direction issued by the President of the Family Division (*Practice Direction Residence and Contact Orders: Domestic Violence* [2008] 1 WLR 1062) which states that where domestic violence is raised as an issue, the court must identify at the earliest opportunity the factual and welfare issues involved. This practice direction was reissued on 14 January 2009 to affirm that a fact-finding hearing is part of the process of trying a case and not a separate exercise; where a case is then adjourned, it remains part-heard.

The courts decide issues relating to contact by having regard to the child's welfare as the paramount determinant and may decide to deny contact, for example, where there has been violence towards the mother although the presumption in favour of contact between children and their parents will generally prevail (see **8.4**).

(b) *Residence order (RO)*. This form of order specifies with whom the child is to live and nothing more, each parent with PR retaining the right to act independently. Orders can be made without notice in exceptional circumstances but an 'on notice' hearing will be listed shortly thereafter to allow both parties to make representations on the issue.

If a residence order is made in favour of a father who is not married to the mother of the child and does not have PR, then the residence order must also give PR to that father (CA 1989, s 12(1)). If a residence order is made in favour of a person without PR, then that person will be given that responsibility (excluding the power to consent to adoption or free for adoption or appoint a guardian) for the duration of the order (CA 1989, s 12(2) and (3)). A residence order gives no power to any person to change the child's surname, or to arrange for the child's removal from the jurisdiction for more than one month without the consent of all persons with PR or the leave of the court (although the court can include in the order general or specific leave to remove the child from the jurisdiction) (CA 1989, s 13). In *Re K (Minor) (Residence Order)* The Times, 8 January 1999 [1999] 1 FLR 583, on an application by the mother for leave to remove the child from the jurisdiction the court found the mother to be untrustworthy (having refused to allow the father to visit his child at an earlier stage). There was therefore concern that the father would not be allowed to see his child and so it was appropriate to refuse the application and also to deny the mother's claim for residence although she was granted contact.

In *Payne v Payne* [2001] 2 WLR 1827, CA, the court held that, in relocation cases, the rights of all the parties have to be balanced under Art 8 of the European Convention on Human Rights and any interference has to be both justified and proportionate. In this case, the Convention did not affect the requirement to balance the factors influencing the operation of the paramountcy of the welfare principle. In such a case, the courts have to balance the reasonable proposals and motivation of the parent wishing to relocate, the effects on the child of seriously interfering with the life of a custodial parent and the denial of contact to the absent parent. The principles stated in *Payne v Payne* have recently been reaffirmed in another Court of Appeal decision (*Re G (Leave to remove)* [2008] 1 FLR 1587. However, the considerations relevant to an application for temporary removal are different. See *Re A (Temporary Removal from Jurisdiction)* [2004] EWCA Civ 1587, where the CA held that weight had to be attached to the value to mother and child of a two-year move to South Africa for future career and development.

Interim residence orders which last for a limited period are possible but should be strictly limited in time to avoid delay. As stated above, applications can be made without notice, although only exceptionally (*Re G* [1993] 1 FLR 910), for example, where a child has been snatched or is in some other immediate danger. In order to challenge an order made without notice, it is necessary to apply for discharge or variation on notice although usually a return hearing will also be listed soon after the 'without' notice hearing.

A residence order may be granted in favour of two or more persons who do not live together (known as a 'shared residence order'). In this instance, the order may specify the periods in which the child is to reside at the different homes. The long held view was that shared residence orders were 'exceptional'. The Court of Appeal in *A v A* (*Minors*) (*Shared Residence Orders*) [1994] 1 FLR 669 moved away from this by indicating that they were still 'unusual' but must incur a positive benefit to the child. Dame Butler-Sloss in *D v D* (*Shared Residence Order*) [2001] 1 FLR 495 endorsed a more relaxed approach to making such orders if the best interests of the child dictated the necessity. In *Re C* (*A Child*) (*Shared Residence Order*) [2006] EWCA Civ 235, the Court of Appeal made it clear that such orders are no longer to be considered exceptional and are in fact appropriate if they reflect the reality of the child's circumstances. It is not necessary for the time to be divided equally between both parents in order for there to be a shared residence order. This more relaxed approach in relation to shared residence orders was further endorsed by the President of the Family Division in *Re A* (*A Child: Joint Residence/Parental Responsibility*) [2008] EWCA Civ 867 where the Court of Appeal stated that any lingering idea that a shared residence order was apt only where the children alternated between the two homes evenly was erroneous. If the home offered by each parent was of equal status and importance to a child, an order for shared residence could be valuable.

A shared residence order may be made in favour of a step-parent or the partner of a parent who is not biologically related to the child, after the parties have separated, for example in *Re G* (*Children*) (*Residence; Same-sex Partner*) [2006] UKHL 43.

(c) *Prohibited steps order* (*PSO*). This form of order prevents a parent with parental responsibility or a third party from taking any step which is specified in the order without the prior consent of the court, for example, taking the child out of the jurisdiction or changing the child's surname. A number of cases have considered the vexed question of changing children's surnames. In *Re PC* (*Change of Surname*) [1997] 2 FLR 730 it was held that where both parents have PR, either may change the child's surname provided the other consents, although such consent need not be in writing. In *Dawson v Wearmouth* [1997] 2 FLR 629 the court held that an unmarried father could apply to have the child's surname changed to his own but the court had discretion to decide whether to grant the application which was of major significance to the welfare of the child. Here, the mother's surname (that of her former husband and other children) was ordered to be retained by the child. This issue was revisited in *Re W, Re A, Re B* (*Change of Name*) [1999] 2 FLR 930 where the court provided a list of factors the court will consider when hearing such an application.

Where a residence order or care order is in place (CA 1989, ss 13(1) and 33(7)), the child's surname cannot be changed without the written consent of every person having PR, or the leave of the court. See *Practice Direction (Child: Change of Surname)* [1995] 1 FLR 458. Leave will only be granted in exceptional circumstances (*Re B (Change of Surname)* [1996] 1 FLR 791). See also *Re C (Minors) (Change of Surname)* The Times, 8 December 1997 and *Re C (A Minor) (Change of Surname)* The Times, 2 February 1998. Where there is no residence order, an application can be made under CA 1989, s 8 either for a prohibited steps order to prevent the surname being changed or for a specific issue order to allow the surname to be changed.

Applications made without notice are possible, the leave of the justices' clerk is required in magistrates' courts (see rule 4(4) FPCR 1991). See *Nottingham CC v P* [1994] Fam 18. Here, the local authority sought an *ex parte* order to oust the father from the family home where there was evidence of the possible sexual abuse of a daughter. The court found that the appropriate procedure here would have been through the public law provisions of the CA 1989. Otherwise, the effect of the application, if granted, would have been a 'no contact order' when the authority had no power to apply for a contact order (see s 9(2) CA 1989). In *Re H* [1995] 1 FLR 638 a prohibited steps order was made to prevent contact between the children and the mother's former cohabitant because of the possible risk to the children. To have made a 'no contact' order would effectively have put the mother under an obligation to prevent contact; the PSO was therefore the more sensible course.

(d) *Specific issue order (SIO)*. This form of order directs the way in which a disagreement about a specific issue which has arisen or may arise in respect of any aspect of PR should be resolved. For example, where those with PR do not agree on the form of education or religious upbringing which the child should have, the matter can be referred to the court for it to make a specific issue order. Applications made without notice are possible, with leave required in magistrates' courts. In *Camden LBC v R* [1993] 2 FLR 757, an application for the court to authorise the use of blood products on a child whose parents were Jehovah's Witnesses was successful. It was considered an appropriate use of the court's powers under the CA 1989, s 8, in preference to wardship, since there was no wider issue concerning the future welfare of the child. A contested issue relating to emergency medical treatment in *Re O* [1993] 2 FLR 149 was thought better dealt with under the wardship jurisdiction, although an application to allow a sterilisation operation to be carried out on a mentally retarded girl could be authorised (see *Re HG* [1993] 1 FLR 587). More recently in *Re S (Specific Issue Order: Religion: Circumcision)* [2004] EWHC 1282 (Fam) the court rejected the application from a Muslim mother who sought permission for both children to become practising members of the Islamic faith and for the 8-year-old boy to be circumcised. The Hindu father sought to promote the children's cultural heritage and the children's right to choose, when old enough, their religious preference.

The court may not make a prohibited steps or specific issue order if the result envisaged could be obtained by making a residence or contact order (CA 1989, s 9(5)). The court may not make a prohibited steps or specific issue order which in effect places a child in the care or under the supervision of a local authority, or which requires the child to be accommodated by or on behalf of the local authority, or confers power on a local authority to determine any issue on parental responsibility which has arisen or may arise.

An s 8 order may contain directions about how it is to be carried out, impose conditions on parents or other persons and specify when it is to come into effect and how long it is to last for, and any other provisions which the court thinks fit (CA 1989, s 11(7)) (see *Re M*, The Times, 10 November 1993). In *Re E (Residence: Imposition of Conditions)* [1997] 2 FLR 638 a mother successfully appealed against the imposition of a condition requiring her to live at a specific address, the court taking the view that the issue of location of residence should have been determined through cross-applications for residence and not through the imposition of conditions aimed at interfering with the ordinary rights of the resident parent. The imposition of conditions on a residence order restricting the primary carer's right to choose his or her place of residence should be seen as exceptional (see *Re B (A Child) (Prohibited Steps Order)* [2008] 1 FLR 613.

An s 8 order will be discharged by a care order (CA 1989, s 91(2)). Orders under s 8 will end after the child has reached the age of 16 unless the court is satisfied that the circumstances of the case are exceptional (CA 1989, s 9(6)). It is also possible for orders to specify a time period during which it shall apply.

8.3.2   Situations in which the court can make an s 8 order

Under CA 1989, s 10, an s 8 order with respect to a child can be made in any family proceedings in which an issue arises with respect to the welfare of the child. The application must either be made by a person entitled to apply for such an order, or where the court has granted leave, or if, in any event, the court considers that such an order should be made.

Equally, orders can be made in other proceedings on the application of a person entitled to make such an application or where the applicant has obtained the leave of the court. The application for leave is governed by the principles in the CA 1989, s 10(9).

8.3.3   What are family proceedings?

For the purpose of CA 1989, family proceedings are defined by s 8(3) and (4) of the act. These subsections are subject to regular update as legislation evolves. Currently the definitions include: proceedings under CA 1989, Parts I (general principles), II (orders in respect of children in family proceedings) and IV (local authority support for children); proceedings under MCA 1973 (ancillary relief, etc); Civil Partnership Act 2004, Sch 5; ACA 2002; DPMCA 1978 (limited financial provision in the magistrates' court); Matrimonial and Family Proceedings Act 1984, Part III (financial relief after overseas divorce); FLA 1996 (injunctions in domestic violence and associated issues) and the Crime and Disorder Act 1998, ss 11 and 12 (child safety orders).

8.3.4   Who can apply for an s 8 order?

Certain people can apply as of right; others require the leave of the court. Those entitled to apply for s 8 orders vary according to the nature of the order sought. For example, where a child is in the care of a local authority, the only order which the court has power to make is a residence order (CA 1989, s 9(1)). Once a child has reached the age of 16, the court has no power to make any s 8 order (except for discharge or variation) unless the circumstances are exceptional (CA 1989, s 9(6)).

Those who can apply as of right without leave are:

Parents or guardians and persons who have a residence order in respect of the child can apply for any s 8 order (CA 1989, s 10(4)). This includes the unmarried father but not former parents whose child has been adopted. Parents can apply for leave on behalf of their child where the child is too young to do so on his or her own behalf, where this would enable the child to receive public funding for representation.

The following persons are entitled to apply for a residence order or contact order without the leave of the court:

(i)   Any party to a marriage where the child is a 'child of the family' of that marriage. 'Child of the family' includes both the natural children of the parties to the marriage and step-children treated as a child of the family, excluding foster children.

(ii)   Any civil partner in a civil partnership in relation to whom the child is a child of the family.

(iii) Any person with whom the child has been living for a period of at least three years (subject to CA 1989, s 10(10)).

(iv)   Other persons who have the consent of the person in whose favour a residence order has been made, or the consent of the local authority which has the child in its care, or the consent of each person with PR can apply for a *residence or contact order* (CA 1989, s 10(5)). Local authorities *cannot* apply for or have such orders made in their favour.

Other persons given standing by rules of court, which may prescribe the circumstances in which others can apply and the orders which can be sought.

All other parties require the leave of the court to make an application for an s 8 order.

Application is in writing and a hearing will only be arranged if the grounds are not made out in the written application (see FPCR 1991, r 3; FPR 1991, r 4.3). Natural parents of an adopted child must seek leave (*Re S* The Times, 8 March 1993), as must a child (see *Re C* [1994] 1 FLR 26; *Re SC* [1994] 1 FLR 96).

Foster parents who have had the child *living with them* within the previous six months cannot apply for leave unless they have the consent of the local authority, they are related to the child or the child has lived with them for the past three years (CA 1989, s 9(3) and (4)).

8.3.5   When will the court grant leave to apply for an s 8 order?

Factors which the court is required to take particularly into account in deciding whether or not leave should be given (in relation to a person other than the child concerned) can be found in CA 1989, s 10(9). Factors include: the nature of the application, the applicant's connection with the child, the risk of harmful disruption to the child's life and, if the child is being cared for by the local authority, any plans which the authority has for the child's future and the wishes of the child's parents (see *Re A* [1992] Fam 182). However, s 10(9) does not provide an exclusive list of the factors to be taken into account. and the CA 1989, s 1(3) checklist does not apply to leave applications nor does CA 1989, s 1(1) (see *Re S (Contact: Application by Sibling)* [1998] 2 FLR 897. It has also been held that the court can have regard as to whether or not the substantive application has a chance of success (but not that it would be bound to succeed) (see *G v Kirklees MBC* [1993] 1 FLR 805 and *C v Salford CC* [1994] 2 FLR 926). *Re J* (*Leave to issue Application for Residence Order*) [2003] 1 FLR 114 emphasised that ECHR Arts 6 and 8 apply to these applications. *Re A* concerned an application by a former local authority foster mother for leave to apply for a residence order over her former foster child. It was held that courts are required to take into account the local authority's plans for the child (see CA 1989, s 10(9)(d)(i)) which must be based on the duty to safeguard and promote the child's welfare. They should not determine the application for leave on the basis that the welfare of the child is the paramount consideration.

There is also concern that cases will involve too many parties and so where, for example, the interests of grandparents coincide absolutely with those of the parents, there is no good reason to grant them leave to be separately represented (see *Re M* (*Sexual Abuse: Evidence*) [1993] 1 FLR 822). However a court may tend to look favourably on an application for leave from grandparents particularly in care proceedings. In *Re J* (*Leave to Issue Application for Residence Order*) [2003] 1 FLR 114, the Court of Appeal gave further guidance on the correct approach to such applications under s 10(9).

Where a child is in the care of a local authority the courts will be circumspect about granting leave when, in effect, the purpose of the application is to act purely as a review of the local authority's decisions in respect of the child (see *Re M* (*PSO: Application of Leave*) [1993] 1 FLR 275).

If the application for leave is made by the child, then the court can only grant leave if satisfied that the child has sufficient understanding to make the proposed application (CA 1989, s 10(8)). Such applications should be determined by the High Court (*Practice Direction* (*Applications by Children: Leave*), Fam D [1993] 1 WLR 313). The s 10(9) guidelines do not apply to applications made by children; there has, however, been a conflict of opinion as to whether or not the welfare principle should be paramount (see *Re C* [1994] 1 FLR 26 and *Re SC* [1994] 1 FLR 96 at **8.3.4**, the latter case following the thinking of the Court of Appeal in *Re A and W* (*Minors*) [1992] 1 WLR 422 that an application for leave does not involve a decision about the future upbringing of the child). The court has recently held the welfare of the child is not paramount (see *M v Warwickshire County Council* [2008] 1 FLR 1093) The current criterion which is taken into account is therefore the likelihood of the success of the application so as to avoid situations where the child is embarking on proceedings which are doomed to failure.

8.3.6   Section 91(14)

The court has the power to require a person who otherwise would be entitled to apply for an order without the need to obtain leave, to obtain leave for a particular application, s 91(14). See *Re R* [1998] 1 FLR 149 for an example and *C v W* [1998] 1 FCR 618 where it was said that the power was not just for hopeless or fruitless applications, but also where a parent pursues litigation unreasonably and in a manner damaging to the interests of the child.

Guidelines on when, and to what degree, such power should be exercised were laid down by the Court of Appeal in *Re P* [1999] 2 FLR 573. *Re C* (*A Child*) [2009] EWCA Civ 674 provides a checklist of the steps the court should undertake when faced with an s 91(14) application. The obvious conflict with the right of access to justice led the court to stress that the power should be used as the exception rather than the rule and that the section should be read in conjunction with the welfare principle outlined at **8.4**.

The power has been exercised where there have been repeated applications which have become or are becoming oppressive; and, pre-emptively, where the conduct has not yet reached that level or where there is no criticism of the applicant's conduct, but nonetheless the interests of the child require it. For example, in *Re M (Section 91(14) Order)* [1999] 2 FLR 553 the children were already confused, unhappy and unsettled and urgently needed to settle down and make their permanent home away from the mother, so contact needed to be put on a new footing and their mother had to come to terms with the arrangement. The court order was intended to be a long-term arrangement and a premature application by the mother would disrupt, upset and confuse the children more. However, s 91(14) orders should not be made in cases where there was substantial contact and the parents find communicating with each other difficult see *Re W (Children) (Restriction on Applications)* [2006] All ER (D) 229.

An absolute prohibition on applications falls outside s 91(14) and any such order would have to be made under the inherent jurisdiction of the court.

8.3.7 Duration of parental responsibility and s 8 orders

Agreements and guardian appointments last until the child reaches the age of 18. Section 8 orders end when the child is 16, unless the CA 1989, s 9(6) applies (ie, the circumstances are exceptional). If s 9(6) applies, the order will end when the child is 18 (CA 1989, s 91(11)).

8.3.8 Enforcement of s 8 orders

The enforcement procedure adopted depends on the type of order and its breach.

Where a person disobeys the terms of a residence order eg, refuses to return the child to the holder of a residence order there are two options available:

1. FLA 1986, s 34 empowers the court to make an order authorising an officer of the court or a police officer to take charge of a child and deliver to another.

2. An order can be sought without notice under the inherent jurisdiction of the court for the tipstaff (an enforcement officer of the Supreme Court) to find and recover a child.

Where there has been failure to comply with a contact order or certain terms of a residence order or injunctive relief this may amount to contempt of court, which is punishable with a fine or imprisonment. In the Family Proceedings Court the court may impose a fine or sentence a person to up to two months in prison of its own motion for breach of a court order under s63(3) of the Magistrates Court Act 1980. In the County court a penal notice may be attached to an order and a subsequent breach may result in a committal to prison. Alternatively, it may be advisable to consider a PSO.

An order is not capable of enforcement unless the order is clear and precise eg, an order providing for 'reasonable contact' would not be enforceable but an order stating that 'the child will be made available for contact every Wednesday between 6 pm–7 pm' is clearly defined and thus enforceable by attaching a penal notice.

A County court judge has jurisdiction to proceed of his or her motion with a committal order where the other party has not requested such action. Such procedure should only be used in exceptional cases and as a last resort where all other remedies have been exhausted (*Re M (A Minor) (Contact Order: Committal) The Times* 31 December 1998).

Generally, committal orders for breach of a contact or residence order are thought to be orders of the last resort but imprisonment is used in exceptional cases. In *AvN* (*Committal: Refusal of Contact*) [1997] 1 FLR 533, a mother who had shown implacable hostility towards contact between the father and the child was committed to prison for flagrant breach of a court order. The court held that the child's welfare was a material consideration but not the paramount consideration and so, even though the child would be affected by the imprisonment of the mother, there was ultimately a limit as to what the court would endure by way of breach of its orders. The Children Act Sub-Committee of the Lord Chancellor's Advisory Board on Family considered, in a report called '*Making Contact Work*', ways in which to address the problems of implacably hostile parents, fines or imprisonment being, in their view, 'crude weapons'. See *Re D* (*Intractable Contact Dispute: Publicity*) [2004] EWHC 727 for Munby J's recommendations on how to resolve the problems. In *VvV* (*Contact: Implacable Hostility*) [2004] EWHC 1215 (Fam) the court made a residence order in favour of the father when the mother had consistently failed to make the children available for contact. The court found the children had suffered emotional harm by the mother and this would continue if the children were deprived of the relationship with their father.

With effect from 1 November 2008, s 11 CA 1989 was amended by the CAA 2006 and provides for a more robust mechanism for the enforcement of contact orders. Under the new provisions, the court can order that a particular activity is undertaken during the period of contact and require CAFCASS to monitor a person's compliance with the activity. The court can also direct CAFCASS to monitor whether a person is complying with a contact order and report to the court. New enforcement powers where a contact order is breached include requiring the person in breach to undertake unpaid work. Financial compensation may also be ordered for losses sustained through non-compliance with a contact order. All contact orders made or varied after 8 December 2008 must have a warning on them, setting out the consequences of not complying with an order.

For detailed consideration of the procedure on applications to commit see **Chapter 13**.

8.4 The welfare principle and the welfare checklist

The CA 1989, s 1 states that the court should have regard to the child's welfare as the paramount consideration when determining any question relating to the child's upbringing or the administration of the child's property. The principle can also apply therefore to wardship proceedings, non-convention (that is, non-European and Hague Convention cases) child abduction cases and the exercise of the inherent jurisdiction in general. However, it does not apply in those cases described above, where the child's upbringing is not directly in issue, for example, where the application is for leave to make an application under s 8, or in restricting publications that might be harmful to a child. In proceedings brought under the ACA 2002 concerning placement orders and adoption orders the welfare of the child is, as in CA 1989 cases, the paramount consideration.. In *Re H* [1994] 2 AC 212, the court held that the welfare of the child on whose behalf the application is made should have paramountcy in the proceedings. The welfare principle is made subject to the general non-interventionist principle that the court shall not make the order or any order *unless it considers that doing so would be better for the child than making no order at all* (CA 1989, s1(5)). This means that the court must be assured that there is actually some benefit to the child in making the order sought.

CA 1989 provides a list of circumstances to which the court is directed to have particular regard when considering whether or not to make an s 8 order, or when deciding whether or not to make, vary or discharge a care or supervision order. These are set out in CA 1989, s 1(3) and are widely known as the welfare checklist. The circumstances include:

(a) The ascertained wishes of the child (subject to the age of the child) ie, what the child has said he or she wants to happen, if he or she is considered old enough or mature enough to reach such a decision. However, in *Re J* [1992] Fam Law 229, the court said that the fact the wishes and feelings of the child were first on the s 1 welfare checklist gave them no priority over other items which included any harm the child was suffering or at risk of suffering. The case concerned a 16-year-old anorexic girl who was in local authority care and who was refusing medical treatment.

(b) The child's physical, emotional and educational needs i.e., who can best provide for all the needs of the child. Issues such as with whom the child has a bonded relationship, the impact which an order is likely to have on the child's sense of security and the importance of maintaining the status quo are of importance here, as is knowing both parents (see *Re F* (*Paternity Jurisdiction*) [2008] 1 FLR 225 where the Court of Appeal confirmed that the court can, where appropriate, order a mother to inform her children of the identity of their natural father).

(c) The likely effect of any change in the circumstances (eg, if another adult is to be introduced into the child's life because one parent is to remarry or cohabit with someone new, a move to new accommodation or to a new school, etc). See *Re H* The Times, 7 September 1992.

(d) The age, sex, ethnicity, background and any other characteristics of the child which the court thinks relevant. In *Re B* [1998] 1 FLR 520, the court stated that there had been a major shift in expert opinion on the weight to be given to the ethnic background of children in residence cases, and so confirmed that two Nigerian boys could remain with their white foster mother who had cared for them since birth and was in accordance with the boys' vehemently expressed wishes. When it comes to the care of a child of either sex, there is not a presumption existing in favour of one or other parent. The courts are keen not to endorse a gender bias when dealing with s 8 cases. You may be aware of pressure groups such as Fathers for Justice, who campaign for a change to the law as they feel that an anti-father bias exists. This is an ongoing debate—but the starting point for the courts is to make no assumptions and to consider how to deal with each case based on its own circumstances. Other issues which may be relevant here relate to bringing up a child in circumstances that could be said to be slightly unusual and hence which might potentially affect the child's welfare, for example, where a parent belongs to religious cult group or is a scientologist, or, where grandparents are seeking an s 8 order, their age may be a relevant consideration.

(e) Any harm which has been suffered or of which there is a risk (eg, where a child has been neglected or physically or sexually abused or it is feared that there is a risk of such abuse).

(f) The ability of the parents or other relevant people to meet the child's needs (eg, where the adult carer suffers from some disability which affects the care which he or she can offer, this will be a relevant consideration). Lesbianism per se will not be seen as making a mother unfit to have the future care of her child (see *C v C* [1991] 1 FLR 223).

(g) The range of powers available to the court in the proceedings (ie, whether it is right for the court to exercise its powers in a particular way).

In *Re P* [1999] 2 FLR 573, the House of Lords held that the Roman Catholic foster parents of a Down Syndrome child born to orthodox Jewish parents could have a residence order made in their favour with reasonable contact to the child's natural parents. The House of Lords confirmed that the benefit to the child of continuing to be brought up by the foster parents, to whom she had become greatly attached, outweighed the benefit to her in being brought up as an orthodox Jew as she did not have the capacity to understand fully or appreciate her Jewish heritage. In effect, this case has added consideration of religious background to the checklist of matters to be taken into account when assessing the welfare principle.

A failure by the court in reaching a decision to run through the checklist may make it easier for a dissatisfied party to appeal against the decision, made on the grounds that the judge below was 'plainly wrong' (see *M v M* [1987] 2 FLR 146).

The general principle in disputed contact cases has been that the child has a basic right to know both its parents, but there are an increasing number of cases in which there have been cogent reasons why the child should be denied that opportunity. In *Re D* [1993] 2 FLR 1, the cogent reason for denying access was the 'implacable hostility' to contact of both the mother and her parents with whom she and the child lived. In *Re D (Contact: Reasons for Refusal)* [1997] 2 FLR 314, the Court of Appeal held that implacable hostility could occur in cases where there were good reasons for that hostility as well as in cases where there were no good reasons for that hostility. In that case, there were good reasons because of the violence of the father to the mother. In *Re L (A Child) (Contact: Domestic Violence)* [2001] 2 WLR 339, it was held that, while there is no presumption against contact simply because of domestic violence, it was one factor among many which might offset the assumption in favour of contact when carrying out the balancing exercise under the welfare principle. Further, in interim contact applications, where allegations of domestic violence have yet to be adjudicated upon, the court should give particular consideration to the likelihood of harm, whether physical or emotional, if contact is granted or denied, and try to ensure that any risk to the child is minimised and the safety of the child and residential parent protected, during, before and after contact. The court further suggested that, under the European Convention on Human Rights, Art 8(2), the interests of the child must prevail where there is a serious conflict between the interests of the child and a parent. In all cases, the power to order no contact or no direct contact should be exercised sparingly.

The FLA, s 11 also makes provision for the making of orders under the CA 1989 over children of the family (either those under 16 or those over that age but in respect of whom the court directs that the section should apply) where there are proceedings for divorce or separation. The concept of the welfare of the child being paramount applies, but in application of that concept the court is required to have particular regard to:

(a) The wishes of the child, having regard to its age.

(b) The conduct of the parties in relation to the upbringing of the child.

(c) The general principle that in the absence of evidence to the contrary, welfare will be best served by:

    (i)   regular contact with those who have parental responsibility and with members of the family;

    (ii)   maintenance of as good a relationship as possible with the parents.

(d) Any risk attributable to:

    (i)   where, and the persons with whom, the child will reside;

    (ii)   any other arrangements for the care and upbringing of the child.

However, FLA 1996, s 11 is not yet in force.

8.4.1 Welfare reports

In order to help the court make an informed decision about the welfare of the child, the CA 1989, s 7 empowers the court to seek expert evidence in the form of a written or oral welfare report (or ask the local authority to arrange for such a report to be made). In the past, such a report would have been compiled by a court welfare officer. In April 2001, the three branches of the welfare services (the Official Solicitors' Department, guardians *ad litem* and court welfare officers) were merged into one body known as the Courts and Family Court Advisory and Support Service (CAFCASS). Unless prepared by a local authority officer, the new title for those compiling court welfare reports is a CAFCASS officer.

The court can ask that such reports concentrate on certain specified matters or ask for a general report. The court can override legal professional privilege in proceedings and order disclosure of reports adverse to a party's interests if it is relevant to a determination (*Re R* [1993] 4 All ER 702).

CAFCASS have the power to interview a child to ascertain wishes and feelings, contact the school, read social services' files and observe contact.

8.5 Rules of evidence

You should note, in particular, that the rules relating to the admissibility of hearsay evidence can be ignored by the court if it considers that any statement or evidence is relevant to any issue before the court (see Children) Admissibility of Hearsay Evidence (Order 1993, SI 1993/621). Civil courts may thus admit hearsay evidence, such as evidence of interviews conducted by psychiatrists and social workers in which children disclose physical or sexual abuse (CA 1989, s 96(3) to (5)). In civil proceedings before a juvenile court, a statement made by a child (or by a person connected with, or having control of the child) that he or she has been assaulted, neglected or ill-treated, or a statement in any report made by a children's guardian or by a local authority, is admissible in connection with any proceedings relating to the upbringing, maintenance or welfare of the child, regardless of whether or not it is also hearsay. In *Re G* [1993] 2 FLR 293 it was suggested that the fundamental rules of evidence should only be relaxed in the most exceptional circumstances amounting to a serious threat to the welfare of the children. The Act also allows civil courts to accept unsworn evidence from young children if the court deems the child capable of understanding the duty to speak the truth and is of sufficient understanding (CA 1989, s 96(2)(a) and (b)).

The CA 1989, s 98 removes the privilege against answering questions which might elicit incriminating replies in any proceedings relating to care, supervision or emergency protection. The witness is, however, protected against the criminal consequences of making a damaging admission but not in proceedings relating to contact and residence orders or proceedings for perjury. The CA 1989, s 98 gives protection against statements being admissible in evidence in criminal proceedings except for the offence of perjury but it does not protect against their use in a police enquiry into the offence (see *Re EC (Disclosure of Material)* [1996] 2 FLR 725).

Each party must file written statements containing the major thrust of the oral evidence to be called at trial and copies of any documents which are to be relied upon, including experts' reports. See also *Re D* The Times, 11 March 1998, as to abiding by Home Office Guidance on interviewing children on video.

Copies must be served on all parties to the proceedings (or their legal representatives) including the children's guardian or CAFCASS officer appointed by the court but is otherwise confidential (except that copies may be supplied to the Legal Services Commission). The timetable for compliance will be fixed at the directions hearing. Evidence which is not disclosed under these rules may not be adduced at trial without the leave of the court (rule 4.17 FPR 1991).

In *Re B* (1993) 143 NLJ 969, it was held that the CA 1989 gave no power to override legal and professional privilege (see also *Oxfordshire CC v M* [1994] 2 WLR 393). But compare the position in wardship under *Re A* [1991] 2 FLR 473. Statements made by either party in the course of conciliation meetings cannot be disclosed (*Re D* The Times, 12 February 1993) unless there are exceptional circumstances suggesting serious future harm to the child.

A witness summons can be issued against a child but only if it would not be oppressive. In *Re N* The Times, 25 March 1996, it was held that where allegations of sexual abuse are made and expert evidence is admitted as hearsay evidence in relation to a videoed interview with the child, it is for judge alone to decide whether or not the child is to be believed. Here, the interview had been very pressured with leading questions being put to the child and so the father's application for contact was ordered to be reheard.

In *Re CH* [1998] 1 FLR 402, the Court of Appeal said that it was undesirable to allow significant discussion about the future care of a child to be held in the judge's private room; rather, any such discussions should be held in private in the court room so that those discussions can be recorded and a transcript made. However see also *Re Z (Children)* [2009] 2 FLR 877 where the Court of Appeal held that the days for private consultations between the judge and counsel were over. The Court of Appeal held that such discussions could not properly survive the HRA 1998.

For procedure, see **9.7**.

8.6 Avoidance of delay

One of the major criticisms of the operation of this area of the law has been the inordinate time that it has taken for cases finally to be resolved by order of the court. Delay in reaching a final decision in these important matters can be extremely damaging to the children concerned, particularly since a child's sense of time is very different from that of an adult. Children can feel extremely insecure while waiting for a case to be resolved. In some cases, courts have been forced to give judicial authority to the *de facto* situation rather than risk the psychological damage which could result from moving the child.

8.6.1 The Private Law Programme

On 21 July 2005 Dame Butler Sloss, then-President of the Family Division, introduced a new framework to the court process when dealing with private law cases. The aim is to assist parents to safeguard their children's welfare by having due regard to the *'overriding objective'* (an expression that you will be familiar with from the Civil Procedure Rules in Civil Litigation). The current President of the Family Division—Sir Mark Potter—is in the process of revising the Private Law Programme. However, it is not known when the new guidance will be issued.

The overriding objective is defined as follows:

to enable the court to deal with every (children) case
(a) justly, expeditiously, fairly and with minimum delay;
(b) in ways which ensure, so far as practicable, that
    a. the parties are on equal footing;
    b. the welfare of the children involved is safeguarded; and
    c. distress to all parties is minimised;
(c) so far as is practicable, in ways which are proportionate
    a. to the gravity and complexity of the issues; and
    b. to the nature and extent of the intervention proposed in the private and family life of the children and adults involved.

Any private law application will now involve three aspects, as set out below.

1. *First Hearing Dispute Resolution Appointment (FHDRA)*
This will be the first hearing in every case, which will be listed at court within 4–6 weeks after the issue of an application. Both parents should attend with their representative, as can any child aged 9 or over in certain court centres. The purpose of this early hearing is to identify the issues between the parties, whether they be resolved or whether a referral to other forms of support is appropriate (eg, mediation, conciliation, Alternative Dispute Resolution schemes). This is also known as the 'conciliation' appointment and its primary purpose is to try to resolve the dispute between the parents by consent without the need for further proceedings.

Where possible a CAFCASS officer (see **8.4.1**) should be present at court to assist with the issues to attempt a resolution.

If matters cannot be resolved the future timetabling of the case will be considered eg, the level of judge required; the evidence that should be filed and whether a CAFCASS report is needed.

2 *Effective court control*
The overriding objective shall be furthered by continuous and active case management of every case to include among others: judicial continuity, the avoidance of unnecessary delay, monitoring and reviewing the outcome of cases and enforcing court orders.

3 *Flexible facilitation and referral* (matching resources to families)
Any decisions and agreements shall be facilitated by any the following:

- use of CAFCASS to facilitate and/or supervise an arrangement to ensure that it works;

- require parties, referral agencies and CAFCASS to report the outcome of any step, eg, observed contact, to the court so that the court can respond by urgent review if necessary;

- in addition, the court can use rehabilitative, training, therapy treatment and enforcement powers when considering an agreement and decision.

The scheme also has information sheets which are made available for parties and children, setting out the venues, facilities, arrangements and alternative resources available—they will be prepared and circulated by the DFJ.

Exceptions

Prior to the matter being listed for an FHDRA, CAFCASS will review the papers and undertake a paper risk assessment. In certain cases (eg, where domestic violence is a feature, or issues are urgent or complex) the matter may need to be listed for separate determination by a judge on how best to manage the case.

8.6.2 Conduct of proceedings

The CA 1989, s 11 attempts to deal with the problem of delay by requiring the court to draw up a timetable and give directions to enable it to deal with the matter without delay. Rules have been made (FPR 1991, r 4.14(2) or FPCR, r 14(2)) to provide for directions appointments in all courts, including the magistrates' courts. Attendance at the hearing is obligatory unless the court directs otherwise. Proceedings are conducted by the clerk in the magistrates' court and by the District Judge in the County court. The appointment will deal with the timetabling of the case, the appointment of a children's guardian or solicitor for the child, the submission of evidence, the preparation of welfare reports, the transfer and consolidation of proceedings, the service of documents and the attendance of the child at hearings. Directions can also be given about the order of speeches and evidence. Directions can be given of the court's own motion subject to the parties having been given notice and having the opportunity to make representations. Directions hearings tend to be oral hearings and parties can be required to attend. In the magistrates' court, directions hearings are held by the clerk whose powers are very restricted.

Section 11(3) gives the court power to make what is, in effect, an interim s 8 order.

8.7 Special Guardianship Orders

8.7.1 How are Special Guardianship Orders made?

Special Guardianship Orders (SGOs) can be made under CA 1989, s 14A and were introduced to the Act by way of an amendment to the ACA 2002. An SGO appoints a person to be the child's special guardian. A special guardian has parental responsibility for a child which he can exercise to the exclusion of other holders of parental responsibility. The aim of the SGO is to provide a child who is placed with a non-parent with some permanence but it is not an adoption. They are considered to be particularly suitable to placements with family members who are not parents which may for example result from care proceedings. In *Re S (Adoption Order or Special Guardianship Order)* [2007] 1 FLR 819, the Court of Appeal gave detailed guidance as to the making of SGOs resulting from a child's placement with a family member. An

SGO, does not entitle the holder to change a child's surname or to remove the child from the UK without the permission of either the court or other holders of PR.

8.7.2   The following persons may apply for an SGO

- a guardian;
- a person with a residence order;
- a person with whom the child has lived for three years;
- if there is a residence order in place any person who has the consent of the person with the residence order;
- if the child is in local authority care any person who has the consent of the local authority; or
- a local authority foster carer with whom the child has lived for at least one year.

8.7.3   SGOs, local authorities and notice period

No person can make an application for an SGO unless it gives at least three months notice to the local authority. If the child is being cared for by the local authority, it must give notice to that authority alternatively notice is to be given to the authority in whose area the child is ordinarily resident.

8.7.4   SGOs, local authorities and procedures

A local authority on receipt of notice must carry out an assessment and complete an SGO report. A list of the factors to be considered and reported on are to be found in the Schedule Special Guardianship Regulations 2005. The Regulations allow the local authority to provide financial and other support to special guardians. In addition a court making an SGO has an obligation to consider the arrangements for contact between the child and its parents. Section 8 contact orders can run alongside SGOs.

8.8   Wardship and the inherent jurisdiction

The CA 1989 has curtailed the powers of the High Court in relation to use of its inherent jurisdiction and wardship. Section 100 provides that the wardship court (be it the High Court or some other court exercising the wardship jurisdiction) does not have the power to put children into the care or under the supervision of the local authority. Equally, local authorities are no longer entitled to use the wardship jurisdiction without the prior leave of the court and leave will only be granted if the court is satisfied that the result which the local authority wishes to achieve could not be achieved through the making of any other order and there is reasonable cause to believe that, if the inherent jurisdiction is not used, the child is likely to suffer significant harm. See *Re J* (1992) 142 NLJ 1123, where the local authority sought leave for a court order for medical treatment of a girl suffering from anorexia nervosa. The court also has power to order that such a child can be detained in hospital until treatment is complete (*Re C* [1997] 2 FLR 180 and *Devon CC v S* [1994] 1 FLR 355). Courts have recommended that applications for AIDS tests on children should be made under the wardship jurisdiction.

The CA 1989, s 100 means that, in effect, the wardship jurisdiction is being used only by those who have no other means of seeking the court's help to protect a child, for example, for some non-therapeutic surgical interventions, to protect the child from the publication of information which might be harmful to that child or where there is a threat of removal from the jurisdiction of the court.

The procedure is by originating summons with an affidavit in support, and is immediate once issued so that no step can be taken without prior court permission. This is particularly useful for threatened child abduction.

In *Kelly v BBC* [2001] 2 WLR 253, it was held that the publication of information about a ward was not of itself a contempt of court. The media did not need the permission of the court to interview a ward or to publish the results of such an interview where the interview did not raise any questions about the ward's upbringing and there was a clear public interest in broadcasting the interview, which, if suppressed, would involve a derogation from the right to freedom of expression, guaranteed by Art 10 of the European Convention on Human Rights.

Likewise, the inherent jurisdiction is invoked by originating summons supported by affidavit; local authorities need the leave of the court. The power in wardship to protect children is probably greater (see *R v Central Television plc* [1994] Fam 192).

The courts will not interfere through either jurisdiction with the exercise of powers clearly vested in other bodies, eg, local authorities, the immigration authorities, or to interfere with the normal criminal process, or to order a medical practitioner to treat a child in any manner contrary to his or her clinical judgement.

Local authorities can use the jurisdictions to help to resolve issues which they have no power to deal with under their statutory powers and must seek leave to apply for the jurisdiction on the basis that they do not have the powers they seek. Section 8 will often provide the powers they need under SIOs or PSOs.

The court can only exercise its jurisdiction where there is evidence that, without it, the child would suffer significant harm, for example, the prevention or sanction of an abortion, medical treatment for an anorexic, sterilisation operations, the continuation of medical treatment and cases where there is no other way to prevent, for example, a paedophile having contact with children (see *Devon CC v S* [1994] 1 FLR 355).

8.9 International custody problems

If it is feared that an attempt may be made to remove a child improperly from the jurisdiction, the child may be made a ward of court or an injunction may be sought preventing the removal of the child.

It is possible for a parent who is worried about a possible improper removal of a child to give notice to the passport office to stop a passport being issued for the child without consent (*Practice Direction* [1973] 3 All ER 194 and *Practice Direction* [1977] 3 All ER 122). The Home Office will try to assist in preventing the illegal removal of a child from the jurisdiction if they are informed.

Because of the problems of international child abduction, the Hague Convention on the Civil Aspects of International Child Abduction of 1980 and the European Convention on Recognition and Enforcement of Decisions Concerning Custody of Children and on the Restoration of Custody of Children of 1980 provide procedures for tracing a child and returning him, put into effect through the Child Abduction and Custody Act 1985. The aim of the Hague Convention is to protect rights of custody and access and to provide for the expeditious return of any child under the age of 16 who has wrongfully been removed or retained in another Contracting State. Under the 1985 Act, it is an offence to attempt to take a child from the UK without requisite consents. The Family Law Reform Act 1987 allows for orders made in one part of the UK to be directly enforceable in another part. If the child has been taken to a non-Convention country, there is little hope, although the UK can enter into bilateral agreements with non-Convention countries (see *Protocol (Child Abduction Cases between the UK and Pakistan)* [2003] Fam Law 199).

Where children are brought from a state which is not a signatory to either the European or Hague Conventions, then the court is free to determine the case on its merits under the wardship jurisdiction, although the court will commonly have regard to the factors specified in the Hague Convention in reaching its decision. If the child is brought from a Convention country, then the provisions of the Convention are applied instead of those of wardship, but the wardship will apply if the Convention application fails.

The Hague Convention makes exceptional provision for the court to consider the welfare of children where the needs of the child require the court to take action other than the summary return to the country of habitual residence under Art 13 (see *Re M (Abduction: Psychological Harm)* [1997] 2 FLR 690). Where the foreign jurisdiction concerned does not take account of the child's welfare in its determinations as to the arrangements for the child's future, the court is justified in refusing return to the court of habitual residence (see *Re JA (Child Abduction: Non-Convention Country)* [1998] 1 FLR 231).

Children's views can be taken into account provided they are sufficiently mature and their views can therefore overturn the presumption of return (see *Re B (Abduction: Children's Objections)* [1998] 1 FLR 667). For these purposes, separate representation is possible (see *Re S* [1997] 1 FLR 486).

For the situation in respect of unmarried fathers, see *Practice Note (Child Abduction and Custody Act 1985): Hague Convention: Applications for Return Orders by Unmarried Fathers* [1998] 1 FLR 491.

It is possible for the court in exercising its inherent jurisdiction to order that a father who had previously abducted one of his children should be required to keep his passport with his solicitors from where it was not to be released without either the order of the court or the consent of the mother (*Re A-K (Minors) (Foreign Passport: Jurisdiction)* [1997] 2 FLR 563).

An interesting development can be seen in *Re T (Staying in Contact in Non-Convention Country)* [1999] 1 FLR 262 where the court required undertakings to be given to apply for 'mirror orders' in Egypt to ensure the child's return from the father's home in Egypt. Egypt is not a party to the Hague Convention. The court emphasised the importance for children to be aware of their cultural identity.

In *Re E* [2000] Fam 62, the court underpinned the importance of the cultural background (unless there are exceptional circumstances, such as persecution or ethnic, sex or other discrimination) in assessing the welfare of the child. The Court of Appeal noted that it would be unrealistic to expect that child welfare would be equally understood and applied throughout the Member States to the Hague Convention.

The Convention on Jurisdiction and Recognition and Enforcement in Certain Family Matters of 1998 regulates concurrent matrimonial proceedings in courts of different Member States involving the same parties and allows for recognition and enforcement throughout the EU. In *Osman v Elasha* [2000] 2 WLR 1037, CA, it was held that, when making an order for the immediate return of a child to his or her habitual residence in a non-Convention country, the court should consider the welfare of the child as the paramount consideration. In that case, the welfare principle had to be considered in the light of Sudanese custom and culture, which applied Islamic law and which was familiar and acceptable to a practising Muslim family.

In *Re M* [1997] 1 FCR 109, a child, who was habitually resident in Scotland but physically present in England, could be subject to the jurisdiction of the English court for the purposes of the court to implement a care plan.

When making applications under the Hague Convention advocates should also consider the impact of the Brussels II (*bis*) Regulation which came into force in March 2005 and which governs the recognition of orders dealing with custody, access and parental responsibility.

8.10   Separate representation of children

8.10.1   When this might occur

As a general rule children are not directly involved in or represented in private law applications for contact, residence, SGOs, etc. However, FPCR 1991, r 9(5) allows the court to appoint a guardian to represent the child if the proceedings are particularly complex, if they involve an international element or if the child's views cannot accurately be ascertained by a CAFCASS reporter. Further guidance is to be found in the *President's Practice Direction on the Separate Representation of Children pursuant to Rule 9.5*, issued on 5 April 2005. In *Mabon v Mabon* [2005] All ER DL, the Court of Appeal made it clear that a court should allow older children to directly instruct solicitors because it was wrong to exclude articulate adolescents from the decision-making process. In proceedings under the Hague Convention, the Court in *Re C (Children) (Abduction: Separate Representation of Children)* [2008] EWHC 517 (Fam) has stated that the proper test for the court in considering the question of party status was whether the separate representation of the child would add enough to the court's understanding of the issues that arose to justify the intrusion, expense and the delay that might result.

8.11   Surrogacy

The term 'surrogacy' basically covers those situations where a woman agrees to have a baby for another couple, whether or not for payment. The law on this area is far from clear, but prima facie parental responsibility for the child will vest in the natural mother, not in the couple who hope to bring up the baby. Although the father can be given PR by agreement or by order of the court (see **8.2.2**), there is a substantial problem over whether any contract to hand the baby over should be enforceable. It seems doubtful that any contract to pay money for a child would be enforceable if the money were not paid voluntarily.

The welfare of the child would be paramount in any case coming to court. In the 'Baby Cotton' case—*Re C (A Minor) (Wardship: Surrogacy)* [1985] FLR 846—it was held that the 'parents' should take the child as the mother was quite happy to hand it over. Also, it seems that the 'parents' can adopt the child (*Adoption Application: Surrogacy*

AA 212/86, The Times, 12 March 1987). Under Human Fertilisation and Embryology Act 1990, s 30, the court can make a parental order on an application of a married couple in respect of a child who is born to a surrogate mother and the gametes used are those of one or other of the couple. However, if the natural mother wished to keep the child, it seems unlikely that she would be prevented from doing so unless she was unsuitable.

It is an offence under the Surrogacy Arrangements Act 1985 to be involved in negotiating or making a surrogacy arrangement on a commercial basis, or to advertise to make such arrangements.

9

Children—public law: procedure and law

9.1 Introduction

This chapter will start with an overview of child protection decision making at local authority level prior to proceedings being issued. It will then consider the legal responses available when a child's parents or carers are considered to be unable to care for him or her properly. You will already be familiar with some of the key concepts from your reading of **Chapter 8**. For example, the concept of parental responsibility (PR), and those of paramountcy of the child's welfare and the no order principle are relevant in public law proceedings too.

The practice of care law is complex, intellectually demanding and emotionally fraught, regardless of which party you appear for. Unlike adoption proceedings, you can become involved in care proceedings at a quite early stage of your practice—for example, you might be asked to represent the parents at an emergency protection order hearing as a matter of urgency. Whatever your level of involvement early on in practice, you will need an understanding of the whole process. This chapter aims to introduce you to the key aspects of the legal framework. The next chapter aims to address the practice of care proceedings work—to familiarise you with the more common practical, evidential and procedural issues in public law—some of these can confront you at very early stages of the process; and to consider some of the common patterns of argument and outcome at final hearings for care and supervision orders.

Be aware that this chapter and the next are designed to give you an 'entry point' for your understanding of this area of law. They are not designed to replace the need for wider reading and regular use of key practitioner texts—rather, they give an overview of the issues for you to use to direct your research using such texts. Probably the key practitioner work in this area is Hershman and McFarlane, *Children Law and Practice*—it is an indispensable source of reference for all practitioners, regardless of experience. Any references to Hershman and McFarlane in this chapter and the next are to the edition as it stood at August 2009. If you cannot find the precise reference, it has probably changed during updating, and should not be hard to find nearby. A handbook which you might find helpful in your early days of practice is David Bedingfield, *Advocacy in Family Proceedings: A Practical Guide*. Both texts are published by Family Law (Jordans Publishing Limited).

9.2 Child protection decision making

9.2.1 Introduction

The local authority's duty to investigate a child's circumstances is dealt with at **9.7.1** below. The Children Act 1989 (CA 1989), s 47 investigations relate to investigation of whether a child is suffering or likely to suffer significant harm—the criteria reflected in the threshold criteria for a full care or supervision order (see **9.4.4** below). The Department of Health publication *Working Together to Safeguard Children* contains vital guidance for all agencies involved in child protection. You can download it from: <www.dh.gov.uk>. Currently at <www.dcsf.gov.uk/everychildmatters/resources-and-practice/IG00060/>.

The current guidance defines the various forms of abuse and neglect of a child as follows (paras 2.2–2.5):

Physical abuse

2.2   Physical abuse may involve hitting, shaking, throwing, poisoning, burning or scalding, drowning, suffocating, or otherwise causing physical harm to a child. Physical harm may also be caused when a parent or carer feigns the symptoms of, or deliberately causes, ill health to a child whom they are looking after. This situation is commonly described using terms such as factitious illness by proxy, or Munchausen's syndrome by proxy.

Emotional abuse

2.3   Emotional abuse is the persistent emotional ill-treatment of a child such as to cause severe and persistent adverse effects on the child's emotional development. It may involve conveying to children that they are worthless or unloved, inadequate or valued only insofar as they meet the needs of another person. It may feature age or developmentally inappropriate expectations being imposed on children. It may involve causing children frequently to feel frightened or in danger, or the exploitation or corruption of children. Some level of emotional abuse is involved in all types of ill-treatment of a child, though it may occur alone.

Sexual abuse

2.4   Sexual abuse involves forcing or enticing a child or young person to take part in sexual activities, whether or not the child is aware of what is happening. The activities may involve physical contact, including penetrative (eg, rape or buggery) or non-penetrative acts. They may include non-contact activities, such as involving children in looking at, or in the production of, pornographic material or watching sexual activities, or encouraging children to behave in sexually inappropriate ways.

Neglect

2.5   Neglect is the persistent failure to meet a child's basic physical and/or psychological needs, likely to result in the serious impairment of the child's health or development. It may involve a parent or carer failing to provide adequate food, shelter and clothing, failing to protect a child from physical harm or danger, or the failure to ensure access to appropriate medical care or treatment. It may also include neglect of, or unresponsiveness to, a child's basic emotional needs.

The guidance in *Working Together* is very informative for those involved in care proceedings. Its 'sister' document, *The Framework for the Assessment of Children in Need and their Families*, provides a framework for the assessment of children in need and children thought to be at risk of significant harm—it is considered in more detail at **10.2.1** and the sections that follow it. You will find it particularly helpful to read the following from *Working Together*.

- Chapter 2 outlines key principles for working to safeguard children, such as 'working in partnership with children and families' (you will find the 15 basic principles of the 'Challenge of Partnership in Child Protection' particularly interesting in terms of comparing how child protection professionals *should* be working with a family, and how they in fact worked with the family in your case).

- Chapter 4 is worth 'skim-reading' in order to gain a sense of which agencies have a role to play in child protection. Any of these can be a source of evidence on which local authority decision making regarding your client is made. In particular, there is reference to the role of the police (3.57–3.64), the Children's Guardian (3.82–3.86—'Guardian *ad Litem*' is simply the former terminology for the Children's Guardian), and the health services.

- Chapter 5, 'Managing individual cases' is a valuable description of the decision-making process which can (in certain cases) lead to the institution of proceedings. The process is summarised below at **9.2.2**.

- Chapter 6 discusses child protection in specific circumstances, such as domestic violence or multiple abuse.

- Chapter 9, which outlines the *impact* of abuse and neglect upon a child; sources of stress for children and their families (eg, drug abuse by a parent, mental health problems, social exclusion, domestic violence); and key lessons to be learned by child protection agencies from research done into the operation of child protection processes.

There are also supplements to the guidance, one dealing with safeguarding children involved in child prostitution, forced marriage, and another dealing with children in whom illness is fabricated or induced (go to <www.dh.gov.uk>, click on the 'policy and guidance' tab, then search for 'safeguarding children involved in prostitution', and for 'children in whom illness is fabricated or induced').

9.2.2 The decision-making framework in child protection

The following is a summary of Chapter 5 of *Working together*, which should assist you to put the information generated by the local authority and disclosed in care proceedings in context. To assist you, you may find the 'Individual Cases Flowchart' produced at Figure 5 of *The Framework* and Appendix 5 of *Working Together* helpful. If a child is found to be in immediate need of protection *at any stage* of the process, the local authority can apply for an emergency protection order (see **9.6.3**)—there is no requirement that the whole process is undertaken *before* action to protect a child is taken if the matter is urgent.

9.2.2.1 Referral

A parent, a professional (eg, the police) or another person (such as a concerned neighbour or family member) may bring to the attention of the local authority concerns regarding a child. Alternatively the concern could arise within the social services department itself as new information is gained on a child already known to the service. The local authority will then seek to clarify the referral and decide on a course of action within 24 hours—usually after checking records and discussing the matter with other agencies involved (eg, police or health visitor). Generally, referral and action on referral should be undertaken with permission from parents unless this would place the child at risk. The result of a referral will be either no further action, or a direct move to provide services to the family, or further investigation of the child's needs (which could then move to CA 1989, s 47 investigation if the child was suspected of being at risk of significant harm).

9.2.2.2 Initial assessment

The local authority is expected to complete an initial assessment within 7 days of the referral. However, the guidance states that where an s 47 inquiry is appropriate, the initial assessment can be undertaken more quickly. It focuses on establishing whether the child is in need, and further whether there is reasonable cause to suspect that the child is suffering, or likely to suffer significant harm (s 47). The process of initial assessment will include seeing and speaking to the child and family members; analysing information from a range of sources (including historical information on the family); and obtaining information from relevant professionals (eg, the child's general practitioner or the health visitor). The family should be informed of decisions taken as a result of the initial assessment (unless this would jeopardise the child protection process, for example, police investigations). 'Ten common pitfalls' of initial assessment are summarised in *Working Together* (p 113)—you may find this interesting from the point of view of the effectiveness of investigations in your case.

9.2.2.3 Next steps where actual or likely significant harm is not suspected

In these circumstances, the local authority will obviously not be considering legal proceedings or the need for a child protection plan. However, if the initial assessment demonstrates that the child is 'in need' (see CA 1989, s 17), a core assessment (see **10.2.1**) may be carried out in order to decide how those needs should be met, including what services the local authority can offer in this regard.

9.2.2.4 Next steps where actual or likely significant harm is suspected

These are the circumstances in which the local authority is obliged to make inquiries (CA 1989, s 47). This will probably involve a 'core assessment' under the *Framework*—see **10.2.1**. The results of that assessment will form part of the local authority's evidence if it commences proceedings for a care or supervision order. At this stage in the investigation, its role is to confirm whether further intervention will be required to protect the child, and if so, what intervention will be necessary—this could be legal proceedings, or some lesser intervention.

Emergency proceedings may be required to protect the child at any stage where it becomes apparent that the child is at immediate risk of serious harm, and normally it is expected that there will be a 'strategy discussion' between social services, the police and other agencies involved before action is taken. Where action is required immediately, this discussion should occur as soon as possible afterwards. Where the immediate removal of a child is needed, the guidance indicates that the local authority should rely on an application for an emergency protection order and not the police protection powers (see **9.6.2** and **9.6.3** below).

9.2.2.5 Strategy discussion

The purpose of the strategy discussion is to enable the social services department and other relevant agencies (eg, education department, health services) to share information, make decisions about initiating or continuing s 47 inquiries, what inquiries will be made and by whom, whether there is a need for action to immediately safeguard the child, and what information about the strategy discussion will be provided to the family. Decisions will be made regarding the provision of any medical treatment, how to handle inquiries in the light of any criminal investigation, and whether other children affected are in need or at risk.

9.2.2.6 Decisions following s 47 inquiries

The outcome of the s 47 inquiries should be discussed with relevant professionals involved in the inquiries, and recorded. The parents should be provided with a copy of that record before any initial child protection conference. There are three possible outcomes according to the guidance in *Working Together*.

First, the concerns may not be substantiated. This may mean that further action is unnecessary, but the local authority should nevertheless consider whether it is appropriate to offer services or support. It may be that the concerns about significant harm remain, but there is insufficient evidence to bring proceedings—in which case, the local authority's response may well be to monitor the child's well-being through, for example, the health visitor.

Second, the concerns are borne out by the investigation, but the child is not considered to be at *continuing* risk of significant harm. This is clearly a more difficult situation for social services. The guidance suggests that a child protection conference may not always be required in such cases, although if another professional involved in the inquiries has serious concerns and requests a conference, social services should agree, and in any event a decision not to call such a conference where the child is shown to have suffered significant harm should not be taken lightly. Where no conference is called, the guidance states that the agencies most involved with the family, social services and the child and family themselves should develop and implement a plan to ensure the child's future well-being. This plan should be clearly developed according to the findings of the assessment, with clear indications of who is responsible for its implementation and what will happen if it is not properly implemented. For circumstances in which this course of action may be appropriate, see paras 5.48–5.51 of *Working Together*.

The third possible outcome is that the inquiries and assessment show that the concerns are substantiated and the child is judged to be at continuing risk of significant harm. In these circumstances, a child protection conference should be convened in order to enable the family, and professionals involved with the family, to assess available information and plan for the protection of the child.

9.2.2.7 Initial child protection conference

If called, this should occur within 15 days of the strategy discussion. The purpose is (para 5.80 of *Working Together*):

- to bring together and analyse in an inter-agency setting the information that has been obtained about the child's developmental needs and the parents' or carers' capacity to respond to these needs to ensure the child's safety and promote the child's health and development;

- to make judgements about the likelihood of the child suffering significant harm in future; and

- to decide what future action is needed to safeguard the child and promote his or her welfare, how that action will be taken forward, and with what intended outcomes.

The guidance in *Working Together* is very specific about who should be invited to the conference—'Those attending conferences should be there because they have a significant contribution to make, arising from professional expertise, knowledge of the child or family or both.' Between the knowledge and expertise of those invited, and the written reports, there should be sufficient information to enable the conference to make well-informed judgements about action to safeguard the child and what is realistic and workable in terms of taking that action. Guidance is also provided about the information which should be provided in advance to the parents.

The decisions to be made by the conference include a decision on whether the child is at continuing risk of significant harm; what an outline child protection plan for the child should contain; and what category of abuse the child should be registered on the Child Protection Register under (see **9.2.1** for the categories of abuse, and **9.2.2.10** for the Child Protection Register).

There is detailed guidance on what decisions need to be made about the child protection plan at paras 5.93 and 5.104 of the guidance. These include appointing a key worker for the child (a social work practitioner), deciding on the membership of the 'core group' of professionals and family members who will develop and implement the plan, establishing the timescales for production of the plan and review meetings, contingency planning and what further assessments if any are required. A date must also be decided upon for a review conference. In particular, the requirements for decisions at the conference on the child protection plan are set out at para 5.100 and include identifying risks of significant harm to the child, establishing short-term and longer-term objectives linked to reducing the risk of harm to the child.

Records of the conference (which are confidential and should not be passed to third parties without the consent of the conference chair or the key worker) should be sent to all persons invited to attend it, including family members. These minutes are listed in the pre-proceedings checklist.

9.2.2.8 Child protection plan, and action following the initial child protection conference

The key worker's responsibility is to act as 'lead worker' and coordinator for the inter-agency protection work with the child and family, and to ensure that the outline child protection plan produced by the initial child protection conference is developed into a detailed working document.

The core group develop the child protection plan in this way. The core group will include relevant family members and the child (if appropriate) as well as professionals (including foster carers) in direct contact with the family. The first meeting should occur within 10 days of the initial child protection conference, and decisions and action agreed at core group meetings should be recorded.

The child protection plan aims to safeguard the child from further harm, promote his health and development, and (if consistent with the protection of the child) to support his family in promoting the child's welfare.

The importance of the family understanding, agreeing to the plan and being prepared to work with it are emphasised. A written agreement as regards implementation of the plan is recommended by the guidance as good practice—this would reflect the causes of concern leading to the child being placed on the Child Protection Register, what needs to change, and what is expected from the parents in order to safeguard the child. From a practical point of view, it is often the case when proceedings are commenced that the family have failed to cooperate with such a plan, and this failure is a large part of the reason for the local authority applying for a care order.

9.2.2.9   The review conference

The progress of the child protection plan will be considered at a review conference. The first of these must occur within three months of the initial child protection conference, and thereafter at intervals of a maximum of six months for the whole of the period of time during which the child's name remains on the Child Protection Register. This aims to prevent 'drift' in the child's case—it ensures that the child's circumstances and protection plan are regularly reviewed. This may involve changes in the plan, including a need for legal proceedings, or de-registration of the child's name from the register if circumstances are sufficiently improved that he or she is no longer at continuing risk of significant harm. The core group is responsible for providing reports to the review conference on each occasion.

9.2.2.10   The Child Protection Register

This is a vital tool for all agencies in child protection. The fact of registration shows an agency looking at the Register that a child is currently considered to be at risk of significant harm and in need of active protection, and the category (eg, 'neglect', 'N') under which a child is registered gives information as to the nature of the risk presenting at the time of registration. The fact that the categories are consistent across all local authorities means that the information the Register provides can be understood in the same way throughout the country. There are strict rules regarding the Register—it is confidential, to be shown only to legitimate inquirers, and must be accessible at all hours to legitimate inquirers. The contact given to inquirers who request it is the name of the child's key worker.

9.3   The statutory framework

9.3.1   Threshold for intervention

Public law children work involves state intervention in the life of the family. It is therefore not surprising that in applications for all types of order, it must be proved that the child's circumstances have reached a sufficiently serious condition before the court even has *power* to intervene in the life of the family by making an order. The test for demonstrating that this point has been reached is commonly referred to as 'the threshold criteria'. This must be proved, as a question of fact, before the court has *jurisdiction* to make the order in question. This is a very important safeguard for the family—local authorities cannot intervene in their lives on a spurious or insufficient basis. However, proving that the threshold criteria exist in relation to the child in question is not the end of the matter. For most of the orders in public law children matters, the proof of the threshold criteria just gives the court the jurisdiction—ie, the power—to make the order in question. The court still has to consider whether in fact such an order should be made, taking into account the paramountcy of the child's welfare and the 'no order' principle. Therefore, for most applications in this area, there are two questions:

- Has the threshold been proved? If not, no orders can be made.
- If so, what order, if any, should be made? This is commonly referred to as the 'disposal' or 'welfare' stage.

Also, the human rights of the people involved must be respected. Any intervention in their family life must be no greater than is proportionate to the risks posed to the children.

The next sections will consider the main orders and procedures that are available in this area. It will begin with the most serious order, the care order, and will then consider in turn each other order or procedure in descending order of seriousness. The more an order interferes in the life of a family, the more serious it is. For each order or procedure, consideration will be given to the *effect* of the order; the *duration* of the order; its *interaction with other orders*; and the *tests to be applied* on the making of the order.

9.4 Care orders

Apart from adoption, a care order represents the most fundamental intervention in the life of a family, and will only be made where the court is satisfied that no lesser measure will protect the child or children in question.

9.4.1 Effect of a care order

By CA 1989, s 31(1), a care order is an order:

placing the child with respect to whom the application is made in the care of a designated local authority.

A care order can only be made in favour of a local authority. It places a duty on the local authority to safeguard and promote the child's welfare, which will include providing for his maintenance and accommodation. It gives the local authority PR. This does not always mean that the child is placed away from his parents—in appropriate cases, the 'care plan' (see **10.6**) can provide that the child is placed with his parents or a member of the maternal or paternal family who is willing and able to care for him. In many cases, however, the plan might be for permanent placement away from the family, eg, adoption or fostering. The plan (now called an s 31A Plan) must be approved by the court before it can make a care order. Independent reviewing officers monitor how local authorities implement the care plan. The independent reviewing officer will chair each review of the care plan in an effort to provide some safeguards to parents and children. The parents must be involved in the decision-making process (*Re G Care: Challenge to Local Authority Decision*) [2003] 2 FLR 42.

9.4.2 Duration

The order can remain in force until a child reaches 18 years. However, it can be ended earlier in a number of ways, such as discharge by the court; discharge by way of a residence or a Special Guardianship Order (SGO) being made; or substitution by a supervision order. It will also end upon the making of a placement order or an adoption.

9.4.3 Interaction with other orders

A care order is incompatible with all s 8 orders (note that contact with a child in care is governed by CA 1989, s 34, not s 8); a supervision order; and an interim care or supervision order. See also Hershman at C 904. For a useful summary of orders that can be made upon the application for a care order, see Hershman at C 983. Many of these are incompatible with a care order but you need to know what orders are available as an *alternative* if the court decides not to make a care order per se.

9.4.4 Grounds for a care order

The court must apply the following tests:

- First, are the statutory threshold criteria satisfied? If not, there is no jurisdiction to make a care or supervision order. This is often referred to as the 'threshold' stage of the decision.

- If so, should an order be made at all?

- If so, what sort of order should be made? These latter two questions relate to the 'disposal' (welfare) stage of proceedings, where the court is deciding what approach best promotes the child's welfare.

- The paramountcy principle, the welfare checklist at CA 1989, s 1(3), and the no order principle do not apply to the question of whether the threshold criteria are satisfied—that is a question of factual proof alone. However, they do apply to the question of whether an order should be made, and if so, the type of order.

- In deciding on whether an order is appropriate, and what sort of order should be made, the court will additionally scrutinise the local authority's care plan (see **10.6**) and proposals for contact with the child (see **9.8**).

The threshold criteria for a care order are laid out at CA 1989, s 31(2):

(2) A court may only make a care order or supervision order if it is satisfied—

(a) that the child concerned is suffering, or is likely to suffer, significant harm; and

(b) that the harm, or likelihood of harm, is attributable to—

(i)   the care given to the child, or likely to be given to him if the order were not made, not being what it would be reasonable to expect a parent to give to him; or

(ii) the child's being beyond parental control.

Clearly, there are two elements to the threshold test—first, establishing the existence, or likelihood, of significant harm to the child; and second, establishing that that harm is *caused by* one of the two circumstances in (b). Both elements must be shown. For example, a child could be suffering significant harm because of a serious disability, but that disability could have occurred without any fault on the part of the parents and their care of him could be totally appropriate, and so the threshold test would not be made out. By contrast, a child might be suffering the consequences of neglect, and the evidence shows that this is due to insufficient care by his parents—clearly, he is suffering significant harm, which is due to inadequate care by his parents, and the threshold is made out.

Note that the test for the adequacy of care given to the child in question is an objective test—by reason of the reference to the care which it would be reasonable for a parent to give. This means that there need not necessarily be blameworthiness on the part of the parent—a parent could be trying their best to care properly for the child and simply be unable to give sufficient care. The threshold would still be met. Where the child's needs are unusual, complex or demanding, it may be that expert evidence is required as to what care such a child would be given by reasonable parents.

9.4.5   Key definitions in the threshold criteria

The threshold criteria in CA 1989, s 31(2) raise a number of issues, for example, what is meant by 'harm', or what constitutes 'significant harm'? Concepts of harm, significance, likelihood and so forth run throughout this area of law so definitions will be provided here. Remember that some of these will apply to the tests for other applications, not just those for care orders.

9.4.5.1   'the child concerned'

This relates to the child who is the subject of the application. It may be that the court is considering applications in relation to several children at one hearing (generally because they are siblings), but decisions as to threshold and order must be made on each child individually. A child is someone under the age of 18 years old, although an application cannot be made in respect of a child who has reached 17 years (16 if married). Further, it is not possible to make an order, or indeed for an application to be made, in relation to a child who is not yet born.

9.4.5.2   'is suffering'

The time at which the child is suffering the harm is an important point. *Re M (A Minor) (Care Order: Threshold Conditions)* [1994] 2 AC 424, [1994] 3 WLR 558, [1994] 2 FLR 577 (HL) provides the key principle: the *relevant date* for deciding whether the child 'is suffering' significant harm is *either*:

- the date of the hearing for a care or supervision order; or
- the date on which the local authority first initiated the procedure for protection of the child, *provided that* the protection has then been continuously in place up to the date of the hearing.

This has an important practical consequence. Generally speaking, care proceedings can take many months to come to a final hearing. During that time, the carers of the child might have made substantial progress in their parenting skills, or in addressing the area of risk. If so, the child's situation at the time of the final hearing could be much improved to the point where it is questionable whether he or she 'is' currently suffering harm. Alternatively, the child's situation could be much improved *because of* protective arrangements made by the local authority (eg, removing the child to foster care). It would then be hard to say that the child 'is suffering' harm at *the time of the final hearing*. This principle enables the court to look back to the time of the initial intervention when assessing the 'is suffering' part of the test, provided that the provision of protective arrangements has not been withdrawn at any time. From a tactical point of view, this makes it unlikely that a local authority would agree to the discharge of an interim care order (for example) unless they had no intention of proceeding to the final hearing in any event.

9.4.5.3   'is likely to suffer'

This part of the test enables the court to intervene in situations where the child has not as yet suffered harm, but there is a likelihood of harm. A classic example might be where there are several children in the household and it can be shown that one or more are suffering or have suffered significant harm due to their parents' care, and yet the other or others are as yet unharmed. The fact of harm to one child, if proved, may provide *evidence* of the likelihood of harm to others in that household. Another example which shows that it is not even necessary for a child to have been in the care of his parents for harm, or likelihood of harm to be established would be where a baby had been born withdrawing from heroin taken by the mother during pregnancy and removed from her care shortly after birth.

The obvious question is to what degree does the applicant have to show that suffering is 'likely'—what does it mean in this context? The key authority is now *Re B (Care Proceedings: Standard of Proof)* [2008] 2 FLR 141, where the House of Lords emphasised that there is only one civil standard of proof: the balance of probabilities ie proof that the fact in issue more probably occurred than not:

The inherent improbabilities are simply something to be taken into account, where relevant, in deciding where the truth lies. [para 70]

As to the time at which 'likelihood of harm' should be demonstrated, see **9.4.5.2** above—the principle is the same.

9.4.5.4   'Harm'

This is defined at CA 1989, s 31(9), as:

ill-treatment or the impairment of health or development including, for example, impairment suffered from seeing or hearing the ill-treatment of another.

Hershman and McFarlane make the point that 'ill-treatment' and 'impairment of health or development' are alternatives—so the ill treatment does not need to have caused some impairment, and impairment does not have to have arisen due to ill-treatment (it could, for example, be due to neglect).

It is also interesting to note that specific recognition is given in the definition of harm that witnessing ill-treatment of another constitutes harm. This is important where, for example, a child has witnessed domestic violence. The child may not have personally been attacked but the attack on another (his mother, say) could be sufficient to establish emotional harm.

The Act provides further definition of the terms within s 31(9):

'development' means physical, intellectual, emotional, social or behavioural development; 'health' means physical or mental health; and
    'ill-treatment' includes sexual abuse and forms of ill-treatment which are not physical.

Clearly, the definitions are cast widely, in order to maximise the chances of protecting children from a wide range of abuses. For example, obvious physical maltreatment, such as physical abuse or sexual abuse, is clearly included, but so are neglect and emotional abuse by reference to treatment which impairs health and development, and the definition extends to impairment of mental health, and to ill-treatment not needing to be physical. It is of course possible, and quite common, that a child has suffered more than one form of abuse.

An obvious question arises as to how to judge whether health and development are 'impaired'. The CA 1989 again provides a clear definition. By s 31(10):

where the question of whether harm suffered by a child is significant turns on the child's health or development, his health or development shall be compared with that which could reasonably be expected of a similar child.

This introduces a need to compare 'like with like'—the child subject to the application is compared to a hypothetical 'similar child'. For example, a child with Down syndrome is inevitably going to be delayed in his development, and it would be misleading for his development to be compared with that of a child without disability. Therefore, the effect of s 31(10) means that his development would be compared with that of a similar child suffering from Down syndrome. From a practical point of view, this will inevitably require expert evidence regarding what level of development could be expected from a similar Down syndrome child and how this child compares. Generally speaking, expert evidence is often required regarding whether a child has suffered 'harm' where the issue is development (as opposed to ill-treatment, which is likely to be more obvious). The 'like for like' comparison that s 31(10) envisages might also mean that other factors are relevant, such as race or culture.

9.4.5.5 'significant' harm

This is a very difficult term to define—as Hershman and McFarlane point out, it is a qualitative term. What matters is that the *harm* is significant—the focus is not so much on the seriousness of the acts that caused it. It could vary according to the child, so for example a nervous and sensitive child could be harmed to a greater extent than a more robust child by the same type of emotional abuse. Alternatively, there may be racial or cultural factors which put a different complexion on the harm. The definition referred to by the courts is: 'considerable, noteworthy or important...' (see *Humberside County Council v B* [1993] 1 FLR 257).

9.4.6 The decision to make a care order

As stated earlier, the court has no jurisdiction to make a care order until satisfied on the balance of probabilities that the threshold criteria with respect to the child in question are made out. This is a question of factual proof. Once the court has decided that it is satisfied as to the existence of the threshold, it then moves to the decision regarding whether to make an order, and if so, what type of order. This stage of the decision making at a final hearing is often referred to as 'disposal'.

9.4.6.1 Applicable principles

The no order principle applies to this stage of the court's decision making. The court must ask itself, in accordance with CA 1989, s 31(9), whether making an order in respect of the child would be better for the child than making no order. Normally, local authorities do not wish to spend precious social services resources upon court proceedings, and therefore the type of cases that come before the courts tend to involve quite serious problems with the parenting of these children. It is therefore frequently the case that the threshold criteria are satisfied and the problems are such that intervention of some sort is required. In care proceedings, therefore, a proper application of the no order principle probably demands that the order or orders made reflect the *least intervention consistent with proper protection of the child's welfare*. See *Re O (Care or Supervision Order)* [1996] 2 FLR 755. Therefore, a care order might not be appropriate where a supervision order would sufficiently safeguard the child's welfare; or where there was insufficient evidence before the court for a final decision to be made and therefore an adjournment under an interim care order was appropriate for further assessment (see **10.7.3.2**).

Such an approach would be consistent with European law. Clearly, the European Convention on Human Rights (ECHR), Art 8, would apply, protecting the right to a family life both for parents and child; equally, Art 6 rights to a fair trial may have an impact on proceedings. Proportionality is a key issue in care law as it is in European law. See further, Hershman at C 965–C 966, *Re C and B (Care Order: Future Harm)* [2001] 1 FLR 611; and *Re B (Care: Interference with Family Life)* [2003] 2 FLR 813.

The welfare principle and welfare checklist are a central part of the court's decision making on disposal. Key checklist factors which are likely to influence the decision will be the child's educational, emotional and physical needs; the parents' capabilities of meeting the child's needs; and the risk of future harm to the child.

The s 1(2) principle that delay is inimical to the welfare of a child is relevant and courts strive to minimise the delay in establishing the child's long-term future. However, you will find that in public law proceedings this does not mean that a final placement must be found at all speed regardless of the cost. In particular, the court will take into account the notion that 'planned and purposeful delay' can be in the best interests of a child.

9.4.7   Discharge of a care order

9.4.7.1   Substitution of a supervision order for the care order

The court can substitute a supervision order for a care order upon the application of a person with parental responsibility, the local authority or the child (see CA 1989, s 39). It cannot do so of its own motion. The principles applicable are the paramountcy principle, and the court will apply the CA 1989, s 1(3) welfare checklist. There is no need to prove that the statutory threshold criteria are still made out (s 39(5)). There are restrictions on repeat applications to substitute—by CA 1989, s 91(15), where an application has been made before, another cannot be made before six months from the disposal of the original application unless the applicant first obtains leave of the court.

9.4.7.2   Discharge of the care order

Section 39 CA 1989 also governs discharge of care orders. The same applicants (see **9.4.7.1**) can apply for the discharge of a care order, and again, by CA 1989, s 39(5) there is no need for the threshold criteria to be shown to still be made out. The same principles—paramountcy, and the welfare checklist—apply, and the same restrictions on repeat applications.

From a tactical point of view, it is difficult for the parents to succeed in applications to substitute or discharge. The child's situation may have substantially improved as a result of the care plan—eg, he may be happy and well settled with a long-term foster family. Even if the parents can show that they have made significant improvements in the matters that led to the initial proceedings (eg, a mother who has successfully overcome problems with depression and drug dependency), they will still need to show that it is in the child's best interests to disrupt his current placement for an untested new placement with themselves. This can be a tough comparison. It is even harder where the parents have not sufficiently addressed the original problems with their parenting. Of course, if the improvement in the parents' position is sufficient to safeguard the child's welfare, and the child's placement under the care plan perhaps is not working well enough, the task will be easier.

9.5   Supervision orders

A supervision order is a less draconian measure than a care order. One crucial difference is that under a supervision order *the local authority does not acquire PR*. The parents or carers of the child are therefore responsible for meeting the child's needs and the local authority has much more limited control of how they exercise their PR (although they may not act inconsistently with the supervision order—CA 1989, s 2(8)). Additionally, there is greater potential for court control of how the supervision is exercised by the local authority, in that the local authority will have to return to court for a care order if the situation deteriorates—contrast the care order where the local authority can simply change the care plan (eg, from rehabilitation with the parents to foster parent care) without further recourse to court.

9.5.1 Effect

A supervision order places a child under the supervision of a designated local authority (CA 1989, s 31(1)) and imposes duties (CA 1989, s 35) on the appointed supervisor to:

- Advise, assist and befriend the supervised child.
- To take such steps as are reasonably necessary to give effect to the order.
- Where the order is not wholly complied with, or the supervisor considers that the order may no longer be necessary, to consider whether or not to apply to court for variation or discharge of the order.

A supervision order without requirements simply requires the supervisor to advise, assist and befriend. It does not appear to give the supervisor the power to give directions to the child, although if the order is not working, the supervisor could apply to court to attach requirements to the order, or even for a care order to be substituted.

9.5.2 Requirements

The court can attach requirements to a supervision order. The available requirements are:

- For the supervised child to comply with directions of the supervisor on certain matters (contained in CA 1989, Sch 3) such as living in a specified place, participating in specified activities, allowing the supervisor to visit him.
- A requirement for the person with whom the child lives to comply with directions of the supervisor—this order requires their consent.
- That the supervised child submit to medical or psychiatric examination.
- That the supervised child undergoes specified treatment for his mental health (provided that certain conditions are satisfied).

For further detail, see Hershman C 1517–C 1532.

9.5.3 Duration

A supervision order will automatically end one year after it was made. It can be made for a period of less than a year. A supervisor can apply for it to be extended, and it can be extended for a period of up to three years from the original order. It will also automatically end if a care order is made (the two orders are incompatible) or the child's eighteenth birthday.

9.5.4   Interaction with other orders

A supervision order is incompatible with a care order. However, on an application for a care order, the court can make a supervision order, and vice versa. They are therefore alternatives. A supervision order is compatible with any s 8 order.

9.5.5   Grounds for a supervision order

The threshold test in CA 1989, s 31(2) applies to supervision orders in exactly the same manner as it applies to care orders. See **9.4.4** above.

The paramountcy of the child's welfare is also applicable to the decision to make a supervision order. The no order principle applies, in particular that the order made should be the least interventionist order possible that is consistent with protecting the child's welfare. See **9.4.6.1** above.

The factors influencing the decision whether to make a care order or a supervision order will be considered at **10.7.3.3**.

9.6   Procedure—the Public Law Outline

9.6.1   Introduction

A new protocol, the Public Law Outline (PLO), was introduced in April 2008 in an attempt to combat the continuing delay in care proceedings. It is set out in full as a practice direction of the President and is reported at *[2008] 2 FLR 668*. At the same time, the Department for Children, Schools and Families (DCSF) revised their statutory guidance for local authorities (The Children Act 1989 Guidance and Regulations).

9.6.2   Key elements of the PLO

- The most significant change introduced by the PLO is the expectation that significant work will be done by local authorities, including involving families, *before* proceedings are instigated. This does not apply where action needs to be taken in urgent circumstances to protect a child.
- There is a detailed pre-proceedings checklist from which it is clear that much of the background assessment work should be done by the local authority *before* proceedings are issued. This checklist includes, for example, a schedule of proposed findings and a care plan
- A letter before proceedings should be written to the parent(s) to alert them of the local authority's concerns and give them the opportunity to obtain legal representation.
- The overriding objective has been restated: the court seeks to deal with cases justly, having regard to the welfare issues involved.
- The expectation is that all parties will co-operate in case management, seek to avoid delay and seek agreement out of court if possible.
- Analysis from a CAFCASS officer is to be available for the Case Management Conference, providing objective quality control to the local authority's position.

- The six stages of the public law protocol have been reduced to four stages: issue to first appointment, case management conference (CMC), advocates' meeting and issue resolution hearing (IRH) and Final Hearing.

- Greater judicial continuity should follow from the allocation of each case to a maximum of two judges.

- The court will set a Timetable for the Child.

- The court will maintain a Case Management Record for each case.

- The Advocates are expected not only to meet to narrow the issues for consideration by the court, but also to draft proposed Case Management Orders.

9.6.3 Developments

It is already apparent that the increase in volume of care proceedings which resulted from the Baby P case has had a significant effect on the workload of CAFCASS officers. In July 2009 the President issued Interim Guidance to assist with this. It is apparent from arrangements for the London family courts, for example, that it has not proved possible for guardians to provide as much input at an early stage as was hoped by the PLO.

At the same time as the PLO was introduced, the court fees for instituting care proceedings rose from £ 150 to £ 4,825. The immediate effect of this was a dramatic reduction in the number of care proceedings being started: there was a fall of 20% in the period between April and September 2008, as compared with the same period in 2007.

Mirroring this, after the dramatic and intensive press publicity surrounding the *Baby P* case, there was a 27% increase in the number of care proceedings started in a 20 day period in November 2008, as compared with the same 20 days in November 2007.

This Manual does not have the capacity to consider these factors in any further detail or to comment on the recommendations of the Laming Report, the text of which is readily available on the web.

9.7 Emergency protection

9.7.1 Introduction

This section will consider the protection of children in an emergency. While care proceedings for some children will commence in quite a measured way, with an application for a care order accompanied by one for an interim care order (see **10.1**), others begin with an emergency. For example, the child might be brought to hospital with injuries highly indicative of physical abuse, and social services and hospital staff are concerned that the parents could discharge the child from hospital and disappear; or the child might come to social services' attention through the police, where the police have been called to an incident and discovered a child they consider to be at risk. There are two principal ways in which children can be protected in such a situation: police protection (which does not require a court order); and an emergency protection order (which does).

9.7.2 Police protection

This is governed by s 46 CA 1989. By s 46 (1):

Where a constable has reasonable cause to believe that a child would otherwise be likely to suffer significant harm, he may—

(a) remove the child to suitable accommodation and keep him there; or

(b) take such steps as are reasonable to ensure that the child's removal from any hospital, or other place, in which he is then being accommodated is prevented.

Clearly, this covers two alternative situations—either the child needs to be *removed* from a situation of risk (s 46(1)(a)) or the child needs to be *kept* in a safe place where removal might put the child at risk (s 46(1)(b)—the specific example used is a hospital).

Neither the police officer taking the child into protection, nor the 'designated' officer who then inquires into the case acquire PR for the child. The child can be kept in police protection for up to 72 hours and no order is required. Thereafter, an emergency protection order will have to be applied for (and the 'designated officer' is one of the persons entitled to apply for such an order on behalf of the local authority).

In terms of how parental rights are affected, although PR is not transferred to the police, a child cannot be removed from police protection unless either the designated officer decides such protection is no longer necessary (according to the test in s 46(1)), or the time limit (72 hours) has expired and no other order—such as an emergency protection order—has been made with regard to the child.

The officer taking the child into police protection has a number of duties. These include informing the local authority, informing anyone with PR as to what has occurred and ensuring that the case is inquired into by the 'designated officer'. The 'designated officer' also has duties, principally doing 'all that is reasonable in the circumstances of the case to safeguard or promote the child's welfare' (CA 1989, s 46(9)(b)). This will also include consideration of appropriate contact, if considered in the child's best interests, with certain people such as those with PR. Where a child has been transferred to accommodation provided by the local authority (as is almost always the case) the obligations regarding contact transfer to the local authority.

Practically speaking, the police officer taking the child into police protection is obliged to inform the local authority. The local authority then has a duty to investigate to establish what action, if any, it should take (CA 1989, s 47(1)). Generally speaking, if the local authority considers that action should be taken, it will itself apply for an emergency protection order rather than requesting the designated officer to do so on its behalf. If the local authority applies, the time limits for the emergency protection order will not include time in police protection, in contrast to an application by the designated officer.

Police protection is therefore very much a 'first aid' provision where a child is at immediate risk. If local authority investigation does reveal cause for concern, matters progress to proceedings taken by the local authority very rapidly. This would often be by application for an emergency protection order.

9.7.3   Emergency protection orders

9.7.3.1   Effect

While in force, by CA 1989, s 44(4), an emergency protection order (EPO) has three effects. It:

(a) Gives the applicant PR for the child (s 44(4)(c)). This does not replace the PR of anyone else who has it.

(b) Authorises removal of the child to accommodation provided by the applicant; or alternatively, the prevention of the child's removal from a hospital or other place in which he was being accommodated immediately prior to the order (s 44(4)(b)).

(c) Operates as a direction to any person who is in a position to do so to comply with any request to produce the child to the applicant (s 44(4)(a)).

Therefore, the order gives the applicant the power to remove the child to, or keep the child in, a safe place; it operates injunctively to demand the handover of a child to the applicant; and the applicant acquires PR. The exercise of that PR is, however, somewhat restricted by s 44(5), whereby it can only be exercised to safeguard and promote the child's welfare, with regard to the duration of the order—in other words, measures must bear in mind that this order is very much temporary—actions and decisions regarding the child with a long-term effect would not be appropriate. During the order, the PR of others who have PR appears to be 'suspended'. For further information on what the applicant can and cannot do during an order, see Hershman C 537–C 570. In particular, action under the EPO must be proportionate (see *P, C and S v UK* [2002] 2 FLR 631); removing—or failing to return—a child where the risk has been removed, for example where a known abuser has been excluded from the home would be disproportionate if it went beyond what was required to safeguard or promote the child's welfare. Further, there is a requirement to allow 'reasonable contact' with a category of persons including the child's parents. Where there are difficulties—such as an inability between the parties to agree 'reasonable' contact, or where the court agrees that a specific person should have no contact at all, this can be dealt with on the hearing by way of directions from the court.

Further directions can be added to the order by the court if it is felt appropriate. These include directions entitling the applicant to enter and search specified premises for the child or for another child; to require any other person to disclose information on the whereabouts of the child; warrants to authorise a constable to assist the applicant, and for a doctor, nurse or health visitor to accompany the constable; directions authorising medical or psychiatric examination of the child; directions with regard to contact with named persons; and exclusion requirements (see **10.5.2**). For further details regarding these important powers, see Hershman C 494–C 534.

9.7.3.2   Duration

An EPO can be made only to last for 8 days at the first hearing (s 45(1)), although there are special provisions where a public holiday falls on the eighth day. If the applicant is a designated officer applying on behalf of the local authority (see above, **9.6.2**), the eight days include any period the child has been in police protection—this is not the case if the local authority applies for itself. Lastly, the order can be extended once, by 7 days (CA 1989, s 45(5)). Normally speaking, an applicant local authority would be expected to have made a decision on whether to apply for a care or supervision order within that time, so reasons will be required by the court as to why the applicant is not ready to proceed.

9.7.3.3   Who can apply?

As seen previously, both the local authority and a designated officer can apply on behalf of the local authority. Additionally, an 'authorised person', normally an officer of the NSPCC can apply. Lastly, 'any other person'—although if the application is to remove the child (rather than to keep the child in his current accommodation), such a person must prove that he has suitable accommodation available. In reality, these applications are almost always made by the local authority.

9.7.3.4   Grounds for the order

An order can be made without notice, and in emergency situations this is often the case. There are detailed rules covering the procedure, the giving of notice and time limits—you should familiarise yourself with these using a text such as Hershman (C 351–C 430).

The court must be satisfied of three matters before an order is made:

(a) that one of the grounds in CA 1989, s 44(1) is made out;

(b) that the child's welfare requires that the order be made (the paramountcy principle); and

(c) that making the order would be better for the child than making no order (the 'no order' principle).

The principal ground in s 44(1), and the ground which is available to all types of applicant, is that the court must be satisfied that.

there is reasonable cause to believe that the child is likely to suffer significant harm if—

(i)   he is not removed to accommodation provided for or on behalf of the applicant; or

(ii) he does not remain in the place in which he is then being accommodated.

This is the most common ground relied upon. Additionally, s 44(1)(b) and (c) provide alternative grounds for local authorities and 'authorised person' applicants only—these relate to where inquiries are being made and there is reasonable cause to suspect that a child is suffering or likely to suffer significant harm. If access to the child for the purpose of such inquiries is being unreasonably refused, these 'frustrated access' grounds can be relied upon in an application for an EPO.

Returning to the first, and most commonly used ground, the test is evidently less stringent than that for a full care order. The applicant only has to prove, as a question of fact, *reasonable cause to believe* that the child is likely to suffer significant harm, although this must be proved objectively ('reasonable')—it is not simply a question of the applicant's personal belief. This lower standard is clearly appropriate to an emergency procedure. There are two other significant differences with the threshold for care and supervision orders. First, here, the facts must relate to *likelihood* of harm—in other words, a future state of affairs. Obviously, the fact that a child can be shown to have suffered, or be suffering significant harm at present will be evidence that this will continue into the future. Second, this ground requires the applicant to show that (depending on the facts of the case) removal from, or retention of the child in, his current accommodation will prevent the harm. For further definitions, see **9.4** above. See *X Council—B (Emergency Protection Orders)* [2005] 1 FLR 341 for 14 key considerations proposed by Munby J.

9.7.3.5   Discharge of order and appeal

Given that the order is quite limited in time, the rules surrounding opposition to the order, application for its discharge and appeal against any decision regarding the EPO application are quite restrictive.

A party may apply to discharge an EPO only if he was not present when it was initially made. Therefore one can oppose the initial making of the order, or one may apply to discharge it—but not both (s 45(8) and (11)). An application to discharge an EPO can be made immediately upon the making of the order, but the court cannot hear it before 72 hours have elapsed from the time of the order. Such applications are always on notice (contrast the making of an EPO, which can be without notice). Again, there are detailed rules on procedure which you will need to be familiar with. Application can also be made to vary directions made on the making of the EPO.

There is no right of appeal regarding any decision on the making or discharge of an EPO—including a refusal to make the order. The only method of review would be judicial review if grounds to support it are present.

In reality, while these rules may appear restrictive, the short-term nature of an EPO needs to be borne in mind. In particular, extensions are often not required, and if the child is not returned the local authority will apply for a care or supervision order, together with an interim care or supervision order within a short space of time. At that point, the parents will have a full opportunity to be heard on the position pending the final hearing.

9.8   Investigation

This section will consider the local authority's powers of investigation of a child's circumstances. Bear in mind that such investigations may not necessarily lead to proceedings being initiated. The result of an investigation could be that the local authority is satisfied that the child's needs are being adequately met by his carers. Alternatively, it may conclude that the provision of services for the child and his carers may best meet the needs of the family at this time. See further **9.2**.

9.8.1   Local authority duty to investigate

The local authority has a specific duty to investigate in a variety of circumstances. Under CA 1989, s 37, a court hearing family proceedings (such as an application for an s 8 order) may be sufficiently concerned about a child's circumstances that it considers that a supervision or care order may be appropriate, and it can order the local authority to investigate. The local authority should consider whether to apply for such an order, or whether provision of services would be appropriate, or whether other action with regards to the child should be taken. There are also duties to investigate in relation to education supervision orders where a court discharges such an order and directs the local authority to investigate; or where a child is persistently not complying with directions under such an order.

Apart from the above requirements, there is an obligation to investigate pursuant to CA 1989, s 47(1). This duty relates to children within the local authority's area. By s 47(1), where a local authority:

(a) are informed that a child who lives, or is found, in their area—

  (i)   is the subject of an emergency protection order; or

  (ii)   is in police protection; or

  (iii) [...]

(b) have reasonable cause to suspect that a child who lives, or is found, in their area is suffering, or is likely to suffer, significant harm, the authority shall make, or cause to be made, such enquiries as they consider necessary to enable them to decide whether they should take any action to safeguard or promote the child's welfare.

The standard *reasonable cause to suspect* is a low threshold—in *Re S (Sexual Abuse Allegations: Local Authority Response)* [2001] 2 FLR 776 it was made clear that this does not require conclusions or facts to be established on the balance of probabilities. The purpose of the investigation is to establish whether action is required to safeguard and promote a child's welfare—in particular, the local authority will be considering whether an application for an order is necessary or whether other powers that it has under CA 1989 should be exercised. The local authority will need to obtain access to the child—and if this is unreasonably refused, then there is a ground for application for an EPO (see **9.6.3.4** above), and the local authority should apply for an EPO, a child assessment order, or a care or supervision order unless satisfied that the child's welfare will be safeguarded without such an order (s 47(6)). By s 47(9) and (11), a variety of organisations are required to assist a local authority with their investigation, including housing authorities, NHS trusts, education authorities, and so forth.

9.8.2   Child assessment orders

Under CA 1989, s 43, a court may make a child assessment order if satisfied that:

(a) the applicant has reasonable cause to suspect that the child is suffering, or is likely to suffer, significant harm;

(b) an assessment of the state of the child's health or development, or of the way in which he has been treated, is required to enable the applicant to determine whether or not the child is suffering, or is likely to suffer, significant harm; and

(c) it is unlikely that such an assessment will be made, or be satisfactory, in the absence of an order under this section.

The point of such an order is to facilitate CA 1989, s 47 enquiries into a child's circumstances where the family or carers of the child are not cooperating with the assessment process—most obviously by denying access to the child.

Clearly, the standard—*reasonable cause to suspect* is relatively low, as is appropriate to an order designed to address a situation where there is concern, but insufficient opportunity to assess the degree of risk, if any, to a child. In terms of seriousness, therefore, it is less interventionist than an EPO. Only a local authority or an 'authorised person' (eg, NSPCC) can apply, unlike the EPO.

If satisfied that these grounds are made out, the court will then consider the no order principle and the paramountcy principle.

The court may treat the application as one for an EPO (s 43(3)), and by s 43(4) must make an EPO rather than a child assessment order if it appears to the court that there are grounds for the EPO and such an order should be made. The court does not have power to make any other kind of order on the application (such as an s 8 order) of its own motion.

The order lasts for seven days only, and there is no provision for it to be extended—at which point the local authority would have to apply for an EPO with directions for assessment or an interim care order in order to continue an incomplete assessment.

The court has considerable control over the assessment process. In particular, the child can only be kept away from home if necessary for the assessment, for such periods as specified in the order only, and only in accordance with directions in the order (s 43(9)). It seems that the child cannot be removed from home without a court direction approving such a measure. Hershman and McFarlane suggest that, given that this type of order is supposed to fall short of the severity of an EPO, then if preventing contact with the child's carers for the duration of an order is necessary, it may be that an EPO is in fact more appropriate. Provision for contact is subject to court direction (s 43(10)).

The order operates as a direction to any person who is able to produce the child to produce him to a person named in the order and to comply with such directions as to assessment as the court specifies in the order (s 43(6)).

A child who has sufficient understanding to make an informed decision may refuse consent to a medical or psychiatric assessment—s 43(8). This would appear to accord with the principles of *Gillick* competence.

While there is no specific guidance on the sort of directions that a court might impose as to the carrying out of the assessment, Hershman and McFarlane suggest a detailed list of matters that need consideration when making such an order. See Hershman C 276–C 280. In particular, directions may be necessary as to who carries out the examinations, the nature of examinations to be permitted, the number of examinations to be permitted and the people who may or must be present during examination. Further, specific directions will be necessary as to what contact the child should have with persons such as his parents during the period of the order.

An order can be varied or discharged on application of specified persons, including the child's parents or carers; and there is a right of appeal with regard to the making or refusal of a child assessment order.

9.9 Contact with a child in care

9.9.1 Powers of the court

Contact with a child in the care of the local authority is governed by CA 1989, s 34. Section 34(1) provides the 'default position' which should pertain whenever there is no specific court order as to contact—the local authority must allow *reasonable contact* with certain people specified by s 34(1), notably the child's parents. Of course, what is 'reasonable' can vary according to the circumstances (eg, once a care order is made, where rehabilitation is planned a higher level of contact is appropriate than where the child is to be placed for adoption). Parents and other relevant persons may be unhappy with the levels of contact granted by the local authority. For this reason there is provision in s 34(3) for persons named in s 34(1) to apply to the court for a contact order (other persons not named in s 34(1) would need the court's leave to make such an application), and in s 34(2) for the child or the local authority to apply for contact orders as well. By s 34(4), the court can authorise the local authority to refuse contact between persons named in s 34(1) and the child. This is an order that should only be made where there is exceptional risk to the child (see *A v M and Walsall Metropolitan Borough Council* [1993] 2 FLR 244), and should never be made routinely as a first step to a care plan entailing adoption. Court orders may carry conditions (s 34(7)—an example might be that the contact be supervised by a named person or take place at a specific address) and when making a care order, a court can make an order for contact under s 34 of its own motion if appropriate. There is an important power for the local authority to suspend contact (even contact ordered by the court) for no more than seven days if necessary to safeguard the child's welfare and an urgent decision is required. If a suspension is required for longer, then clearly the local authority would have to apply for an s 34 contact order, or even an order authorising refusal of contact. By s 34(11), the court is required to scrutinise and invite parties to comment upon the plans for contact put forward by the local authority before granting a care order. Section 34 applies to interim care orders as well since by s 31(11) the definition of 'care order' includes interim care orders.

There is a particularly important provision to remember when making an s 34 contact application—by CA 1989, s 91(17), where an application is made and *refused*, the applicant may not make another application under s 34 for a further six months, unless the court gives leave for such an application. This is to prevent the potentially destabilising effect on the child of frequent, unmeritorious applications. You should note that this applies to all care orders, including interim care orders—and so careful consideration needs to be given to the timing and merits of any application made prior to the final hearing since it may prevent a further application being made at the time of the final hearing.

Just as with an s 8 contact order in private proceedings, 'contact' includes all forms of contact, such as staying or visiting contact, supervised contact and indirect contact (telephone calls, letters and so forth).

9.9.2 Applicable principles

The paramountcy principle applies to contact proceedings under s 34. Contact with a child in care raises particular difficulties in that what is in the child's best interests will depend to a large degree upon what his likely future is to be. The court has to balance the value of contact to the child against how that contact might affect the child's long-term placement—and in some cases, where there is any doubt, the long-term placement will have to be prioritised, as being the child's greatest need. Where the person seeking contact is not able to take full-time care of the child (such as a parent whose parenting abilities are such that he or she cannot meet the child's needs), the degree of contact that is appropriate will depend on the likely long-term placement of the child and whether and to what degree contact would destabilise that placement. For example, if the care plan is for the child to be placed for adoption, direct contact between parent and child will almost certainly be inappropriate. If rehabilitation is intended, then contact will be essential and will probably be at an increasingly high level. If the child is to be fostered by an experienced foster family long term, some direct contact could be appropriate but at a level that enables the child to integrate properly into his foster family and which is not unduly disruptive to the life of the foster family. In such a situation, the parent who can be supportive of the child's new home is likely to be more successful in gaining direct contact than the parent who seeks to undermine the new home in the child's eyes. It is also important that the parent seeking contact can demonstrate that he or she will be consistent and maintain contact so as not to undermine the child's sense of security and self-worth.

The fact that a care order is made with a care plan for placement away from the family does not necessarily mean that there will not be long-term contact between the child and his family—much depends on the child's placement, as mentioned above. There are certain advantages that contact with the birth family gives a child and which may be important enough in the individual case to be worth preserving. These were considered in *Re E (A Minor) (Care Order: Contact)* [1997] 1 FLR 1—Simon Brown LJ:

In short, even where the s 31 criteria are satisfied, contact may well be of singular importance to the long-term welfare of the child; first in giving the child security of knowing that his parents love him and are interested in his welfare; second, by avoiding any damaging sense of loss to the child in seeing himself abandoned by his parents; thirdly, by enabling the child to commit himself to the substitute family with the seal of approval of the natural parents; and fourthly, by giving the child the necessary sense of family and personal identity. Contact, if maintained, is capable of reinforcing and increasing the chances of success of a permanent placement, whether on a long-term basis or by adoption.

See also *Re B (Minors) (Care: Local Authority's Plans)* [1993] 1 FLR 543.

The issue of contact to a child in care is dealt with comprehensively, both as to substantive law and as to procedure in Hershman and McFarlane, Section C.

Children—public law: preparation and practice

Introduction

Policy responsibility, together with associated statistics for the social care of children, has passed from the Department for Children, Schools and Families (DCSF). If you go to the DCSF website <www.dcsf.gov.uk>, you can look at statistics relating to social care services, and in particular, statistics relating to children in need. The main entry pages for children and family matters, at the time of writing, are in the section entitled 'Every Child Matters' <www.dcsf.gov.uk/everychildmatters/>. There are about 60,000 children being looked after by local authorities in England at any one time. This includes children subject to a care order (under s 31 CA 1989) and those who are being looked after under a voluntary agreement with their parents (under s 20 CA 1989). Statistics from the recent past, for example show for the year ending 31 March 2003, the number of children and young people on the Child Protection Register in England was 26,600, or 24 children per 10,000 people under 18. Of these, 39 were registered at risk of neglect, 19 at risk of physical abuse, 18 at risk of emotional abuse and 10 at risk of sexual abuse. Fifteen were registered in mixed categories. The figure for core assessments was 55,700 (see **10.2.1**), which were carried out to establish whether a child was at risk or in need. For the year ended 31 March 2003, the total number of children looked after by local authorities at any time in England was 94,300, or 85 children per 10,000 people under 18. Of the 60,800 looked after at the time of the survey, 65 were in care under a care order, and 31 were being voluntarily accommodated by agreement with their carers. Sixty-eight were accommodated with foster parents, 13 in children's homes or residential schools and 10 were placed with their parents. Fifteen had had three or more placements in one year. The figures on children adopted from care in England in 2002–2003 show that 3,500 were adopted from care, 59 of whom were aged 1–4 years old, and 29 were aged 5–9 years old. The average time to complete the adoption process was 2 years and 9 months, although 81 of the children were placed for adoption within 12 months of the 'best interest' decision (in other words, placed with their proposed adopters within 12 months of the final hearing). The purpose of including these figures is to give you an idea of the scale of the problem. The figures have been extracted from the summaries of information in each survey, and should of course be understood subject to the guidance and caveats in those survey reports. You may also wish to look at the statistics on 'Outcome Indicators for Looked After Children' in England in the 12 months to 30 September 2003. These measure outcomes such as educational achievement, health and criminal involvement. Sadly, although perhaps not surprisingly given their difficult upbringings, these children seem to significantly underachieve compared to the general population of children.

This chapter will first consider the investigative process in care proceedings, including the use of interim care and supervision orders to maintain a 'holding position' between local authority and parents to protect the child prior to a final hearing, discussion of local authority evidence, expert evidence and the role of the Children's Guardian in proceedings. Some of the main issues which can arise at any stage in the care proceedings will then be summarised. There will then be consideration of arguments and outcomes at a final hearing.

10.1   Interim care orders and interim supervision orders

Children may become the subject of court proceedings in a variety of ways. An application for a care or supervision order may be made after a Children Act 1989, s 47 (CA 1989) investigation (see **9.7.1**) as a result of a core assessment prepared for that investigation; or following a child being taken into police protection (see **9.6.2**) and becoming the subject of an emergency protection order (see **9.6.3**). The PLO requires the local authority to carry out significant work before proceedings are instigated. While it is possible for a child to remain in his parents' care, or in voluntary accommodation with the local authority whilst care proceedings are ongoing, it would be unusual for the local authority to accept this situation if there is concern that the child could be at risk—generally, it will feel the need to share parental responsibility (PR) under an interim care order (ICO), so that it can protect the child without further recourse to the court if need be. See also **9.4.5.2** regarding the importance of maintaining protective arrangements continuously to the date at which the court will assess whether the child is suffering significant harm.

10.1.1   Grounds for, effect of, and duration of interim care and interim supervision orders

An interim order can be made whenever an application for a care or supervision order is adjourned. They are made under CA 1989, s 38(1), and are intended to be a strictly neutral step to preserve the status quo, giving no advantage to the local authority in terms of the final hearing. See *Re G* (*Minors*) (*Interim Care Order*) [1993] 2 FLR 839. While the guidance (*The Children Act 1989 Guidance and Regulations, vol 1, Court Orders*) suggests that this is never a 'routine' step in proceedings, in reality, where the evidence shows that there are real child protection concerns it would be unusual for one not to be granted.

The effect of an interim care order is to pass PR to the local authority for the duration of the ICO. The PR of the parents is not extinguished, but just as for a final care order, they cannot exercise their PR inconsistently with that of the local authority—for example they cannot remove a child from a foster care placement chosen by the local authority. The ICO therefore has similar effects to the final order, but for a time-limited period. However, unlike with a final order, the court has much more control over the local authority's actions. In particular, it can prescribe what assessments the local authority can carry out both by way of the requirement for the court's leave to undertake an assessment (see **10.3**) and the power under CA 1989, s 38(6) to *direct* that the local authority carry out certain assessments (see **10.5.1**). The local authority is obliged under the PLO to produce a care plan for the court's scrutiny at the outset of proceedings and it will be considered again when deciding whether or not to grant the

ICO. See *Re L* [2008] 1 FLR 575 for the tests to be applied when the care plan at ICO stage involves removal of the child from the parents.

An interim supervision order (ISO) is simply a supervision order limited in time. For supervision orders, see **9.5**.

On first application for an ICO, the initial order can last for up to eight weeks from the date it is granted. It may be granted for a lesser period of time (quite often the initial ICO is granted for a short period to safeguard the child until court time can be found for a contested hearing where the parents indicate that they do not agree to the making of an ICO—see CA 1989, s 38(10)). After expiry of the initial order, it can be renewed for up to four weeks at a time. Most courts have a system of automatic renewal, unless a party gives written notice prior to renewal that he or she objects and wishes to contest a renewal, and this is in accordance with current guidance (see the *Handbook of Best Practice in Children Act Cases*, hereafter 'the Handbook').

The grounds for such an order follow the pattern of applications for full care and supervision orders in that there is a threshold to be met as a question of factual proof, and thereafter the paramountcy principle, the welfare checklist and the no order principle apply to the decision whether or not to make an order. The major difference with a full care or supervision application is that the threshold is lower—the court need only be satisfied that *'there are reasonable grounds for believing that the circumstances with regard to the child are those required to satisfy the statutory threshold criteria'*—ie, that the child is suffering or likely to suffer significant harm due either to not receiving the care that it would be reasonable for a parent to give to him, or being beyond parental control. Because the threshold is lower ('reasonable grounds to believe'), a finding of fact that the threshold criteria are met for an ICO *does not* constitute a finding that the threshold criteria are met for a full order—the local authority will have to prove this to the higher standard in CA 1989, s 31 at a final hearing. The court hearing an application for an ICO should not seek to make findings on whether the threshold is met for a final order. It is possible for parents to concede that the threshold is met for the ICO or interim supervision order and go on to argue 'disposal' (whether an ICO should be made, or another order, or no order) in just the same way as for a full care or supervision order—see **10.7.2** below.

ICOs can also be relevant at a final hearing—see **10.7.3.2**.

10.2 Local authority evidence

10.2.1 The Framework for the Assessment of Children in Need and their Families

This guidance, produced by the Department of Health in June 2000, is a key document for professionals involved in child protection work. Assessments produced pursuant to this guidance (usually called 'Core Assessments') surface very frequently in care proceedings and therefore, time invested by you in familiarising yourself with its contents will be time well spent. It will provide you with an insight into social service decision making in the individual case, and may well inform the decisions you make about how to undermine the local authority's case (or defend it, depending on your client). The entire document can be accessed through the Department of Health website. Go to the Department's website and follow the links, or key the following into a browser <www.dh.gov.uk/en/Publicationsandstatistics/Publications/PublicationsPolicyAndGui dance/DH_4008144>. There is a very useful summary of the '*Framework*' at Appendix 2 of *Working together to safeguard children* (see **9.2.1**). You will also find the standard re-cord forms for initial and core assessments (designed to be child age and development specific); and the Complete Family Pack of Questionnaires and Scales. These latter documents provide useful insight into the investigations that social services carry out on families for the purpose of assessments.

10.2.2   Ascertaining whether a child is 'in need'

The purpose of the guidance is to assist social work practitioners to identify whether a child is 'in need', including whether he is suffering or likely to suffer significant harm, and how his needs might best be met via appropriate provision of services to the child and his family. This is key to fulfilling the local authority's statutory duty under CA 1989, s 17 to safeguard and promote the welfare of children in need within its area. It is intended to provide a *systematic way of analysing, understanding and recording* what happens to a child within his family. It does not have the force of statute but must be complied with unless circumstances are exceptional. One of the crucial principles behind its use is that it is a *framework and not a practice manual*. Social work practitioners are expected to adapt its requirements to the needs of the individual case rather than apply it in a dogmatic and 'tick box' way. It also aims to facilitate effective collaborative work between professionals from different disciplines and agencies so that parents and children do not experience inconsistent treatment by these professionals. A vast array of different agencies may have had dealings with the family—chapter 5 of the Framework will give you an indication of who these are likely to be. They include education and health professionals, the police (in some cases) and many others. They will frequently be required to assist in and contribute information and/or professional skills to an assessment.

Throughout the Framework, there is emphasis on the importance of communication with the family and the child (as far as the child is able to understand), information sharing with the family, and seeking where possible to secure their agreement to plans made as a result of assessment. The PLO requires the involvement of the parents at an early stage. Key principles informing the mindset of child protection professionals include that it is in a child's best interests to be brought up by his family wherever possible; and that parents have a right to call upon the local authority for services, including voluntary accommodation (CA 1989, s 20), and help, when needed. To this end, whilst the focus is always clearly on the child, services might address needs of the adults (eg, counselling) if that will have an impact upon the child's welfare. One of the main messages of the guidance is that assessment and provision of services are not mutually exclusive—the family should not have to wait for the completion of an assessment for services to be provided if their necessity is clear during the assessment. In the individual case, you will be looking to see whether, and to what extent, these principles have informed the way professionals have worked with the family so far. Has proper and timely support been provided to enable this child to be brought up by the family as far as possible? There are many cases in which social work practitioners have worked very hard with the family and explored all possibilities to enable the child to be cared for by them, despite which the family have made insufficient effort, or are simply incapable of providing adequate care. There are others in which intervention by the professionals has been poorly targeted, or issues have been prejudged and not properly assessed.

The principles underpinning the assessment of a child in need are summarised at chapter 1.33 of the Framework, and developed in more detail at 1.34–1.60.

10.2.3 How does the carrying out of a core assessment under the Framework relate to care proceedings?

A core assessment does not necessarily have to be carried out with legal proceedings in mind. Primarily, they are begun where initial assessment has demonstrated that the child may be a child in need, and they are aimed at giving the local authority the necessary information to develop a 'child in need plan' for that child and identify necessary services for that child and his parents. However, legal proceedings may become an issue at any time in the assessment process if the professional(s) carrying out the assessment suspects that the child is suffering or is likely to suffer significant harm. At this point, the assessment would not end, but the local authority would have to consider its CA 1989, s 47 obligations to inquire and decide whether action is necessary to protect the child. The focus and pace of the assessment may change at that point to focus on establishing whether the child is suffering harm and whether action is necessary. This could result in proceedings for a care order—beginning with an application for an interim care order. If the situation is truly urgent, then an emergency protection order could be sought.

The PLO requires disclosure by the local authority of all the relevant assessments when proceedings are instituted. The Timetable for the Child and the CMC should ensure that the court has control over all further necessary work by the local authority and other professionals. In contested care proceedings, the professional who undertook the core assessment will often have to 'speak to the report' (give evidence) orally and be cross-examined on it.

In contested care proceedings, the professional who undertook the core assessment will often have to 'speak to the report' (give evidence) orally and be cross-examined upon it.

10.2.4 What is being assessed?

From the point of view of legal proceedings, the assessment may provide evidence to support the local authority's case as follows:

- proof that the threshold criteria are met; and/or
- evidence demonstrating what the child's welfare requires; and/or
- evidence justifying and supporting the care plan or part of the plan.

More widely, whether the core assessment relates to legal proceedings, or whether it simply seeks to identify whether the child is in need and what support the local authority can provide to promote his welfare, there are three key elements being assessed (known within the Framework as 'domains'):

- the child's developmental needs;
- the capacity of the parents to respond appropriately to those needs;
- family and environmental factors and their impact upon the parents' capabilities and the child.

Summaries of the various aspects of these three domains can be found (in chapter 2) at pages 19, 21 and 36 of the Framework. *You should refer to these*, as well as to Figure 2, which is a pictorial summary of how the three domains relate to the child's welfare. Assessors are strongly advised to *observe* the interactions between parents and child as well as discussing these with the parents. Further, assessment will take in the impact of the parents' relationship with each other on their abilities to respond to the child's needs. This may involve considering a distinction between an abusing parent and a potentially protective parent. In particular, it is sometimes the case that one parent could parent better alone than if the parents are together.

Chapter 3 considers the process of assessing, including the need for contact and information-sharing with agencies who may have previous knowledge of the family (such as health visitors or the school), and the timescales for the assessment. It makes clear that the child himself should be seen. There may be pre-existing assessments on the family by other professionals which need to be obtained to inform the core assessment, and to avoid duplication.

Sections 3.39, 3.40 and 3.42 are of particular interest in understanding the different methods by which information is gathered during a core assessment and the importance of sharing records, plans and reports with the family, including providing copies. Section 3.42 makes particular reference to what 'direct work' with the child will involve.

10.2.5 Decision making and judgements

This section will be of particular interest to the lawyer, dealing as it does with the conclusions drawn from the core assessment process and subsequent planning. The process of analysis should lead to the following results:

- identifying the child's needs and the parents' ability to respond appropriately to those needs;
- identifying whether, and if so, what intervention is necessary to secure the well-being of the child;
- a realistic plan of action, including what services should be provided to the family, and a timetable and process for review.

At 4.15 the crucial judgements to be made are outlined:

- determining what has been happening and whether this is a child in need or a child suffering significant harm;
- understanding the child and family context sufficiently to be able to secure the child's well-being or safety;
- assessing the likelihood of change;
- and later, on review, reviewing whether such change is being achieved.

The latter two judgements are often the crucial points for the lawyer in care proceedings—likelihood of change is a fundamental issue when considering the 'disposal' (welfare) stage of the final hearing. The decisions of and plans by the local authority will be apparent from its care plan, disclosed at the outset of proceedings.

The remainder of chapter 4 is very important in terms of local authority planning for the child, and you should read it. In particular, at 4.21, the guidance states that the content and timing of the plan for the child is informed by three key aspects of the child's health and development:

- ensuring the child's safety;
- remembering that a child cannot wait indefinitely;
- maintaining a child's learning.

Again, the particular issue for the lawyer is likely to be the second of these points. Where parents have not improved their parenting sufficiently for return of a child at a final care hearing, the argument on their behalf will usually relate to allowing more time for assessment of their abilities, or a new type of work or assessment. The concern is the child's timescales—children cannot wait for a permanent placement forever and to expect them to do so could cause them harm in itself. The younger the child the more urgent the need for permanency and secure attachments with a carer become. Sections 4.22 and 4.25 raise the importance of secure attachments between parents and child in deciding the future of the child, and the issues of permanent placement elsewhere.

Sections 4.26, 4.28 and 4.30 are of particular interest for the lawyer since they identify criteria indicative of poor, or good, prospects for reuniting a child with his family. In making judgements about the long-term placement of the child, the professionals involved are likely to have relied upon a combination of such factors. At 4.26, the following criteria are identified as suggesting a poor outcome for reuniting the child with abusive parents:

- the abusing parent completely or significantly denies any responsibility for the child's developmental state or abuse;
- the child is rejected or blamed outright;
- the child's needs are not recognised by its parents, who put their own needs first;
- parents have frequently failed to show concern, or acknowledge, long-standing difficulties such as alcoholism or psychiatric problems; and
- during therapeutic interventions, the relationships within the family and with professionals are at breaking point.

One imagines that many of these issues must have been seen in the *Baby P* case, but were not followed up.

Key themes in the care case will therefore be whether the parents *minimise* the problems rather than being realistic about them; whether they *accept responsibility* for the problems in their parenting or deny that they exist (in particular, do they blame the child or do they have some insight into their own responsibility?); whether the parents put the child's needs first and above their own (eg, does the mother in an abusive relationship continue that relationship 'because she can't help it' or seek to end it in order to protect the children?; or a parent with an addiction to narcotics makes insufficient effort to give up, putting their need for their addiction before their children's needs to be properly parented); whether the parents *deny* that they have their own problems (such as alcoholism) or acknowledge them and attempt to resolve them; and whether the parents are *able to work with professionals, or resist attempts to improve their parenting*.

Therefore, when looking at the evidence in a case where the local authority's care plan is for permanent placement away from the family, the lawyer needs to identify and evaluate evidence demonstrating these factors, and evidence which suggests the contrary. For example, in a case where the mother is alleged to have failed to cooperate with the professionals, is there evidence that she has in fact attended appointments made for her? Is there reason for non-compliance, for example that she was suffering from post-natal depression which was undiagnosed at the time? See further, **10.2.7** below.

10.2.6   The initial social work statement

This is a document which will only be prepared for care proceedings (unlike the core assessment, which has a number of roles in child protection work). Under the PLO, the initial social work statement must be filed on the issue of the application. The PLO outlines its contents.

A social work chronology will also be filed in the prescribed format.

As regards the initial statement, see further *Re R (Care: Disclosure: Nature of Proceedings)* [2002] 1 FLR 755.

As you can see, the initial statement will to a large extent contain the history of social services' dealings with the family and agencies involved with them, together with details of the arrangements for the child and the action to assess the case and work with the parents that the local authority proposes to undertake during the proceedings. It is normally made by the child's allocated social worker, who would not usually be the same person as the author of the core assessment (whether one already exists or is proposed to take place during the proceedings). Further statements may well be filed in accordance with the court's directions at stages during the proceedings. These later statements will update the court on events occurring since the initial statement and progress of assessments and work with the family, if any, which are ongoing.

10.2.7   Challenging the local authority evidence

It will immediately be noted that the local authority evidence has a distinct advantage over that of the parents. The evidence that the parents will give about past events may well be confused and incomplete. It may be that their recollection is affected by the problems they face, for example drug abuse or depression or simply chaotic lives. They certainly will not have recorded salient details as they occur! By contrast, social services will have routinely recorded their interaction with the family throughout their involvement, as will other agencies (eg, the health visitor) coming into contact with the family. It can also be difficult to challenge the local authority version of events because—at least in theory—it relies upon observation by professionals who have no personal interest in the outcome, in stark contrast to the parents. That is not to say that the credibility of local authority witnesses cannot on occasion be undermined, for example there may be evidence to show that a key social work practitioner allowed personal feelings of dislike towards a parent to affect her professional judgement, or prejudged the outcome (eg, failing to investigate an important allegation made by the mother which later proves to be true; or failing to consider a realistic alternative to some quite draconian step without good reason).

Of course, you must always take your client's instructions on the history of the matter, and look at each case on its facts. There may be good evidence to contradict historical allegations of fact, or those made may be susceptible to being undermined. But in many cases, the focus of the lawyer will be less on challenging the past and more on trying to demonstrate change in the parents' attitudes and abilities. The factors referred to in 4.26 of the Framework (see **10.2.5** above) will provide a starting point in many cases for what you have to attack—both historically, and in relation to the events during the lifetime of the proceedings. Parents, unfortunately, frequently react to social services' intervention by denying all the problems, minimising their own responsibility, and refusing to cooperate—or at least cooperate in any meaningful way—with those professionals trying to work with them. These attitudes will be something the lawyer will need to explore with the clients in conference, and advise them about as early as possible in the case—a continuation of this behaviour is likely to prove disastrous for their prospects of success. Where parents cannot see that there is any cause for concern regarding their parenting, their motivation for change will be low—and demonstrating potential for change will often be the key argument. The lawyer will be looking at all times for the following, for purposes of cross-examination (whether at contested ICO hearing or a final hearing) and argument:

- Evidence of cooperation with professionals from the parents. For example, an open attitude to social services' visits (rather than refusing to open the door, or being away from home when a visit is prearranged) and engagement with social work practitioners (attending planning meetings, being prepared to discuss assessments and so forth). More importantly, evidence of engagement with assessment and therapeutic work—eg, regular attendance at parenting work sessions and a clear attempt to put what is learned into practice. The lawyer will attempt to 'accentuate the positive' by putting to the social work practitioner the instances of positive engagement by the parents. The more it can be shown that the parents are cooperating, and are likely to continue to cooperate with professionals in the interests of the child, the better the chance of a successful outcome.

- Demonstrations of insight into the problems by the parents. Are there examples of attempts to really understand the problems by the parents? Do they accept any responsibility for the problems, and what instances demonstrate this? What work has been done with them, or is planned, to assist them to gain insight into these issues? Insight is important because an understanding and acceptance of the problems is a good indication that change will be possible.

- Are there good reasons for a failure to cooperate, or to properly engage with work designed to improve their skills? It may be that attention can be turned on the way in which the social work practitioners handled the situation—for example, contrary to the principles of the Framework, there may have been little effort to consult parents about key decisions and include them in decision making (eg, were there genuine efforts to invite them to planning meetings and share information with them?). It may be that parents have a good relationship with one practitioner and not with another—was this taken into account in decisions about who would deal with the family? More fundamentally, there might be good reason for the parents' inability to engage with work—they may have low learning ability, and the intervention, however well meaning, did not take this into account; or one might have been suffering depression in a way which reduced their motivation, and this was untreated at the time they are alleged to have failed to cooperate.

- Have the right assessments been undertaken, or the right work targeted? Some interventions, however well-intentioned, may be ineffective compared to others—a classic example would be where learning difficulties were not taken into account.

- What efforts have been made to support compliance by the parents? For example, if a resource is not available locally, was assistance given to enable the parents to travel? What resources could have been supplied by the local authority but were not? Again, while the social services department cannot make decisions about housing and provision of accommodation, they can, under CA 1989, s 27, ask the housing authority for assistance—have enquiries been made?

- Consider the key principles outlined in the Framework. Does social services' intervention demonstrate a commitment to those principles or not? For example, given the key principle that *where possible*, children should be brought up in their families, on deciding that the child could not be permanently placed with the parents, did the social worker make a genuine effort to consider placement within the wider family (eg, grandparents) if that was an option on the facts of the case?

- To a degree, social work practitioners have some similarities to expert witnesses (see **10.3** below). Their evidence may be susceptible to being undermined in terms of important assumptions they have made about the facts, or key information relied upon by them which has come from other sources being incorrect, in particular where a fact is subsequently shown to be false.

10.3 Expert evidence

Care proceedings do not simply focus on past events—unlike many forms of litigation, there is a strong focus on the likely future. The court is trying to predict the future in order to decide what the child's welfare will demand. If a care order is not made, will the child suffer significant harm? Will the parents be able to meet the child's needs in the long term? Will the therapy or work needed to enable the parents to meet the child's needs be successful—and how quickly? Would the child's needs be better met by adoption or fostering? These are a few of the questions that the court may be seeking to answer in a typical care case.

The local authority evidence discussed at **10.2** will in part seek to answer these questions. Additionally, expert evidence may be sought to help the court predict the future in this way. It may also play a role in determining past events, for example, whether a child has suffered non-accidental injuries, sexual abuse or emotional damage as a result of the care given to him. Many care cases will therefore involve some element of expert evidence and it is usually of great importance. For this reason, your cross-examination of an unfavourable expert can be vital. In the modern context, this can become even more difficult because it will frequently be expected that parties will jointly instruct one expert and therefore you do not have the benefit of an expert instructed by your party who can assist you to identify appropriate cross-examination of other experts in the case.

This section will look at the legal requirements for expert evidence, the role of the expert in proceedings, and throughout the discussion, practice requirements for the instruction of experts. There will also be some brief consideration of the methods of undermining unfavourable expert testimony.

10.3.1 Leave for the instruction of experts

By FPR 1991 r 4.18(1) and FPC (CA 1989) R 1991 r 18(1), leave of the court must be obtained for a child to be medically, psychiatrically or otherwise examined. Further, by FPR 1991 10.20A(2)(vii) and FPC (CA 1989) r23, disclosure of the case papers to the expert should only happen once the court has authorised the instruction of an expert. A failure to obtain leave for these purposes means that the evidence thereby obtained may not be adduced without leave of the court.

Clearly these rules are important—they ensure that the court has control over any assessment of the child. This protects the child from unwarranted intervention which may not be in his best interests and helps to protect the privacy of the family.

There is another important rule relating to litigation privilege—in other words, the privilege that attaches to expert evidence and other evidence prepared for pending or anticipated litigation. In CA 1989 proceedings, litigation privilege does not apply. Therefore, if the court gives leave to disclose the relevant case papers to an expert, any resulting report from the expert *must be disclosed* to the court and other parties, even if unfavourable to the party commissioning the report. (Litigation privilege should be contrasted with legal professional privilege—communications between client and lawyer for the purpose of obtaining legal advice—which *does* apply to CA 1989 proceedings to protect the confidentiality of lawyer–client communications.)

On 1st April 2008, the Practice Direction: Experts in Family Proceedings Relating to Children came into force ('Experts' Practice Direction—EPD'). It supersedes all previous directions and guidance under the previous protocol. The full text can be found in Section N of Hershman & McFarlane and also by searching for 'expert evidence in children cases' on the courts service website: http://www.hmcourts-service.gov.uk. The aim of the EPD is to help the court identify at an early stage what matters are outside its expertise, to encourage the early identification of any experts and to formulate the questions for them. Under the PLO, expert evidence must be addressed by or at the CMC. It is clear from the Active Case Management section of the PLO (para 3.15) that the court will control the use and cost of experts; the combination of the PLO and EPD give the clear impression that the court is seeking to reduce both these elements.

10.3.2 Role of the expert in the proceedings

Any expert witness should be referred to Wall LJ's *A Handbook for Expert Witnesses in Children Act Cases* (2nd edition). As its title suggests, it is aimed specifically at the expert body and has useful summaries of current practice and guidance. When an expert is instructed before proceedings are issued, it should be made clear to the expert that he may in due course be reporting to the court and should consider himself bound by the EPD.

As with any other proceedings, the purpose of expert evidence is to provide evidence and information on areas outside the court's expertise. Experts can give opinion evidence on any matter within their expertise which is relevant to the court's decision. That can include the ultimate issue, although the decision is that of the judge—and the judge makes that decision on the basis of all the evidence in the case, not just that of the expert.

Following *M v R* (*Child Abuse: Evidence*) [1996] 2 FLR 195, it was established that a suitably qualified expert can give evidence as to the credibility or accuracy of a child or other witness. This might be important for example in a sexual abuse case where the physical evidence is limited or even non-existent and reliance is placed on allegations by the child or another witness.

10.3.3 Instructing the expert

One of the first points to note about the instruction of an expert is that generally it is inappropriate for an expert involved in therapeutic treatment of a child to make a forensic report to the court. There are several good and obvious reasons for this—the therapeutic expert will probably have built up a relationship of trust with the child—and/or with the parents—which might be compromised by the same expert having duties to the court; equally that relationship could make it difficult for the treating expert to fulfil the role of court reporter objectively due to sympathy for the child's plight. It is generally better that an independent expert reports and makes recommendations for the child's future. That is not to say that a treating expert will not be expected to give evidence or be involved in proceedings at all—for example, they may have valuable factual information to give on the child's medical history which they are best placed to provide, and indeed, their information as to the child's history will probably form part of the reporting expert's investigations. For consideration of when the treating clinician may be useful as an expert, see *Oldham Metropolitan Council v GW & PW* [2007] 2 FLR 597.

What sort of expert is appropriate? Different expertise might be required for different stages of the court's decision-making process. For establishing the threshold criteria, the type of expert evidence required depends very much on the type of harm the child has suffered and which is feared might occur in the future. For a case of neglect (the most common form of abuse), generally speaking, a child psychiatrist would be appropriate to comment upon the emotional harm occasioned by the neglect. Where there are allegations of non-accidental injury or, less dramatically, physical harm occasioned by neglect, a consultant paediatrician would be appropriate. It may very well be necessary to instruct a consultant radiologist as well should there be bony injuries to be assessed. For suspected sexual abuse, there will be a need for medical evidence regarding the child's physical condition and also a child psychiatrist to consider other evidence regarding the abuse, and the emotional effects of abuse that is shown to have occurred.

It may well be that different types of expertise are required in the same case at the 'disposal' (welfare test) stage. The issues in the case will dictate who is required. For example, in a non-accidental injuries case, there may be a need for expert evidence from a psychiatrist or psychologist regarding the abusing parent's ability to control their anger as well as the attachments between the child and the parents and the prognosis for successful rehabilitation of the child to his parents. This evidence will be essentially 'forward looking' in an attempt to predict the outcomes.

Duties are placed on the advocates to identify any proposed experts and draft questions for them (in accordance with the EPD) at the Advocates' Meeting which must take place before the CMC. Detailed consideration will, therefore, need to be given to all these matters as early as possible in the proceedings. The questions must be clear and precise.

An example might be the case of a couple whom social services suspect have neglected their 4–year-old child. The child appears to be suffering from developmental delay—she is not putting on weight or growing at a normal rate; she is still in nappies; she was late to learn to walk and her speech and comprehension seem to the social worker to be delayed. Her parents appear largely indifferent to her presence and are not noted to interact with her in a frequent or meaningful way.

You will probably need to instruct a consultant child psychiatrist to consider the following:

(a) To what extent is this child's development delayed by comparison with other children of her age?

(b) What reasons are there for any delay established—in particular, what indications are there that the delay is due to parental neglect?

(c) Comment on the nature and quality of attachment between the child and her parents?

(d) Comment on the degree of insight and understanding her parents have in relation to their child's emotional and developmental needs?

(e) To what extent are her parents capable of meeting her needs at present?

(f) To what extent are her parents capable of improving their capacity to parent, including consideration of their insight into their parenting skills problems and their motivation to address those problems?

(g) What work and resources are likely to be necessary for such improvement to take place?

(h) Over what timescale is such improvement likely to take place, and at what point, if at all, would rehabilitation be feasible?

Questions (a)–(c) are relevant to establishing the threshold by addressing the question of what developmental harm, if any, the child has suffered, and the causation of that harm. Note the comparison to a child of her age without developmental difficulties—CA 1989, s 31(10), see **9.4.5.4**. Questions (c)–(h) address 'disposal'—the child's welfare—by addressing the issue of the parents' ability to understand and overcome problems in their parenting, together with the issue of what resources will be necessary and what timescale is likely. This will help the judge to decide whether a rehabilitation to the parents is feasible and in the child's best interests. The questions asked are very clearly defined according to the issues in the case.

10.3.4 The duties of the expert and the contents of his report

An expert in family proceedings in relation to children has an overriding duty to the court which takes precedence over any obligation to the person from whom he has received his instructions or by whom he is paid (para 3.1 EPD). This now mirrors the position in civil proceedings under Part 35 of the Civil Procedure Rules. The EPD sets out details for experts of their duties:

1. to assist the court in accordance with the overriding duty;

2. to provide advice which conforms to the best practice of the expert's profession;

3. to provide an independent opinion;

4. to limit his opinion to material issues and to matters within his area of exepertise;

5. to alert those instructing to areas outside his expertise on which his advice has been sought and volunteer an opinion as to whether another expert is required;

6. to take into consideration all material facts including those arising from ethnic, cultural, religious or linguistic contexts, when providing his opinion;

7. to inform those instructing without any delay of any change in opinion and the reasons for such change.

In addition, para 3.3 of the EPD gives detailed guidance on the content of the report.

The expert's report shall be addressed to the Court and filed in accordance with the Court's timetable and shall:

1. Give details of the expert's qualifications and experience.

2. Contain a statement setting out the substance of all material instructions (whether written or oral) summarising the facts stated and instructions given to the expert which are material to the conclusions and opinions expressed in the report.

3. Identify materials that have not been produced whether as original medical or other professional records or in response to an instruction from a party.

4. Identify all requests to third parties for disclosure and their response.

5. Make clear which facts in the report are within the expert's own knowledge.

6. State who carried out any test, examination or interview which the expert has used for the report and whether or not the test, examination or interview has been carried out under the expert's supervision.

7. Give details of the qualifications of any person who carried out the test, examination or interview.

8. In expressing an opinion:

   (a) take into account all material facts as set out under his duties at 6 above and give details of any literature or other research material upon which the expert has relied in giving an opinion;

   (b) describe his own professional risk assessment process and process of differential diagnosis;

   (c) indicate whether a proposition is a hypothesis (in particular a controversial one) or an opinion deduced in accordance with peer-reviewed and tested technique, research and experience accepted as consensus in the scientific body.

   (d) indicate whether an opinion is provisional or qualified and giving necessary consequential details.

9. Where there is a range of opinion:

   (a) summarise the range;

   (b) highlight and analyse within the range an 'unknown cause', (eg too little information to form a scientific opinion);

   (c) give reasons for any opinion expressed, the court finding it of great assistance if a balance sheet approach is used with factors that support and undermine the opinion.

10. Contain a summary of the expert's conclusions and opinions.

11. Contain a statement that the expert understands his duty to the Court and has complied with that duty.

12. Contain a statement that the expert has no conflict of interest (other than one already disclosed), does not consider that any disclosed interest affects his suitability as an expert in the case and that he will notify the instructing party if there is any change in this.

13. Be verified by a statement of truth in prescribed form.

The EPD in this way seeks to ensure that the basis of the report is made clear—the factual assumptions made, the ambit of the expert's instruction, the methods used must all be stated. This is important since any of these matters can form the basis of cross-examination to test the reliability and significance of the report.

10.3.5 Dealing with expert evidence at a hearing

This section will focus on the cross examination of experts. Experts do give evidence-in-chief but this tends to be quite limited—rather like a witness statement, their report stands as their evidence-in-chief and so examination-in-chief is restricted to explaining and expanding matters which are not clear from the report and/or obtaining the expert's views on any new matters which have arisen since the time of the report.

It may be that the expert is never called to give evidence and the report is accepted. In addition, if there is more than one expert, an expert's meeting (see the Protocol) may have narrowed the actual disagreements between them quite sharply, so that their evidence and your cross examination can be narrowly focused on those areas.

Cross-examining any expert is a considerable challenge for an advocate. The expert inevitably knows far more about his area of expertise than you do. There are a number of matters that it is useful to bear in mind.

First, there are particular differences between the evidence of an expert and the evidence of most other witnesses.

- Experts tend to speak in 'probabilities' rather than absolutes. For example, when predicting the child's future, a child and adolescent psychologist may state that it is 'unlikely' that the parents can improve their parenting difficulties sufficiently 'within an appropriate timescale' for the child. He cannot say definitely that they will or will not, or what that timescale truly is—nobody can. He is having to express an *opinion* based on facts and analysis of what is known so far.

- Normally, experts draw conclusions and give evidence without first-hand knowledge of many of the facts they rely on. Of course, an expert will have direct experience of some facts—eg, if they have observed a play session between parent and child they can give direct evidence of what they saw as a question of fact. But much of the information on which an expert relies in drawing conclusions is second hand—provided by others, for example, social work records and the papers disclosed with leave of the court.

With this in mind, David Bedingfield states three questions that an advocate must consider when preparing to cross-examine an expert.

(1) How did the expert conduct his assessment? The advocate must always seek to understand the methods used by the expert in order to reach the opinion that was reached.

(2) What did the expert assess? The advocate must seek to understand the factual matrix used by the expert, and seek to pin down the expert on what factual assumptions were made.

(3) Why is the assessment wrong?/Why did the assessment reach a conclusion that was reached?

(David Bedingfield, *Advocacy in Family Proceedings: A Practical Guide*, Jordan's Family Law, 2005).

As Bedingfield goes on to point out, in order to undermine the expert's evidence, the expert must be shown to have made an error on one of these three fundamental questions. Cross-examination will therefore seek to show a problem with the expert's method(s), and/or an erroneous factual assumption on which the conclusion is based which then renders the conclusion unreliable (or where a fact relied on is the subject of dispute in the proceedings, that the expert would have concluded differently if the fact relied on was incorrect—disproving the fact relied on is then an issue for cross-examination of the witness who provided the challenged fact).

As Bedingfield explains, challenging the expert on an error on the third question will almost always fail unless a successful attack can be made on either or both of the first two questions—unless there is other evidence in the case which contradicts the expert's conclusion—normally a report from an equally well-qualified expert disagreeing with the expert in question.

You should never attempt to prepare or carry out a cross-examination without having a clear idea of what you want to be able to say about this witness's evidence in a closing speech—and experts are no exception. Have a clear idea about what helpful evidence this expert could give for your case; and in what way he or she damages your case.

The content of your cross-examination will be driven by the issues in the case, but the following grounds of challenge may be appropriate:

- **Difference between your case and expert's view is a question of degree**. Because experts speak in probabilities (see above), a major aim of cross-examination will often be to establish that the difference between your case and his view is a question of degree—and obviously, the closer the case, the more powerful this point. For example, say you are acting for the local authority. Your case is that even if the parents could improve their parenting and overcome drug dependency with intensive work, they cannot do so soon enough—this child is 2 years old and needs permanent placement very soon. The parents' expert has stated that progress could be made by the parents within three months. In cross-examination you will be seeking to 'extend' that period to introduce doubt—so you will make reasonable suggestions such as that a lapse in the drug rehabilitation programme could easily extend the time the parents need by many months. The expert would probably agree—enabling you to 'chip away' at the parents' suggestion that they can improve in a time suitable for the child.

- **Expert has based conclusions on facts reported by others**. It is therefore possible to 'separate' the facts on which the expert relies from his personal expertise and credibility—you are not attacking his judgement, rather the facts on which he has drawn conclusions—if the facts were different, would his conclusion have been different? Usually the answer will be 'yes'. You will then aim to undermine the important fact(s) when cross-examining the witness who reported them.

- **Alternative version**—you can suggest alternative versions of the facts to an expert to establish how that would change his conclusions. You *must* ensure that those alternative versions are facts for which you have evidence in support (such as the evidence of the parents) and that the facts you suggest accurately reflect the version of events that your other evidence will prove—otherwise a positive answer from the expert proves nothing. As with all these questions, be very careful how you prepare the line of questioning—if it becomes muddled, the effect is lost.

- **Alternative interpretations of facts**—this can be quite a tricky area. Evidently you will never be as 'expert' on the area as the person you are cross-examining, but you will have made an effort to try to understand the area. The same facts relied upon might support other interpretations. For example, petechial marks on a child's neck (these are little rash-like areas of tiny red dots—they are the result of little capillaries bursting) can be highly indicative of abuse—but an alternative cause is a child having a coughing fit while wearing a collar that is too tight; or a badly fitting seatbelt.

- **Reasonable suggestion**—provided the alternative facts or the alternative interpretation you put is reasonable, an expert who resists such a suggestion too strongly looks less credible.

- **Method**—the methods employed by the expert may have weaknesses—eg, a test may take account of one feature of someone's personality, but take insufficient account of, or be a poor test of, another feature. It might be reliant on the quality of the information 'fed into' the test, which might be erroneous or contain assumptions. Certain factors may have been overlooked or gone untested. This area of cross-examination would be easier if you are fortunate enough to have an expert instructed for your party who can advise you on the adequacy of the other expert's methods.

- **Bias**—it is very rare for an expert to lie, but it is not unknown for them to be biased or in some way have a personal interest. It may be helpful to find out prior to cross-examination whether the expert tends to give evidence for one side (eg, local authority, or parents) rather than the other. Equally, the expert may be strongly identified with a 'pet theory' and therefore feels his personal reputation is as much at stake as the interests of the parties in the proceedings. Occasionally, experts have 'relied upon' facts which have not been observed by either themselves or any other witness—clearly, that would lend doubt to the expert's credibility.

- **Qualifications**—exceptionally, the expert's qualifications to provide the evidence may be insufficient. This would, however, be most unusual in care proceedings, and there would almost certainly be fault on the part of the lawyer or lawyers instructing him for such an expert to be chosen in the first place.

Further reading and information

- Expert Witness Pack—draft letters of instruction, guidelines for report writing, etc. Published by the Expert Witness Group, and Family Law

- *Child Psychiatry and Child Protection Litigation*, Julia Brophy (ed) (Gaskell, 2001)

Experts—key authorities

- *Oldham Metropolitan Borough Council v GW & PW* [2007] 2 FLR 597

- *Re U (Serious Injury: Standard of Proof); Re B* [2004] 2 FLR 263—guidance on treatment of expert evidence by courts post-*R v Cannings*

10.4 Role of the Children's Guardian

10.4.1 Appointment of the Children's Guardian

Apart from the local authority and the parents, there is almost always another party to the proceedings—the Children's Guardian (see CA 1989, s 41(1), for presumption favouring appointment of a Children's Guardian in specified proceedings—which include applications for care and supervision orders). This will be a person drawn from the Guardian ad Litem and Reporting Officer Service of the Children and Family Court Advisory and Support Service (CAFCASS), and the Children's Guardian is an officer of the court. Appointment and duties of the Guardian are governed by FPC (CA 1989) R 1991, rr 10 and 11 in the Family Proceedings Court, and by FPR 1991, rr 4.10 and 4.11 in the High Court and County court—see also the Protocol, regarding timing of the appointment. The Children's Guardian acts for the child in public law proceedings since a child is, by law, a person under a disability. The Children's Guardian will usually select a solicitor to act as advocate in the proceedings on the instructions of the Children's Guardian—it would not be compatible with the Guardian's obligations as a witness in the proceedings for the Guardian to also act as advocate. For rules governing appointment of a solicitor for the child, and what happens when the child is sufficiently mature to instruct the solicitor for himself, see Hershman and McFarlane at C 2708 and C 2811–20. In relation to the law on Children's Guardians and the responsibilities of the solicitor for the child generally, see section 6 of part C, Hershman and McFarlane.

The local authority has obligations to consult with the Children's Guardian where one is appointed. It would be wrong for the local authority to change a child's circumstances in a major way without first discussing the matter with the Guardian; equally, an application for a care or supervision order should not be withdrawn without such prior discussion.

10.4.2 Responsibilities of the Children's Guardian

By s 41(2)(b), the Children's Guardian is under a duty to safeguard the interests of the child in the manner prescribed by the rules. Upon appointment, he or she must appoint a solicitor for the child (see **10.4.1** above). The requirements imposed by the rules can be summarised as follows:

- give advice to the child as appropriate to his age and understanding;
- instruct the solicitor representing the child on matters relevant to the child's interests;
- notify any person whose joinder to the proceedings would assist in safeguarding the child's interests (in the Guardian's view) of their right to apply to be joined;
- attend all hearings unless excused by the court, and give advice to the court;
- prepare a written report where ordered to do so, and in any event prepare a written report for the final hearing; and
- accept service of documents on behalf of the child and advise the child on the contents of the documents in as far as appropriate given his age and understanding.

Most importantly, the Children's Guardian is empowered, and indeed obliged, to investigate and advise the court on the basis of that investigation. He or she will give evidence at a final hearing (and if appropriate at earlier hearings, such as a contested ICO), and will be cross-examined by the other parties in the normal way. The Guardian's background is almost always as a child protection social work practitioner, and they therefore tend to be regarded as independent social work—ie, child care—experts. Their views carry significant weight with the court. The Guardian must have regard to the principle of the Children Act that delay is likely to be prejudicial to the welfare of the child, and the elements of the welfare checklist (CA 1989, s 1(3)).

10.4.3 Investigation by the Children's Guardian

This is a vital part of the Guardian's role. The Guardian has access to relevant records of the local authority (see CA 1989, s 42), including the right to take copies, and can bring relevant records and documents to the court's attention. The Guardian's access is quite wide ranging (see Hershman and McFarlane at C 2747–C 2749) and will include certain records held by voluntary organisations and registered children's homes.

Further, the Guardian may interview those persons he or she considers relevant, and as directed by the court. Evidently, this will involve seeing the child (on a fairly regular basis), the family, the social work practitioners involved, health visitors and other agencies involved with the family, plus other professionals who have been involved in the child's care (eg, hospital staff, day nurseries, etc).

The Guardian may also obtain other professional assistance where necessary. The Guardian's expertise in child care—it would therefore be wrong for him or her to attempt to express expertise in other areas, such as paediatrics. In such cases, the Guardian can obtain expert evidence to assist, with the leave of the court.

10.4.4 The Children's Guardian's report

The Children's Guardian may be asked to assist the court at interim hearings—this might be by way of written evidence or oral report. Examples could be as to the desirability of an assessment of the child being sought by another party, or on the question of a contested application for an ICO. At a final hearing, a written report must be filed in advance of the hearing, and the guardian will give evidence and be cross-examined. The report for a final hearing will summarise the Guardian's investigations and his or her conclusions from those investigations as to the options available to the court and the suitability of the local authority's care plan. A Children's Guardian can make specific recommendations, and a court should not depart from these without giving reasons in the judgment (*Re D* (*Grant of Care Order: Refusal of Freeing Order*) [2001] 1 FLR 862). See further Hershman and McFarlane C 2751. The report is confidential and distribution of the report carefully controlled beyond its provision to the parties in the case.

10.5 Key issues during proceedings prior to a final hearing

This section aims to provide you with a starting point to consider a number of common problems and issues which can confront you prior to (and sometimes even at) a final hearing.

10.5.1 Section 38(6) CA 1989 directions for assessment

As you have seen, there is often a considerable body of assessment available at the early stages of proceedings—eg, a core assessment by the local authority. Once proceedings have commenced, the court's leave is required for any assessment of the child (see **10.3.1**). It may be that the parties can agree that further assessment is required, and on the specific type of assessment—alternatively, there may be disagreement on these issues. Under CA 1989, s 38(6), the court can direct that further assessment be carried out, whether by the local authority or upon instruction by another party. The section reads as follows:

Where the court makes an interim care order, or an interim supervision order, it may give such directions (if any) as it considers appropriate with regard to the medical or psychiatric examination or other assessment of the child; but if the child is of sufficient understanding to make an informed decision he may refuse to submit to the examination or other assessment.

This is an important section—the local authority may have PR under an ICO, but this is one example of the fact that the court has some control over its exercise—the court can order an assessment in an appropriate case even if the local authority does not want it.

There was once a distinction drawn by the courts between 'assessment' and 'therapy'—the former was permissible, the latter was not. This distinction was problematic—for example, some organisations (eg, The Priory) provide assessment which has elements of therapy. The distinction is now abandoned—the chief question in deciding whether to direct assessment is: 'Can what is sought be broadly classified as an assessment to enable a court to obtain the information necessary for its own decision?' (see *Re G*, cited below).

The key point in a s 38(6) application is whether or not the assessment is *necessary for a court to have sufficient information* before it to make the final decision in the case. 'Assessment' is wider than psychiatric or medical assessment, and can include assessment of the *parents* together with their child (often as a *residential assessment*)—a significant point in many cases where the ability of the parents to care properly is doubted. The court will not ignore the resource implications for funding by the local authority—some assessments are simply prohibitively expensive—although the court can direct the assessment is funded in any event. Section 38(6) CA 1989 can be used to prohibit an assessment. It is essential that you are familiar with the key authorities in this area before you seek to argue such an application.

Key authorities

- *Re C (A Minor) (Interim Care Order: Residential Assessment)* [1997] AC 489, [1997] 1 FLR 1 HL

- *Re G (Interim Care Order: Residential Assessment)* [2004] EWCA Civ 24, [2004] 1 FLR 876

- *Re J (Care: Rehabilitation Plan)* [1998] 2 FLR 498

- *Kent County Council v G & Others* [2005] UKHL 68, [2006] 1 FLR 601

- *Lambeth London Borough Council v F* [2005] 2 FLR 1172

10.5.2 Exclusion orders in care proceedings

The ability to attach an exclusion requirement to an ICO under CA 1989, s 38A(2) is a relatively recent power, and a welcome addition to the court's armoury. The order is dependent on an ICO being made, and s 38A(2) sets the following conditions:

(a) there is reasonable cause to believe that, if a person ('the relevant person') is excluded from a dwelling-house in which the child lives, the child will cease to suffer, or cease to be likely to suffer, significant harm, and

(b) that another person living in the dwelling-house (whether a parent of the child or some other person)—

(i)   is able and willing to give to the child the care which it would be reasonable to expect a parent to give him, and

(ii) consents to the inclusion of the exclusion requirement.

The exclusion order can include a provision requiring the relevant person to leave a dwelling-house in which he or she is living with the child; prohibiting the relevant person from entering a dwelling-house in which the child lives; and excluding the relevant person from an area in which a dwelling-house in which the child lives is situated (s 38A(3)). The court has power to attach a power of arrest to such an order (s 38A(5)). You should familiarise yourself with the other provisions of s 38(A). By s 38(B), the court has power to accept an undertaking from the relevant person instead—a power of arrest may not be attached to an undertaking but it is otherwise enforceable as an order of the court. Note that both the order and the undertaking would cease to have effect if the child is removed from the house in question for more than 24 hours continuously. For procedural requirements, see Hershman and McFarlane C 1455–C 1475.

The significance of these powers is clear. It may be apparent on the evidence that the harm, or threat of harm to the child would be eliminated or sufficiently reduced if an abuser in his household were to be removed. For example, the father may have perpetrated appalling violence on the mother of which the child is aware. If the father is excluded, the immediate risk reduces (provided that the mother stays away from him) and this may mean that the child does not have to be removed from his home or main carer. Notice the need for consent to the order from the person remaining to care for the child. Another example would be where one adult in the household is suspected of physical or sexual abuse of the child and another adult is willing to accept the need to protect the child. These powers are important in such circumstances because where possible, it is likely to be far less disruptive for a child to remain with familiar carers and significant adults in his life, and to stay in his home.

10.5.3   Split hearings

The final determination of the case is often dependent on the nature of the findings of fact made about the abuse suffered by the child. The difficulty is that in the classic final hearing, the court considers whether the proven facts meet the threshold criteria, and then what the decision should be on the child's future (disposal) *at one hearing*. However, the findings of fact relevant to the threshold *inform and determine* the shape of the investigation that occurs during the proceedings, and sometimes it is necessary to prove the relevant facts for the threshold *before* the final hearing in order to decide what assessments and information the court needs to make the decision on disposal at the final hearing. In a typical neglect/emotional harm case, there may be little need to prove facts in order to work out what assessments are required—the key focus will often be on how parents respond to intervention and parenting skills work done during the life of the case. However, in other, perhaps more dramatic, situations, it may be essential to decide what the factual position is *first* in order to work out what assessments if any are then necessary for the court to make a final decision. Take this example:

The parents are a young married couple. They take their 14-month-old child to the casualty department at the local hospital, explaining that the child had a fall the previous evening and still seems to be uncomfortable. The treating consultant paediatrician is suspicious of their story, which seems to vary in the detail, especially as to when the fall occurred. Radiological examination shows multiple injuries of apparently different ages, some of which are indicative of non-accidental injury.

The local authority's case is that this is non-accidental injury. The parents deny this, saying the injuries must be the results of accidents.

Clearly, this is essential to a finding on the threshold criteria at a final hearing—and also to decisions on disposal. There are three possibilities—the injuries were deliberately inflicted—a very serious form of abuse; the injuries were a result of innocent events which were nevertheless avoidable—indicating a failure to provide proper care by not keeping the child safe; or the injuries were from innocent causes which were simply unlucky and not due to a failure of care.

The difficulties for the court, if findings of fact have to wait to a final hearing, are that the response and required assessment in order to have the right information for a final decision on the child's future, would be quite different for each circumstance. For the deliberate abuse, assessment would have to focus upon trying to assess which parent was the abuser and which was not; whether the abusive parent accepts responsibility and has insight into the causes of the loss of control; whether the non-abusive parent is able to protect the child from the abusive parent and put the child's safety before their own needs to trust the other parent and have a relationship with the other parent; and whether the abusive parent can change their behaviour. Clearly the degree of risk is high, and will require specialist assessment. For the 'neglect' circumstances, the assessment will probably focus on work with the parents to improve their ability to recognise risks and protect the child from such risks—in order to provide an important aspect of child care properly. It may be that other aspects of their care—which would be assessed by way of a local authority core assessment—are acceptable. The final scenario—accident which the reasonable parent's care could not have avoided—probably does not even require intervention.

Other examples might be where it is unclear who the perpetrator of the abuse was; or whether the child has suffered sexual abuse.

It is in cases like these, where the facts need to be established in order to determine what information will be necessary for the court to make a final decision on the child's future, that a split hearing is likely to be required. Fact finding hearings are regularly held as the first part of a contested care case. The findings will then inform the preparation for the disposal hearing, which must be heard by the same judge: *Re B (Care Proceedings: Standard of Proof)* [2008] 2 FLR 141.

There is one special class of case in which split hearings could be appropriate, and which is worth specifically mentioning here. Situations arise in which a child has apparently suffered significant harm, but it is unclear *who the perpetrator is*. For example, a child may have suffered non-accidental injuries, but neither parent admits responsibility. In this case, it is hard to tell who presents the risk to the child, and therefore what the future level of risk is, what future assessments need to be carried out, whether the risk can be ameliorated by intervention (eg, anger management counselling with the abusing parent) and whether the child could be safely placed with one parent if the other parent were no longer part of the household. It makes future planning for the child very difficult indeed. The situation can be complicated still further if the parents seek to blame their babysitter, or child minder, or another family member—any of whom may be responsible because the child has at relevant times been in their care. Not only does this present problems for future work with the family and the assessment of risk for long-term planning—it also causes difficulties in establishing whether the threshold is met, since it has to be shown that the significant harm, or risk of significant harm is due to the child not receiving the care that a reasonable parent would give.

In regard to the threshold criteria, the leading authority is *Lancashire County Council v B* [2000] AC 147, where the House of Lords held that the threshold can be met by a finding that the child suffered harm in the care of his parents or other carers—there is no need to precisely prove who was responsible for the injuries.

For purposes of the welfare part of the decision (disposal), it is obviously better if the perpetrator of the harm can be identified for the reasons given above. The judge hearing the preliminary hearing should attempt to give such assistance as is possible for social services and those experts having to carry out assessment as to the facts. For further consideration of this issue see Baroness Hale in *Re B* (below) at para 59–61.

Key authorities

- *Re S (Care Proceedings: Split Hearings)* [1996] 2 FLR 773

- *Re M and MC (Care: Issues of Fact: Drawing of Orders)* [2002] EWCA Civ 499, [2003] 1 FLR 461

- *Re G (Care Proceedings: Split Trials)* [2001] 1 FLR 872

- *Re Y and K (Split Hearing: Evidence)* [2003] EWCA Civ 669, [2003] 2 FLR 273

- *Re B (Care Proceedings: Standard of Proof)* [2008] 2 FLR 141

10.5.4 Criminal proceedings and care proceedings

It is often the case that the circumstances that have given rise to the concerns for the child such that child protection proceedings have been commenced may also have simultaneously become the subject of criminal proceedings, or at least a criminal investigation. This is scarcely surprising—assault, sexual abuse and similar allegations in care proceedings are criminal offences as well as child abuse. However, the fact that there are two sets of proceedings ongoing can cause difficulties. First, the standard of proof in care proceedings, being civil proceedings, is lower than that in criminal proceedings (where the allegation must be proven beyond reasonable doubt). This has two effects—if the factual allegation is proven in the criminal proceedings, then it has been proven to a higher standard than it would have been in care proceedings. Conversely, the finding of a fact against a respondent in care proceedings who is also facing criminal charges arising out of the same circumstances is of little relevance to the criminal proceedings given the standard of proof. The main principle is that pending criminal proceedings are not necessarily a reason to adjourn the care proceedings. Obviously, findings of guilt in criminal proceedings on an allegation common to the care and criminal proceedings can be helpful in the care proceedings—however, the disadvantage of awaiting the result of the criminal proceedings is likely to be substantial delay in determining the future of the child.

The most important issue relates to the sharing of information between police (or the Crown Prosecution Service—CPS) conducting an investigation, and the local authority involved in child protection. This section will look at the following issues; the position on confidentiality of documents and on the privilege against self-incrimination in care proceedings; the court's power to direct disclosure of documents filed in care proceedings to third parties, in particular the police; and the obtaining of documents from the police for use in child protection and care proceedings. For wider questions of public interest immunity, refer to section 5 of part C, Hershman and McFarlane. This is a particularly complex area.

10.5.4.1 Confidentiality of documents

By FPR 1991, r 4.23, all documents 'held by the court' in the proceedings (save a record of the order) cannot be disclosed *without leave of the court*, except to the parties and their legal representatives, the Children's Guardian, the Legal Services Commission (for the purpose of obtaining funding), and an expert whose instruction has been authorised by the court (see **10.3.1**). A similar provision is to be found in FPC (CA 1989) R 1991, r 23. This therefore means that documents are confidential—but that confidentiality is not absolute. The court can order disclosure to a third party for specific purposes.

10.5.4.2   No privilege against self-incrimination in care proceedings

By CA 1989, s 98:

(1) In any proceedings in which a court is hearing an application for an order under Part IV or V, no person shall be excused from—

   (a) giving evidence on any matter; or

   (b) answering any question put to him in the course of his giving evidence on the ground that doing so might incriminate him or his spouse of an offence.

(2) A statement or admission made in such proceedings shall not be admissible in evidence against the person making it or his spouse in proceedings for an offence other than perjury.

It is therefore clear that there is no privilege against self-incrimination in care proceedings. This is perhaps unsurprising, given the prime importance of protecting the welfare of children. Section 2 seems to give some protection against use of statements and admissions made in care proceedings being then used in criminal proceedings. However, this provides less protection than would at first appear. While 'statement or admission' is given a wide meaning—it includes statements while giving oral evidence and in a written statement of evidence filed in the proceedings, and admissions made to the children's guardian and to expert witnesses while preparing assessments—as Hershman and McFarlane point out (C 307-3025), the protection is *only against such statements being admissible in criminal proceedings*. It would not prevent, for example, the court granting leave for disclosure of the material to a third party such as the police for use in a criminal *investigation*.

10.5.4.3   Disclosure to the police

A distinction needs to be drawn between disclosure of documents held on the court file and other information gathered by (for example) the local authority.

Documents held on the court file (ie, those filed in the proceedings) are subject to the confidentiality referred to at **10.5.4.1** above and therefore require leave of the court for disclosure to the police. The key principles in an application to the court for disclosure of such documents to the police are to be found in *Re EC* (see 'key authorities' below). The court will seek to balance the welfare of the child, the importance of encouraging frankness in the care proceedings by maintaining confidentiality, the public interest in the proper administration of justice and prosecution of serious crime, and fairness to the person who has incriminated himself where CA 1989, s 98(2) applies. There is obviously a difference between cases where there is a factual link between the care proceedings and the criminal proceedings, and those where they are unconnected. There can be no guarantee of confidentiality in any case.

Where the documents that the police wish to see are not filed with the court in Children Act proceedings, different rules apply. If the documentation or information is not covered by r 4.23 FPR 1991, social work practitioners are encouraged to share information with the police as part of an inter-agency cooperative approach to child protection. The situation may be very different with the Children's Guardian—their report and investigations are subject to r 4.23 and it is for the court to decide if that material should be disclosed.

10.5.4.4   Disclosure to third parties generally

The court has power to order disclosure of documents filed in CA 1989 proceedings to non-parties—*Re L (Police Investigation: Privilege)*—see 'key authorities' below. The test to be applied on an application for disclosure is the need to balance the public interest in encouraging frankness by providing confidentiality, against the public interest of a fair trial in a criminal case—*Re D (Minors) (Wardship: Disclosure)*—see below. Hershman and McFarlane summarise the factors that the court must balance as follows (C 2967):

(a) the need to protect the interests of the children;

(b) the need to encourage candour from all involved in the proceedings;

(c) the public interest of free exchange of information between agencies; and

(d) the public interest in protecting the vulnerable members of the community (ie, parents as potential defendants).

Hershman and McFarlane also reproduce (at C 2967) Munby J's examination of these factors in *Re X (Disclosure of Information)*. You should read this section of the judgment (citation below) and also the summary (at C 2968) of cases where disclosure has been allowed for a variety of purposes. See also *Re R (Securing Editing of Documents)* [2007] below, in relation to documents where key information *must* remain confidential.

Key authorities—10.5.4.2 to 10.5.4.4

- *Re D (Minors) (Wardship: Disclosure)* [1994] 1 FLR 346
- *Cleveland County Council v F* [1995] 2 All ER 236, [1995] 1 FLR 797
- *Re X (Disclosure of Information)* [2001] 2 FLR 440
- *Re L (Police Investigation: Privilege)* [1995] 1 FLR 999
- *Re EC (Disclosure of Material)* [1996] 2 FLR 725
- *Re L (Care: Confidentiality)* [1999] 1 FLR 165
- *Re R (Securing Editing of Documents)* [2007] 2 FLR 759

10.5.4.5   **Obtaining documents from the police for use in care proceedings**

Of course, it often happens that matters are 'the other way around'—the local authority in particular may wish to obtain documents from the police for use in care proceedings. As Hershman and McFarlane point out, there are actually two stages to the issue of disclosure in such circumstances:

(a) disclosure by the police to the local authority; and

(b) further disclosure by the police or local authority to parties to the care proceedings.

(See *Nottinghamshire County Council v H* [1995] 1 FLR 115.) The normal procedure would be a witness summons against the chief constable for the force in question requiring production of the material requested. The test for the court is to balance the public interest in maintaining confidentiality of materials whose disclosure could prejudice an investigation or prosecution against the public interest in ensuring that a local authority has available all material which will assist in proper development of proposals for the future of the child in question. See further, Hershman and McFarlane C 2976–C 2977 for the full procedure and specifically the procedure regarding further disclosure of information obtained by the local authority to other parties in the care proceedings.

Where there are no pending care proceedings, the rules are different—it is again a question of inter-agency sharing of information for effective child protection.

10.6 The care plan

10.6.1 Purpose of the care plan

In every application for a care order, the local authority must produce a 'care plan' for the court's scrutiny s. 31A CA 1989. Indeed, scrutiny of the care plan is an essential part of the 'disposal' decision on such applications, but will also be scrutinised regularly by the court and when an ICO is sought. The purpose of the document is to provide the essential information about long-term planning for the child—this enables the court to see what the local authority's plans are for that child if the order sought is granted. The proposals should be supported by evidence and proper details of proposed placements should be given.

10.6.2 What should the care plan contain?

There is specific guidance on the contents of a care plan given in Local Authority Circular LAC (99) 29, 'Care Plans and Care Proceedings under the Children Act'. This is reproduced in Hershman and McFarlane Division N, section 2. Alternatively, log on to the Department of Health website <www.dh.gov.uk>, go to 'publications and statistics', and search the letters and circulars library. The main purpose of the circular was to provide consistency of approach to preparation and implementation of care plans across the country. Detailed guidance is given on the format of care plans, the need to give reasons for choosing the placement and for particular courses of action, together with the need to identify achievable timescales and specific outcomes—with a view, in particular, to reviewing implementation and progress of the care plan. The plan should encompass five sections. The first is 'overall aim', which is a summary of the plan and its timetable; the second, 'child's needs including contact' identifies issues such as the child's needs, the child's wishes and the extent to which these have been acted on, and the arrangements for contact, including proposals to restrict or terminate contact.

The third section covers 'views of others', explaining the extent to which views of other significant persons such as the parents have been obtained, and any action taken as a result; the fourth section is 'placement details and timetable', containing details of placement, any proposals for rehabilitation of child and family (if appropriate), arrangements for health care, education, and so forth; and the last section, 'management and support by local authority' provides details of who is responsible for the plan's implementation, the timing of reviews, and contingency planning should the plan fail.

10.6.3 Permanent placement options

The care plan will indicate where the local authority proposes to place the child should the order be granted. The most common alternative possibilities are now considered.

- Rehabilitation with parents/family. This would obviously be the preferred option for the family. The local authority will have taken the view from evidence available from the various assessments and work with the family during the care proceedings that the parents have shown sufficient improvement in the aspects of parenting skill that had caused initial concern, and that the child can now be returned to their care within a suitable period of time. This will usually be pursuant to a careful plan for phased return (eg, increasing contact over a period of time coupled with ongoing work on parenting skills or counselling). Sometimes, this will have begun by the time of the final hearing (in consultation with the Children's Guardian). Under the care order, the local authority will continue to share PR with the parents (see **9.4.1**), so can act quickly to protect the child should things go wrong. If rehabilitation is successful, the parents might apply at some suitable time in future to discharge the care order, for a residence order in their favour (automatically discharging the care order) or to substitute for a supervision order (see **9.4.7**). Sometimes rehabilitation to the parents is not possible, and placement is planned with another family member who has been assessed as suitable and who is willing to assist. This could be under a care order—an alternative possibility is that that person is granted a residence order or a Special Guardianship Order and the local authority does not share PR. This could occur if it is clear that such a placement will eliminate the risks.

- Permanent placement with foster parents. In this situation, the foster parents do not acquire PR—this is held by the local authority under the care order. The parents continue to hold PR, but cannot exercise it inconsistently with that of the local authority. The foster family will become the child's main home, providing all care for the child and a permanent substitute family. The parents (and possibly other significant members of the child's natural family) will usually be granted contact with the child as appropriate to the child's welfare—see **9.8**, and proposals for contact will become an important part of the court's decision. Generally, contact will be encouraged although there may be a need to restrict it where it undermines the child's sense of security with the foster family (often because of undermining tactics by the parents). As a very general rule of thumb, foster care tends to be a suitable disposal where the child is too old (or possibly too damaged by his experiences) for adoption—very approximately, children of about 5 years of age and above may be unsuitable for adoption. Because foster care therefore concentrates largely on older children, many of those children have suffered abuse or neglect over some considerable period of their lives, and can present considerable challenges to foster carers.

- Adoption. This is perhaps the most extreme outcome for parents. Upon adoption, the parents lose their PR for the child (as indeed does the local authority, for the care order would also lapse), and the adoptive parents acquire it. It is effectively a 'family transplant'. There is likely to be very little contact allowed to the birth family. Direct contact is almost never allowed, there may or may not be some heavily controlled provision for indirect contact (such as a birthday card for the child once a year), and 'life story' work will at some stage usually be done with the adopted child so that he or she has a sense of their own identity. Birth parents may be permitted to provide photographs and the like for that purpose. This is usually the preferred option where the child is relatively young—the younger the child, the more likely the success of the adoption. There are often issues where the child has older siblings who cannot be adopted—a desire to maintain the children's relationships with each other can in such situations either indicate fostering for all the children, or some agreement for contact with siblings where some of the children are adopted.

- Care homes, special schools. These are obviously the least preferable outcome for any child, since they do not involve a family environment. There are some children for whom rehabilitation is not possible, and who are unsuitable for fostering or adoption. An example may be a child who has been sexually abused and who has become a threat to other children as a result of sexualised behaviour; or a child whose behaviour is so challenging that it cannot be handled within a family environment. Specialist professional care could be the only option. In these cases, contact with the birth family may be feasible, again with due consideration for its effect on the child's welfare.

10.6.4 Care plans and human rights

Clearly, permanent placement away from the natural family has the potential for interference with the Art 8 rights of the child and those of the family for family life with each other. This is all the more so with adoption, involving the permanent destruction of ties between child and family. There are, of course, the competing Art 8 rights of the child to proper care and a stable, loving permanent home. The court must balance these competing rights when making a final decision on whether to grant the care order with the care plan proposed. The principle of proportionality in European human rights law is of particular importance. In *Re C and B (Care Order: Future Harm)* [2001] 1 FLR 611, Hale LJ stated:

The principle has to be that the local authority works to support, and eventually reunite the family, unless the risks are so high that the child's welfare requires alternative family care.

And later:

Intervention in the family must be proportionate, but the aim should be to reunite the family when the circumstances enable that, and the effort should be devoted towards that end. Cutting off all contact and the relationship between the child and their family is only justified by the overriding necessity of the interests of the child.

There are further human rights issues which arise with respect to care plans, considered in the next section.

10.6.5 The court cannot alter the local authority's care plan

The scheme of the statute, the CA 1989, empowers the court to decide whether to make, or withhold, the care order. However, once the care order is made, the court has no ongoing control over the way in which the local authority implements its care plan. This presents two problems. First, the court may consider that a care order is necessary to safeguard the child's welfare, but that the local authority's care plan is inappropriate. An example might be that the local authority plans that the child should be adopted, whilst the court considers that a proper attempt should be made to rehabilitate the child to the parents. *The court has no power to order the local authority to change the care plan*—it can only make, or refuse to make, the care order. The court could be faced with an awkward situation—the child will not be safe unless the local authority shares PR with the parents under a care order, but if the care order is made, the child's ties with his parents will end because the local authority will pursue adoption. This—and similar dilemmas—can result in a sort of 'stand-off' situation between the local authority and the court. In such situations the court will encourage negotiation between the parties over the care plan, and it retains the power to make contact orders under CA 1989, s 34. More importantly, and perhaps more controversially, the court has power to continue to make ICOs in the proceedings to safeguard the child and retain control of the child's position whilst still withholding a full care order (at which point control passes to the local authority), and may do so in an effort to put pressure on the local authority to reconsider the plan. This is a very difficult situation—the court can properly use ICOs to postpone the final decision on a care order if there is a need for further assessment or further clarification of the care plan because this is 'planned and purposeful delay' and so does not offend the principle that delay is damaging to the child's welfare (see **10.7**). However, in a situation where the necessary information is available to the court and it is simply a question of disagreement over permanent placement of the child the question arises whether the continuing postponement of the decision on the child's future by way of a series of ICOs is appropriate in terms of the no delay principle. At some point, the court has to choose between leaving the child with the parents without the protection of the care order, and making a care order with a care plan of which it does not approve. As was stated in *Re S and D (Children: Powers of Court)* [1995] 2 FLR 456, the court may be forced to choose the lesser of the two evils.

The second situation that can arise is that the court approves the care plan proposed by the local authority and makes a care order. The court then plays no further role unless a party makes a further application (eg, to discharge the care order). The local authority may subsequently change the care plan. This can have profound consequences, for example, a change from a permanent foster placement where the parents could have good contact, to adoption, where their ties with the child are cut. However, do also refer to **9.4.1**, where the new provisions of CA 1989, s 26 are discussed, whereby independent reviewing officers now monitor how local authorities implement the care plan. The difficulties of challenging a care order where the parents cannot realistically offer adequate alternative care for the child are discussed at **9.4.7.2**. This is also a difficult area for the court, since courts have no power to intervene regarding how local authorities exercise their statutory powers once the care order is made. Once the care proceedings are concluded, the alteration of a care plan in such a way as to breach the parents' human rights can be challenged by way of an application for the court to exercise its powers under ss 7 and 8 of the Human Rights Act 1998 (HRA 1998). A local authority is a 'public authority' and may therefore not act incompatibly with the European Convention on Human Rights (ECHR)—to do so is unlawful under HRA 1998, s 6. The difficulty with breaches of human rights is that although an applicant may establish a breach, this does not necessarily mean that he or she will be given a remedy. However, under HRA 1998, s 8, the court has access to remedies including the power to grant an injunction restraining a breach of human rights. Of course, it should be remembered that alteration of the care plan is not automatically a breach of human rights—it may have been done as an essential response to the requirements of the child's welfare, which could have significantly changed since the production of the original care plan. Whilst proceedings are pending, the challenge should be made in the course of the care proceedings. For an excellent review of the law in this area, see Hershman and McFarlane Section C, C 1138–C 1141.

10.6.6   Twin-track planning

Twin-track planning is a very important aspect of an interim care plan where (as in many cases) the alternatives at a final hearing are likely to be rehabilitation of the child with the family (depending on progress made and assessment done during the proceedings), and permanent placement in an adoptive family. The aim is to minimise delay in permanently placing the child should rehabilitation fail, or not be feasible in the first place. The effect is that at the same time as the possibility of rehabilitation is being explored in the care proceedings, the local authority will also have taken the child's case before the adoption panel, and identified suitable adopters. This means that the court has full information on the two possibilities at the final hearing. In addition, should rehabilitation not be chosen, the adoption can proceed much more quickly than if the process had not been started before the final care hearing, and this means that the child can have a permanent placement much sooner. This is certainly desirable from the point of view of the child's emotional development and security. There is also a similar process known as 'concurrent planning', whereby work is done towards rehabilitation whilst at the same time establishing a plan for alternative placement elsewhere. See *Re D and K (Care Plan: Twin-Track Planning)* [1999] 2 FLR 872.

Further reading and key authorities

- *Re J (Minors) (Care: Care Plan)* [1994] 1 FLR 253
- *Re C and B (Care Order: Future Harm)* [2001] 1 FLR 611
- *Re B (Care: Interference with Family Life)* [2003] 2 FLR 813
- *Re S (Minors) (Care Order: Implementation of Care Plan), Re W (Minors) (Care Order: Adequacy of Care Plan)* [2002] 1 FLR 815
- *Re D and K (Care Plan: Twin-Track Planning)* [1999] 2 FLR 872
- LAC (99) 29—see reference at **10.6.2**

10.7 The final hearing—arguments and outcomes

This section aims to give you an outline understanding of common issues and arguments at a final hearing. Of course, every case turns on its own circumstances, but there are some common patterns of argument which you need to be familiar with.

10.7.1 Threshold, disposal and standard of proof

You will recall from **9.4.4** that there are two basic stages to the court's decision—the decision on the *threshold criteria*, which determines whether or not the court has the jurisdiction to make a care or supervision order at all, and which depends on the test in CA 1989, s 31; and if the threshold is established, the decision on *disposal*, where the court decides whether a care order is in the best interests of the child, given the care plan, or whether another order, or no order at all, would best serve the child's welfare.

Whether or not the threshold criteria are established is a *question of fact*, to be proven in the normal way. Suspicion is insufficient, however serious the allegation. The child's welfare has no relevance to this particular decision—it is simply a question of whether the local authority applicant can prove that the facts of the case are such that the child is suffering or likely to suffer significant harm due either to the care being given to him not being what it would be reasonable to expect a parent to give, or to his being beyond parental control. The court has to be 'satisfied' that this is the case. The standard of proof is the ordinary civil standard—the balance of probabilities. The standard of proof is the ordinary civil standard—the balance of probabilities. *Re H and Others (Minors) (Sexual Abuse: Standard of Proof)* [1996] 1 FLR 80, was approved by the House of Lords in *Re B (Care Proceedings: Standard of Proof)*, see **9.4.5.3**.

10.7.2   Conceding threshold

If you are able to undermine the evidence relied upon by the local authority as establishing the threshold, then of course you should seek to persuade the court that the threshold criteria are not met and therefore there is no jurisdiction to make the care or supervision order. However, as indicated in **10.2.7**, the evidence amassed by the local authority regarding the concerns for the child at the outset of proceedings can often be very hard to challenge, and it is often the case that the best line of attack relates to the 'disposal' stage of proceedings, where the argument may be that the parents have now made sufficient progress with parenting skills for rehabilitation, or that there is further assessment required before the court has enough information to decide (see **10.7.3.2**). In other words, frequently more is to be gained by looking at the parents' capacity to change than by trying to defend the (sometimes indefensible) past. If your case falls into this category, you may well need to consider 'conceding the threshold'. This basically means that your client *concedes* (ie, admits) that the threshold criteria are satisfied as a matter of fact, and that the court has jurisdiction to make a care or supervision order. This is not the same as consenting to the care order—it leaves you free to argue the 'disposal' side of the case—whilst you accept that the court has jurisdiction to make a care order if it considers it appropriate, your argument is that it should not make a care order, or that the current care plan is inappropriate, or that a supervision order is more appropriate than a care order, and so on. The benefits of such a course of action are first that you *may* be able to limit the findings of fact against your client—although see below—and, second, that there could be a significant saving of court time because this will limit the issues.

However, you cannot simply concede the threshold criteria without more. The court has to be 'satisfied' of facts sufficient to meet the threshold criteria. If for a parent, you will need to identify the *factual basis* upon which your client concedes the threshold. Your client will need to admit facts which are sufficient to show that *at the relevant time* (see **9.4.5.2**), the child was suffering or likely to suffer significant harm due to the care he was receiving not being what it would be reasonable for a parent to give. Tactically, you will want to admit sufficient facts for this purpose and no more, and careful discussion with and advice to the client will be required.

These are *admissions of fact*, and they are for the respondent parents to make. They are therefore not something which the local authority is in a position to dictate. However, if you represent the local authority, you will need to consider the conceded facts with care. First, do they meet the threshold? If not, you will need to prove the facts of the local authority's case further in any event. Second, it may be important to the local authority to prove facts beyond what the parents are prepared to concede because of the arguments on the 'disposal' decision. For example, in a case involving serious neglect and emotional abuse, the parents make admissions of fact regarding the neglect which are sufficient to satisfy the threshold criteria. However, the admissions they make are fairly limited—taken at face value, they would support the need for a supervision order, but not for the child to be placed for adoption under a care order. The local authority takes the view that it needs a care order, and proposes to place the child for adoption because the neglect and emotional abuse was far greater than the parents concede, and the child has suffered considerable developmental delay. In these circumstances, the local authority will wish to prove the full extent of the abuse and neglect in order to *justify the need for a care order and the type of care plan that they propose*.

Therefore, if representing the parents you may be able to 'limit the damage' on the findings of fact about the past by conceding threshold on your terms, but be aware that the local authority may want to prove further and more extensive facts which it considers relevant to the next stage of the decision, disposal.

The issue of conceding threshold by admitting facts will also arise on an ICO hearing—however, bear in mind that the threshold is lower, simply being 'reasonable cause to believe' that the CA 1989, s 31 criteria are met.

Conceding threshold—key authorities

- *Re G (A Minor) (Care Proceedings)* [1994] 2 FLR 69
- *Stockport Metropolitan Borough Council v D* [1995] 1 FLR 873
- *Re M (Threshold Criteria: Parental Concessions)* [1999] 2 FLR 728

10.7.3   Final hearing—disposal issues

10.7.3.1   Possible outcomes

There are a number of possible outcomes on the final hearing, and it may be that the parties can agree on one of these courses. First, the court could decide that the threshold criteria were not made out and the local authority's application would fail. This is highly unusual. If the threshold criteria are made out, the court may decide that a final care order is appropriate, and that the care plan is in the child's best interests, in which case a final care order will be made. It may be that the court feels that a care order is disproportionate and that a supervision order is sufficient to protect the child's welfare, with or without requirements (see **9.5**). The court may decide that a care order is appropriate, but does not approve of the care plan—as to which, see **10.6.5** above. The court may decide that neither a care nor supervision order is actually required, in which case it may make no order, or it might make a residence order in favour of the parents or some other family member who has been assessed and is willing to care for the child. A common argument, which sometimes succeeds, is that the court has *insufficient information* on which to make a final decision and that further ICOs should be made until that information is available, at which point there should be a further hearing to consider the final decision. This situation is considered in the next section.

10.7.3.2   Final or interim care order?

It is often the case that the parents' representatives argue at a final hearing that the court is not in possession of all the information it requires to make a properly considered final decision. Usually, the argument will be based on the suggestion that there is a further issue or new circumstances that require assessment, for example, the parents have recently separated and there is no assessment of their ability to care for the child alone, as opposed to as a couple (it is sometimes the case that some parents cope better alone, for example because the other parent undermined their parenting ability due to violence). Sometimes, an expert's report produced for the final hearing raises the possibility that the child could be rehabilitated with the family and that this needs to be further assessed. It is also sometimes the case that the care plan is insufficiently clear and specific, although in some cases this is unavoidable and specifics can only be worked out some time after the final hearing.

The lawyer will therefore argue that the court cannot make a final decision on disposal unless this further assessment is available, and so ICOs should be made and the case relisted for final hearing once the report has been completed. Where this course of action is contested, the most obvious argument for the opponents (usually the local authority, often with the guardian's support) will be that the further assessment will cause considerable delay that the child cannot afford. There is likely to be extensive cross-examination of the expert regarding the length of time that such an assessment would require and the likelihood of the parents successfully completing it.

If the court accepts this argument, an interim care order will be granted. It is established that whilst delay is normally harmful to the child's welfare, 'planned and purposeful delay' can be in a child's best interests. You must familiarise yourself with the key authorities in the table below before seeking to argue such an application.

Key authorities—interim care orders at a final hearing

- *Re S (Minors) (Care Order: Implementation of Care Plan), Re W (Minors) (Care Order: Adequacy of Care Plan)* [2002] 1 FLR 815
- *C v Solihull Metropolitan Borough Council* [1993] 1 FLR 290
- *Hounslow London Borough Council v A* [1993] 1 FLR 702
- *Re J (Minors) (Care: Care Plan)* [1994] 1 FLR 253

10.7.3.3 Care or supervision order?

It may be that it is obvious that the court will not consider that the child's welfare will be properly protected if there is no court order. Whilst the parents may be unable to argue that there should be no order, they may seek to argue that a supervision order will provide sufficient protection to the child. It would give the local authority a statutory basis to remain involved in the family and able to 'keep an eye' on the child's progress, without the draconian step of allowing the local authority to share PR. Whilst a supervision order does have this effect, which can be strengthened by the addition of requirements (see **9.5.2**), it is a much less powerful order than the care order. There is little sanction for its breach (generally, the local authority would have to reapply for a full care order) and the local authority cannot remove the child without further recourse to court (an emergency protection order if the circumstances justify it, and application for an interim care order).

When deciding to make a care or a supervision order, the court will need to carefully weigh the level of likely future harm to the child, and the harm which will be caused by removing him from his family. Only if protection of the child demands, will the stronger order, the care order, be made rather than a supervision order.

Again, the court is considering the issue of proportionality of response to the feared harm.

Key authorities—care or supervision order

- *Re S (Care or Supervision Order)* [1996] 1 FLR 753
- *Re V (Care or Supervision Order)* [1996] 1 FLR 776
- *Oxfordshire County Council v L (Care or Supervision Order)* [1998] 1 FLR 70
- *Re S(J) (A Minor) (Care or Supervision Order)* [1993] 2 FLR 919

Mediation in the context of the family

11.1 Defining mediation

Mediation is one of a number of settlement-seeking processes that include negotiation, collaborative law and conciliation. These processes come under the heading of Alternative Dispute Resolution (ADR). 'Alternative' in this context is generally understood to mean alternative to court proceedings. 'Appropriate Dispute Resolution' would be a more accurate term, because mediation is often used in conjunction with court proceedings and not as a substitute for them. In some countries, mediation provides the normal way of settling disputes, with the court as the alternative.

The Legal Services Commission (LSC) provides public funding for family mediation (but not for collaborative law) through the Community Legal Service (CLS), defining it as 'a neutral third party, the mediator, working with the parties to help them arrive at a voluntary and mutually satisfactory resolution of the dispute' (CLS Decision Making Guidance April 2003, 7.1.(d)). Mediation is encouraged because it offers 'a swift and fair resolution of disputes without unnecessary or unduly protracted proceedings in court' (ibid, 7.2.(a)). Family mediators define it as 'a process in which an impartial third person assists those involved in family breakdown, and in particular, separating or divorcing couples, to communicate better with one other and reach their own agreed and informed decisions concerning some or all of the issues relating to separation, divorce, children, finance or property' (UK College of Family Mediators, Code of Practice 1995).

11.2 Similarities and differences between mediation and conciliation

The terms 'mediation' and 'conciliation' are sometimes used synonymously. It is useful, however, to distinguish 'in-court conciliation' from the voluntary and independent process of 'mediation' that takes place out of court and mainly prior to the issue of proceedings. Although the courts may refer cases to independent family mediation services, in-court conciliation appointments are mainly undertaken by the Children and Family Court Advisory and Support Service (CAFCASS). CAFCASS officers also undertake risk assessments and provide reports for the court in contested cases. Normally a different officer would prepare a report from one who has previously acted as conciliator in the case concerned.

Mediation differs from in-court conciliation in a number of ways. Both processes are needed and they complement each other.

Family mediation	*Court conciliation*
Mainly pre-court, most cases referred by lawyers, may avoid proceedings	Court-referral—later stage, after issue of court proceedings
Voluntary and independent of the courts	Carries the court's authority
Private, informal, out of court	Usually on court premises
May cover all interrelated issues concerning children, property, finance etc. Not only separation and divorce—other family cases.	Conciliation meetings held on children issues (residence and contact). Separate FDR (Financial Dispute Resolution) hearings held before a judge promote early settlement on finance/property matters.
Independent, qualified mediators, no contact with judges	Family court social workers (CAFCASS), who communicate with judges
Impartial and non-directive	Not neutral—pro contact taking place, may be directive
Confidential and legally privileged	Not confidential, outcomes and some information may be reportable
Facilitates full discussion, more sessions	Quick settlement of limited issues
Wide spectrum from cooperative to high conflict Children do not usually participate	Difficult and more entrenched disputes. The court may ask parties to bring children, who may be seen by the conciliator at the conciliation appointment.

Mediation and conciliation are similar in the sense that they take place 'in the shadow of the law'. Mnookin and Kornhauser (1979) observed that separating and divorcing couples do not negotiate in a vacuum: they 'bargain in the shadow of the law ... The outcome that the law would impose, should no agreement be reached, gives each parent certain bargaining chips'. These bargaining chips are their relative chances of winning their case in court, depending on established legal principles and presumptions and also on the jurisdiction in which the proceedings are taken.

11.3   Why do legal practitioners need to understand conciliation and mediation?

Lawyers need to understand different methods of settling disputes for two main reasons. First of all, there is a requirement to refer clients eligible for Legal Help to a family mediation service recognised by the LSC, because the client must receive information and consider the option of mediation, before legal aid can be obtained for an application to the court in family matters (see s 11.4). Second, legal advisers need to advise clients, including private clients, on cost-effective ways of settling matters. Under Law Society protocol, solicitors should advise any new client of the benefits of settling through mediation, any difficulties or drawbacks they might face in mediation and the availability and costs of their nearest mediation service. Judges may also propose referral to mediation at a later stage of proceedings. Legal advisers could even face complaints of professional negligence if they fail to draw clients' attention to the possibility of settling through mediation. There should be no fear of clients entering into an agreement in mediation without the benefit of legal advice, because mediators encourage clients to take legal advice in the course of mediation and particularly on any proposals for settlement, before they enter into any agreement solicitors and mediators generally understand each other's role and clients benefit from their willingness to refer to each other.

Solicitors, barristers and judges who have taken training in mediation find that many of the techniques and skills are valuable in their day-to-day work without practising mediation per se, because these techniques can be used in negotiations towards settlement and in advising clients who are caught up in disputes. Many family law practitioners offer mediation as an additional service offered by their firm or chambers, sometimes in conjunction with non-lawyer co-mediators. Judges support mediation as a 'firmly established, significant and growing fact of English procedure' (Mr Justice Colman, *Cable & Wireless v IBM*, reported in The Times, 26 November 2002). They support increased use of mediation 'as the only available recourse of those who cannot afford the costs and risks of litigation, and the chance of justice it affords' (Mr Justice Lightman, 'Breaking Down the Barriers', The Times, 31 July 2007). Mr Justice Lightman goes on to explain that referral to mediation 'does not interfere with the right to a trial: at most, it merely imposes a short delay to allow an opportunity for settlement . . . Such is the impact of mediation that parties who enter it unwillingly become infected with the conciliatory spirit and settle'. Judges recommend that mediation should play a central role in the legal system and form part of the training of law students and judges, because 'the saving of court and judicial time currently expended on avoidable litigation . . . must provide more than a complete return—and an entirely satisfactory method of fulfilling the state's duties under article 6 of the European Convention on Human Rights (the right to a fair trial)' (Law Society's *Gazette*, 13 February 2003). The President of the Family Division of the High Court, Sir Mark Potter, has emphasised the view of senior judges that it is not too late to consider referral to mediation after court proceedings have started. Mediation should be considered where a dispute seems likely to become protracted. With the consent of both parties and their lawyers, such cases may be adjourned so that mediation can take place out of court.

Even at Court of Appeal level, it is not too late to consider mediation. In his concluding judgment in the Court of Appeal, Lord Justice Thorpe, who had referred the case to mediation, stated: 'This appeal emphasised the importance of availability of mediation at an appellate level. There was no family case, however conflicted, that was not potentially open to successful mediation, even if mediation had not been attempted or had failed during the trial process' (*Al-Khatib v Masry* [2005] 1 FLR 381).

11.4 The requirement to consider mediation

The major reform of divorce law introduced in the Family Law Act 1996 (FLA 1996) was abandoned as unworkable. However, FLA 1996, Part III, covering family mediation was implemented and re-enacted in the Access to Justice Act 1999.

A person shall not be granted representation for the purpose of proceedings relating to family matters, unless he has attended a meeting with a mediator—(a) to determine—(i) whether mediation appears to be suitable to the dispute and the parties and all the circumstances, and (ii) in particular, whether mediation could take place without either party being influenced by fear of violence or other harm; and (b) if mediation does appear suitable, to help the person applying for representation to decide whether instead to apply for mediation.

The requirement applies to private law cases within the definition of Family Proceedings under the Funding Code and covers family relationships including:

(a) marriage;

(b) heterosexual or homosexual relationships between partners, whether cohabiting or not;

(c) blood relationships;

(d) step-relationships; and

(e) adoption or long-term care of children such that they may reasonably be regarded as part of a family.

The requirement does not apply to family proceedings under:

(a) Matrimonial Causes Act 1973, s 37; or

(b) Inheritance (Provision for Family and Dependants) Act 1975. Although proceedings under the Inheritance (Provision for Family and Dependants) Act 1975 are exempt from the requirement to attend an assessment meeting, mediation may take place in such cases or in other family proceedings where the mediator deems the case, the parties and all the circumstances to be suitable.

11.5 Legal Help and referrals to family mediation

The requirement to consider mediation comes at the end of Level 2, immediately prior to the issue of contested proceedings (<www.legalservices.gov.uk> LSC Family Mediation Fee Scheme). The Level 2 fee covers work undertaken by solicitors, including negotiation, where there is a significant family dispute relating to children and/or finance, up to the issue of proceedings. If referral to mediation is made at this stage, much of the work involved in gathering financial disclosure and exploring options for settlement can be done in mediation. When mutually acceptable proposals for settlement are reached in mediation, the mediator prepares a legally privileged memorandum of understanding and 'open' statement of financial information and the clients take these documents to their lawyers for legal advice. There may be minor adjustments, but in many cases the petitioner's solicitor draws up a consent order based on terms set out in the memorandum of understanding. The solicitor receives a higher fee for settling the case, benefiting from the groundwork done by the mediator. This saving in solicitors' time creates an incentive to refer to mediation. Even if the case does not settle through mediation, options may have been considered and differences narrowed.

11.6 Exemptions

The client is exempted from the requirement to attend an information and assessment meeting with a mediator in the following circumstances:

1   **Inability of the client (ex) partner or other party to the mediation to attend a meeting with a mediator where**

   (a)   due to any disability, inability or restriction on the client (ex) partner or other party, s/he is unable to travel to see a mediator, eg, client (ex) partner or other party is under bail conditions which prevent contact between the parties, is hospitalised or imprisoned.

   (b)   where, due to any relevant disability or inability of the client (ex partner) or other party, mediation is unavailable, eg, where one of the party's hearing is impaired and there are no mediators available with appropriate facilities.

2   **Domestic abuse**

   The client has made an allegation of domestic abuse against a potential party to the mediation *and* this has resulted in a police investigation or the issuing of civil proceedings for the protection of the client within the last 12 months.

3   **Available appointment**

   (Applicable only after at least three or, if less, all approved mediation suppliers, within the prescribed travelling distance, have been contacted.)

   (a)   Where the mediation service is required to undertake the willingness test (see **11.7** below) and there is no mediator available to hold an assessment meeting within 15 working days of the date of first contact with the mediation service.

   (b)   Where no willingness test is undertaken and there is no mediator available to hold an assessment meeting within 10 working days.

4   **Availability of the client (ex) partner or other party to attend a meeting with a mediator because they:**

   (a)   live abroad; or

   (b)   live further away from a mediation service than a 45-minute journey time (each way), by the fastest method of transport reasonably available to them.

5   **Bankruptcy**

   The mediation concerns financial issues and the client or (ex) partner or other party to the mediation is bankrupt and cannot deal with their own financial affairs.

6   **The parties are in agreement and there is no dispute to mediate on**

7   **Previous assessment of suitability**

   There has been a previous, negative assessment by a mediator of suitability of the parties and the dispute for mediation within the last four calendar months.

8   **Whereabouts of the opponent are unknown, and reasonable attempts to locate them have been unsuccessful**

9   **Any other reasons why the client should not be referred to a mediation service**

11.7   The 'willingness test'

The client who is referred to mediation may attend the information and assessment meeting alone, or may attend jointly with the other party, if both are willing. Alternatively, under the 'willingness test', the client can ask the mediation service to contact the other party to find out if he or she would be willing to consider mediation. If the other party declines mediation or does not reply within 10 days, the client is not required to attend an assessment meeting.

At the information and assessment meeting the mediator:

(a) explains how mediation works and its potential benefits;

(b) assesses whether the client is eligible for publicly funded mediation. This is free of contribution and exempt from the statutory charge;

(c) explains the costs of mediation for those paying privately, making some comparison with estimated average costs of litigation;

(d) identifies issues for mediation, whether child issues, property and finance issues or all issues;

(e) checks whether mediation is suitable in all the circumstances and in particular ascertains whether either party is in fear of violence or other harm and/or concerned about child protection issues;

(f) discusses with both parties, separately or together, whether, having understood the process, they are willing to take part in mediation; and

(g) provides information about other services if mediation is not suitable, such as further legal advice, counselling, welfare benefits advice or other form of help.

There is no limit to the number of mediation sessions that clients may attend, but under the fixed rates for publicly funded mediation there is economic pressure to achieve settlement within three sessions. Where mediation is not suitable, not accepted or breaks down, the mediator completes a CLSAPP7 certificate and sends it to the client or his legal adviser, so that Level 3 Family Help can be obtained for legal representation.

In assessing whether mediation is suitable, the mediator needs to take account of the level of conflict, any language difficulties or special needs and different kinds of power imbalance. Any indications of fear or intimidation need to be explored and considered carefully. Mediators must see each party separately at least briefly, even if they attend the assessment meeting together, to check for particular concerns or fears that would make mediation unsuitable. Research has shown that some experience of domestic violence in the past does not necessarily rule out mediation, if there is no risk of continuing violence and both parties wish to address matters jointly. Mediators are trained to screen for domestic abuse and child protection issues. Where there has been some incident in the past and one client is nervous about meeting the other, special arrangements can be offered, including separate waiting areas and different leaving times so that an anxious client can arrive and leave the building safely, without fear of being followed afterwards. These arrangements are explained in advance to both parties and have been found to work well.

Family mediators need to take account of the needs of clients from ethnic minorities, including the need to translate information and provide access to interpreters. Even if the mediator comes from the same ethnic background as one or both clients, no assumptions can be made, since family traditions vary within ethnic groups and every family is unique.

11.8 Principles of family mediation

The principles and Code of Conduct for family mediation distinguish it from advising, counselling, arbitrating and adjudicating.

The main principles are:

- **Voluntary participation:** the principle of voluntary participation is a fundamental tenet of family mediation in the UK (see **11.7** above). Any participant, including the mediator, may terminate the mediation at any time.

- **Safety in mediation:** as explained above, mediators must assess at the pre-mediation information meeting whether mediation is suitable in all the circumstances. Domestic violence includes verbal and psychological abuse. Some women find sustained verbal and psychological abuse even more damaging than physical abuse. Provided mediation is suitable and accepted by both parties, ground rules may be agreed to ensure equal participation and to prevent threatening or abusive language or behaviour in or around mediation meetings.

- **Independence and conflicts of interest:** 'Mediators must not have any personal interest in the outcome of the mediation and...must not mediate in any case in which they have acquired or may acquire relevant information in any private or other professional capacity' (College of Family Mediators, Code of Practice 2000, s 4.4. 1–2). A conflict of interest check must be carried out on each referral to mediation. The Law Society's Code of Practice for Family Mediation (1999) states that mediation should not take place 'if the mediator or a member of his or her firm has acted for any of the parties in issues not relating to the mediation, unless that has been disclosed to the parties as soon as it is known and they consent' (s 3.4.3).

- **Party control and impartiality:** 'Mediators must at all times remain neutral as to the outcome of mediation. They must not seek to move the participants towards an outcome which the mediator prefers, whether by attempting to predict the outcome of court proceedings or otherwise. They may, however, inform participants of possible solutions, their legal and other implications, and help participants to explore these' (UK College of Family Mediators, Code of Practice s 4.2). Mediators have no powers to impose decisions on participants. They facilitate dialogue between them and consideration of options, assisting them to agree, if possible, their preferred solution and arrangements.

- **Privacy, confidentiality and limits to confidentiality:** the mediation process is confidential and legally privileged. In *Cutts v Head* [1984] Ch 290, Oliver LJ stated at p 306 that: 'parties should be encouraged so far as possible to settle their disputes without resort to litigation and should not be discouraged by the knowledge that anything that is said in the course of negotiations...may be used to their prejudice in the course of the proceedings'. As a general rule, the only person who can waive the protection of privilege is the person to whom the privilege attaches. The privilege attached to all without prejudice discussions between both parties cannot be waived by one of them unilaterally. Baron J in *DB v PO* [2004] EWHC 2064 stated that 'it was wholly inappropriate for the mother to invade the privilege of the mediation process by exhibiting the draft parenting agreement'.

- In its ruling in *Re D (Minors)* (11 February 1993), the Court of Appeal used the term 'conciliation' synonymously with 'mediation' in recognising that 'parents would not achieve a compromise unless they approached conciliation openly and were prepared to give and take. They would not make admissions or conciliatory gestures unless they were confident that these could not be used against them. Any attempt at conciliation must be off the record but there were exceptions.'

The Court of Appeal went on to say that: 'The practice of conciliation had evolved over the last ten years, in court and out of court ... Resolution of disputes by parents locked in acrimony and controversy had taken over from efforts to preserve the marriage. Conciliation did not form part of the legal process but was becoming an important tool in many family courts. That underlined the importance of preserving a cloak over all attempts at settlement of disputes over children.' This ruling established that evidence may not be given in proceedings under the Children Act 1989 (CA 1989) of statements made by one or other of the parties in the course of meetings held, or communications made, for the purpose of conciliation, 'the only exception would be in rare cases where a statement made during conciliation indicates that the maker has caused or is likely to cause serious harm to a child' (*Re D*, above). 'Where a mediator suspects that a child is in danger of significant harm, or it appears necessary so that a specific allegation that a child has suffered significant harm may be properly investigated, mediators must ensure that the local Social Services (England and Wales) or Social Work Department (Scotland) is notified' (College of Family Mediators, Code of Practice s 4.5.2). The participants must be informed, verbally and in writing, of the extent of the confidentiality provided and the circumstances in which it could be breached by the mediator.

It must also be made clear to participants that 'mediators must not discuss or correspond with any participant's legal adviser without the express consent of each participant. Nothing must be said or written to the legal adviser of one, which is not also said or written to the legal adviser of the other(s)' (College of Family Mediators, Code of Practice s 4.5.2).

- **Open financial disclosure:** although what is said in mediation cannot be used in court if mediation breaks down, this 'does not apply to factual information given during the mediation process, such as details of income and property. This can be used in any later court proceedings and passed to solicitors (<www.legalservices.gov.uk> CLS, Mediation).

  In the agreement to mediate signed by both parties, they undertake to make full financial disclosure on the understanding that this information may be made available to legal advisers and may be used in later court proceedings. This assists the formalisation of agreements and avoids wasteful duplication, if financial disclosure had to be made again through lawyers. Each party is asked to complete an open financial statement and provide necessary supporting documents. Mediators make it clear that they do not investigate and verify the information provided. However, information is shared and clarified through questions asked by either party and the mediator. This process helps to identify discrepancies or (generally unintentional) omissions and addresses the need for valuations or other documentation. The financial disclosure gathered in mediation is summarised by the mediator in an open statement of financial information provided to each party, with copies of supporting documents attached. The parties are encouraged to take the financial statement and the financial forms completed by each of them to their legal advisers, to check the adequacy of the disclosure. Mediators may terminate the mediation if a participant refuses to provide information or provides information that appears to be deliberately incomplete or inaccurate.

- **Consideration of children's needs:** 'Mediators should have a special concern for the welfare and best interests of children whilst respecting their impartiality and neutrality and should remind parents of the need to inform and consult their children about what is happening, and that family disputes and prolonged conflict have a severe negative impact on children' (Council of Europe Committee of Ministers Explanatory Memorandum to Recommendation No R (98)1, 21 January 1998, para 45). Participants are encouraged to consider their children's needs, feelings and views and to cooperate as parents over arrangements for their children.

- **Non-binding:** proposals for settlement reached in mediation are recorded as not legally binding and subject to independent legal advice to each party.

- **Informed consent to mediation:** before commencing mediation, both parties are invited to sign an agreement to mediate which sets out the principles and objectives of mediation, the role of the mediator, the extent and limits of the confidentiality provided, any charges involved and the need for full and accurate financial disclosure on an 'open' basis.

- **Standards of training and practice:** there should be 'appropriate mechanisms to ensure the existence of procedures for the selection, training and qualification of mediators (and) standards to be achieved and maintained by mediators'. National associations of family mediators represented in the Family Mediation Council e have requirements and standards that regulate family mediators' training and practice. Publicly funded family mediation is regulated under the LSC Quality Mark Standard for Mediation (December 2002).

11.9 Does mediation work?

The National Audit Office (NAO) examined the effectiveness of public expenditure on mediation in family breakdown and concluded that 'mediation is generally cheaper, quicker and less acrimonious than court proceedings and research shows it secures better outcomes, particularly for children ... On average a mediated case takes 100 days and costs £752, compared with 435 days and £1,682 in cases where mediation is not used' (NAO Review, March 2007). Forty-two per cent of clients who had not been referred to mediation said that they would have been willing to accept it, had they known about it. 'Confrontation in court cannot always be avoided, but the alternative of mediation should be pursued wherever possible—to the benefit of disputing individuals and the taxpayer'. To help increase awareness, the government has set up a Family Mediation Help Line to provide information to callers about family mediation, the availability of publicly funded mediation and the location of the nearest service. Support for mediation is also strengthened by research findings that contested court proceedings over children are more likely to exacerbate parental conflict than to resolve it (Trinder *et al.*, 2002).

A large-scale study coordinated at the University of Bristol and funded by the LSC (Davis *et al.*, 2000) examined a sample of 4,593 cases in which one or both parties were publicly funded: 70% were referred by lawyers, 12% by the court and the remainder were self-referred. The experience of mediation was generally very positive. 82% of participants considered that the mediator had been impartial and 70% found mediation very or fairly helpful; 71% said that they would recommend mediation to others in a similar situation. Of those who reached some agreement, 59% said they expected to be able to negotiate any further changes between themselves. The researchers concluded that mediation as a process has its own distinctive and positive features and that mediation should be supported as a separate system running in parallel to the court system.

11.10 Different approaches to family mediation

11.10.1 Co-mediation

The majority of mediators work as sole mediators but some also offer co-mediation. The Family Mediators' Association (FMA) developed a model of co-mediation in which a lawyer mediator is teamed with a mediator experienced in working with couples and families, generally from a social work background. Both of them must be trained in mediation (Parkinson, 1989). Co-mediation helps to manage high conflict or particularly complex cases, or may be arranged to meet special needs. A gender balance between the mediators is very helpful. The LSC will pay for co-mediation but it must be justified on the case file. Co-mediators offer combined expertise, different perspectives and a wider range of strategies in managing the powerful emotions and conflicts that often surface in mediation.

11.10.2 Shuttle mediation

Although the initial information and assessment meeting may be held with each party separately, family mediation normally requires face-to-face meetings with both together, unlike civil and commercial mediation where separate meetings (referred to as 'caucusing' or 'shuttle mediation') are the norm. In family mediation, the aim is to help participants to engage in dialogue directly, especially parents who need to be able to communicate directly over arrangements for their children, after mediation ends. If, in emergency or for exceptional reasons, one party is seen alone, this is on the basis that all communications between one party and the mediator must be capable of being shared with the other party. This is different from the practice of civil/commercial mediators who hold information in confidence, including each party's 'bottom line' for settlement. The more information the mediator holds from each party without the other's knowledge, the more powerful the mediator becomes. Family mediators seek to 'empower' both parties as much as possible in reaching their own fully informed decisions.

11.10.3 Attendance of legal advisers

It is normal practice in civil and commercial mediation for lawyers to attend mediation sessions with their clients and for the mediator to meet separately with each party and their lawyer in different rooms and to 'shuttle' between them. In some American states, lawyers attend family mediation meetings as well. However, in the UK advising lawyers do not normally attend family mediation meetings. Separated couples, especially parents, need to be able to talk and negotiate directly with each other. They could be inhibited by their lawyers' presence in discussions that are often very personal and emotional. Advising lawyers might try to take control and could gather information from the legally privileged mediation process that they could use in some way in later court proceedings. On the other hand, if the parties can take time out from a mediation meeting to consult with their lawyers on the spot, further delay could be avoided. Lawyers, unlike mediators, can advise a client that their position is unrealistic or unreasonable. Advising lawyers can be very helpful in assisting negotiations and fine-tuning the terms of settlement. If both parties want their legal advisers to attend mediation with them, the ground rules covering their lawyers' involvement need to be clarified and the lawyers asked to sign a document recognising the confidentiality of the mediation process. It needs to be clear that the mediator is not responsible for paying the costs of the lawyers' attendance. This is not covered in publicly funded mediation and private clients may wish to pay their lawyers' charges as well as the mediator's fees. Lawyers who took part in a study in Florida admitted that they attended mediation in order to learn about the mediation process and the mediator's abilities. Once they were satisfied that the mediators were competent and knowledgeable, they were comfortable to allow their clients to participate. The survey showed that after first-hand experience of attending mediation sessions, lawyers recognised that the benefits of mediation outweighed any potential disadvantages to their client.

11.11 Why do people go to mediation?

A follow-up consumer study conducted by researchers at the University of Newcastle (Walker, McCarthy and Timms, 1994) asked people why they had gone to mediation. They gave the following reasons (not listed in order of priority):

- needing to sort out issues they were unable to deal with by themselves;
- wanting to work out agreements together, rather than via solicitors;
- wanting to do their best for the children;
- wanting an amicable divorce and to stay on friendly terms with each other;
- needing someone impartial, objective and knowledgeable to help to manage discussions;
- wanting to reduce their legal costs;
- wanting practical and emotional help at the same time;
- hoping mediation may lead to reconciliation;
- wanting to be told 'what's fair' (mediators do not offer this).

One husband said he went to mediation hoping for a miracle. Although he and his wife did not get back together, he found it a great help 'to get things resolved' (op cit,, at p 38). Another client saw mediation as 'somewhere we could have a more structured discussion where the focus would be brought back to what were really the major issues' (ibid, at p 37).

11.12 The main stages of family mediation

The process normally consists of a series of stages to enable participants to define the issues they need to settle, to identify their options and priorities and to work towards an agreed outcome that takes account of the immediate and long-term needs of all concerned. Mediation on all issues would normally consist of the following stages.

Stage 1 Signing the agreement to mediate
After both parties have received information on mediation and expressed their willingness to take part, they receive a written explaining the aims and principles, the mediator's role and confidentiality. In signing this agreement, participants confirm their acceptance of mediation and undertake to make full disclosure of financial information, with supporting documents as necessary.

Stage 2 Identifying issues for mediation and agreeing the agenda
Participants are invited to explain what they need to settle through mediation and to agree an agenda, at least for the first meeting. The agenda needs to be balanced and urgent issues need to be prioritised. The next stage of the process can then be planned.

Stage 3 Focusing on the children
Where there are issues concerning children, parents generally wish these issues to take priority over financial or other issues. Immediate attention may be given to working out contact arrangements, possibly on an interim basis. Interim arrangements help to provide reassurance and reduce conflict, increasing willingness to move forwards. Most parents recognise that children need a continuing relationship with them both, although they may disagree over the frequency or length of visits or over the involvement of third parties.

Stage 4 Gathering and sharing information
Gathering and sharing information is central to the process, before options can be explored. Financial forms completed by each party are copied and shared with them both. Mediators request supporting documents, clarify discrepancies and help participants to gain a full picture of their financial situation, with independent legal and financial advice as necessary.

Stage 5 Exploring options
All available options and their pros and cons need careful consideration. Mediators help by asking 'reality-testing' questions and by inviting participants to complete a schedule of actual and/or projected average monthly expenditure, to check their borrowing capacity and monthly payments and to take account of child support and other outgoings.

Stage 6 Negotiating towards settlement
Proposals for settlement may involve short-term and/or long-term arrangements on all or some of the issues. These could be confined to contact arrangements or could set out a proposed full and final settlement on all issues.

Stage 7 Gaining the cooperation of children and others involved
Children and new partners need to understand and cooperate with decisions and arrangements, if they are to work in practice. Parents may need to discuss how to explain new arrangements to their children and how to give children the reassurances they are looking for.

Stage 8 Drafting the memorandum of understanding and open financial statement
The legally privileged memorandum of understanding sets out proposals for settlement. Financial information is summarised in the 'open' statement of financial information, with supporting documents attached. Participants are invited to confirm the accuracy of these documents before seeking independent legal advice on them.

Stage 9 Ending mediation

Mediation may end at any stage, with or without agreement. Where there is partial agreement or none at all, mediation has not necessarily 'failed', because the issues may have been clarified and often narrowed, and participants may have considered their options and gained a better understanding of their differences. The dispute may then settle more quickly if it goes to court. Mediation helps parents to talk to each other about their children and to understand each other better.

11.13 Examples where mediation worked well

Case A

An English mother and Dutch father who had not yet separated, worked out detailed arrangements on separation and divorce, including arrangements for their children, the family home, division of assets, pensions and debts. They attended three mediation meetings and undertook tasks between meetings, such as obtaining valuations and filling in financial forms. They brought their proposals for settlement to the final mediation meeting and the mediator incorporated them in a memorandum of understanding used by their solicitors to draw up the consent order.

Case B

An unmarried couple, 'Sam' and 'Marie', who had two sons aged 16 and 18, had cohabited for many years and separated a year previously. Sam continued to live in their jointly owned property, while Marie was renting and seeking a sale of the property and equal division of the net proceeds. They came to mediation to address their financial and property issues. There was intense conflict over financial contributions and consequent entitlements. Sam demanded production of Marie's bank accounts over the past 15 years. Marie was willing for Sam to specify a sample of bank statements that he would be free to examine. Sam seemed reluctant to take this further, however. Rather than using factual problem-solving techniques, the co-mediators observed that both Marie and Sam were still acutely distressed by the breakdown of their relationship. Recognition of their powerful emotions was cathartic and led to a shift of stance and atmosphere. Sam then put forward a proposal for a balanced and straightforward settlement with which Marie readily concurred.

Case C

A middle-aged couple accepted a joint pre-mediation information meeting. Communication between them had broken down completely. The wife was filing a divorce petition and they had put their home on the market, without knowing where either of them would live. Facilitating a dialogue in mediation helped them to start talking again. The wife subsequently withdrew her petition and the couple reconciled. If the divorce had proceeded, it is unlikely that court referral to mediation on financial issues would have led to reconciliation, because it would have been too late. Although reconciliation is not the aim of mediation, this can be the outcome, especially if mediators use techniques and skills that are not too business-like and not confined to settling the presenting issues.

Case D

An elderly couple living in separate nursing homes were no longer able to manage their affairs. They each had an adult daughter from a previous marriage. These two adult daughters, each representing their own parent, used mediation to consider the sale of their parents' property and disposal of possessions, settling these issues by agreement and thus being able to fund the costs of their parents' nursing-home care.

11.14 Power imbalances in mediation

It is not easy to manage the complex power imbalances that couples bring to mediation, while at the same time maintaining balance and impartiality. Concerns have tended to centre on whether women are liable to be put at risk or disadvantaged. Irving and Benjamin (1995) discuss feminists' concerns and conclude from their research that mediation does not disadvantage women, since most of them said they found mediation more helpful than they believed litigation would have been. A mother who retains day-to-day care of the children and occupation of the family home may seem to be in a more powerful position, despite financial difficulties, than a father who may earn more but lives in rented property and sees his children for limited periods of time. One party may be more willing to compromise than the other and this can create an imbalance that mediators need to manage.

Power relationships tend to shift during separation and divorce. Although some patterns remain the same, in separation and divorce previous power imbalances may change in critical ways. One partner's decision to leave the other may alter the previous balance of power. Women are often more strongly placed than men in disputes over children, whereas men often have greater knowledge and control of financial assets. In mediation, participants may work out how to share or reallocate different areas of control and responsibility through recognising mutual interests and common concerns.

Mediators are impartial, but they cannot be entirely neutral in managing the mediation process. They need to enable a less articulate person to speak and encourage those who feel emotionally overwhelmed. They need to restrain individuals who try to dominate and take over the mediation. These shifts from a midway position need not be perceived as biased, provided there is rapport with both parties and balance is maintained overall. If one party tries to bulldoze the other into accepting a settlement, the mediator needs to restrain or challenge this person, while making space for the other one to be heard. A co-mediator can help to manage imbalances, while keeping both parties engaged in the mediation. In any case, proposals for settlement are reviewed by advising lawyers and mediators should identify the questions and aspects on which legal advice is particularly needed.

11.15 Disadvantages and drawbacks of mediation

There could be disadvantages if:

- either party takes part under duress. This should be avoided, however, by pre-mediation assessment to check and confirm each party's willingness;
- mediation is used inappropriately or without adequate safeguards (as above);
- mediation delays proceedings without achieving settlement, thus increasing the costs and timescale. Mediation can usually be arranged quickly and may take place in the interval before a court date is arranged, without delaying the proceedings. Financial information may be gathered more quickly in mediation and can be used in court. Issues have often been clarified and options explored in mediation, so that if litigation ensues, the parties do not go back to square one;

- face-to-face discussions with a former partner may intensify conflict or distress. Mediators' training and experience should enable them to intervene if discussions become confrontational or destructive. A cooling-off may be needed, or the mediator may refocus the couple from irreconcilable grievances towards their future needs and those of their children;

- either party is not mediating in good faith: a competent mediator should spot this, however, and if necessary terminate the mediation;

- power imbalances are not recognised or managed adequately; and

- the mediator is perceived as showing a bias towards one party, or is directive. The agreement to mediate that clients sign at the outset explains the complaints procedure. Considering the anger that clients bring to mediation, it is surprising that few complaints are received. Research findings show generally high levels of consumer satisfaction.

There can be no guarantee of reaching agreement through mediation. Possible disadvantages need to be weighed against potential benefits. However, when clients recognise the potential benefits, especially the major savings in legal costs, most decide to give mediation a try.

11.16 Children and mediation

The need for family mediators to have special concern for the well-being and best interests of children has been mentioned as a principle of mediation (see **11.7**.) The LSC's regulations for publicly funded family mediation require mediators, where there are children of the family:

,to have arrangements designed to ensure that the parties are encouraged to consider:

(a) the welfare, wishes and feelings of each child; and

(b) whether and to what extent each child should be given the opportunity to express his or her wishes and feelings in the mediation.

(CLS *Funding Code Procedures* R9 April 2003, Part D 5.3.)

Under their Code of Practice, mediators encourage participants to focus on the needs of the children, as well as their own needs. They must 'explore the situation from the child's point of view . . . and must encourage the participants to consider their children's own wishes and feelings. Where appropriate, they may discuss with the participants whether and to what extent it is proper to involve the children themselves in the mediation process in order to consult them about their wishes and feelings' (College of Family Mediators, Code of Practice 2000, s 4.7.1–2).

In order to help participants to consider what the children may be feeling and what would help the children to adjust to the changes taking place in their lives, family mediators need some knowledge of child development and children's experience of parental separation and divorce. There have been a number of research studies carried out with children of different ages, comparing the experience of children in 'intact' families with those who have experienced parental separation, one or more times. The findings show that children's needs and feelings are all too often ignored when parents are caught up in their own conflicts. The level and duration of conflict between parents has been found to be a more significant factor in the child's longer-term adjustment to separation than the separation per se.

When separated parents continue to cooperate over their children, the children do well and may even show some benefits in terms of increased maturity and understanding of human relationships. However, when parents cannot agree, communication often breaks down not only between the parents but also between parent and child. If children do not receive sufficient explanation, understanding, reassurance and support, their distress may result in failure to progress at school, loss of self-esteem, acting-out behaviour and sometimes longer-term depression and difficulty in forming relationships as adults. A study carried out at the Department of Child Health at the University of Exeter (Cockett and Tripp, 1994) found that:

- Fewer than half the children whose parents had separated had regular contact with the parent they no longer lived with. Half these children did not even know where the other parent was living.

- Only 6% of children had been given a joint explanation from both parents of the impending separation or divorce. In over 70% of families, it was left to the mother to tell the children. In some cases the mother told the children only that their father had left, without giving them any explanation or reassurance.

- Most of the children had been very aware of the conflict between their parents. When the children were asked what they thought would have helped them, most said that they needed much more information, explanation and reassurance from their parents than they actually received.

- Many children felt they should have been involved in decisions about contact. This does not mean that they want to be given responsibility for decisions. A significant minority, however, had made their own arrangements to keep in contact with the non-resident parent, because their parents were unable to agree or because their parents were no longer speaking to each other.

- Children were also likely to lose touch with grandparents and other relatives who played an important part in the children's lives, prior to the parents' separation.

Mediators help parents to consider how they will explain their decisions and future arrangements to their children and reassure them that the separation or divorce is not their fault (as children often imagine). Children are also reassured to know that their parents want to take their wishes and feelings into account, depending on the child's age and maturity, without asking the child to choose between them. Most parents prefer to talk with their children at home, without using outside agencies or involving their children directly in mediation. However, some parents want older children to have the opportunity to express their views, feelings and needs to someone outside the family, possibly meeting with the mediator on their own or with a child counsellor who works alongside the mediation service. Some children ask for this too.

In practice, children meet with the mediator in only a small minority of cases and this needs careful consideration and planning with the parents. There must be agreement between both parents and the mediator that it is appropriate for the child or young person to be invited to take part, clarity about the objectives and agreement about the nature of the involvement. Where both parents and the mediator consider it appropriate and the child is willing to attend, an older child or young person may meet with the mediator, with siblings or separately, without the parents being present. Children's acceptance needs to be sought carefully, without any pressure to come against their will.

With both parents' consent, the mediator may write to the child directly. The confidentiality of discussions with a child in mediation needs to be explained fully and included in a written agreement signed by the parents and talked through with the child. Mediators are required to have additional training before they may involve children directly. Feedback from children in such cases indicates that they found it very helpful to have the opportunity to talk with the mediator and that consultation with children and young people assists parents to reach agreements that meet their children's needs, without children being given responsibility for choices or decisions (Parkinson, 2006).

11.17 Family mediation in international cases

Mediation is recommended as an appropriate means of resolving international disputes in cases with a cross-border element. The expansion of the European Union to twenty-seven Member States and the mobility of individuals and families across state boundaries increase the need for international cooperation. In 1998 the Council of Europe's Committee of Experts on Family Law reported that 'research in Europe, North America, Australia and New Zealand suggests that family mediation is better suited than more formal legal mechanisms to the settlement of sensitive, emotional issues surrounding family matters. Reaching agreements in mediation has been shown to be a vital component in making and maintaining co-operative relationships between divorcing parents: it reduces conflict and encourages continuing contact between children and both their parents' (Committee of Ministers Explanatory Memorandum to Recommendation No R (98)1, 21 January 1998, para 7).

The Committee's recommendations were adopted by the Council of Europe's Committee of Ministers:

Realizing that a number of States are considering the introduction of family mediation (and) convinced of the need to make greater use of family mediation . . . [the Committee of Ministers] recommends the governments of member States—

i. to introduce or promote family mediation, or, where necessary, strengthen existing family mediation:

ii. to take or reinforce all measures they consider necessary with a view to the implementation of the following principles for the promotion and use of family mediation as an appropriate means of resolving family disputes.

(Recommendation No (98) 1, 21 January 1998, ss 9–11)

The Recommendation defines family mediation as 'a process in which a third party, the mediator, impartial and neutral, assists the parties to negotiate over the issues in dispute and reach their own joint agreements' (ibid, s 10) and refers to research results showing that the use of family mediation has the potential to:

- improve communication within the family;
- reduce conflict between parties in dispute;
- produce amicable settlements;
- provide continuity of personal contacts between parents and children;
- lower the social and economic costs of separation and divorce for the parties themselves and states;
- reduce the length of time otherwise required to settle conflict (ibid, s 7).

The Explanatory Memorandum to the Recommendation points out that family disputes have special characteristics that need to be taken into account:

1 There are usually continuing and interdependent relationships. The dispute settlement process should facilitate constructive relationships for the future, in addition to enabling the resolution of current disputes.

2 Family disputes usually involve emotional and personal relationships in which feelings can exacerbate the difficulties, or disguise the true nature of the conflicts and disagreements. It is usually considered appropriate for these feelings to be acknowledged and understood by parties and by the mediator.

3 Disputes that arise in the process of separation and divorce have an impact on other family members, notably children, who may not be included directly in the mediation process, but whose interests may be considered paramount and therefore relevant to the process. (Memorandum, para 15)

The Committee of Ministers of the Council of Europe agreed that 'mediation should not, in principle, be compulsory' (Recommendation No R (98) 1).

International Conventions (such as the Hague Convention on the Civil Aspects of International Child Abduction 1980) and the harmonisation of legal systems in Europe aim to avoid conflicts between different jurisdictions following different legal principles and presumptions.

The Regulation known as Brussels II Revised (Council Regulation (EC) No 2201/2003 of 27 November 2003, which came into force on 1 March 2005) applies to all EU Member States, except Denmark. It takes precedence over the European Convention on Recognition and Enforcement of Decisions concerning Custody of Children and on Restoration of Custody of Children 1980 and over the Hague Convention, but preserves the Hague Convention for dealing with applications for the return of a child and gives directions on how the Convention is to be applied as between Member States.

European Code of Conduct for Mediators
The European Code of Conduct for Mediators was published by the European Commission in July 2004 as a voluntary instrument designed to improve quality and trust in mediation. Mediation is defined in the European Code of Conduct as 'any process where two or more parties agree to the appointment of a third-party—hereinafter "the mediator"—to help the parties to solve a dispute by reaching an agreement without adjudication'. The European Code of Conduct is intended to apply to:

• any type of mediation that falls within the above definition;

• any type of dispute within civil or commercial law; and

• any legal, social or cultural context within the European Union.

On 21 May 2008 the European Parliament and the European Council published a Directive (2008/52/EC) entitled 'Certain Aspects of Mediation in Civil and Commercial Matters' in which it is recognised that 'agreements resulting from mediation are more likely to be enforced voluntarily and are more likely to preserve an amicable and sustainable relationship between the parties. These benefits become even more pronounced in situations displaying cross-border elements'.

An international group of family mediation trainers convened by International Social Service in Geneva in 2005 agreed the following definition: 'Family mediation is a process in which qualified and impartial third parties (mediators) assist the parties to negotiate directly or indirectly on the issues that need to be resolved and to reach considered and mutually acceptable decisions that reduce conflict and encourage co-operation for the well-being of all concerned' (ISS Family Mediators Trainers Group, Geneva, 2005). Although face-to-face discussion in the same location is the essence of mediation, this may be impossible to achieve when distances and costs of travel are too great, as they are in many cross-border mediations where the parents live far apart, possibly in different continents. The ISS definition covers different forms of 'tele-mediation', including video-conferencing and Skype. These resources can enable mediation to take place, however wide the geographical distance. But to work effectively, mediators in different countries need to have common principles and shared objectives and above all, be able to communicate well.

The Council of Europe held its 7th Family Law Conference in March 2009 on the subject of International Family Mediation. It was recognised that:

> training for international family mediators is a sensitive subject which needs to be further developed, as there are currently many different standards and systems regarding the requirements for a family mediator, and great disparities in terms of curricula, certificates obtained and training possibilities in general. Some systems are more formalistic, while others put an emphasis on practical training. Both systems present advantages and disadvantages. Very concretely, the unanimous conclusion is that: Firstly, we need to harmonise those systems, their qualifications and agree equivalences, and, second, we should create a centralised register of competent accredited mediators, who would assist individuals and authorities to identify and contact certified and qualified mediators.
>
> (Conference Conclusions by Winter R., Judge and Chair of the International Association of Youth and Family Judges and Magistrates, Austria)

The Hague Conference on Private International Law
Following the recommendations of the Third Malta Judicial Conference, the Members of the Hague Conference decided at the Meeting of the Council on General Affairs and Policy of the Conference (31 March–2 April 2009):

> In the context of the Malta Process, and subject to the availability of the necessary resources, the Council authorised the establishment of a Working Party to promote the development of mediation structures to help resolve cross-border disputes concerning custody of or contact with children. The Working Party would comprise experts from a number of States involved in the Malta Process, including both States Parties to the 1980 Child Abduction Convention and non-States Parties. It would also include independent experts.

Other bodies actively involved in supporting these developments include GEMME (Groupement Européen des Magistrats pour la Médiation) and a number of national projects (Belgium, the Netherlands and Reunite in the UK) and bilateral projects (Germany–Poland and Germany–USA) coordinated by MiKK in Berlin (Mediation bei internationalen Kindschaftskonflikten).

11.18 Training and practices in family mediation

There are approximately 1,000 trained family mediators currently in practice, half of whom are qualified and experienced family lawyers with additional training in family mediation, while the other half are mainly qualified social workers who may have experience in family therapy or family court work. Most mediators offer mediation on a part-time basis either within their legal practice or at a recognised mediation centre.

Family mediators wishing to undertake publicly funded mediation in England and Wales must have completed a recognised course of training. Family mediation training is provided by the Family Mediators' Association, National Family Mediation and Resolution (formerly the Solicitors Family Law Association). In order to be recognised by the LSC to undertake assessment meetings and publicly funded family mediation, the mediator must be a member of one or more of the above associations, must mediate in a recognised family mediation centre or legal practice and must have passed successfully the Assessment of Competence in Family Mediation. The assessment is based on a portfolio explaining how the mediator uses mediation techniques and skills at each stage of the mediation process, illustrated with examples from five completed mediations. There must be case commentaries and a testimonial from the mediator's supervisor. The CLS Quality Mark sets out further detailed standards and requirements. There must be regular reviews of mediation files, supervision and continuing training.

Experienced family lawyers who have taken family mediation training said that they gained additional understanding and skills including:

- dealing with people in a different way—understanding the emotional side and feelings involved;
- taking a non-adversarial and non-directive approach in working with both parties jointly;
- helping people in conflict to communicate better;
- picking up signals from speech, body language and eye contact;
- acquiring and developing new skills, eg, balancing, reframing and mutualising;
- gaining greater understanding of children's needs and reactions to parental separation;
- giving information in a balanced and impartial way;
- developing options and reality-testing; and
- summarising clearly, orally and in writing.

The use of language is particularly important in mediation in easing and clarifying stressful exchanges and in 'reframing' negative statements to help to bring out underlying fears or needs in more constructive ways.

11.19 Summary of the main benefits of family mediation

- participants are helped to reach their own decisions and to retain control over their own affairs, instead of having decisions imposed on them by the court;
- disputes can be settled at an early stage, before positions become entrenched;
- participants are encouraged to look to the future, rather than focusing on past grievances;
- separated parents are helped to manage ongoing communications concerning their children;
- children's needs are kept in the forefront of discussions. Parents are helped to take full account of their children's needs and feelings, as well as their own;
- misunderstandings can be cleared up or avoided;
- stress, animosity and bitterness can be reduced;
- available options can be explored in joint discussions, before decisions are taken;

- possibilities of reconciliation are not ruled out and may emerge through discussion;

- arrangements can be tailored to particular family circumstances and needs;

- meetings are informal and can be arranged quickly, compared with the formality and delays of court proceedings;

- face-to-face discussions reduce the costs and delays of lengthy correspondence;

- legal costs may be greatly reduced, especially if litigation is avoided;

- mediation addresses issues that participants see as interlinked in practical and emotional terms, whereas in the legal system, children issues are dealt with separately from financial matters.

11.20   Mediation—keeping the balance

Getting an agreement is not the sole goal of mediation. Helping separated couples and their children to communicate more easily with each other is also very important, so that they can negotiate future changes on their own. The values and proposals that some individuals bring to mediation can seem eccentric, but it is not the mediator's role to determine what is normal or acceptable. The whole process of mediation is a balancing act. Mediators need good balance to stay on their tightrope, managing the power imbalances and tensions that threaten mediation both internally and externally. At a personal level, mediators need stamina, patience and a sense of humour to resist the downward drag of unremitting disputes. Practical common sense is needed to test the reality of workable arrangements, yet intuition and imagination are equally important in sensing what is unsaid and what may need to be elicited.

Mediation is now used in many different spheres, nationally and internationally, including family law, education, health services, community and neighbourhood, intellectual property and environmental disputes. Mediation cannot be a universal panacea and is not always suitable, but the availability of mediation and its benefits need to be understood and encouraged as widely as possible.

11.21   Suggested further reading

Brown H., and Marriott A., *ADR Principles and Practice* (Sweet & Maxwell, 1993).

Cockett M., and Tripp J., *The Exeter Family Study: Family Breakdown and its impact on children* (University of Exeter Press, 1994).

College of Family Mediators, *Standards and Code of Practice 1995* (reissued 2000).

Community Legal Service, *Funding Code Procedures and Decision Making Guidance*, R9 April 2003.

Irving H., and Benjamin R., *Family Mediation—Contemporary Issues* (Sage Publications, 1995).

Legal Services Commission, *Quality Mark Standard for Mediation*, December 2002.

Mnookin and Kornhauser, 'Bargaining in the Shadow of the Law: The Case of Divorce' [1979] *Yale Law Review*, 88: 950.

Parkinson L., 'Co-mediation with a Lawyer Mediator' [1989] *Family Law*, 48: 48–9, 135–9.

—— *Family Mediation* (Sweet & Maxwell, 1997).

—— 'Child-inclusive Family Mediation' [June 2006] *Family Law*, 483–8.

Roberts M., *Mediation in Family Disputes: Principles of Practice* (Ashgate, 2008).

Trinder L. *et al.*, *Making Contact: How Parents and Children Negotiate and Experience Contact after Divorce* (Joseph Rowntree Foundation Research Findings 092, October 2002).

Westcott (ed), *Family Mediation—Past, Present and Future* (Family Law, 2004).

Relevant principles of taxation

12.1 Principles

It is important to be familiar with the way that maintenance is taxed, as many barristers early in practice may be asked to deal with such cases. Those who are going to specialise in family law must be conversant with the tax provisions relevant to divorce.

There has been no very coherent policy on the taxation of husband and wife. The historical concept of the husband and wife as one person was used for income tax and capital gains tax (CGT), taxing the married couple as one unit, but inheritance tax applies to each spouse independently. Increasingly, the approach has been to limit special reliefs and allowances available to spouses, and since 1990/91 spouses have been considered separately for income tax and CGT. There are some provisions to prevent tax avoidance within the family. Civil partners are generally in the same position for tax as spouses. Generally, a child is taxed separately from his or her parents, the child being separately taxable on any income he or she receives and having a personal tax allowance from the time of birth, but again there are provisions to stop tax avoidance.

For more information and helpful guides, see the HM Revenue & Customs website (<www.hmrc.gov.uk>).

12.2 Income tax

12.2.1 Spouses married and living together

Each married person is independently liable for tax on her/his own income with an individual personal allowance, a figure of £6,475 for 2009/10. An additional personal allowance is available for someone over 65, depending on the level of their income.. A married couple's allowance was available where one spouse was born before 1935, but this is ending in 2009–10.

The situation as regards tax allowances for children has changed over the years. The current position is that a child is liable for tax on any personal income with an individual tax allowance. A Child Tax Credit is available to any parent who is single, married or living with someone and has at least one child under the age of 16 living with them, or a child up to 20 in full-time education or training. There are also tax credits available to assist with child care costs in some circumstances. If parents are not liable to higher-rate tax, this allowance can go to either of them or be shared. If either of the parents is liable to higher-rate tax, the allowance goes to that parent, and the allowance tapers off to no benefit a little way into the higher-rate tax band. The higher-rate tax threshold is £37,400 for 2009/10. A Working Families' Tax Credit is available for families with very low income, and should be researched if appropriate.

12.2.2 Separation and divorce

Provisions for the taxation of maintenance payments are set out in the Finance Act 1988, ss 36–40, see **12.6**.

12.3 Capital gains tax

12.3.1 Spouses married and living together

As with income tax, the principle of joint assessment of husband and wife survived for many decades, but as with income tax this was abandoned in 1990. Each spouse is separately liable for tax on their own gains, and each has a separate annual allowance of £10,100 for 2009/10.

Married couples have a substantial advantage in that disposals between spouses are treated as being at no gain, no loss, so that no CGT will be payable on such a disposal (Taxation of Chargeable Gains 1992 (TCGA 1992), s 58). Note, however, that the original acquisition price of the asset will be retained for calculating gains on a later disposal by the recipient spouse. On the operation of this section, see *Gubay v Kington* [1984] 1 WLR 163.

12.3.2 Separation and divorce

It is important to note that disposals made as part of financial provision on divorce are not necessarily exempt from CGT, and the divorce settlement should be considered carefully to avoid CGT, as it will potentially apply at 18% to any gain that is realised, See *M v M (Sale of Property)* [1988] 1 FLR 389. In *Aspden v Hildesley* [1982] 1 WLR 264 a husband agreed to transfer his share in a second home to the wife but it was held that this transaction was not exempt so he would have to pay CGT on the value of his share.

As suggestions for avoiding CGT:

(a) Make disposal or agreement before separation and divorce, so it will be at no gain/no loss (but remember the original acquisition cost is retained for calculating later gains).

(b) Use exempt assets for provision, eg, a car.

(c) Remember a sterling lump sum will not be liable to CGT (but consider how such a sum could be raised).

(d) Remember that a main private residence is not liable to tax.

(e) After separation and divorce, the spouses will not be 'connected', so it may be possible to argue market value should not be taken.

12.4 Inheritance tax

12.4.1 Spouses married and living together

Spouses are separately liable for inheritance tax on their own estates with their own allowances and own cumulative totals. This can be important in tax planning: assets can be divided between the spouses to ensure that each makes full use of the nil rate band of £325,000 each for 2009/10.

Transfers between spouses are exempt (Inheritance Tax Act 1984 (ITA 1984), s 18); and they can benefit from other exemptions and reliefs, such as provision for maintenance (ITA 1984, s 11) and gifts in consideration of marriage (ITA 1984, s 22).

12.4.2 Separation and divorce

While there is no complete exemption for provision on divorce, it is unlikely that inheritance tax will bite on divorce provision. There will be no tax on the divorce, but only potentially when one spouse later dies. The provision that dispositions for maintenance of the family are not transfers of value applies to maintenance on divorce (ITA 1984, s 11), and if there is provision under a court order it can be argued that there is no intention to confer a gratuitous benefit (ITA 1984, s 10).

12.4.3 Death of one spouse

Tax will be chargeable on the estate of the deceased, including their share of jointly owned property, subject to their cumulative total. Property passing to the surviving spouse will be exempt, but will be chargeable to tax when the survivor dies, so exemptions should be used carefully.

12.5 Cohabitees

12.5.1 Income tax

Couples living together will each be taxed as a single individual, paying tax on their own income with a single personal allowance each..

12.5.2 Capital gains tax

Each cohabitee will be separately taxed and will have their own allowances. Disposals between them will be potentially taxable, which may be a problem if they split up and need to divide assets..

12.5.3 Inheritance tax

Each cohabitee will be separately taxed and will have their own allowances and cumulative total. Transfers between cohabitees will not be exempt, but they may be 'potentially exempt transfers' if they are gifts. A problem can arise if one cohabitee dies, as assets left to the other will not be exempt.

12.6   Taxation of maintenance payments

12.6.1   Generally

The approach of the tax system to maintenance payments has varied over the years. The current system is relatively straightforward, but confusion may be caused if dealing with a variation in a case where an original order was made some years ago. Payments made under obligations entered into before 15 March 1988 were taxed under a complex process by which tax was paid in advance by the payer, but then became a tax credit of which the payee might be able to reclaim all or part depending on his or her own tax position. The current approach is that maintenance payments should have limited and simple tax consequences, because the payer pays tax, but then no further tax is payable by the payee It is very important to take this into account in looking at appropriate figures for maintenance. The same rules apply to former spouses and former civil partners.

12.6.2   Tax effects for the person paying maintenance

Maintenance payments are not deductible for tax purposes and must be paid in full from taxed income. This applies to payments to or for a former spouse or a child, including assessments under the Child Support Act 1991.

Until 2000/01, an additional personal allowance was available to someone paying maintenance to a former spouse. From 2001/02, maintenance payments relief is only available where the payer or the former spouse is over 75, and it only provides a very limited tax deduction.

12.6.3   Tax effects for the person receiving maintenance

Whether the recipient of the payments is a former spouse or a child, the payments will not be taxable in his or her hands (though obviously he or she will be fully liable to tax on any other income he or she has). The recipient will not be able to set any tax allowance against the maintenance payment, or be able to reclaim any tax paid by the payer in respect of the payment.

12.7   Illustration of tax issues relevant to divorce

Jasper and Fiona married in 2004 and separated in 2008, since when they have not lived together. They have one child, Gemma, currently aged 7.

Fiona has petitioned for divorce and has been granted a decree nisi. Financial provision is currently being negotiated, and Fiona has proposed the following terms. Advise Jasper on any potential tax implications of each term to help him to decide how he should respond.

(a) Jasper should transfer to Fiona his share in the former matrimonial home, which is registered in their joint names and which is currently valued at £250,000. The house was purchased in 2004 for £180,000.

(b) Alternatively, the former matrimonial home should be settled, to be sold when Gemma becomes 18, the proceeds then to be divided with 75% to Fiona and 25% to Jasper.

(c) Fiona should transfer to Jasper a yacht that was purchased in 1998 for £20,000. Although the purchase price was provided by Jasper, the yacht was put into Fiona's name as Jasper at the time had a slight fear that he might go bankrupt. The yacht is now worth £50,000.

(d) Fiona should keep a Volvo car bought for her by Jasper which is currently worth £10,000.

(e) Jasper should pay to Fiona a lump sum of £20,000. To raise this sum he would have to sell shares that he purchased in 1993 for £2,000, and they are now worth £30,000.

12.7.1 *Advice to Jasper*

(a) There will be no inheritance tax consequences as all the transfers would apparently be to meet reasonable claims on divorce and would therefore be 'non-gratuitous' (ITA 1984, s 10).

(b) There is an apparent capital gain of £70,000 on the matrimonial home; however, the gain will be exempt from CGT, as it relates to a main private residence (TCGA 1992, s 222; and see also Extra-Statutory Concession D6, as the couple are already living separately).

(c) If the house is settled, it will become the main private residence of Fiona alone. Therefore, when the home is eventually sold (or if Fiona later buys out Jasper's interest), then the gain that Jasper makes will be subject to CGT (calculated as the gain his 25% has made since the settlement). This must be considered in deciding how attractive this option is.

(d) The yacht has apparently gained £30,000 in value. If Fiona transfers ownership to Jasper, this gain will prima facie be liable to tax at Fiona's marginal rate of income tax, and reduced by Fiona's annual allowance of £10,100 if this has not yet been used for another transaction.

(e) There is no disposal if a spouse keeps an asset, and in any event motor cars are not subject to CGT.

(f) The transfer of money will not in itself attract CGT as sterling is not liable to the tax. However, the gain of £28,000 that will accrue on the sale of the shares will attract CGT at Jasper's marginal rate of tax, reduced by his annual allowance of £10,100 if this has not yet been used on another transaction, and also reduced by the costs of sale. If a capital sum is to be paid, it is always important to consider how it will be raised.

Applications for committal orders—checklists

13.1 Introduction

13.1.1 When committal orders may be sought

A committal to prison is the ultimate means by which a court may enforce an order to do an act (other than to pay money except in circumstances prescribed by Debtors' Act 1869, s 5 and Administration of Justice Act 1970 (AJA 1970), s 11 and Sch 8) within a prescribed time where the individual concerned has failed or refused to obey the order. Similarly a committal order may be made where person has done an act which he was ordered not to do. Undertakings given to the court may be enforced in the same way.

There are many different kinds of orders in family proceedings which may be enforced by committal to prison. These include orders restraining an individual from molesting another, regulating or forbidding the occupation of the family home (under Family Law Act 1996 (FLA 1996), Part IV); interlocutory orders concerning the filing of evidence or the disclosure of documents or information; orders requiring the attendance of parties at hearings; and orders made under the Children Act 1989 (CA 1989), ss 8 and 14A, 14B(2)(b), 14C(3)(b) and 14D.

The party who obtained the order which may require enforcement by committal to prison is entitled to have a 'penal notice' endorsed on the order drawing the attention of the receiving party to the consequences of disobedience. Save in exceptional circumstances no order for committal may be made unless such a warning has been drawn to the attention of the alleged contemnor.

A penal notice may not be endorsed on an order made under CA 1989, ss 8 or 14 without the leave of the court (Family Proceedings Rules 1991 (FPR 1991), r 4.21A).

In any event, in family proceedings, committal orders are viewed as a last resort, when all other reasonable means of enforcement have been tried or are inapt to the occasion.

While in proceedings concerning children, the welfare of the child is not the paramount consideration when considering whether to make an order to commit a contemnor to prison, it may be a highly relevant consideration.

This is well illustrated by *M v M* (*Breaches of Orders: Committal*) [2006] 1 FLR 1154. A father was found on more than 60 occasions to have breached an order forbidding him from having contact with his children. Nonetheless the court decided not to commit him to prison. The older children were likely to revolt against the idea of their father being sent to prison. This would have made them unmanageable for their mother in whose care they lived, which would have resulted in care proceedings. This would have been detrimental to their welfare. In the circumstances their welfare was the decisive factor in determining that a committal order should not be made.

No order will be enforced by committal unless it is clear and unambiguous in its terms. Thus an order simply requiring a parent to allow the other parents 'staying contact on dates to be arranged' is not enforceable as it did not require the residents parent to do an act by a particular time (*D v D* (*Access; Contempt: Committal* [1991] 2 FLR 34.)

The court will not enforce an order to do an act by a particular date unless it is proven that the order was served before that date.

No committal order will, be made in respect of a trivial breach of an order. The applicant for such an order is likely to have costs awarded against him (*Adam Phones Ltd v Goldschmidt* [1999] 4 All ER 486).

13.1.2 The importance of abiding by correct procedure

The Court of Appeal has stressed in several cases that, because committal for contempt of court is concerned with offences of a quasi-criminal nature and the liberty of the subject is at stake, the relevant rules of court must be complied with and the prescribed forms must be used. However, 'any procedural defect in the commencement or conduct by the applicant of a committal application may be waived by the court if satisfied that no injustice has been caused to the respondent by the defect' (Practice Direction—Committal Applications, para 10, supplemental to RSC Ord 52 and CCR Ord 29).

In *Nicholls v Nicholls* [1997] 1 FLR 649, Lord Woolf MR gave the following guidance (p 661E):

(1) As committal orders involve the liberty of the subject it is particularly important that the relevant rules are duly complied with. It remains the responsibility of the judge when signing the committal order to ensure that it is properly drawn and that it adequately particularises the breaches which have been proved and for which the sentence has been imposed.

(2) As long as the contemnor has had a fair trial and the order has been made on valid grounds the existence of a defect either in the application to commit or in the committal order served will not result in the order being set aside except insofar as the interests of justice require this to be done.

(3) Interests of justice will not require an order to be set aside where there is no prejudice caused as the result of errors in the application to commit or in the order to commit. When necessary the order can be amended.

(4) When considering whether to set aside the order, the court should have regard to the interests of any other party and the need to uphold the reputation of the justice system.

(5) If there has been a procedural irregularity or some other defect in the conduct of the proceedings which has occasioned injustice, the court will consider exercising its power to order a new trial unless there are circumstances which indicate that it would not be just to do so.

The Human Rights Act 1998 (HRA 1998) has affected the manner in which all committal proceedings must be approached. The President's Direction (Committal Applications and Proceedings in which a Committal Order may be made) [2001] 1 FLR 949 states, at para 2:

In any family proceedings (to which the Civil Procedure Rules Practice Direction Supplemental to RSC Ord 52 and CCR Ord 29 relates) in which a committal order may be made, including proceedings for the enforcement of an existing order by way of judgment summons or other process, full effect will be given to the HRA 1998 and to the rights afforded under that Act. In particular the European Convention for the Protection of Human Rights and Fundamental Freedoms 1950, Art 6 of is fully applicable to such proceedings. Those involved must ensure that in the conduct of the proceedings there is due observance of the HRA 1998 in the same manner as if the proceedings fell within the CPR direction.

See also *Mubarak v Mubarak* [2001] 1 FLR 698—although this case related to an application for a judgment summons, it is instructive on the requirement of strict compliance with Art 6.

The checklists which follow are designed to cover the practical points which most often arise, and need to be considered, in preparation for, and in the course of, committal hearings. They are not comprehensive of every point which has reached the Court of Appeal.

13.1.3 Committal procedure: forms, rules and practice direction

Whichever prescribed form of committal application is required, the form 'must set out in full the grounds on which the committal application is made and should identify, separately and numerically, each act of contempt' (Practice Direction—Committal Applications, paras 2.5 and 2.6, and *Harmsworth v Harmsworth* [1987] 3 All ER 816). This requirement and the need to support the application with suitable evidence and give due notice to the respondent are the most important steps to ensure that an application for committal can achieve an effective hearing.

The Civil Procedure Rules 1998 (CPR 1998) and the Practice Direction—Committal Applications, supplemental to RSC Ord 52 and CCR Ord 29, have incorporated some of the previous case law and practice, but have made the selection of appropriate forms and rules more complicated. This affects family practitioners as orders and committals under the Protection from Harassment Act 1997 (PHA 1997) are governed by the CPR 1998.

Committal procedure is governed in the High Court by RSC Ord 52 (preserved in CPR 1998, Sch 1) and, in civil proceedings, by Practice Direction—Committal Applications and, in the Family Division, by the FPR 1991, r 7.2. In County courts, CCR Ord 29 (preserved in CPR 1998, Sch 2) and, in non-family proceedings the same *Practice Direction*, applies. In family proceedings courts, the Family Proceedings Courts (Matrimonial Proceedings etc) Rules 1991 (FPC(MP)R 1991), r 20 applies.

Under the President's Direction, the Civil Procedure Rules Practice Direction supplemental to the RSC Ord 52 and the CCR Ord 29 applies to all applications in family proceedings for a committal order in the same manner and to the same extent as it applies to proceedings governed by the CPR 1998 subject to:

- the FPR 1991;

- the limited application of the CPR 1998 in family proceedings.

Further important points arising in the CPR Practice Direction are:

(a) Where the alleged contempt is in connection with existing family proceedings (other than contempt in the face of the court) or with an order made or an undertaking given in existing proceedings, the committal application shall be made in those proceedings.

(b) Following the FPR 1991, r 7.2, committal applications in the High Court are to be made by summons. In the County court, applications are to be made as prescribed by the CCR Ord 29. References in the CPR Practice Direction to 'claim forms' and 'application notice' are to be read accordingly.

(c) Where the CPR Practice Direction requires more information to be provided than is required to be provided under the RSC and the CCR, the court will expect the former to be observed.

(d) The court will ensure that adequate time is afforded to the respondent for the preparation of his or her defence.

(e) The CPR Practice Direction applies to breaches of exclusion requirements made in interim care orders under the CA 1989 and to orders made under the FLA 1996, Part IV.

The prescribed form for initiating a committal application in family proceedings in the County court is Form N78 (FPR 1991, r 1(3) and CCR Ord 29, r 1(4) and 2(3)). In family proceedings in the High Court, the application is made by summons (FPR 1991, r 7.2(1)).

In civil proceedings in the High Court and the County court, a committal application, where final judgment has been given, must be commenced by a Part 8 claim form (SC Practice Direction 52.2). The claim form is form N208. This procedure should be followed for applications for breach of injunction made under the PHA 1997.

If the committal application is commenced by claim form, the CPR, Part 8 applies as though references to 'claimant' were references to the person making the committal application, and references to 'defendant' were references to the person against whom the committal application is made (in SCPD 52 referred to as the 'respondent': see SCPD 52.2.5).

If the application is made in existing proceedings, it must be commenced by the filing of an application notice in those proceedings.

An application to commit for breach of an undertaking or order must be commenced by the filing of an application notice in the proceedings in which the undertaking was given or order was made (SCPD 52.2(1) and (2)). The application notice must be in form N244.

County court Forms N78 and N79 were designed to ensure that the procedural requirements of the rules were met, and the requirements for common disposals would be complied with. The Forms can be used as checklists as they incorporate the essential requirements in all committal applications and, in the case of Form N79, the menu of common disposal orders. In family proceedings courts, similar Forms FL418 and FL419 apply. Practitioners are strongly recommended to use these Forms as simple checklists for ensuring that the essential procedural requirements are followed. Form N78 remains a convenient guide as to the contents required for a committal application by summons in the Family Division or committal application under CPR 1998, Part 8, which must be issued in application notice in Form N244 or in claim form in Form N208. The checklists appearing after this introduction provide a sequential and extended framework for following good practice.

Form N79, the prescribed form for a committal order in County courts, and Form FL419 for family proceedings courts, contain most of the usual orders made on proof of disobedience of an injunctive order or breach of an undertaking. The court—judge or justices and clerk—can delete the orders not required, and enter the precise details of the orders made. Forms N79 and FL419 are supplied to courts with explanatory guidance notes attached and they can be used as a checklist at the time of making an order.

13.1.4 Committal hearings

In general terms, hearings of committal proceedings are in many respects similar to hearings of criminal charges. Thus the burden of proof rests on the person making the allegation of contempt; the standard of proof is the criminal standard; the respondent must be allowed to cross-examine witnesses and to call evidence; the respondent is entitled to submit that there is no case to answer; if a contempt is found proved the contemnor must be allowed to address the court by way of mitigation or seeking to purge his or her contempt; and autrefois acquit and autrefois convict apply.

The court is entitled to require the respondent to file sworn witness statements or affidavits from himself and his witnesses (*Re B (Contempt of Court: Affidavit Evidence)* [1996] 1 FLR 239. This rule is now subject to the *President's Practice Direction, Committal Applications* which requires the application of the CPR Practice Direction to applications for committal orders in family proceedings. Those rules provide that a respondent may give oral evidence and may call witnesses notwithstanding that he has not filed any written witness statements.

High Court Contempt proceedings are civil proceedings although they incorporate the criminal standard of proof. Thus hearsay evidence is admissible subject to the requirements of Civil Evidence Act 1995 and the European Convention of Human Rights, Art 6 (*Daltel Europe Ltd (in liquidation) v Makki* (The Times, 8 March 2006). The same approach probably applies in the County court.

The European Convention on Human Rights, Art 6(3)(c) provides that 'a defendant is entitled to defend himself in person or through legal assistance of his own choosing or, if he has not sufficient means to pay for legal assistance, to be given it free when the interests of justice so require'.

The Legal Aid Act 1988, s 29 gave the court power to grant legal aid if it appeared to the court desirable to do so in the interests of justice in cases where a person was liable to be committed or fined under the County Court Act 1984 (CCA 1984), ss 14 or 118 (ie, not in FLA 1996, Part IV proceedings). The AJA 1999 repealed this provision but did not replace this power.

In *Re K (Contact: Committal Order)* [2003] 1 FLR 277, the Court of Appeal held that a mother's rights under Art 6 had been breached by the making of a committal order at a hearing at which she did not have legal representation. She was entitled (Art 6(3)(c)) to have legal representation at a hearing at which deprivation of her liberty was at stake and the Legal Services Commission (LSC) should have expedited her application for emergency funding for her to be represented. Legal representation might have also made a difference to the outcome which affected her family life by separating her from her children. Thus, her right to respect for family life under Art 8 was also affected by denial of representation.

Under the old law, a judge's failure to inform the respondent of his or her right to legal aid was a material irregularity which would lead to a committal order being quashed (*King v Read and Slack* [1999] 3 FLR 423). In the light of *Re K*, a court would be wise to inform the respondent of his or her right to apply for public funding under the AJA 1999 and the regulations made under that act.

Judges (including District Judges) have power to commit for contempt under:

(a) The CCA 1984, s 118—contempt in the face of the court—one month's imprisonment and/or a level 4 fine (the section is wide enough to protect witnesses on their way to or leaving court—*Manchester City Council v McCann* [1999] 2 WLR 590).

(b) The CCA 1984, s 14—assault on officer of the court in execution of his duty—three months' imprisonment and/or level 5 fine.

(c) The Attachment of Earnings Act 1971, s 23—14 days' imprisonment and/or level 2 fine.

(d) The Housing Act 1996, ss 152 and 153—breach of injunction to prevent antisocial conduct/breach of a tenancy term—two years' imprisonment and/or level 4 fine.

(e) The FLA 1996, Part IV—two years' imprisonment and/or level 4 fine.

In the case of a contempt in the face of the court, if the facts are not in dispute there is no objection to the judge before whom the contempt took place making findings regarding the contempt. Although the principle that a judge should not be a judge in his own cause does not apply as the purpose of the jurisdiction is to protect the administration of justice, not the judge personally, it is often sensible for the matter to be referred to another judge to forestall any appearance of bias (*R v Murray* [2006] 150 SJ 1191 and see below: (*Re G (Contempt Proceedings)* [2003] Fam Law 471)).

In any other case where the court has the power to commit a person for contempt of court and no limitation applies to the period of committal, the committal must be for a fixed term. The maximum sentence in the High Court and County court is two years' imprisonment; in the magistrates' court one month (Contempt of Court Act 1981, s 14).

Alternatively the High Court or County court may impose a fine. There is no limit on the amount.

The court may sequester the contemnor's assets (see *Hale v Tanner* [2000] 2 FLR 879).

In the High Court and County court the court may make a hospital order, a guardianship order or an interim hospital order under the Mental Health Act 1983, ss 37 or 38 where the person is suffering from mental illness or severe mental impairment (Contempt of Court Act 1981, s 14(4)). A person may be remanded for a report of his mental condition where it is suspected that he is suffering from mental illness or severe mental impairment.

In respect of persons between the ages of 18 and 21 years, any sentence of committal must be served in a Young Offenders' Institution (see Criminal Justice Act 1982, s 9(1), and *Re H (Respondent under 18; Power of Arrest)* [2001] 1 FLR 641.)

There is, theoretically, power to sentence a person between the ages of 18 and 21 to an attendance centre order. However before such an order is made, the Minister of Justice must notify the court that such a centre is available. At present no such notification has been given.

A person under the age of 18 may be fined, subject to his means. He may also be made the subject of orders under the Mental Health Act 1983 (see s 14(4) above). In any other circumstances he may not be detained (see Criminal Justice Act 1982, s 9(1); and *Re H (Respondent under 18; Power of Arrest)* [2001] 1 FLR 641.)

There is a distinction between a case where a party to proceedings is alleged to have been in breach of an order of the court made in the proceedings, and one where a party has done something that, although not in breach of a specific order is, nevertheless, a contempt of court. In the latter case, there may be more than one way of dealing with it. If the breach is admitted, a warning, together if necessary with a specific undertaking or injunction in terms to prevent a recurrence of the breach, may be sufficient.

A committal order, even if suspended, is a last resort normally reserved for serious, intentional, and in most cases, repeated contempts of court that have been established by due process. If the contempt is not admitted and is sufficiently serious and culpable for a court to contemplate a committal order, due process is obligatory. Nearly all contempt proceedings require adjournment to a separate hearing, often to a different judge. An adjournment would be necessary if the first judge had heard evidence from a party alleged to be in contempt, that he or she would not be obliged to give for risk of self-incrimination if he or she were faced with an allegation of contempt (*Re G (Contempt Proceedings)* [2003] Fam Law 471).

13.1.5 Sentencing powers

Upon finding a contempt has been proved, whether by evidence or admission, the court has a range of powers. For a brief summary, see *Hale v Tanner* [2000] 2 FLR 879, CA. When considering the length of any sentences of imprisonment for contempt due regard must be had to the maximum allowable for the contempt under the provisions mentioned in the previous section. In one case a person who was over 18 but under 21 was found to be in breach of an order which had excluded him from a specified area. The Court of Appeal allowed his appeal against a sentence of two years' detention because the maximum sentence must be reserved for the worst case, and in any event the sentence was excessive (*Turnbull v Middlesbrough Borough Council* [2003] EWCA Civ 1327.)

The objective of a judge sentencing for breach of an injunction is to uphold the authority of the court, and not simply to punish the offence itself. Nonetheless where sentences were passed for breaches of an order under FLA 1996, Part IV, the Court of Appeal held that they should generally be kept in line with penalties imposed for similar misconduct under the PHA 1997, albeit that the latter were charged as criminal offences (*Lomas v Parle* [2004] 1 All ER 1173). It is appropriate that the approach in sentencing for contempt for non-compliance with an order should take into account criminal sentencing cases. Although the maxima are different in contempt proceedings, guidance given for sentencers in criminal proceedings in Criminal Justice Act 2003, ss 142–144 should be taken into consideration. These, in summary, set out the purposes of sentencing in criminal cases (punishment; reduction of crime, reform and rehabilitation, public protection and reparation); the means of determining the seriousness of the offence (regard being had to the offender's culpability, the degree of harm done by him, his previous record); any acceptance of responsibility and at what stage such acceptance was expressed).

The disposal must be proportionate to the seriousness of the contempt, reflect the courts' disapproval and be designed to secure compliance in future. The principle of proportionality between the seriousness of the contempt and the rigour of the punishment presumes a process of graduated sentences. The court must ask itself whether the contempt is so serious that only a sentence of imprisonment could be justified. If it is not, then imprisonment will be wrong in principle. Thus a suspended sentence should not be imposed unless, but for the special factors justifying suspension, immediate imprisonment would have been appropriate. It should not be imposed merely because the contemnor cannot afford to pay a fine (see *Re M (Contact Order)*, Court of Appeal, The Times 18 April 2005. The court should briefly explain its reasons for the choice of disposal.

Where a first breach of an injunction is serious, an immediate committal to prison may be imposed and there is no principle that a first breach cannot result in a sentence of imprisonment: *Jordan v Jordan* [1993] 1 FLR 533, *Thorpe v Thorpe* [1998] 2 FLR 127. In an extreme case, a mother who prevents contact which is in the interests of a child may be sent to prison: *A v N (Committal: Refusal of Contact)* [1997] 1 FLR 533. However, all other remedies should be tried first: *Re M (Contact Order: Committal)* [1999] 1 FLR 810. In children cases the welfare of the child is not the paramount consideration in deciding whether a contemnor should be committed to prison. The objective is to uphold the authority of the court. If its authority is undermined any orders it makes in the best interest of children will not serve their purpose. Thus where a mother had flouted contact orders, failed to attend the court and had abused the court with obscenities, a sentence of 7 day's imprisonment suspended on terms, was fully justified (*Re S (Contact Order: Committal)* [2005] 1 FLR 812.)

Where there has been a really substantial error leading to a demonstrable injustice to the victim of a contempt, the Court of Appeal can allow an appeal by the claimant and increase the sentence: *Manchester County Council v Worthington* [2000] 1 FLR 411; *Wilson v Webster* [1998] 1 FLR 1097, CA. A contemnor contemplating an appeal should be warned that the sentence can be increased. There is no jurisdiction to release a contemnor on his or her application to purge his or her contempt by suspending the unserved balance of the prison sentence: *Harris v Harris* [2002] 1 FLR 248. The level of sentencing for contempt of court in connection with domestic violence had increased in recent times to reflect the needs of contemporary society. Sentences should not be manifestly discrepant with those passed in the criminal courts for like offences. Thus where a father had assaulted his children's grandmother and uncle in front of the children which had resulted in a non-molestation order being made, four further incidents of verbal abuse, intimidation including one of violence where he grabbed the grandmother by the throat and forced her onto the bonnet of a car merited a sentence of nine months' imprisonment (*H v O (Contempt of Court: Sentencing)* [2005] 2 FLR 329).

Although an attack on a judge in court would be treated as serious contempt in the face of the court, in exceptional circumstances prison may not be justified. The Court of Appeal allowed an appeal against sentence *four days after the contemnor had completed the sentence*. He was understandably upset and frustrated by the way in which he had been treated. He interrupted proceedings being conducted by the judge who had sentenced him, throwing eggs and shouting out passages from the Court of Appeal's judgment in his case. While his behaviour was a deplorable affront to the dignity of the court, the reality of the situation could not be ignored. His sentence for his contempt in the face of the court was reduced from two months to 28 days (*Hammerton v Mammerton (No 2)* [2007] EWCA Civ 465).

13.1.6   The Domestic Violence, Crime and Victims Act 2004

Hitherto it was possible for there to be parallel criminal proceedings relating to the same facts as were the subject of the contempt proceedings. This led to an unsatisfactory duplication of effort, and was wasteful of resources and was time consuming. It was stressful for the victim to have to go through two sets of proceedings. As sentence in the contempt proceedings needed not to be delayed to await decisions in the concurrent criminal proceedings (*pace: Smith v Smith* [1991] 2 FLR 55), from the respondent's point of view he suffered a double jeopardy. In one case, where the husband had been prosecuted, convicted and sentenced in the criminal courts under the PHA 1997 and in proceedings in the County court for breach of orders under FLA 1996, the sentence for contempt had to be reduced to reflect the criminal sentencing (see *Lomas v Parle*) [2004] 1 FLR 812.

This anomaly has now been remedied by The Domestic Violence, Crime and Victims Act 2004 which has inserted a new s 42A FLA 1996. This provides that where a person, without reasonable excuse, does anything that he is prohibited from doing by a non-molestation order he is guilty of an offence (s 42A(1)).

Where a person is convicted of an offence under s 42A in respect of any conduct, that conduct will not be punishable as a contempt of court (s 42A(3)). Equally, where a person has been punished for conduct as a contempt of court, he cannot be convicted for an offence under s 42A in respect of that conduct (s 42A (4)).

The maximum sentence on indictment will be five years' imprisonment; after summary trial, 12 months (s 42A). Breach of a non-molestation order may be disposed of either as a crime under s 42A or as a contempt pursuant to arrest by warrant or the notice to show cause procedure (using form N78) under CCR, Ord 29 (see below at **13.4.1**)

The non-molestation order may have been made ex parte. Where this has occurred, to bring criminal or contempt proceedings, there must be proof that the order was brought to the attention of the Respondent.

Under the PHA 1997 duplicated punishments from both contempt of court and an offence under the Act for breach of an injunction granted under s 3(3)(a) in civil proceedings are excluded (s 3(7) and (8)).

The Act came into force on 1 July 2007. The principle procedural changes is that although a breach of an order remains a contempt of court, the court may no longer attach a power of arrest to a non-molestation order made under FLA 1996, s 42. Occupation Orders made under ss 33 to 38 will have an existing penal notice endorsed and may have a power of arrest attached. Orders made under s 42 will have endorsed on them a modified penal notice alerting the respondent to the new criminal offence and sanctions, but without any power of arrest. The new forms and procedures have been introduced by the Family Proceedings (Amendment) Rules 2007 and the Family Proceedings Courts (Matrimonial Proceedings etc) (Amendment) Rules 2007. Rules 3.9 and 3.9A which relate to the hearing of applications and enforcement of orders made under FLA 1996, Part IV have been amended accordingly.

It is important to remember that separate orders must now be drawn using form FL 404 for occupation orders and FL 404a for non-molestation orders.

As one of the possible consequences of breach of an order may be a criminal conviction, the question has arisen as to whether the standard of proof required when making the original order should be the criminal standard. It has been held that applications for Anti Social Behaviour Orders in civil proceedings should be determined applying the criminal standard because applications involve allegations of criminal conduct, and the serious consequences of breach (*Manchester CC v McCann* [2002] 4 All ER 593 (HL)). However as nothing in the FLA 1996 as amended expressly alters the standard of proof, it is probably still the civil standard that applies.

A problem arises from the overlap between FLA 1996, ss 33–38 and s 42. The former sections enable the court to make occupation orders which may still be enforced with a power of arrest. These provisions permit a court to exclude a respondent from a defined area in which the dwelling-house occupied by the applicant is included (see s 33(3)(g); s 35(5)(d), s 37(2)(d) and 38(3)(d)). An order to the same effect can also be made under s 42 to prevent molestation. Thus it is still possible for an individual to be both prosecuted under s 42A and made the subject of contempt proceedings for breach of order made under ss 33–38 for same infraction. It is submitted that should such an occasion arise the court must ensure that the wrongdoer is not punished twice over for the same wrong (following May LJ in *H v O* [2005] 2 FLR 329 at 338.)

This overlap in the jurisdiction conferred by ss 33–38 and s 42 makes it all the more important to ensure that the order made is drawn up using the correct form. Errors could result in a criminal sanction being imposed for breach when this never intended to be the means of enforcement.

A further problem may result from the contrast between wording of s 33(1) and (3)(g) of the Act, and in ss 35–38. Section 33(1) defines the term 'dwelling-house' as used in the section as the place which 'is or at any time has been the home of the person entitled and of another person with whom he is associated' or 'was at any time intended by the person entitled and any other such person to be their home'.

It will be immediately obvious that the phrases 'another person' and 'any other person' are wide enough to include any associated person (as defined by s 62(3) of the Act) and not just the respondent.

It follows that if the applicant has fled the former matrimonial home with her children to escape the respondent's violence, and has obtained a tenancy for them all elsewhere, the new address would appear to be covered by the section as well as the matrimonial home. The applicant would inevitably wish for the respondent to be excluded from an area around the new address. This would be possible, on the literal wording of s 33(1) and s 33(3)(g).

In contrast s 35 is confined, in cases of former spouses or civil partners, to dwelling-houses which were at any time their matrimonial/civil partnership home. Section 36 in cases of cohabitants and former cohabitants is confined to dwelling-houses in which they cohabit, have cohabited or intended to cohabit. Sections 37 and 38 relates to a dwelling-house which neither party is entitled to remain in occupation (for example where they are licensees or squatters) is confined respectively to the matrimonial/civil partnership home or the home in which the parties cohabited. Thus the area of the possible exclusion zone must be defined geographically around that dwelling-house and nowhere else. Hence the scope of these provisions is narrower than under s 33(3)(g). If a person who cannot bring themselves within s 33 requires an exclusion zone around a dwelling-house which was not the home in which she dwells, dwelled or intended to dwell with the respondent, he/she must apply under s 42.

Where the protection of the applicant requires the exclusion of the respondent from a specified area around the family home, it is likely that many applicants will prefer to opt for orders under ss 33–38 rather than s 42 on the grounds that while they require protection from a former partner or spouse, they may have no wish to run the risk of criminalising him,. This may be especially so if he is still the main financial provider and has as a continuing relationship with the children of the parties.

13.2 Checklist 1: preparing an application for committal for disobedience of an injunctive order or breach of an undertaking

13.2.1 Form of injunctive order or document recording an undertaking

(1) Was the order one which the court had jurisdiction to make?

If made in proceedings other than family proceedings, does the order support a legal right, eg, forbid a recognised tort or harassment within the PHA 1997, s 1, or protect a legal or equitable interest?

If made in family proceedings (under FLA 1996, Part IV, CA 1989, matrimonial proceedings begun by petition, or under the inherent jurisdiction of the High Court), was the order available as a non-molestation or occupation order? Or was the order available for the protection of family property? The High Court has further injunctive powers under the inherent jurisdiction.

An injunctive order or an undertaking must be obeyed, even if it is irregular, until it is discharged, but want of jurisdiction may affect the conduct of an application to commit and/or the approach to sentence for a contempt.

(2) Was the instruction to the other party, or the undertaking, precise and explicit as to what the person was required to do or abstain from doing? (See CPR, PD 25 (Interim Injunctions), para 5.3.)

And, if the doing of an act was required, did the injunctive order specify when or by when the act was to be done, as required by RSC Ord 42, r 2(1), CCR Ord 22, r 3 or FPC(MP)R 1991, r 20(6)(b); or did the undertaking specify when or by when the act was to be done?

(3)(a) In the case of an injunctive order:

(i) In the High Court, was there 'prominently displayed on the front', of the copy of the order for service, a warning (penal) notice, as required by RSC Ord 45, r 7(4) and CPR, PD 40B, para 9.1?

Note: In the High Court the party wishing to have the penal notice endorsed on the order must do so himself (RSC Ord 45, r 7).

(ii) In a County court, was the injunctive order issued with a penal notice endorsed or incorporated, as required by CCR Ord 29, r 1(3) or FPR 1991, r 3.9A(5) and CPR, PD 40B, para 9.1; was it issued in prescribed Form FL404 or N16 or N138 or with Form N77 endorsed or incorporated?

Note: a warning (penal) notice cannot be endorsed on or incorporated in an order under the CA 1989, s 8 unless a judge has so directed: FPR 1991, r 4.21A.

Note: (i) In the County court the penal notice is endorsed by an officer of the court. It s a mandatory requirement, but carried out as a purely administrative functions (CCR Ord 29, r 1(3) and *R v Wandsworth County Court ex p Munn* (1994) 26 HLR 697).

(iii) In a family proceedings court, was the injunctive order issued in Form FL404 or was it issued with a penal notice endorsed or incorporated, as required by FPC(MP)R 1991, r 20(7)?

(b) In the case of an undertaking:

(i) In the High Court or a County court, was the undertaking recorded in an order or form of undertaking in which a penal notice was incorporated or endorsed in accordance with CPR, PD 40B, paras 9.2 and 9.3, and in a County court as required by CCR Ord 29, r 1A? Also, was it acknowledged by signature of the giver upon the direction of the court under CPR, PD 40B, paras 9.3 and 9.4? In a County court, Form N117 should be used and, in the Family Division, practice form D787.

(ii) In a family proceedings court, was the undertaking recorded in Form FL422, as required by FPC(MP)R 1991, r 20(14)?

13.2.2 Service of injunctive order or record of undertaking

(1)(a) In the case of an injunctive order:

(i) Was personal service of the order, with a warning or penal notice prominently displayed on the front **(High Court)** or endorsed on it or incorporated in it **(County or family proceedings court)**, effected?

Personal service is required by RSC Ord 45, r 7(2), CCR Ord 29, r 1(2) or FPC (MP) R 1991, r 20(11) unless (i) the order recites that personal service was dispensed with, or (ii) the terms of the order are only prohibitory, and do not require an act to be done and, pending service, have been communicated to the other party.

(ii) If the injunctive order required the other party to do an act, was the injunctive order served personally before the expiration of the time within which he or she was to do the act, as required by RSC Ord 45, r 7(2)(b), CCR Ord 29, r 1(2)(b) or FPC(MP)R 1991, r 20(6)(b)?

Note *Davy International Ltd v Tazzyman* [1997] 3 All ER 183 and *Jolly v Hull; Jolly v Jolly* [2000] 2 FLR 69, as to the powers to dispense with service of the order at the hearing of a committal application, under RSC Ord 45, r 7(7) and CCR Ord 29, r 1(7).

(iii) If served, is personal service proved?

Proof is usually by affidavit of service in judge courts and by Form FL415 in family proceedings courts.

(b) In the case of an undertaking:

(i) Was the Form FL422, D787 or N117 or the order recording the undertaking delivered to or served on the giver of the undertaking?

Personal service of a document recording an undertaking is not necessary to render the undertaking enforceable because it is the giving of the undertaking which makes it effective (see *Hussain v Hussain* [1986] Fam 134). However, unless either the giver of the undertaking signed the Form FL422, D787 or N117 or the court papers, or a document recording the undertaking was delivered to or served upon the giver, difficulties may arise on an application to commit (see *Hussain v Hussain* (above) at pp 140 and 142).

In a County court, CCR Ord 29, r 1A requires delivery by the court, to be recorded on the back of Form N117, or alternatively personal service is required. FPC(MP)R 1991, r 20(14) is to like effect.

13.2.3   Form of the application to commit and the requirement of an affidavit or statement in support

(1)(a) **In civil proceedings in the High Court and County courts, does the Claim Form N208 or Application Notice N244 give the essential information to the respondent and to the court?**

There is no separate prescribed form specific to committal applications. The prescribed requirements are in Practice Direction—Committal Applications, paras 2.2, 2.5 and 2.6. County court Form N78 is a useful guide.

(b) **In family proceedings, does the summons in the Family Division (FPR 1991, r 7.2(1)), or the Form N78 in a County court, or the form FL244 in a family proceedings court, give the essential information to the respondent and the court?**

In particular (all courts: Practice Direction—Committal Applications, paras 2.5–2.6, CCR Ord 29, r 1(4A), FPC(MP)R 1991, r 20(9)).

(i) Does the application accurately identify the terms of the injunctive order or undertaking of which breach is alleged (CCR Ord 29, r 1(4A))?

(ii) Does the application 'list' (CCR Ord 29, r 1(4A)) or 'identify', separately and numerically, each alleged act of contempt (Practice Direction—Committal Applications, paras 2.5 to 2.6)?

(iii) Does the application clearly inform the respondent when and where he or she must attend to show reason why he or she should not be sent to prison?

The ways in which the party alleged to be in contempt is alleged to have committed the contempt(s) *must* be sufficiently clear to inform him or her what case he or she has to meet.

(2) Is the application supported by an affidavit as required by RSC Ord 52, r 4(1) and Practice Direction—Committal Applications, paras 2.5 to 2.6 and 3.1 or CCR Ord 29, r 1(4A) or a statement signed and declared to be true as required by FPC(MP)R 1991, r 20(9)(c)?

13.2.4 Service of the application to commit and the affidavit or statement in support

(1) Is personal service of the application and the affidavit or statement proved (in judge courts usually by an affidavit of service, in family proceedings courts by Form FL415) **as required by RSC Ord 52, r 4(2), Practice Direction—Committal Applications, paras 2.5 to 2.6, CCR Ord 29, r 1(4) or FPC(MP)R 1991, r 20(8) (9) unless the court has dispensed with service under RSC Ord 52, r 4(3), CCR Ord 29, r 1(7) or FPC(MP)R 1991, r 20(12), or has provided for substituted service under RSC Ord 65, r 4(2), CCR Ord 13, r 4(1) (substituted service is not available in magistrates' courts)?**

(2)(a) In family proceedings, was personal service achieved at least two days, not counting Saturdays, Sundays or bank holidays, before the hearing, as required by RSC Ord 8, r 2(2), or at least two court office business days as required by CCR Ord 13, r 1(2) and Ord 1, r 9(4), FPC(MP)R 1991, r 3A(5) unless the court has abridged time under RSC Ord 3, r 5(1), CCR Ord 13, r 4(1) or FPC(MP)R 1991, r 3A(6)?

(b) In civil proceedings, was personal service achieved at least 14 days before the hearing unless the court has directed otherwise (Practice Direction—Committal Applications, para 4.2)?

The Court of Appeal has emphasised the need for the County court to pay particular attention to the requirement that the hearing of the application should not be less than 14 days after service (*Turnbull v N Middlesbrough BC* [2003] EWCA Civ 1327).

13.2.5 Evidence

(1) Is there sufficient evidence to prove, to the criminal standard of proof, the alleged contempt(s)?

(2) Is/are the witness(es) relied on available for cross-examination?

13.3   Checklist 2: Preparing for hearing following an arrest under a power or a warrant of arrest granted under s 47 of the FLA 1996 or arrest under a warrant of arrest granted under PHA 1997, s 3

13.3.1   Introduction: summary committal following arrest

Some practitioners and judges consider that upon production in court of an arrested alleged contemnor it is good practice to adjourn, to remand the respondent if the arrest was under the FLA 1996, s 47, and to expect the applicant to issue an application for committal. However, the FPR 1991, r 3.9A(4) specifically authorises the established practice that when a person is brought before the court following an arrest under the FLA 1996, s 47, the court 'may (a) determine whether the facts, and the circumstances which led to the arrest, amounted to disobedience of the order, or (b) adjourn the proceedings...' RSC Ord 94, r 16(5)(a) specifically authorises summary trial in the case of an arrest under the PHA 1997, s 3. Form N79, for recording a finding of contempt, specifically provides for proceeding on the basis of the respondent being before the court upon an arrest without there having been served an application for committal in Form N78, in the case of an arrest under FLA 1996, s 47, or in a claim form, in the case of an arrest on a warrant under the PHA 1997, s 3(5).

Where a person is arrested under either the FLA 1996, s 47 or the PHA 1997, s 3, and is brought before the court within the powers under the Acts, and there is sufficient evidence to proceed with a summary trial, and the arrested person is able to put his case adequately before the court, there clearly is power to proceed forthwith, without requiring preparation or service of a form of committal application. Further, there is no power to remand under the PHA 1997. Where the court does proceed forthwith without a form of committal application being prepared, the arrested person is before the court only for the matter upon which he or she has been arrested, previous alleged contempts are not before the court, and the court must be clear about what the circumstances of the arrest and alleged contempt are. Summary disposal in this way is convenient particularly where the respondent admits the contempt. Where he or she denies the alleged contempt, and he or she may need witnesses to support his or her denial, an adjournment will be appropriate.

13.3.2   Form of injunctive order

(1) Was the order one to which the court had power to attach a power of arrest under the FLA 1996, s 47? (There is no power under the PHA 1997 to attach a power of arrest.)

Section 47(1), Family Law Act 1996, which enabled power of arrest to be conferred for breaches of non-molestation orders made under the FLA 1996 has been repealed (Domestic Violence, Crime and Victims Act 2004 (DVCVA 2004), Sch 10, para 38).

A power of arrest remains available in respect of breaches of occupation orders made under the 1996 Act. A copy of the order containing the power of arrest must be delivered to a police station in Form 406 (r 3.9A(1), FPR 1991).

Where both a non-molestation order and an occupation order have been made, care must be taken to distinguish between them. Thus if an order prohibited a respondent from harassing the applicant by entering or going within 50 metres of her address then, although it may have been intended to have the same effect as an order simply prohibiting entry or attempted entry into the premises, its *form* is that of a non-molestation order made under FLA 1996, s 42(6), and a power of arrest cannot be attached to it.

In other words, was there evidence on which the court which granted the power could have concluded that the respondent had used or threatened violence against the applicant or a relevant child? If not, the arrest was unlawful and the respondent must be released.

In the case of arrest under a power of arrest, the 'relevant provisions', ie, the arrestable provisions and no other clauses of the injunctive order, should have been delivered to the appropriate police station in prescribed Form FL406: FPR 1991, r 3.9A(1), FPC(MP)R 1991, r 20(1).

A power of arrest cannot be attached to an undertaking: FLA 1996, s 46(2); it must be an order, non-molestation or occupation.

(2) If the arrest was under a warrant of arrest, were there injunctive non-molestation or occupation provisions available as the foundation for a warrant, ie, provisions to which no power of arrest had been attached?

(3) Has the warrant been properly issued?

Warrants of arrest are still available for breaches of non-molestation and occupation orders (FLA 1996, s 47(8), as amended by DVCVA 2004, Sch 10, para 38.

The warrant must be substantiated on oath (FLA 1996, s 47(9)). The application for the warrant must be made in form FL407. The warrant must be in form FL408.

(4) If the warrant is sought for breach of an undertaking, was the undertaking properly received by the court?

Undertakings can no longer be accepted without enquiry by the court. This will require a hearing and, presumably, a finding. Thus, if a person denies the allegations of the applicant, but offers an undertaking, the court may not be able to accept it without hearing evidence and making a finding of fact against the respondent. This appears to be the effect of an amendment to FLA 1996, s 46 (DVCVA 2004, Sch 10, para 37). Section 3A has been inserted to provide that:

The court shall not accept an undertaking under s 46(1) (which allows undertaking to be given both in respect of non-molestation and occupation of premises) instead of making a non-molestation order in any case where it appears to the court that—

(a) *the respondent has used or threatened violence against the applicant or a relevant child; and*

(b) *for the protection of the applicant or child it is necessary to make an order so that any breach may be punishable under s 42A.*

An undertaking is enforceable to the same extent and in the same way as an occupation or non-molestation order (s 46(4)).

13.3.3 Service of the injunctive order

(1)(a) Is personal service proved, as required by RSC Ord 45, r (7)2(a), CCR Ord 29, r 1(2)(a) or FPC(MP)R 1991, r 20(6)?

Proof is usually by affidavit of service in judge courts and by Form FL415 in family proceedings courts. Note powers to dispense with service under RSC Ord 45, r 7(7) and CCR Ord 29, r 1(7) and see *Davy International Ltd v Tazzyman* [1997] 3 All ER 183 and *Jolly v Hull; Jolly v Jolly* [2000] 2 FLR 69. Where a respondent has been repeatedly required to comply with an order, it is unreal to argue that waiver of the requirement for service of further orders for compliance is in any sense 'retrospective'. To allow otherwise would be tantamount to encouraging persistent offenders to rely on technicalities to evade liability for contempt (*Benson v Richards* [2002] EWCA Civ 1402).

Or:

(b) **Was the arrested person aware of the terms of the injunctive order either by being present when it was granted or by being notified of its terms?**

If so, under RSC Ord 45, r 7(6), CCR Ord 29, r 1(6) or FPC(MP)R 1991, r 20(11) he or she may be dealt with for the matter for which he or she was arrested if it was something he or she was forbidden to do. The arrested person cannot be dealt with unless he or she was aware of the terms, because contempt involves disobedience and unless the respondent was aware of the terms he or she cannot be guilty of contempt.

13.3.4 The arrest

(1) **In the case of arrest under a power of arrest under the FLA 1996, s 47(6):**

(a) **Was the operative period of the power of arrest, as recited in the injunction and prescribed Form FL406, still running at the time of the arrest?**

(b) **Was the arrest by a constable who had 'reasonable cause for suspecting' the arrested person of being in breach of a provision of injunctive order to which the power of arrest was attached (FLA 1996, s 47(6))?**

If not, the arrest was unlawful and the arrested person must be released.

(2) **In the case of arrest under a warrant of arrest under the FLA 1996, s 47(8), (9):**

(a) **Were there injunctive non-molestation or occupation provisions available as the foundation for a warrant, ie, provisions to which a power of arrest had not been attached? and**

(b) **Was there evidence on oath before the court which granted the warrant on which it could have had reasonable grounds for believing that the respondent had failed to comply with the injunctive order or the undertaking?**

Note that there is doubt as to whether a warrant can be granted for breach of an undertaking given in proceedings under the FLA 1996, Part IV.

In the case of a warrant of arrest under the PHA 1997, s 3(3) (5), was there evidence on oath before the court which granted the warrant on which it could have had reasonable grounds for believing that the defendant had failed to comply with the injunction?

Note that a warrant cannot be granted for breach of an undertaking in proceedings under the PHA 1997.

13.3.5 The hearing

(1) **In the case of arrest under a power of arrest under the FLA 1996, s 47(6), will the hearing before the judge begin within the period of 24 hours beginning at the time of the arrest (no account being taken of Christmas Day, Good Friday or any Sunday) as required by the FLA 1996, s 47(7)(a)?**

If not, the proceedings are *ultra vires*, there being no power to detain the arrested person beyond the statutory period, and the arrested person must be released.

However, the court may remand the arrested person (FLA 1996, s 47(7)(b)) and adjourn the hearing to be resumed within 14 days of the arrest: FPR 1991, r 3.9A(4)(b)(i), FPC(MP)R 1991, r 20(4)(b)(i). If the court does adjourn the hearing, the arrested person may be remanded (s 47(7)(b)) or released (FPR 1991, r 3.9A(4)(b), FPC(MP)R 1991, r 20(4)(b)); where the court does adjourn, the arrested person must be dealt with within 14 days of the day on which he or she was arrested, whether by the same or another judge, and the person must be given not less than two days' notice of the adjourned hearing (FPR 1991, r 3.9A(4)(b)(ii), FPC(MP)R 1991, r 20(4)(b)(ii)). Personal service of the notice of the adjourned hearing should be effected, unless the arrested person was given notice before being released (see *Chiltern DC v Keane* [1985] 1 WLR 619 at p 622A).

If the arrested person is not dealt with within 14 days, FPR 1991, r 3.9A(4), FPC(MP)R 1991, r 20(4) permit the other party to request the issue of Notice to Show Good Reason under CCR Ord 29, r 1(4) or FPC(MP)R 1991, r 20(8).

(2) **Following any arrest, is there sufficient evidence to prove, to the criminal standard of proof, the alleged contempt?**

13.4 Checklist 3: conduct of hearing of application for committal or following arrest under a power or warrant of arrest

13.4.1 Preliminary requirements

(1)(a) **If the application is made** (civil proceedings) **by Claim Form N208 or Application Notice N244 or** (High Court Family Division) **by summons or issued** (County court) **in Form N78 or** (family proceedings court) **in Form FL418, is breach of a specific, explicit (not implied) direction in an injunctive order or a promise in an undertaking alleged? And has the notice of application been served personally on the alleged comtemnor (RSC Ord 52, r 4(2), CCR Ord 29, r 1(4), PD Committal Applications, paras 2.5 and 2.6, FPC(MP)R 1991, r 20(8) (9)) two clear or office days before the hearing in family proceedings (RSC Ord 8, r 2(2), CCR Ord 13, r 2(2), CCR Ord 13, r 1(2) and Ord 1, r 9(4), FPC(MP)R 1991, r 3A(5), or 14 days before the hearing in proceedings under CPR (PD Committal Applications, para 4.2)?**

(b) **Or, if the respondent has been arrested upon a power of arrest or warrant of arrest and brought before the court, was he or she arrested for an arrestable disobedience and, where arrested under a power of arrest, has the hearing begun within 24 hours of the arrest?**

And, *should the hearing proceed or should an adjournment be allowed to enable the case and evidence to be prepared?* FPR 1991, r 3.9A(4) and FPC(MP)R 1991, r 20(4) (and, under the PHA 1997, CCR Ord 49, r 15A(7)) allow the court to deal forthwith with the matter upon which the respondent was arrested without service on him or her of a Notice to Show Good Reason or dispensation with this under CCR Ord 29, r 1(7) or FPC (MP) R 1991, r 20(12). Alternatively, the court may adjourn proceedings for not more than 14 days. In proceedings under the FLA 1996 there is a general power to remand in s 47(7)(b) and (10) and power to remand for a medical report under s 48. There is no power to remand under the PHA 1997.

(2) **Was the respondent a party in the proceedings to whom the injunctive direction was ordered?**

With few exceptions, an injunctive order cannot be made against someone who is not a party. Quaere whether a non-party can give an undertaking without becoming a party.

(3) **Was the injunctive order (with a warning notice prominently displayed on the front (High Court) or penal notice endorsed or incorporated (County or family proceedings court)) personally served or, if it was prohibitory (not mandatory), was the respondent present when the order was made, or has he or she been notified of it?** (RSC Ord 45, r 7(6), CCR Ord 29, r 1(6), FPC(MP)R 1991, r 20(11).)

Or, was the undertaking recorded in County court Form N117, Principal Registry Form D787 or family proceedings court Form FL422 or, in the Chancery or Queen's Bench Divisions of the High Court, in a document in which the giver signed a statement to the effect that he or she understood the terms of his or her undertaking and the consequences of failure to comply with it in accordance with CPR, PD 40B, paras 9.3 and 9.4? *Was that document delivered to or served on or acknowledged by signature of the respondent?*

(4) **Was the direction or promise either:**

(a) **To do a specified act or specified acts at or before a specified time?**

If so, is the act one which the court has power to enforce by committal proceedings? Committal for contempt is not available, for example, to enforce payment of a money judgment (except where judgment summons is still available; see *Nwogbe v Nwogbe* [2000] 2 FLR 744 (CA)), or a declaratory order such as a defined pattern of contact with a child. *Also, was the order served before the time specified in the order for the act to be done, as required by RSC Ord 42, r 2(1), CCR Ord 22, r 3 or FPC(MP)R 1991, r 20(5)(b)?* Or

(b) **To abstain from doing a specified act or acts?**

Note the powers to dispense with service under RSC Ord 45, r 7(6) (7) and CCR Ord 29, r 1(6) (7) and see *Davy International Ltd v Tazzyman* [1997] 3 All ER 183 and *Jolly v Hull; Jolly v Jolly* [2000] 2 FLR 69.

(5) **In the case of arrest under a warrant of arrest granted under the PHA 1997, s 3(5), has the person arrested already been convicted of an offence in respect of the alleged contempt?**

If so, he or she cannot be punished in contempt proceedings: s 3(7).

13.4.2 Trial procedure

PRELIMINARY PROCEDURAL POINTS

(1) Is the court following normal criminal procedure?

If the court is embarking on a re-hearing after a previous hearing in the absence of the respondent, either because the court dispensed with service of notice on him or her or the court accepts that his absence was not his or her fault, the entire procedure must be followed. No short cuts. Note that on a review on notice of a committal ordered in the absence of the respondent, the sentence cannot be increased.

(2) **In the case of proceedings under the FLA 1996, should the court remand, before or after deciding whether the contempt(s) is (are) proved, for a medical report under the FLA 1996, s 48?**

(3) **If the respondent is not legally represented, should a solicitor within the precincts of the court be invited to represent the respondent under the Assistance By Way Of Representation scheme?**

(Regulation 8 of the Legal Advice and Assistance (Scope) Regulations 1989, SI 1989/550; reg 7, ABWOR representation might, by amendment to the Schedule, art 2(b), become available in family proceedings courts.) (Legal aid under the Legal Aid Act 1988, s 29 is **not** available for a person answering an allegation or breach of an injunction or undertaking.) See also *Re K* (*Contact: Committal Order*) [2003] 1 FLR 277.

CONDUCT OF HEARING

(1) **In civil proceedings under CPR, Part 8 and Practice Direction—Committal Applications, has the respondent filed affidavits giving any evidence in opposition to the committal application (Practice Direction—Committal Applications, paras 3.1 and 3.2)? But the respondent does not need permission to adduce oral evidence if he or she has not filed affidavits (Practice Direction—Committal Applications, paras 3.3 and 3.4).**

In family proceedings also it is good practice to file affidavits in opposition to a committal application.

(2) **Amendment of the committal application can be permitted by the court (PD Committal Applications, para 2.6.3)).**

(3) **Does the respondent admit the allegation(s) and, if so, precisely what does he or she admit?**

The exact finding(s) of contempt will have to be recorded in the committal order (Form A85, High Court; Form N79, County court; Form FL419, family proceedings court). *Are the admissions adequate to enable the court to proceed to consideration of penalty without hearing evidence?*

(4) **Burden of proof on applicant.**

(5) **Normal sequence of evidence.**

Chief, affidavit or statement and/or oral; cross-examination; re-examination. Applicant and his or her witnesses first; respondent and his or her witnesses after. The alleged contemnor is not compellable as a witness at the instance of the applicant or the judge (*Comet Productions UK v Hawkex Plastics Ltd* [1971] 2 QB 67) and cannot be directed to give information (PD Committal Applications, paras 6 and 7).

The privilege against self-incrimination applies in civil contempt proceedings: *Memory Corp plc and another v Sidhu and another* [2000] 1 All ER 434.

(6) **Respondent entitled to submit 'no case'.**

(7) **Actus reus and mens rea must be proved.**

Mens rea is knowledge of the injunctive direction plus deliberate conduct which in fact is a breach. Not necessary to prove that the respondent understood the nature of the court's procedures provided he or she knew what was forbidden (*P v P* (*Contempt of Court: Mental Incapacity*) [1999] 2 FLR 897, CA).

(8) Criminal standard of proof.

(9) Contempt)(s) found proved must be specified and recorded in committal order. (Form A85, High Court; Form N79, County court; Form FL419, family proceedings court.)

(10) A finding of contempt should not be based on hearsay evidence.

(*R v Shokoya, The Times*, 10 June 1992; *Re B* (*A Minor*) (*Contempt: Evidence*) [1996] 1 WLR 627.)

The defendant is not obliged to give evidence—if he or she has been cross-examined in connected proceedings, he or she may invoke the privilege against self-incrimination to be tried for contempt by a different judge (see *Re G* (*Contempt Proceedings*) [2003] Fam Law 471).

13.4.3   Consideration of penalty

RANGE OF POWERS AND APPROPRIATE APPROACH TO CHOICE OF DISPOSAL

The disposal must be proportionate to the seriousness of the contempt, reflect the disapproval of the court and be designed to secure compliance in the future (*Hale v Tanner* [2000] 2 FLR 879, CA, where the range of powers is summarised).

1   **Does the contemnor wish to mitigate or attempt to purge his or her contempt?**

2   **In family cases, does the applicant wish to give his or her views?**

3   **Is the contemnor eligible for imprisonment being aged 21 or more, or eligible for detention being aged 18 or over and less than 21, or is no custodial sentence available the contemnor being aged less than 18?**

4   **If available, is an immediate custodial sentence the only appropriate disposal? What alternatives are available?**

Note that there is no principle that 'a first breach [of an injunction] cannot result in a sentence of imprisonment'. Where the disobedience of an injunction or undertaking is serious, an immediate custodial sentence may be imposed (*Jordan v Jordan* [1993] 1 FLR 169, *Thorpe v Thorpe* [1998] 2 FLR 127).

General guidance was given by Hale LJ in *Hale v Tanner* [2000] 2 FLR 879:

(a) Imprisonment was not an automatic response to a breach of an order, although there was no principle that imprisonment was not to be imposed on the first occasion.

(b) Although alternatives to imprisonment were limited, there were a number of things the court could consider—especially where no violence was involved.

(c) If imprisonment was appropriate, the length of the committal should be decided without reference to whether or not it should be suspended.

(d) The seriousness of the contempt had to be judged not only for its intrinsic gravity but also in the light of the court's objectives both to mark its disapproval of the disobedience to the order and to secure compliance in the future.

(e) The length of the committal should relate to the maximum available, ie, two years;

(f) Suspension was possible in a wider range of circumstances than in criminal cases, and was usually the first way of attempting to secure compliance with the order.

(g) The court had to consider whether the context was mitigating or aggravating, in particular where there was a breach of an intimate relationship and/or children were involved.

(h) The court should consider any concurrent proceedings in another court, and should explain to the contemnor the nature of the order and the consequence of breach.

Where a person has been convicted of an offence under FLA 1996, s 42A for any conduct, he cannot be punished for that conduct as a contempt of court; conversely he cannot be convicted of an offence in respect of any conduct which has been punished as a contempt of court (FLA 1996, ss 42A(3) and (4)).

Where the maximum sentence for a contempt is two years' imprisonment, that length of sentence should be reserved for the worst possible case. In determining the length of sentence, two years must therefore be regarded as at the top of the scale of seriousness, and the case in question must be dealt with accordingly.

In cases of serious violence, an immediate custodial sentence is almost inevitable (*Wilson v Webster* [1998] 1 FLR 1097; *Ticehurst v Ticehurst* (1996) 10 CL 204).

(5) What penalty should be imposed for each separate contempt found proved?

If more than one contempt, should penalties be consecutive or concurrent? Is the total appropriate? The maximum total imprisonment that can be imposed on one occasion is two years in a judge court, two months in a family proceedings court. Sentences can be consecutive, including an implemented suspended sentence, but the total cannot exceed the maximum of two years or two months.

(6) Should imprisonment (of contemnor aged 21 or more) be suspended or should consideration of penalty be adjourned with liberty to restore? If so:

(a) **For how long? and**

(b) **What conditions should be ordered to define the event(s) which would render the contemnor liable to implementation or imposition of a penalty?**

The period of suspension or adjournment should be fixed, but an indefinite suspension can be valid: *Griffin v Griffin* [2000] 2 FLR 44 (CA). The power to remand an arrested person under the FLA 1996, s 47(7) (10) is not available where the contemnor appeared in answer to a Notice to Show Good Reason, therefore the case law which established that sentence could not be deferred by remand in custody, after finding contempt proved, should still apply.

13.4.4 Preparation of the order of committal or other disposal

(1) **What should be recorded in the order of committal (Form A85, High Court; Form N79, County court; Form FL419, family proceedings court)? In particular:**

(a) **What precise findings of contempt? and**

(b) **What precise terms of disposal have been ordered?**

Form N79 or Form FL419 should be checked and initialled by the judge or the chairman or bench of justices.

(2) If an immediate custodial sentence is ordered, can the committal order be issued in time to be served when the respondent is detained upon the warrant of committal?

In a County court, CCR Ord 29, r 1(5)(a) requires that the committal order be served when the warrant is executed, unless the warrant is signed by the judge; if the judge signs the warrant, 36 hours is permitted for preparation and service of the committal order (Ord 29, r 1(5)(b)). FPC(MP)R 1991, r 20(10) permits the committal order to be served within 36 hours after execution of the warrant.

13.4.5 Appeal

Where there has been a really substantial error leading to a demonstrable injustice to the victim of a contempt, the Court of Appeal can allow an appeal by the claimant and increase the sentence: *Manchester County Council v Worthington* [2000] 1 FLR 411, CA; *Wilson v Webster* [1998] 1 FLR 1097, CA. A contemnor contemplating an appeal should be warned that a sentence imposed for contempt can be increased. A sentence for contempt for breach of an order under Family Law Act 1996, s 42 will not be increased on appeal unless it is shown to have been not merely lenient, but unduly lenient. Thus, where a husband subjected his estranged wife to 'an appalling history of intimidation and abuse' despite a series of proceedings taken against him under the PHA 1997 in the criminal courts, and under the FLA 1996 in the County court, the Court of Appeal regarded a sentence of 4 months' imprisonment as unduly lenient. A sentence of not less than 10 months was merited (*Lomas v Parle* [2004] 1 FLR 812).

The Court of Appeal has recently held that the level of sentencing for contempt associated with domestic violence in the older cases did not fully reflect contemporary requirements and opinion, which now demanded more condign deterrent punishments for such offences. Sentences in committal proceedings for breaches of injunctions under FLA 1996, s 42 should, so far as possible, reflect this range of opinion. The mere fact that a breach of a non-molestation order occurred in the context of a father wishing to have contact with his child was not in any way a mitigating factor; if anything, it was the reverse. As it was essential to have regard to the statutory maximum sentence of two years' imprisonment in Contempt of Court Act 1981, s 14. Subject to that caveat, sentences for breaches of injunction for harassment should not be discrepant with sentences for harassment under the PHA 1997. Similarly sentences for breaches involving violence or threats of violence should be congruent with sentences passed for similar conduct in the Crown Court. For an attack by a father on a grandmother involving verbal abuse, threats of violence, and physical assault by grasping her throat and forcing her onto the bonnet of a car, and three other instances of intimidation and abuse, a sentence of 9 months' imprisonment was held to be the right level for a man of previous good character (*H v O* [2005] 2 FLR 329).

APPENDIX A
PRACTICE DIRECTION (ANCILLARY RELIEF PROCEDURE) [2000] 1 FLR 997

Pre-application protocol

1 Introduction

1.1

1.1.1 Lord Woolf in his final Access to Justice Report of July 1996 recommended the development of pre-application protocols:

> to build on and increase the benefits of early but well informed settlement which genuinely satisfy both parties to dispute.

1.1.2 In April 2000 the Lord Chancellor's Ancillary Relief Advisory Committee recommended that there be a Protocol for ancillary relief applications and this recommendation has been accepted by the Lord Chancellor.

1.2 The aim of the pre-application protocol is to ensure that:
   (a) Pre-application disclosure and negotiation takes place in appropriate cases.
   (b) Where there is pre-application disclosure and negotiation, it is dealt with
       (i)   Cost effectively;
       (ii) In line with the overriding objectives of the Family Proceedings (Amendments No 2) Rules 1999;
   (c) The parties are in a position to settle the case fairly and early without litigation.

1.3 The court will be able to treat the standard set in the pre-application protocol as the normal reasonable approach to pre-application conduct. If proceedings are subsequently issued, the court will be entitled to decide whether there has been non-compliance with the protocol and, if so, whether non-compliance merits consequences.

2 Notes of guidance

Scope of the protocol

2.1 This protocol is intended to apply to all claims for ancillary relief as defined by FPR r 1(2). It is designed to cover all classes of case, ranging from a simple application for periodical payments to an application for a substantial lump sum and property adjustment order. The protocol is designed to facilitate the operation of what was called the pilot scheme and is from 5 June 2000 the standard procedure for ancillary relief applications.

2.2 In considering the option of pre-application disclosure and negotiation, solicitors should bear in mind the advantage of having a court timetable and court managed process. There is sometimes an advantage in preparing disclosure before proceedings are commenced. However solicitors should bear in mind the objective of controlling costs and in particular the costs of discovery and that the option of pre-application disclosure and negotiation has risks of excessive and uncontrolled expenditure and delay. This option should only be encouraged where both parties agree to follow this route and disclosure is not likely to be an issue or has been adequately dealt with in mediation or otherwise.

2.3 Solicitors should consider at an early stage and keep under review whether it would be appropriate to suggest mediation to the clients as an alternative to solicitor negotiation or court based litigation.

2.4 Making an application to the court should not be regarded as a hostile step or a last resort, rather as a way of starting the court timetable, controlling disclosure and endeavouring to avoid the costly final hearing and the preparation for it.

First Letter

2.5 The circumstances of parties to an application for ancillary relief are so various that it would be difficult to prepare a specimen first letter. The request for information will be different in every case. However, the tone of the initial letter is important and the guide lines in para. 3.7 should be followed. It should be approved in advance by the client. Solicitors writing to an unrepresented party should always recommend that he seeks independent legal advice and enclose a second copy of the letter to be passed to any solicitor instructed. A reasonable time limit for a response may be 14 days.

Negotiation and Settlement

2.6 In the event of pre-application disclosure and negotiation, as envisaged in para. 2.2 an application should not be issued when a settlement is a reasonable prospect.

Disclosure

2.7 The protocol underlines the obligation of parties to make full and frank disclosure of all material facts, documents and other information relevant to the issues. Solicitors owe their clients a duty to tell them in clear terms of this duty and of the possible consequences of breach of the duty. This duty of disclosure is an ongoing obligation and includes the duty to disclose any material changes after initial disclosure has been given. Solicitors are referred to the Good Practice Guide for Disclosure produced by the Solicitors Family Law Association (obtainable from the Administrative Director, 366A Crofton Road, Orpington, Kent BR2 8NN).

3 The protocol

General Principles

3.1 All parties must always bear in mind the overriding objective set out at FPR Rule 2.51B and try to ensure that all claims should be resolved and a just outcome achieved as speedily as possible without costs being unreasonably incurred. The needs of any children should be addressed and safeguarded. The procedures which it is appropriate to follow should be conducted with minimum distress to the parties and in a manner designed to promote as good a continuing relationship between the parties and any children affected as is possible in the circumstances.

3.2 The principle of proportionality must be borne in mind at all times. It is unacceptable for the costs of any case to be disproportionate to the financial value of the subject matter of the dispute.

3.3 Parties should be informed that where a court exercises a discretion as to whether costs are payable by one party to another, this discretion extends to pre-application offers to settle and conduct of disclosure. (Rule 44.3 Paragraph 1 of the Civil Procedure Rules 1998).

Identifying the Issues

3.4 Parties must seek to clarify their claims and identify the issues between them as soon as possible. So that this can be achieved, they must provide full, frank and clear disclosure of facts, information and documents which are material and sufficiently accurate to enable proper negotiations to take place to settle their differences. Openness in all dealings is essential.

Disclosure

3.5 If parties carry out voluntary disclosure before the issue of proceedings the parties should exchange schedules of assets, income, liabilities and other material facts, using Form E as a guide to the format of the disclosure. Documents should only be disclosed to the extent that they are required by Form E. Excessive or disproportionate costs should not be incurred.

Correspondence

3.6 Any first letter and subsequent correspondence must focus on the clarification of claims and identification of issues and their resolution. Protracted and unnecessary correspondence and 'trial by correspondence' must be avoided.

3.7 The impact of any correspondence upon the reader and in particular the parties must always be considered. Any correspondence which raises irrelevant issues or which might cause the other party to adopt an entrenched, polarised or hostile position is to be discouraged.

Experts

3.8 Expert valuation evidence is only necessary where the parties cannot agree or do not know the value of some significant asset. The cost of a valuation should be proportionate to the sums in dispute. Wherever possible, valuations of properties, shares etc. should be obtained from a single valuer instructed by both parties. To that end, a party wishing to instruct an expert (the first party) should first give the other party a list of the names of one or more experts in the relevant speciality whom he considers are suitable to instruct. Within 14 days the other party may indicate an objection to one or more of the named experts and, if so, should supply the names of one or more experts whom he considers suitable.

3.9   Where the identity of the expert is agreed, the parties should agree the terms of a joint letter of instructions.

3.10   Where no agreement is reached as to the identity of the expert, each party should think carefully before instructing his own expert because of the costs implications. Disagreements about disclosure such as the use and identity of an expert may be better managed by the court within the context of an application for ancillary relief.

3.11   Whether a joint report is commissioned or the parties have chosen to instruct separate experts, it is important that the expert is prepared to answer reasonable questions raised by either party.

3.12   When experts' reports are commissioned pre-application, it should be made clear to the expert that they may in due course be reporting to the court and that they should therefore consider themselves bound by the guidance as to expert witnesses in Part 39 of the Civil Procedure Rules 1998.

3.13   Where the parties propose to instruct a joint expert, there is a duty on both parties to disclose whether they have already consulted that expert about the assets in issue.

3.14   If the parties agree to instruct separate experts the parties should be encouraged to agree in advance that the reports will be disclosed.

Summary

3.15   The aim of all pre-application proceedings steps must be to assist the parties to resolve their differences speedily and fairly or at least narrow the issues and, should that not be possible, to assist the court to do so.

APPENDIX B
ANCILLARY RELIEF PROCEDURE TIMETABLE

Outline Ancillary Relief Procedure

Note: the overriding objective in Rule 2.51B governs all steps

Phase 1: to end of First Appointment (FA)

	Step	Party	Timing	FPR
1	Filing of Ancillary Relief Notice (Form A)	Either	Any time after filing Petition	2.61A(1)
2	Fixing of First Appointment 12–16 weeks ahead (Form C) NB: No vacating of date without permission	Court	When Form A is filed	2.61A(4)(a) 2.16A(5)
3	Service of copy of Notice in Form A on Respondent	Court	Within **4 days** after Form A filed	2.61A(4)(b)
4	Filing and **simultaneous exchange** of **Form E**, completed and sworn by each party and containing the information and attaching the documents **required** by the Form and any other documents **necessary** to explain or clarify the information. The **required** documents are • property valuations obtained in last 6 months • most recent mortgage statements • last 12 months' bank statements Most recent investment(s) statement • surrender value quotes of insurance policies • last 2 years' business accounts • valuation of pension rights • recent income information (eg last 3 payslips and most recent P60)	Both	At least **35 days** before FA	2.61B(1) (2)
5	Service of documents required by but unavoidably not attached to Form E (with explanation); but otherwise	Either	At earliest Opportunity	2.61B(5)
	NO general discovery before FA	Neither		2.61B(6)
6	Filing and service of		At least **14 days** before	2.61(B)(7)
	• Concise statement of issues;	Both		
	• Chronology;	Both	FA	
	• Questionnaire, **referable to the statement of issues**, seeking further information and documents; and	Both		
	• Notice (**Form G**) stating whether that party will be able to proceed to FDR at the FA and confirmation of service under FPR 2.59(3) & (4), and applicable 2.70(4)	Both Applicant		2.61(B)(9)
7	Produce first costs estimate (Form H)	Both	Immediately prior to FA 24 hours prior to FA	2.61F(1)
	If a party intends to seek a summary assessment of costs, produce a Woolf costs schedule			2.61F(2)

8	THE FIRST APPOINTMENT			
	Objective: to define issues and save costs	Both parties to attend personally unless otherwise ordered FPR 2.61D(5)	On date fixed 12–16 weeks after filing of Form A (Step 2)	2.61D(1)
	Directions as to:			2.61D(2)(a)
	• answering questions and producing documents; and any further **necessary** documentation; 2.61D(2)(b)			2.61D(2)(a)
	• valuations (joint where appropriate) and experts			2.61D(2)(b)
	• evidence to be adduced by each party, further chronologies, schedules			2.61D(2)(b)
	District Judge *shall* then:			
	either direct FDR (this will be the norm)		Date for FDR on Form D	2.61D(2)(c)
	Or (if FDR inappropriate) direct:			2.61D(2)(d)
	• hearing for further directions; or			
	• hearing for interim order; or			
	• final hearing; or			
	• adjournment for mediation, negotiation or generally.			
	The District Judge *may* in addition			2.61D(2)(f)
	• make urgent interim order, provided application duly made in accordance with 2.69F returnable on that occasion;			
	• having regard to forms g (see step 6), treat as FDR			
	• direct pensions valuation			
	Costs			
	• produce written estimate to DJ	Both		2.61F
	• DJ must consider making an order for costs where appropriate because of the litigation conduct of the party in relation to the proceedings			2.61D(2)(e)
				2.71(4)

Phase 2: to end of Financial Dispute Resolution Appointment (FDR)

	Step	Party	Timing	FPR
9	Comply with all directions made at FA	Both	As per Direction Order and by FDR date	
	Any further discovery only with court permission	Both	By application	2.61D(3)
10	Where FDR has been ordered:			
	Notice to court of all offers, proposals and responses, Produce second costs estimate in Form H	Applicant	At least 7 days before	2.61E(3)
				2.61F
	prior to FDR	Both	Immediately	
11	**THE FDR APPOINTMENT**			
	Objective: best endeavours to reach agreement	Both parties to attend personally unless otherwise ordered: FPR	On date fixed at FA	2.61E
				2.61E(6)
	Ground rules:			2.61E(9)
	• FDR treated as held for discussion and negotiation purposes: see Practice Direction [1997] 3 All ER 768, [1997] 1 WLR 1069			2.61E(1)
	• Conducted by a DJ who will not have anything else to do with the case			2.61E(2)
	• Offer details lodged are not to be kept on court file after FDR			2.61E(5)
	District Judge may then:			
	• adjourn from time to time;			2.61E(7)
	• make appropriate consent order;			
	• give further directions; and			2.61E(8)
	• fix final hearing			
12	**Application for interim order**			
	• An application for an interim maintenance or variation order must be made returnable on 14 days notice	Either	at any time	2.69(F)
	• Unless the applicant has filed Form E it must be accompanied by a short sworn statement about his means and why the application is necessary			
	• the other party must file and serve a short sworn statement of means not less than 7 days before the hearing	Either	At any time	2.69(F)
	• A party may at any stage apply (without notice if necessary) for other interim orders			

Phase 3: to final hearing

	Step	Party	Timing	FPR
13	**Direction Order made at FDR to be complied with appropriately**	Both	As per Direction Order	
14	Statement of Open Proposals • To be drafted	Both	After FDR **14 days** before final hearing	
	• File with court and serve on other party	Applicant Respondent	**7 days after** receipt of Applicant's statement	2.69E(1) 2.69E(2)
15	**Further Directions/adjourned FDRs**	Either party may apply or court may direct	Any time	2.61D(4)
	A written statement of costs in Form H must be produced at every Court hearing			2.61F
16	**THE FINAL HEARING** NB: Final costs estimate in Form H1 required, unless court orders otherwise	On date fixed at First Appointment (Step 8) or at FDR (Step 11) or otherwise		
	Re Bundles for trial, see *Practice Direction (Family Proceedings: Court Bundles) (Universal Practice to be Applied in all Courts other than the Family Proceedings Court)* [2006] 2 FLR 199			
17	**Cost after judgment** • The general rule is that the court will make no order as to costs, unless a party's litigation conduct justifies such an order. See *President's Direction (Ancillary Relief: Costs)* [2006] 1 FLR 865			2.71(4) 2.71(5)

Index